People of the Bomb

People of the Bomb
Portraits of America's Nuclear Complex

Hugh Gusterson

 University of Minnesota Press
Minneapolis
London

Copyright 2004 by the Regents of the University of Minnesota

Published by the University of Minnesota Press
111 Third Avenue South, Suite 290
Minneapolis, MN 55401-2520
http://www.upress.umn.edu

Library of Congress Cataloging-in-Publication Data

Gusterson, Hugh.
    People of the bomb : portraits of America's nuclear complex / Hugh Gusterson.
        p.   cm.
    Includes bibliographical references and index.
    ISBN 0-8166-3859-4 (hc : alk. paper) — ISBN 0-8166-3860-8 (pb : alk. paper)
        1. Nuclear weapons—Moral and ethical aspects—United States.
    2. Nuclear weapons—Moral and ethical aspects.   3. War—Moral and ethical aspects—United States.   4. War—Moral and ethical aspects.   5. Military scientists—United States.   6. World politics—20th century.   I. Title.
        U264.3.G87 2004
        172'.422—dc22

                                                                        2004003476

Printed in the United States of America on acid-free paper

The University of Minnesota is an equal-opportunity educator and employer.

12 11 10 09 08 07 06 05 04   10 9 8 7 6 5 4 3 2 1

For Graham,
in the hope that his world will be better

Everything . . . from the young writers impatient of a long creative life to the deconstruction of our critics; every variety of intellectual retreat, of conformism, every small loss of moral acuity, I see collectively as the secret story of American life under the bomb. We have had the bomb on our minds since 1945. It was first our weaponry and then our diplomacy, and now it's our economy. How can we suppose that something so monstrously powerful would not, after forty years, compose our identity?

—*E. L. Doctorow*

Contents

Acknowledgments

This book is the product of fifteen years of research and writing. Fieldwork—at the Lawrence Livermore National Laboratory in California, the Los Alamos National Laboratory in New Mexico, among weapons scientists and activists in Russia, and in Washington, D.C.—would not have been possible without a series of fellowships and grants: a Mellon New Directions Fellowship and a Social Science Research Council–MacArthur Fellowship when I was a graduate student; a Weatherhead postdoctoral fellowship at the School of American Research; an Old Dominion fellowship and the Levitan Prize from the Massachusetts Institute of Technology; a John D. and Catherine T. MacArthur Foundation Grant in Research and Writing in the Program on Peace and International Security; a fellowship from Stanford University's Center for International Security and Arms Control; and grant number SBR-9712223 from the National Science Foundation's Program on Societal Dimensions of Engineering, Science, and Technology.

Unlike academics who conduct research in archives or from published sources, ethnographers are at the mercy of the human beings they study. This book would have been impossible without the willingness of countless weapons scientists, policy makers, and activists to talk to me with the promise of no reward beyond the possibility that I would quote them accurately. In retrospect it is remarkable how few, even at the highest levels of the national security bureaucracy, declined to talk to me. In keeping with my promise as an ethnographer to those I interviewed, those with whom I spoke are (unless they gave permission to be quoted by name) quoted anonymously in these pages and their identity is often, in accordance with standard anthropological practice, shielded with pseudonyms. I hope they will not feel that their trust in me was misplaced and might even feel in some way enriched by their glance at themselves in the ethnographic mirror.

Each essay in this book is accompanied by a list in the notes of particular interlocutors who helped shape it; I will not repeat those names here. Over the years these interlocutors have included weapons scientists and activists as well as academics drawn eclectically from anthropology, security studies, science studies, and other fields. All have given generously of their time in responding to drafts of my ideas, not infrequently ideas that irritated them, and I appreciate their comments enormously. Writing is a strange business: we writers sit on our own in quiet rooms organizing thousands of words that then get distributed to libraries and bookstores, but we have only a partial sense of who reads them or what they make of them. The responses of colleagues and interviewees to my drafts over the years helped bridge this gap and forced me on many occasions to rethink arguments whose weakness I had failed to see.

Special thanks go to Jennifer Poole and Nancy Boyce, who did superb jobs reconciling different versions of the manuscript and undertaking some of the detailed drudgework necessary to turn a plurality of essays into a single book, and also to Diana Witt for her indexing. Of course, my strongest appreciation goes to my wife, Allison Macfarlane, sternest critic and strongest supporter, for her intellectual companionship, homecooked food, and more child care than I can easily repay. The book is dedicated to our own joint project, Graham.

Introduction
Securityscapes

I met my first nuclear weapons designer in 1984.

I had just dropped out of a graduate program in anthropology at an Ivy League university and moved to California, where I resolved to work as a political activist. I had originally been drawn to anthropology by a vague attraction to its liberal, relativist ethos and by the opportunity to claim to know why other people behaved as they did. As it happened, my entry into graduate school had coincided with President Reagan's arrival in Washington. In the early 1980s, as I watched Congress cut aid to the poor, the nuclear arms race intensify amidst loose talk of "winnable nuclear wars,"[1] and an American-incited cluster of civil wars take shape in Central America, my assigned readings on kinship terminology, patrilateral cross-cousin marriage, and totemic symbolism among Australian Aborigines began to seem increasingly disconnected from things I cared about in the real world. My preparation to fill in a tiny and esoteric piece of the ethnographic mosaic in Africa seemed irrelevant to what really mattered, and so I had left for California to explore activism as a vocation.

I arrived in San Francisco just as the Nuclear Freeze movement was gathering force. This massive grassroots antinuclear movement was rousing itself to contest the Reagan administration's plans to deploy the MX, cruise, and Pershing missiles and to demand, instead, an end to the arms race—a nuclear freeze.[2] Thanks to a chance encounter in the Berkeley Rose Garden on a beautiful Sunday afternoon, I was offered a job on the staff of the Nuclear Freeze Campaign in San Francisco. I was twenty-four years old. Although I was only beginning to master the basic facts about nuclear weapons—the result of many evenings spent poring over the eye-straining pamphlets in the campaign's office—it was part of my job to speak on the dangers of the nuclear arms race to any audience that would listen: church groups, college classes, women's circles, whatever. And so on this particular day in 1984 I found myself standing before a classroom of fresh-faced teenagers at San Francisco's Lowell High School ready to debate Tom, a middle-aged nuclear weapons designer from the nearby Lawrence Livermore National Laboratory. Livermore scientists had designed the nuclear warheads—weapons many times more powerful than the bomb that destroyed Hiroshima—for the MX and ground-launched cruise missiles, and they were deeply reviled by local antinuclear activists. The previous year about thirteen hundred protestors had been arrested in a single day for civil disobedience at the gates of the laboratory. A local judge who was a member of the John Birch Society inadvertently turned them into martyrs in the eyes of many in the San Francisco Bay Area when he held them for a week in circus tents in the local prison grounds in an attempt to break their will and force them to promise not to protest at Livermore again. The judge eventually backed down.[3]

My encounter with Tom took place before a class that had evidently been well prepared by a very liberal teacher. My impassioned warnings about the economic costs of the arms race, the immorality of nuclear weapons, and the dangers of nuclear war were well received. Meanwhile Tom, a shy and diffident man, sick that day with a cold, tried with earnest sincerity to defend nuclear deterrence and the work of his laboratory as the students, winked at by their teacher, tore into him. One girl in the class—to my satisfaction, I confess—even attributed his weapons work to perverse sexual desires. This San Francisco classroom was one of the few places in Ronald Reagan's America where an antinuclear activist could feel he had the upper hand over the nuclear complex.[4]

In the fullness of time, however, the bloom faded on the activist rose. If I had left graduate school frustrated at the irrelevance of my work there to the pain and injustice I encountered every day in the media, life in the ragged office of a nonprofit was disfigured by the constant search for funding and by the dull ache of repetitive bureaucratic tasks largely disconnected from the rewards of a deep intellectual project. The treadmill of filing and phoning made it hard to find time to read and to think, and the need to stay "on message" precluded truly free thinking. In my encounter with Tom, for example, finding myself at last just a few feet away from one of the, until now, faceless weapons makers whose work so vexed me, I was too constrained by my combat-ready role as activist to have a meaningful dialogue with a man who, I realized, I was as fascinated to understand as to debate. Scoring debating points after cramming from pamphlets and at workshops was no substitute for an intellectual life, and so I returned to graduate school, this time to a program at Stanford University with a reputation for politically engaged anthropology.

Three years later, fortified by a new round of training in a more avant-garde graduate program, I embarked on a more sustained and challenging encounter with the scientists of Livermore. In 1987, my academic advisers having consented to a very unconventional choice of fieldwork site, I moved to the suburban town of Livermore to commence an anthropological study of the nuclear weapons laboratory there and, to a lesser extent, of the antinuclear activists who opposed it. For the next two years, adapting as far as possible the traditional anthropological method of participant observation to the study of a top-secret facility employing eight thousand people and its geographically dispersed communities of opponents, I shared housing with nuclear weapons scientists, went to church with nuclear weapons scientists, drank at bars with nuclear weapons scientists, played sports with nuclear weapons scientists, and collected detailed life histories from more than a hundred of them, while driving in the evenings and on weekends to observe antinuclear meetings, document antinuclear protests, and interview antinuclear activists—many my former colleagues and friends from the movement. A little to my surprise, I found that I got on well with the nuclear weapons scientists of Livermore, many of whom became genuine friends, much to the puzzlement of my former comrades in the antinuclear movement. When, some years after my initial fieldwork, I got married, the ceremony took place in a Livermore scientist's garden. (The wedding was attended by both weapons scientists and activists, who sat at adjacent tables eyeing one another suspiciously.)

At the simplest level my question during that initial fieldwork was why weapons scientists and activists had chosen to do what they did and how they were sure they were in the right. In the course of investigating this question I became interested in the religious lives of scientists and protestors, in the symbolism of the body in the nuclear age, in the effects of secret weapons work and activist overtime on family life and the self, in protests and scientific experiments as different kinds of rituals, and, above all, in the rhetorical strategies through which each side made its beliefs real. Under the influence of the French theorist Michel Foucault, I came to see discourse as the fabric of the self and, melding Foucault with insights from interpretive anthropology, sought to understand how discourse and experience worked to constitute the self in the context of the nuclear weapons debate. These investigations resulted in my book *Nuclear Rites* and in a number of the chapters in this book, most of which have appeared over the years in journals and edited collections and are finally gathered here in one volume. I have discussed the methodological and psychological problems inherent in a critical study of a top-secret facility and in conducting research in two communities bitterly opposed to one another elsewhere.[5]

Those years of fieldwork in Livermore from 1987 to 1989 are only the starting point for the larger project captured in this book, however. I began to realize that I could not understand the people I was meeting and the struggles I was chronicling in the San Francisco Bay Area without doing further fieldwork in distant but intimately connected places: the other nuclear weapons laboratory in Los Alamos, New Mexico; the bureaucratic centers of nuclear decision making in Washington, D.C.; and the nuclear weapons communities in Russia. Over the course of the 1990s this ethnographer and his notebook showed up in all these locales. Also, in search of a larger context in which to situate my interviewees, I began to investigate systematically the functioning of militarism in news coverage, in politicians' speeches, in popular culture, and in the dry journals of international security specialists. I realized, for example, that I might better understand the reaction of weapons scientists to the end of the cold war if I looked at the astonishing failure of leading international security scholars in the late 1980s to acknowledge the end of the cold war as a possibility (the topic of chapter 6); that I would see Hiroshima in a new light if I looked at media coverage of the Gulf War (chapter 4); and that I needed to watch science fiction movies to understand the cultural psychology of many of the weapons scientists I was meeting (the topic of chapter 3). The result is the book you now hold in your hands—an attempt, based on research over a period of fifteen years, to understand on a broad canvas the functioning of American military ideology, particularly nuclear ideology, during the cold war and in the turbulent decade or so following the end of the cold war.

The End of the Cold War and After

In 1987, when I first embarked on the research that produced this book, the American nuclear complex was coming under pressure from Mikhail Gorbachev's energetic attempts to end the arms race and from a powerful, if declining, international grassroots movement against nuclear weaponry. Although it was far from clear at the time, the cold war and the nuclear arms race were expiring. For the weapons laboratories and the Pentagon, it was still largely business as usual, however. For the roughly eight thousand employees of the Livermore Laboratory this meant a budget of about $1 billion a year, two-thirds of which was spent on developing new nuclear weapons and on ballistic missile defense work. As my research continued into the 1990s, the international securityscape mutated: the Soviet Union collapsed, nuclear testing ended, bipolarity gave way to globalization, and rogue states replaced the Soviet Union as a locus of nuclear threat. Throughout these changes the nuclear complex, and American military programs more broadly, endured and adapted despite prophecies of a new era of demilitarization. (At the end of the cold war, the U.S. military budget was around $300 billion; the military budget for FY2004 is $380 billion, not including the price of the "War on Terrorism," which is paid for separately.)

Immediately after the end of the cold war, in the shadow of the new millennium, public discourse on international security issues took on a millenarian tinge. For example, antinuclear activists, who, only a few years earlier, had been struggling to stop a single nuclear weapons system from being deployed, now declared, even before the nuclear test ban treaty had been negotiated, the complete abolition of nuclear weapons to be their immediate goal. Undeterred by the financial implosion of their organizations in the years after the end of the cold war, they formed an umbrella organization called Abolition 2000 dedicated to securing the worldwide abolition of the Bomb by the millennial year.[6]

But it was not only activists on the left who discerned utopian possibilities on the millennial horizon. Further to the right, Francis Fukuyama, a well-regarded thinker at the State Department, declared (in a 1989 article and then a 1993 book filled with earnest references to Hegel) that the end of the cold war was poised to bring about the global triumph of Western democracy and, therefore, "the end of history"—an argument that was, astonishingly, taken seriously by the media. At about the same time Bill Clinton's first national security adviser, Tony Lake, proclaimed that democracies do not fight one another and foretold an unprecedented era of peace and prosperity as democracy and free trade spread around the world under American tutelage. Meanwhile, on the apocalyptic end of the millennial spectrum, Harvard University's Samuel Huntington forecast that the end of the cold war and the intensification of globalization would accelerate a worldwide conflagration in the form of a global "Clash of Civilizations"—a much discussed thesis I analyze and contest in chapter 7.

The new world orders foretold at the cusp of the third millennium were stillborn. Instead of the spread of liberal democracy and the end of history, we got the Gulf War and the war in Kosovo and the hideous butchery of Bosnia and Rwanda as U.S. diplomats, trying hard to look the other way, squeamishly debated whether or not they should use the word *genocide,* with all the moral obligations it entailed, to describe what was happening.[7] On the nuclear front, the Clinton administration was able, thanks to a Herculean diplomatic effort, to win an indefinite extension of the Non-Proliferation Treaty in 1995 and to conclude the Comprehensive Test Ban Treaty in 1996, but was unable to prevent India and Pakistan from crossing the nuclear Rubicon with their nuclear tests of 1998. According to some sources at least, North Korea also crossed the threshold in these years, discreetly building an untested nuclear weapon with assistance from Pakistan.[8]

Nor, despite its proclaimed commitment to arms reductions and to the long-range goal of a nuclear-free world, was the Clinton administration able or willing to retrench the nuclear complex in the United States. In spite of predictions in the early 1990s that, as the junior weapons laboratory, the Lawrence Livermore National Laboratory would face closure or conversion,

Livermore continues today to rely on weapons work for the vast majority of its funding and its employees have not seen forced layoffs since the 1970s. In a story told here in chapter 9, the Livermore and Los Alamos National Laboratories were able to replace nuclear testing at the Nevada Nuclear Test Site with lavishly funded experiments to simulate nuclear testing and, as their price for acquiescing in the nuclear test ban, they were able to insist on a continuation of the two-laboratory system and an increase in their budgets for nuclear weapons research and development—this despite the fact that no new nuclear warheads were slated for deployment. Astonishingly, by the end of the second Clinton administration, nuclear weapons research and development was, in constant dollars, better funded than it was, on average, during the cold war. As Lawrence Korb, a former Pentagon official in the Reagan administration, put it, "The Cold War is over and the military-industrial complex has won."[9]

This does not mean, however, that nothing changed for weapons scientists. The weapons laboratories, whose work routines and status hierarchies had been defined throughout the cold war by the rhythms of nuclear testing and new weapons deployments, now had to adjust to a life with neither nuclear testing nor new weapons commissions. Chapters 8 and 9 explore the meaning of nuclear testing during the cold war for both weapons designers and their opponents in the peace movement and tell the story of the laboratories' increasingly futile struggle to save nuclear testing followed by their surprisingly graceful adjustment to virtual testing and to a mission of weapons stewardship rather than weapons development.

This transition at the weapons laboratories was accompanied by a broader mutation of the global nuclear system. In an ironic turnaround, as Russian utility companies threatened to cut off the supply of electricity to nuclear weapons facilities in arrears on their bills and Russian nuclear weapons designers threatened to strike over months' of unpaid wages in the early 1990s, American military planners went in a few short years from fearing the power of the Russian nuclear complex to fearing the possibly disastrous consequences of its collapse. Afraid that Russian nuclear materials, weapons designers, or even complete nuclear weapons might find their way into the hands of the Mafia, international terrorist organizations, or so-called rogue states, the U.S. Congress, in a move that was a little surreal, began to send taxpayers' money to Russian nuclear facilities and encouraged American nuclear weapons designers to learn Russian and collaborate on experiments with their Russian colleagues in an attempt to bind them to the U.S. nuclear complex. By the mid-1990s it was not uncommon to hear Russian being spoken in the Los Alamos National Laboratory's main cafeteria. Where British weapons scientists once were the most common foreign visitors to Los Alamos, now it was Russians.

One of the themes of this book is the extraordinary ability of American leaders to make real in the public mind new threats and new alliances (often with old enemies) as times change. Chapter 5 explores the rhetorical strategies adopted by the Truman administration shortly after World War II as it sought to persuade the American public to support the new NATO alliance (which included such recent enemies as Germany and Italy) and to fear its new enemy, until recently its ally, the Soviet Union. After the end of the cold war, as the world moved into the second nuclear age, a similar process of ideological transmutation took place. Now the Soviet Union was reconstructed (again) as an ally, and Iraq, until recently the recipient of substantial U.S. military aid even after it used chemical weapons against its own people, was transformed into a new entity—a "rogue state"—and demonized as the embodiment of all that was most dangerous in the new world order. Chapter 4 examines U.S. media representations of Iraq during the first Gulf War and chapter 2, the most important in the book, analyzes the Western discourse on nuclear proliferation, which was to the 1990s what anticommunism was to the 1950s. It was largely through this discourse that the new category of rogue states, now the justification for all manner of military programs, was made real. In chapter 2 and in the postscript on nuclear rhetoric in George W. Bush's America, I suggest that the category "rogue state" is incoherent and vacuous, and that the pronouncements of media pundits and defense intellectuals regarding the dangers of nuclear weapons in the hands of Third World nations are based on an indefensible double standard and, ultimately, neocolonial stereotyping disguised under a thin patina of rational thought: if nuclear weapons are safe in American hands, why not in Indian or Pakistani hands, too? I also try to suggest that the discourse on rogue states and proliferation, by miscasting the nuclear danger, prevents us from recognizing other threats to our security.

When I have presented these arguments at public forums, they have often proved controversial, but I believe that they engage the key issues of the second nuclear age. This age is dominated not by an arms race between two superpowers, as during the cold war, but by the schism between those countries reaping the benefits of globalization and those countries reaping the whirlwind. Militarily this age is characterized by a divide between a few countries with advanced nuclear and conventional weapons and other countries (and even subnational groups) interested in acquiring them. If past is prelude, the wars of the second nuclear age will often be high-tech neocolonial wars in which the United States, in varying degrees of coalition with other advanced industrial countries, fights so-called failed states and rogue states. While many of these wars, waged in part to secure access to oil and other strategic resources, might be described as resource wars, they will (as in the 2003 attack on Iraq) be presented to the public as human rights wars and as what Jonathan Schell calls "disarmament wars."[10] The belief that certain countries have no right to acquire "weapons of mass destruction," and the parallel public silence or amnesia about the massive American stockpiles of these same weapons, will be vital in the legitimizing of these disarmament wars.

Securityscapes

I am often asked, thankfully not so much by anthropologists anymore, what my work has to do with anthropology. The glib answer is that anthropologists study anything human. A more serious answer would be that, in recent years, a number of anthropologists have begun to systematically investigate a triad of phenomena at stake in this book: the cultures of science, the properties of the global system in the era after bipolarity, and ideologies of violence. Anthropological work on the latter two has been facilitated by important funding initiatives by the MacArthur Foundation, without which my own work would not have been possible. The MacArthur Foundation was determined to introduce anthropological voices into public and expert discussions of international security, and in the process, it has helped move the center of gravity of anthropology away from where it was when I first dropped out of anthropology in the early 1980s because I could not discern its relevance to a world engulfed in arms races and civil wars.

These positive developments notwithstanding, there is one respect in which, I fear, anthropology has developed a blind spot, though not irretrievably so, in recent years. Most anthropological theorizing of globalization and of the global system has accented global flows of migrant workers, refugees, capital, and popular culture that cut across the grain of the nation-state and, heeding Arjun Appadurai's emphasis on emergent "postnational" forms of identity,[11] has ignored the nation-state or even, unwittingly echoing the ideological formulas of corporate executives, spoken of the nation-state as increasingly marginal. If this intellectual trend was suspect from the start, it is even more so following the retrenchment of the national security state after the attacks of September 11—attacks increasingly understood in American public discourse as enabled by dangerous flows of Third World people and capital inherent to globalization.

There is a threefold danger in this kind of anthropological theorizing about the global system. The first is that, if we leave the military state out of our stories of globalization, the kinds of political violence studied by anthropologists in such places as Guatemala, Sri Lanka, or Mozambique may implicitly be understood by anthropologists not as an essential component of globalization but, as in the deeply suspect theories of such popular pundits as Thomas Friedman and Robert Kaplan,[12] taking place in states left behind by, or out of, globalization—what political scientists call "failed states."[13] The second danger is that the emergent narrative of globalization in anthropology may render invisible, or at least extrinsic to anthropological investigation, the continuing accumulation of weaponry and surveillance powers by national security states in the West as well as the Third World—a process of accumulation that is itself a product of globally coordinated flows of corporate products and security experts or, in other words, of globalization itself. The third danger is that an anthropological narrative of globalization without the state, especially the national security state, runs the risk of reinstantiating the damaging division of intellectual labor in the academy after World War II whereby international security as an object of expertise was surrendered to the political scientists, while anthropologists largely wrote about the world as if nuclear weapons and the cold war did not exist.

So, in a friendly amendment to Appadurai's portrait of the world after bipolarity as a fluid panorama of "ethnoscapes," "technoscapes," "financescapes," "mediascapes," and "ideoscapes," I suggest that we should also be on the lookout for "securityscapes." In chapter 9, I define securityscapes as "asymmetrical distributions of weaponry, military force, and military-scientific resources among [and I might add, within] nation-states and the local and global imaginaries of identity, power, and vulnerability that accompany these distributions." Key social actors in these securityscapes are weapons scientists, military officers, defense intellectuals, international relations professors, weapons contractors, the directors and casts of Hollywood war movies, war reporters, international aid personnel, antiwar activists, and many others. We need anthropological investigations of the microworlds of these actors and accounts of the ways in which these worlds clash and fit together. In its polymorphous investigation of the linked realities of weapons scientists, antinuclear activists, Hiroshima survivors, media pundits, the specialized journals of defense intellectuals, and Hollywood movies the present book seeks to demonstrate the potential power of such a project.

In keeping with the heterogeneous nature of the phenomenon under investigation here, not only are the topics of the following chapters diverse, but so are the fieldwork sites I present, the sources I draw upon, and the styles in which I discuss them. This is a tactic I have referred to elsewhere, theorizing an alternative to the straitjacket of participant observation in conventional anthropology, as one of "polymorphous engagement."[14] Whereas some chapters mainly rely on anthropological fieldwork in a variety of sites, others draw heavily on media sources or expert journals. And, although most chapters are written in what I hope is readable academic prose, chapters 1 and 3 are more reflexive and dialogic, constructed as they are around portraits of individual weapons scientists I found particularly interesting (for example, the Japanese American physicist in chapter 1 who has composed a life in which she works on nuclear weapons for the state that interned her father during World War II and bombed her aunt in Hiroshima in 1945). The entire enterprise is unified by persistent themes that cut across the various chapters: the power of language to make weapons programs seem natural and safe or to erase from consciousness the suffering of those maimed and killed in war; the circumstances in which the national security state loses its power to define reality and, on the other hand, the extraordinary power of the military state to recuperate moments of rupture such as the end of World War II or the end of the cold war; the formulation of "the other" in our collective imagination of threat; the relation between emotion and reason in the discourses of science and war; and, more reflexively, the possibility of using the perspectives of weapons scientists as a vantage point from which to critique the liberal shibboleths of the academy.

Disciplinarity

In this introduction so far, I have emphasized my credentials as a card-carrying anthropologist, but the essays in this book are by no means intended only for anthropologists, and, in writing them, I have profited greatly from reading work across a number of disciplines: critical security studies and conventional international relations theory, science and technology studies, women's studies, and media studies in particular. I hope that these essays may return something of use to these fields and enlarge the circle of dialogue in the humanities and social sciences.

Turning first to international relations theory and security studies in political science, I have found a field, to be frank, oddly divided. In the United States the leading departments at the major universities are dominated by people who, regardless of age, largely rehearse the arguments—with slight embellishments for the post–cold war era—that dominated the field twenty or even thirty years earlier. For the most part these people are unreflexive positivists who are unfamiliar with the work of the poststructuralist, postcolonial, and feminist theorists who turned intellectual life upside down in neighboring disciplines in the humanities and social sciences in the 1980s. As I write these words today, at a time when history, anthropology, and literature have taken a strong interpretive turn, mainstream political science in the United States is dominated by rational choice theory—an intensification of the positivist framework that has dominated the discipline in recent decades. Meanwhile there is a group of international relations theorists who do boldly creative work grounded in critical theory, but they and their students are largely marginalized in second-tier departments or are concentrated in political science departments in Britain or Australia, where such work is more warmly embraced. To simplify, the first group assumes that the international system is an anarchic sphere in which states ruthlessly pursue their self-evident interests, and that objective generalizations can be formulated about these states' behavior; the second group assumes that interests do not exist outside ideology, that statesmen are cultural as much as profit-maximizing beings, and that social science, since it deals with conscious human beings rather than particles, is an interpretive enterprise.[15]

The essays here are, explicitly or implicitly, haunted by an engagement with the divided fields of international relations and security studies. Although I find the often turgid language and dense theorizing of critical security studies vexing, the essays that follow are deeply informed by the perspective to be found in that literature, and chapters 5 and 6 were originally written to extend the arguments of critical security studies for an international relations audience. As for mainstream security studies and international relations theory, it is partly of interest to me because it offers a worldview so closely cognate to that of weapons scientists who sometimes draw upon it to legitimate their work. As a practitioner of science studies I also find the mainstream security studies literature fascinating because of the ways in which, less convincingly than the "hard sciences," it draws upon the rhetoric of proof and certainty to secure its knowledge claims. Science studies built itself as a field by deconstructing these kinds of maneuvers in physics and biology but has largely ignored the rhetoric of science in international relations theory. In chapter 6, working within the framework of contemporary science studies, I undertake an analysis of some of the knowledge claims made in mainstream international relations and security studies at the end of the cold war, asking how well they functioned to explain the sudden transformations of that period and in what sense they could be understood to be "scientific." I hope this chapter will be of interest to mainstream political scientists as well as others.

This book has also been shaped by my reading of feminist theory. Any student of nuclear culture over the past two decades would have to be blind not to see the relevance of gender to that topic. Nuclear weapons designers are overwhelmingly male while many of the most important leaders of the antinuclear movement, not to mention much of its rank and file, have been women. Meanwhile, as Carol Cohn has pointed out in a celebrated article, the language of weapons scientists and defense intellectuals is saturated with the metaphors of male sexual prowess ("penetrating the enemy's defenses," "hardening our missiles," and so on).[16] Nevertheless, especially in the context of debates about essentialism in women's studies in the 1980s and 1990s, I have found myself particularly interested in a phenomenon that does not quite fit the conventional feminist analysis of war, namely, women who enthusiastically embrace military roles—the kind of women, for example, who belong to the mischievously named ladies' crocheting and nuclear weapons design club at the Los Alamos Laboratory. Elsewhere, I have written about what I call "feminist militarism"—the growing number of women who identify the cause of women's rights not with the struggle against militarism but, in a context where women now constitute roughly 15 percent of U.S. military personnel, with the unfettered right to secure career advancement free from male obstructionism in weapons laboratories or in the armed services.[17] Chapter 1, which explores the world of a self-proclaimed feminist nuclear weapons designer, is intended as a human portrait of feminist militarism and as a way of giving a new twist to the old debates on essentialism in women's studies.

This volume is also intended as an intervention in the burgeoning new field of science and technology studies. In the United States many programs in science, technology, and society were originally established by maverick scientists in the 1970s to address newly urgent questions about the social responsibility of scientists in an era of militarism and environmental concern—the years of the Vietnam War, the Pentagon Papers, and Love Canal. Since then the field has largely fallen out of the hands of these maverick scientists and has been professionalized around a body of theory imported from Europe that closely explores the processes by which scientists construct scientific facts.[18] This broadly constructivist literature in science and technology studies has, however, achieved its considerable successes at the cost of marginalizing politics as conventionally understood. Instead of investigating the connections between scientific research and larger political structures, it has focused on the microprocesses within scientific laboratories and disciplines by which facts are made real. It has been more interested in the politics of academic faculty rooms and conferences than of national parliaments and mass movements, and it has tended to ignore the relationship between science and the state. One of my goals is to bring the state back into science and technology studies. Although the essays in this book are deeply influenced by the constructivist perspective that now dominates science and technology studies, they seek to reconnect that perspective with the social and political questions about scientific ethics, militarism, and the environment that prompted the original birth of the field only to fall largely out of sight in the 1980s and much of the 1990s.

Finally, the selections included here have been informed by recent work in the humanities and social sciences on mass media. Some of the most interesting contributions to this literature, influenced by the Birmingham school and by "reader-response theory," emphasize the ways in which popular culture can serve as a locus of resistance to dominant institutions in Western society, and they accent the agency of individual consumers who find their own meanings in, say, films and television shows. Chapter 3 is very much in this tradition. But as a scholar of militarism in the era of cable news and the consolidation of mass media ownership, I increasingly find myself impressed by the remarkable power of the American mass media, particularly the news media, to shape the subjectivity of consumers and constrain their ability to perceive certain questions, facts, or ideas. For example, as the Bush administration sought to build the case for an invasion of Iraq in 2003, surveys found that a majority of Americans, particularly those who largely relied on television news, believed (quite erroneously) that "some or all of the Sept. 11 hijackers were Iraqi."[19] A number of essays in this book explore the extraordinary ability of mass media to construct reality for ordinary citizens—an increasingly urgent topic of investigation for those of us concerned to protect and extend democracy in the West and to make sure, in an era of globalization, that Americans can grasp and visualize the lives of others with whom their own are increasingly intertwined. In chapter 4, I argue that American mainstream media coverage of the Gulf War in 1991 made it difficult for ordinary Americans to fully grasp the fact that about 200,000 Iraqis died in a war that looked as much like a video game as a conventional battlefield to many television viewers.[20] Chapter 5, in which I analyze a 1949 radio speech by the U.S. secretary of state, shows how skillful politicians can use the media to reshape public perceptions of foreign policy. And in chapter 2, I show how print and television media can collaborate in the construction of a common sense—here about nuclear proliferation—that, when subjected to close scrutiny, reveals itself to be highly suspect and ideological.

People of the Bomb is, then, an ambitiously polyglot offering. It covers a wide range of topics, draws from diverse literatures, and aims to speak to multiple audiences—in anthropology, security studies, science studies, media studies, and women's studies. But in this regard it is well tailored to its subject. American militarism is one of the most complex and powerful phenomena of our era. It shapes the careers our young scientists choose, the way our news is reported, the films our Hollywood studios decide to make, and the fears that bring mass movements into being. For better or worse, militarism is all around us—in our politics, in our economy, and in our culture—and it is in danger of becoming so large and so much a part of our common sense that we lose the ability see it in its entirety and with the kind of critical perspective that might enable us to take control of it rather than unconsciously inhabit it. The essays in this book are intended to help bring the profound influence of militarism on our lives back into focus.

Part I

Encounters with the Other

1

Becoming a Weapons Scientist

This chapter is about the charged intersection between my own life and that of Sylvia,[1] a key subject in my fieldwork, at a moment when we were both undergoing important processes of transition and apprenticeship in our professional lives. At the time I was carrying out an ethnographic study of the Lawrence Livermore National Laboratory—a federal laboratory near San Francisco that has, for the past forty years, devoted about two-thirds of its resources to nuclear weapons design. It was Livermore scientists who designed, for example, the warheads for the MX and ground-launched cruise missiles.

Sylvia, who is my age, had earned a Ph.D. in physics from MIT. Although she had not yet designed a nuclear device when I first met her in January 1989, she was in the process of mastering her trade and joining the tiny and mysterious elite within the Lawrence Livermore Laboratory by becoming a nuclear warhead designer. I had, in the mid-1980s, been an antinuclear activist with the Nuclear Freeze Campaign in San Francisco, an organization dedicated to the termination of the Livermore Laboratory's principal mission. By the time I met Sylvia I had completed coursework in graduate school, ceased my work on behalf of the Nuclear Freeze, and was attempting to master my new trade as an anthropologist. Making a highly unconventional choice of fieldwork site, I was earning my own Ph.D. by studying Sylvia and her colleagues rather than the peasants, nomads, and slum dwellers who are more customary targets of the anthropologist's exoticizing gaze. Although I did not know it at the time, my writing about Sylvia and her colleagues would eventually lead me, in another professional transition, away from Livermore to MIT, the university where Sylvia was trained as a physicist, and where I now teach the anthropology of science and train students to study scientists like Sylvia.

Thus ran our lives, then, both parallel and opposed. At a moment when anthropologists are questioning the grounds of cultural knowledge and the established canons of ethnographic writing, I would like to speak here about Sylvia's world in conventional ethnographic terms but also, more reflexively, as an entity that has been refracted in my writing through the prism of symmetries and contrasts between our two lives. My account, then, will seek to shed light on Sylvia's world, but in doing so it will also accent the ways in which my knowledge of Sylvia and her world is what Donna Haraway has called "situated knowledge"—knowledge that is, without being untrue, never finally true; knowledge that is partial; knowledge whose shape is de-termined in part by the particular questions, angles of insight, and blind spots that I brought to my research as someone who is, in spite of my best efforts to be "detached," an actor with my own social history and my own positioning in a web of social and intellectual relationships. I say "in part" because, while my history and identity affect the way I tell Sylvia's story, it should also become apparent that her story often ruptured the schemas with which I intended to contain it. This is what it means to say that doing fieldwork and writing ethnography are dialogic processes.

But before we go any further, let me tell you about Sylvia.

A Typical Weapons Scientist?

Looking back through my field notes, I find these scattered remarks about Sylvia written after our first encounter:

> Sylvia has worked at the lab for about two years. She is 30 and lives in a suburban house on her own except for a huge golden Labrador . . . On the phone I was struck by her openness and friendliness. The interview was fairly short because she gets self-conscious talking at great length and soon trails off in embarrassed laughter. Before the interview she asked me to give her some suggestions for reading in the history of sociology. At the end of the interview she peppered me with questions about the protesters. Why do they do what they do? What do they think about the Russians? Do they know anything about science? At one point in the interview we're interrupted by a phone call from a computer programmer who's running one of her programs. (It's 8 p.m., but work never ends.) He can't get into one of her files. To my amazement she rattles off the file name by memory, and it goes something like this: AB666589:!!$#:lllbm58745.

After Sylvia and I got to know one another better she once said jokingly to me, "I think of myself as a six-foot-tall, blond, blue-eyed male." Since

Sylvia is rather less than six feet tall, dark-haired, dark-eyed, and Japanese American, this is a striking remark. It is also an ambiguous remark. It hints at the possible psychological costs inherent in working as a minority woman among Livermore's predominantly white male physicists, but it also bespeaks, metaphorically, a self-confidence that, over time, I came to see as an integral part of Sylvia's persona. She is, to my knowledge, the only nonwhite member of the laboratory's elite cadre of warhead designers. Having lived for a year in Japan, Sylvia speaks Japanese and says she identifies quite strongly with her Japanese ancestry. During World War II her mother lived in Japan and her father, who is now a successful engineer, was put in an internment camp by the U.S. government. On the day the first atomic bomb was dropped Sylvia's aunt was taking her grandfather to Hiroshima. She sustained a dose of radiation high enough to induce radiation sickness, though she did survive and now lives in California. During one of our conversations Sylvia recounted for me her aunt's experience that day in 1945, as it had been told to her by her aunt, complete with a horrifyingly powerful image of the aunt standing on a bridge on the edge of Hiroshima looking down into a river choked with corpses and red with blood. How does your family feel about your nuclear weapons work? I ask. "They have this unspoken way of expressing themselves," she says quietly. "I think they're against it. They'd rather I was a doctor."

Sylvia's account of her aunt's experience in Hiroshima affected me deeply. When I was an antinuclear activist I, like many other antinuclear activists I knew in the 1980s, had had nightmares about dying in a nuclear war. Once, while sitting on a hill overlooking San Francisco, I had even had a strange waking vision of a mushroom cloud over the city. During my fieldwork, as I explain in more detail later, these nightmares and fears receded. But the night of my conversation with Sylvia about her aunt, I had a nightmare that there was a bloodstained body in my bedroom. It was the only nightmare I had during my final year of fieldwork.

When I first met Sylvia I was bewildered that anyone whose aunt had been bombed at Hiroshima could now earn a living designing nuclear weapons. Surely she of all people should know better, I thought. However, such an attitude on my part preempted the fundamental question in regard to nuclear weapons—the basic question at stake in my fieldwork: namely, whether nuclear weapons protect their bearers from danger or are themselves the danger from which we need to be protected. My own evolution into an antinuclear activist in my early twenties was associated with a sense of awakening, of pulling off layers of numbness and denial about the terrible things nuclear weapons could do to nations and to bodies. For me, any sense as intimate as Sylvia's of what nuclear weapons actually do to people could only be linked to an antinuclear sensibility. Sylvia confronted me with a different reality: for those who are persuaded by the arguments in favor of nuclear weapons, a stark knowledge of what happened at Hiroshima may simply reinforce the notion that it is important for one's own country to have such weapons. Just as those whose relatives have been shot may decide to buy guns, so those whose relatives have been atom-bombed may decide to work on atom bombs. The antinuclear movement of the 1980s sought in its literature and iconography to appropriate the shattered bodies of Hiroshimans as incontestable signs of our own imminent extinction should the arms race continue, but this is not the only way these bodies can be read.

At least as puzzling for me as Sylvia's relationship to Hiroshima was the fact that she was a woman. The antinuclear movement in which I had participated in the early 1980s was deeply shaped by an array of feminisms from mainstream equal rights feminism to ecofeminism and the separatist feminism that informed the vision of the large, women-only peace camps at Greenham Common in Britain and Seneca Falls in New York.[2] I had learned from the movement that, to put the message in caricature, men make war and women make peace. And, indeed, many of the most influential and charismatic national leaders in America's antinuclear movement were women: Randall Forsberg, Helen Caldicott, Pam Solo, Jane Gruenebaum, and Jesse Cocks, for example. Meanwhile the disparate but connected ideas of such feminist writers as Starhawk, Carol Gilligan, Susan Griffin, Nancy Chodorow, Gloria Steinem, and Ursula Le Guin pulsed in pristine and mediated forms through the movement, which, however imperfect its actual record in regard to women, was permeated by women's symbolism and women's consciousness. Many antinuclear affinity groups, for example, took women-oriented names such as Ovary Action, Princesses Against Plutonium, Spiderwomyn, and Moms Against Bombs. There were also such groups as Women's Strike for Peace, Women's Action for Nuclear Disarmament, and the Women's International League for Peace and Freedom, the oldest peace group in the United States. At antinuclear demonstrations it was commonplace to see signs such as Pay Mothers, Not the Pentagon; Take the Toys Away from the Boys; and (accompanied by a satellite photo of the earth) Love Your Mother. In this movement, especially in the more radical direct-action wing, it was in varying degrees taken for granted, by many men as well as women, that the militarist project was in some sense a masculine one, that women (especially mothers) represented a "different voice," a more peaceful voice, and that—as Carol Cohn, Cynthia Enloe, Sara Ruddick, and others have argued—the project of making peace was deeply connected with the transformation of America's gender system.[3] As the handbook for the women's peace camp in Seneca Falls put it:

> Feminism is a value system which affirms qualities that have traditionally been considered female: nurturance of life, putting other's well-being before one's own, cooperation, emotional and intuitive sensitivity. . . . These traits have been discounted by societies which teach competition, violent conflict resolution, and materialism. Feminism insists that the qualities traditionally considered female be recognized as deserving respect and manifesting great power.[4]

The general sentiments of this passage, if not necessarily its essentialist phrasing, were widespread in the movement, and it was within the movement that I myself received my earliest and most thoroughgoing exposure to feminist thinking and practice.

In terms of the framework I had internalized in the antinuclear movement, then, a woman warhead designer was an anomaly indeed. Sylvia, however, does not see things this way. Although she works on weapons, she describes herself as a feminist, and I found her acutely aware of the problems women face in science. She was well aware, for example, that women accounted for only 26 percent of the employees at the laboratory, that most of these women were secretaries or were concentrated in the fields of biomedicine, computer science, and environmental science, and that there was evidence suggesting women at the laboratory tend, statistically speaking, to be paid less than men for comparable work.[5] Just under 6 percent of the laboratory's physicists are women—a number that is in line with the number of Ph.D.'s in physics given to women nationally. Among the elite caste of warhead designers at the laboratory, I knew of only three women, including Sylvia. "The only other women that I see regularly [at the laboratory] are computer analysts and secretaries," she says. "There aren't that many engineers or scientists who are women and, in general in science, as soon as women move into a field, the average salary drops." Sylvia has strong feelings about the male-dominated culture of university science departments, and is particularly critical of MIT: "My observation was that it was all right for a graduate student to be a woman because the professors had control over the students, but the competition from male faculty if you were a woman was something else. I know women faculty there, actually, who have had the chairman of their department saying that they will never get tenure as long as they were the chairman there."

At the laboratory Sylvia has had no problem finding mentors among the senior male warhead designers, two of whom have worked closely with her and have passed along a substantial body of cultural as well as technical knowledge to her. On the whole Sylvia finds the laboratory's treatment of women more favorable than MIT's. Still, she has run into a few problems—technicians who, perhaps deliberately, open drawers containing centerfolds, even though such pictures are officially banned at the laboratory, and invitation lists to design review meetings from which her name is omitted. Attendance at such meetings is important because this is how designers maintain a profile in their community while assuring access to the latest ideas and data. Sylvia said she was not finally sure whether her name was, in her early years at the lab, sometimes left off because she was a woman or simply because she was a new designer.

I once asked Sylvia what it meant to her to call herself a feminist. Arguing firmly against versions of feminism that essentialize or sentimentalize women by attributing to them a different voice, a separatist agenda, or a unique consciousness grounded in the particular experience of motherhood, she replied: "I'm fighting for everybody's rights, not just women. I just wish that people would let people be the way that they are, and not put them in little boxes." I asked if she saw a connection between masculinity and the arms race on the one hand and mothering and participation in the peace movement on the other. She replied: "I think I'm protecting children. I feel as if I'm protecting, helping to protect the country. Anyway, I don't think that looking after children is inherently men's or women's work. I think that we get socialized to take it that way." She added mischievously: "I'm looking forward to the day scientists make it possible for a man to carry a baby. Then I can get on with my work." Her response, eschewing the essentialist grounding of womanhood in motherhood so popular in the peace movement,[6] appropriated Nancy Chodorow's vision of shared parenthood as a basis for the mutual liberation of men and women but on behalf of a militarist-feminist program of liberation. When I left the field, Sylvia was busy raising money in her spare time to fund a special summer workshop to prepare local high school girls for careers in science.

Sylvia says she is not very political, but as an undergraduate she did protest her university's investments in South Africa. "If I had to label myself," she says, "I'd say I was a Humphrey Democrat." The reader may be as surprised by this as I was. When I arrived at Livermore I expected its weapons scientists to all be communist-hating, Reagan-Bush-loving conservatives, but it turned out that I was wrong and that Sylvia was far from unusual.

Take Sylvia's colleague, Clark. He used to be a warhead designer and is now making a name for himself in weapons policy studies at the laboratory. Clark has also been a member of the Sierra Club, an active supporter of women's rights, an opponent of U.S. intervention in Central America, a supporter of gun control, and, in the 1970s just before he came to the Livermore Laboratory, an active protester against the Vietnam War.

A number of the scientists I interviewed said they had been opposed to the Vietnam War. Others were environmentalists who had been active members of the local Sierra Club before it took a position in favor of a nuclear freeze in the early 1980s, at which point its Livermore membership plummeted. One young scientist at the laboratory told me she was so enraged by the *Exxon Valdez* oil spill in Alaska that she cut her Exxon card in two, soaked it in oil, and mailed it back to the company. And Mark, a weapons designer on whose living room wall I noticed a Gandhi poster, told me about his occasional daydreams of saving whales—a cause as classically liberal as his methods were not: "I had fantasies of being Captain Nemo in *Twenty Thousand Leagues under the Sea,* torpedoing the whaling ships. What's wrong with that? They're willing to kill whales, so why not blow up their ship and leave them to figure out where to go from there?"

Many laboratory scientists had also been active in the civil rights movement. One warhead designer had helped organize a campaign in Livermore in the 1960s to prohibit racial discrimination in jobs and housing. Jeremy, a deeply religious man who was now employed as a weapons physicist, had spent part of the 1950s working with an activist priest for racial integration in the American South before coming to the laboratory. And Phil, a warhead designer who had some union-organizing experience and who liked to complain to me about the domination of American politics by corporate interests, told me he left his church because the minister opposed a social action program on behalf of minority inner-city residents. He also got into an argument with some high-ranking military officials when they visited the laboratory: "We had some colonels or lieutenant colonels over, and they were talking about something, and it was, they were here to defend capitalism versus communism. And I called them on it. I said, 'You've got things all screwed up. I'm not supporting this country because it's a capitalistic country. I'm supporting it because of its form of government.'"

Just before the 1988 election, one weapons designer took a straw poll of his colleagues to see for whom they planned to vote. He found they were split down the middle between George Bush and Michael Dukakis—roughly the same spread I found in my own interview sample (two of whom told me they had voted for Jesse Jackson in the primary).

So, the laboratory was, to my surprise, a place of political diversity. It was a place where Reagan-Bush supporters, those with no great interest in politics at all, and liberals who had struggled for civil rights and against the Vietnam War could all work together in the development of nuclear weapons.

Thinking through Identity

As my fieldwork proceeded, I began to wonder about the grounds of this collaboration. How were conservative and liberal scientists able to work together on nuclear weapons in the context of a society that, in the decade of Reagan's defense buildup and the Nuclear Freeze movement, was contentiously divided, largely along liberal-conservative lines, about the need to keep building nuclear weapons? How were liberals—some of whom had participated in the peace movement of the sixties and seventies and were critical of many Reagan administration policies in the 1980s—able to feel committed to their work developing nuclear weapons for Ronald Reagan's arms buildup? And if the kinds of overt political ideologies—liberalism and conservatism, Democratic and Republican Party political affiliation—celebrated by the American media as the schismatic indexes of political identity were not the ideological glue holding the laboratory together, then what was? Evidently I had to think about political identity and ideology in new ways, not simply in terms of conventional American political labels, if I was to understand the political integration of the laboratory that enabled its mission to proceed.

Thus, instead of thinking about the laboratory's integration solely in terms of its ability to recruit a particular type, I began to think about the practices through which the laboratory resocializes recruits and actively produces new thinking, feeling, believing, acting selves among its scientists. I also began to think about science itself—the ideology that claims not to be one—as a source of binding energy capable of holding the scientists together despite their apparent political differences. I began to see Livermore's scientists as united not by a commitment to any overtly political program (for example, "push the Soviets out of Eastern Europe") but by a shared dedication to a technocratic program ("make sure the nuclear arsenals are safe and stable") that was avowedly transpolitical. I began to think of the socialization of scientists into the laboratory as, in part, a process whereby political questions were transformed into technocratic questions, and I became interested in how this process was accomplished and experienced.

Insofar as other writers about weapons professionals have adopted a processual perspective, and I am thinking of Robert Jay Lifton and John Mack in particular here,[7] they have tended to present the processes involved as largely repressive or subtractive: ethical questions are avoided, feelings are denied, and fears are repressed. In such analyses, weapons professionals are defined as much in terms of what they lack as what they are. Although part of the work of becoming a weapons scientist does indeed involve learning not to attend to particular fears, feelings, and questions—just as part of the work of becoming an antinuclear activist also involves a selective learned inattention—it also involves the active learning of discourses, feelings, and practices. To take the example of ethics, as I have argued elsewhere,[8] rather than ignoring the ethical dilemmas of their work, weapons scientists learn by listening to their colleagues and other members of the local community to resolve these dilemmas in particular socially patterned ways. They learn, for example, to think about the ethical problems of weapons work in private, not to raise them in public or over lunch with their colleagues. They also learn to think of these issues in instrumentalist, technocratic terms, and to reject discourses that do not recast these moral problems in technocratic terms. In other words, becoming a weapons scientist involves much more complex and creative social and psychological processes than repression and avoidance. As Michel Foucault says in *Power/Knowledge,* "Power would be a fragile thing if its only function were to repress" (59). The power of the social processes sustaining the laboratory's work lies in their ability to teach scientists new ways of thinking, to positively reshape the identities and discourses of its employees as they are transformed from neophytes into mature weapons scientists.

The process of social and psychological engineering involved here is ideological, but in a more fundamental way than we often mean when we use the term *ideology.* Raymond Williams argues in *Marxism and Literature* that we must think of ideologies not only in terms of discourses and ideas but also as "structures of feeling"—ways of experiencing and living in the world that profoundly reshape our emotions, bodily reflexes, and fantasies, as well as our ideas and beliefs. As Sharon Traweek has put it, taking up some of Williams's ideas in her own ethnographic study of physicists at the Stanford Linear Accelerator in California and the KEK facility in Japan, "Novices . . . must become unself-conscious practitioners of the culture, feeling the appropriate desires and anxieties, thinking about the world in a characteristic way."[9]

I should add here that my awareness of the culturally transformative power of particular milieus and social practices derived partly from a process of reflection on changes in my own identity as my fieldwork progressed. When I arrived in Livermore in 1987 I was no longer a practicing peace activist, but in many ways I still had the consciousness of a peace activist. I had been very concerned about the potentially catastrophic consequences of the arms race, a concern that had manifested itself in, among other things, insurgent and graphic mental images of nuclear destruction; and, during my first interviews with Livermore scientists, I felt deeply conflicted about my role as polite ethnographer, which felt a little like a pose, and I wondered if I should stop even trying to find out how these people had become deranged enough to work on nuclear weapons. However, over the two years that I spent talking, eating, hiking, worshiping, and celebrating with nuclear weapons scientists, through a process I still find mysterious, my fear of nuclear war receded, my nightmares about nuclear war disappeared, and I began to find the dark apocalyptic rhetoric of antinuclear activists increasingly quaint, even tiresome. Moreover, after months of disciplined interviewing, note taking, hypothesis testing, and academic writing, the notion that I was an anthropologist, which had at first seemed so hollow, took on increasing substance and became the anchoring principle of my existence. By behaving like an anthropologist, I had become one.

But enough about my voyage of initiation. Let us return, instead, to Sylvia's.

Becoming a Weapons Scientist

Moral philosophers have distinguished two basic positions in the debate on nuclear ethics: the deontological and the consequentialist. Deontologists believe that, if it is wrong to destroy an entire city, then it is wrong to threaten to do so. Consequentialists believe that actions should be judged not by their intrinsic purity but by their consequences; hence, if threatening to destroy an entire city helps save the city, then it is moral to make the threat.

Unsurprisingly, Livermore scientists are consequentialists, and part of the process of becoming a nuclear weapons scientist involves internalizing a commitment to what we might call the central ideological axiom of laboratory life: that scientists at the laboratory design nuclear weapons to ensure, in a world stabilized by nuclear deterrence, that nuclear weapons will never be used. The pragmatic spirit of this central axiom enables it to transcend conventional political divisions of left and right and to unite weapons scientists, in theory at least, around the technocratic project of figuring out what works best. To antinuclear activists and laboratory critics this central axiom of laboratory life seems like a hollow and dangerous cliché, but then it is in the nature of deeply held ideological beliefs that they appear to those who hold them so self-evident that they require no elaboration, whereas to others they may seem so bafflingly wrong that they defy explanation—one group's common sense is another group's nonsense. Part of the process of maturing as a weapons scientist, quite apart from learning the physics and engineering, is coming to see the laboratory's central ideological axiom not as an empty cliché but as a comfortable truth, of coming to feel in one's bones that theories of nuclear deterrence describe the world as it really, inevitably is.

From the perspective of laboratory critics, antinuclear psychologists, and peace activists this process is one of denial, avoidance, and repression. Critics and antinuclear activists often accuse weapons scientists of spiritual deadness and a lack of imagination, and say they do not think about the moral issues raised by their work. For example, Hugh DeWitt, an internal critic who has called for an end to weapons research at the laboratory, calls his colleagues Ph.D. peons who cannot see beyond their "high pay, job security, good benefits, excellent physical facilities, travel to scientific meetings, and good retirement programs."[10] He says they do not think about the ethics of their work.

I will leave it to professional psychologists to decide whether Sylvia is "in denial," but we certainly cannot argue that she has not thought about her work, and it became increasingly clear to me that Sylvia deliberately sought out highly conflictual situations in order to incite such thinking. She approached these conflictual situations as if they were experiments.[11] For example, the summer after she accepted the job at Livermore, but before she arrived at the laboratory, Sylvia made a point of traveling to the Soviet Union, and even telling some Russians what kind of job she had been offered, to see if she would still feel comfortable working on nuclear weapons by the end of the trip. She did. Later, she went to Hiroshima and visited the Peace Museum, which memorializes in the most graphic ways the damage inflicted on the people of that city by the first atomic bomb. She also, at one point, asked if I would take her to an antinuclear meeting and, on another occasion, asked if she could borrow an antinuclear video I had so that she could see for herself what antinuclear activists were saying.

My discussions about nuclear ethics with Sylvia and her colleagues often surprised me. I was surprised, for example, when Sylvia told me of her disgust at the effects of American nuclear testing in the 1950s on Pacific Islanders. "It was very disturbing to me to see that these people had been screwed. Their land was taken away. If I had been around then, I hope that they wouldn't have done that. Either that or I would have quit." And I was surprised that, although Sylvia felt comfortable working on nuclear weapons, she said she would have difficulty working as a defense lawyer trying to secure the freedom of criminals. I was also surprised by her colleague Clark, who told me he felt more comfortable working on nuclear weapons than he would working on conventional weapons. From my perspective as a lapsed antinuclear activist, nuclear weapons were more immoral than conventional weapons because they could kill so many people and kill them so indiscriminately: they were genocidal weapons. For Clark, however, it was precisely because conventional weapons were less destructive that they were routinely used to kill people and, for this reason, he would have had difficulty working on them. As one of Sylvia's colleagues put it, "The moral questions aren't simple. Your conscience should trouble you either way. If you do work on nuclear weapons, think of all the people those weapons might kill. If you don't work on nuclear weapons, think of all the people you may be endangering by leaving them undefended."

Seen in this light, then, in a situation of grave ethical and practical ambiguity, the process of becoming a weapons scientist is one of becoming increasingly certain that nuclear weapons are reasonably safe, and this has been one of Sylvia's central achievements in her first seven years at the laboratory. Sylvia had largely completed this process of self-assurance by the time the cold war ended, and she now believes that nuclear weapons work should continue in a post–cold war world in order to improve the safety of the nuclear stockpile.

When I asked Sylvia why she took the job at Livermore, her response, compared to those of other weapons scientists answering the same question, was unique. Most scientists at Livermore told me they accepted job offers at the laboratory because the work seemed interesting and challenging, and they liked the laid-back, collaborative ambience of the laboratory (as opposed to the cut-throat competitiveness of university physics departments). One of Sylvia's senior colleagues, for example, explained his decision to come to the laboratory many years earlier in these words:

> I had seen enough at MIT of young professors coming in and the scramble to achieve tenure and the tactics that were required or seemed to be required for them to receive good standing in the eyes of the department head and so forth, and I thought that was really disgusting. At the same time, when I talked to people at Lockheed, I really felt uncomfortable about any sense of freedom; I really felt uncomfortable about the push based on the profit motive. I had seen enough of Livermore to know that it seemed to offer quite a bit of academic freedom, quite a bit of time for self-improvement and for satisfying things that were interesting specifically for you—a characteristic of the university without that "after three years you will be put on the auction block and either accepted or rejected from this particular institution." And there was a great deal of adventure in those days. With atmospheric testing, the way you collected samples was by climbing in the backseat of an air force airplane and taking off and having filter papers on either wing, and after the bomb goes off and you have a *lovely* mushroom cloud, then in an hour or so you make a quick pass through the cloud and expose the filter papers and collect samples and bring these back to the laboratory . . . I thought that sounded *absolutely* wonderful.

The explanation Sylvia gave me of her decision to work at Livermore was decidedly different. Unlike the account any other weapons scientist gave me, Sylvia's explanation foregrounded her own initial doubts and fears about nuclear weapons themselves. "The work is quite interesting, and that was definitely a consideration. But I decided to work at the lab, I think, because I had a fear of big weapons. I really wanted to see what was happening for myself. I wanted to see what was going on, rather than take other people's word."

My own fear of nuclear calamity, a fear that was socialized by the antinuclear movement and abetted by the extravagant military rhetoric about winnable nuclear wars during the first Reagan administration, was organized around scenarios of nuclear wars blundered into or started deliberately by leaders who were either mad or so hyperrational about the calculus of terror that they had lost touch with the human consequences of war. Projecting my concerns onto Sylvia, I presumed that she too feared an all-out nuclear war and was perplexed that she could hope to allay such a fear by learning more about the processes of nuclear weapons design rather than international relations and psychology. It took me awhile to realize that she presumed our leaders too rational to start a nuclear war. "I'd say the odds of a nuclear war in my lifetime are very small and very low. I don't think any rational person would use them," she said. What mainly concerned her was not a deliberate nuclear war but the possibility of an accidental explosion of a nuclear weapon. We had each turned nuclear safety into the kind of problem we felt equipped to solve—in my case, a social and political problem; in her case, a technical one.

I have argued elsewhere that nuclear weapons tests are ritual simulations of human control over the awesome power of life and death embodied in nuclear weaponry, and that it is by participating in nuclear tests that nuclear scientists become confident in their mastery over these weapons.[12] Drawing on Bronislaw Malinowski's notion that rituals alleviate anxiety about human vulnerability in the face of cosmic mysteries,[13] I have suggested that nuclear tests matter to warhead designers, not only as scientific experiments, but also as rituals that experientially validate the designers' claims that nuclear weapons are indeed subject to human control. I have also suggested that nuclear tests might be seen as rites of passage in which young scientists are transformed into established designers by displaying their mastery over nuclear weapons to the community of weapons scientists at large—an argument, I might add, that has not, on the whole, been well received at the laboratory.

In the course of my research, Sylvia worked her way through the nuclear cycle. While I was doing my fieldwork, she participated as a neophyte mastering her trade by assisting other designers in their tests. Throughout, at the same time as she was on her personal odyssey to discover whether nuclear weapons were indeed safe, she was learning, both culturally and technically, how nuclear tests are done. Finally, just as I was finishing my dissertation, completing my own professional rite of passage, she oversaw her first test as lead physicist—a test that, so far as I have been able to ascertain, went well.

The last few times I spoke to her Sylvia seemed changed in subtle but important ways. When I first met her, she was fascinated by the counterculture of Berkeley, whose streets she liked to roam while thinking through difficult calculations, and she sometimes talked about moving there from her suburban home. The last time I spoke to her, however, she had given up thoughts of moving to Berkeley—"I'm working much harder now, and the commute would take up too much time. It's better to live close to the lab." Sylvia seemed preoccupied. Although she had been publishing in unclassified areas so that she could get a job outside the laboratory if she needed to, she was concerned that the U.S. government's restrictions on nuclear testing were creating a logjam of experiments, thus slowing down her and her colleagues' work. She opposed an indefinite suspension of nuclear testing, which the government subsequently implemented, much more confidently than she had when I first met her:

> I would like to see testing of things that have already been built, just to make sure nothing has happened, like quality of the sample, because things change. So knowing nothing, I mean, knowing incomplete information and then having that information change on you is very risky. Of course this would be my personal bias. I like to poke things and tear them apart. I would like these systems to be as predictable as possible.

Sylvia had become a weapons scientist.

Dialogue

As the reader will probably have gathered by now, although she has been subjected to the same social processes as other weapons scientists, Sylvia has worked her way through them in her own unique fashion. For me Sylvia was fascinating for her willingness to place herself in conflictual situations and for the ebullient uniqueness of her life—a life that fulfilled the career ambitions of an upwardly mobile Japanese American family and of a generation of feminists but in the most improbable way either could have imagined. I also found myself drawn to Sylvia because of her energetic interest in reflecting on the laboratory and her life within it, and in understanding something about the antinuclear activists who stood opposed to the direction her life had taken. Traditionally anthropologists call people such as Sylvia—"natives" with an unusual interest in reflecting upon and explaining their own culture—key informants. I dislike this term not only because of the connotations of surveillance and betrayal inherent in the word *informant,* but also because the hierarchy built into the word fails to convey the discursive, mutually challenging nature of my conversations with Sylvia—conversations that, despite the roles of native and ethnographer that formally underpinned them, were informative, challenging, and rewarding for both of us. Thanks to these interactions not only did I learn about the laboratory but Sylvia learned about the antinuclear movement, and every time she violated my expectations about warhead designers, I learned about myself and my own unexamined assumptions.

These conversations with Sylvia became conduits for all kinds of communications that would not otherwise have taken place. For example, Sylvia used her relationship with me to find out more about the protesters, about whom she was greatly curious, and once even asked me, only half playfully, I think, to let the protesters know that her division had enjoyed the theatrical nature of the latest demonstration at the laboratory gates and that she had admired the giant puppets they had made for the occasion. As for me, thanks to my friendship with Sylvia, I was able to find out what it meant to her to be a weapons designer, as well as what her colleagues thought of particular hypotheses I was developing or papers I was writing, and how I was perceived by the community of warhead designers. Among other things I learned, for example, that the warhead designers sometimes joked about collaborating in feeding me plausible but spurious accounts of their secret lives behind the barbed wire fence.

Above all, the reflexive nature of my conversations with Sylvia helped me realize the extent to which, despite my best efforts, I often read into the lives of Livermore scientists a pervasive sense of guilt and conflict about their work that, I now believe, existed far more in my mind than in theirs. A brief anecdote will illustrate the point. Sylvia once asked me if I would take her to an antinuclear meeting to rally supporters for an upcoming protest at the Nevada nuclear test site. As we drove back from the meeting it was clear to me that Sylvia was upset about something. I presumed that the meeting, where speakers held forth at length about the evils of the arms race and the moral callousness of weapons scientists, had brought to the surface her deep psychic conflicts about her work. No wonder she was upset. No, she said, she was angry at me because, on the way to the meeting, I had told her exactly what to expect in such a way that I had, as she put it, "ruined the experiment."

Since I started to write about my fieldwork, Sylvia's response to my ideas has been ambivalent. When a series of my articles about the laboratory's reaction to the end of the cold war appeared in a local newspaper in Livermore, Sylvia wrote to tell me, "People on my corridor brought me zillions of copies of all three articles—they all thought, as do I, that the articles accurately reflected the mood around the lab." She also felt, unlike many of her colleagues, that there was something to my notion of nuclear tests as rituals, even if she did not completely agree with it. Just after her own nuclear test she wrote to me:

> I wanted to convey my congratulations to you on the completion of your Ph.D. At about the time you were in Palo Alto [submitting your dissertation], I was probably in Nevada, going through a ritual you may have described in your dissertation. The note that Harry [her mentor] sent a couple of months ago was shown to me before going out—I regret not adding my own comments to balance and temper his, but I was in the midst of the process. Let me just say I enjoyed reading about the rituals A-Division designers go through (I actually saw them do some of them) during a test. Harry believes you were misled because he's never seen this stuff, but some of it happens.

She was much less happy, however, about a passage in my dissertation in which I analyzed one of our conversations. In that passage I mentioned that she had watched a television docudrama about the bombing of Hiroshima and had answered my question about the feelings the program aroused in her by saying, "It was poorly executed. They were quite accurate about the physical effects of the explosion, but the accents were all wrong." I used this response to illustrate my observation that a scientist's learned attentiveness to detail and objectivity could distance him or her from the suffering of human bodies. Sylvia responded quite angrily to this:

> It is very natural and automatic for me to be able to distinguish between native and nonnative Japanese speakers. I was not able to suspend my belief that this was not "real," just as I am not able to do so at a badly done film of any kind, and so it was difficult for me to empathize with the pain that those actors were trying to portray because, to me, they couldn't be real bomb survivors. But that does not mean I do not or cannot feel pain for the bomb victims. I remember your expression of disbelief when I described how some physicists have cringed when driving by a roadkill. But why is *this* so hard for you to believe? Why didn't you use *that* as an example of something?

For better or worse, Sylvia and I have become part of one another's lives. I must live with her criticisms of my work, and she must live with my interpretations of her life. The intrusiveness of this situation is encapsulated nicely in a card I once received from her when she was traveling in Japan: "I had a very strange dream about going through the Peace Museum in Hiroshima with a tape-recorded tour piped into my ear, except that the headphones were attached to a microphone into which *you* were speaking. And there was no stop button."

Conclusion: There Is None

When I applied for funding for my research from the National Science Foundation, one anonymous reviewer recommended that I be denied funding because, as a former antinuclear activist, I would not be objective about nuclear weapons scientists. Just as I have left it to others to decide whether Sylvia is "in denial," I will leave it to the reader to decide whether I have been "objective" about weapons scientists. Returning to Donna Haraway's notion of "situated knowledge" I will say, however, that no knowledge is disinterested, no ethnographer capable of what Haraway calls the "God's-eye view from nowhere." From my perspective it is my very identity as a former antinuclear activist that gave me an angle, a set of questions, a terrain of engagement in my encounter with the weapons scientists. Many of my earlier presumptions about nuclear weapons scientists perished on that terrain of engagement, as I have tried to show here by giving a processual rather than a finished account of my fieldwork—by, to adapt a phrase of Bruno Latour's, giving the reader ethnography in the making rather than ethnography ready made. Following Latour, I have taken it as axiomatic here that a postmodern stratagem of objectivity would be a reflexive one that interrogated itself while focusing on the making as well as the presentation of interpretation. This is one reason for the dialogic mold of this chapter. Let me now turn to some others.

Sylvia's allegorical observation that our encounter came without a stop button evokes a characteristic feature of anthropology as it is practiced in the late twentieth century that is particularly marked in the case of my own project. Where fieldwork used to be a bounded and hierarchical encounter between the knower and the known aiming to produce an authoritative summation of the observed culture, today it often has more of the qualities of an ongoing, albeit asymmetrical, dialogue.

To begin with, the ivory tower from which I write no longer affords that "God's-eye view from nowhere," in part because my location has been situated and problematized by Sylvia and her colleagues. If in my writing I raise questions about the way they make their living and the institution for which they work, I cannot help but notice that, in their answers to my questions about their choices, they raise questions about perceived sexual discrimination and abuse of junior faculty at the institution where I work, saying they would rather work at a nuclear weapons laboratory than at a university like mine. The process of cultural critique here, while not equal, is mutual, and it leaves me with a lot more to think about than just the socialization of weapons scientists and the contradictions of other people's lives.

Moreover, unlike a former generation of ethnographers whose works were not read by their subjects, anthropologists today must live with our subjects' responses to our work—especially if we practice "repatriated anthropology." The days when our subjects had culture and we had culture theory are, if they ever existed, now gone. In my case, before I interviewed Sylvia, she quizzed me about the interpretive turn in anthropology, and, after I wrote my dissertation, she disputed the terms of some of my interpretations. Other "informants" disputed my reading of Foucault and so on. Addressing this kind of situation, Renato Rosaldo has written in *Culture and Truth* that

> we should take the criticisms of our subjects in much the same way that we take those of our colleagues. Not unlike other ethnographers, so-called natives can be insightful, sociologically correct, axe-grinding, self-interested, or mistaken. They do know their own cultures, and rather than being ruled out of court, their criticisms should be listened to and taken into account, to be accepted, rejected, or modified, as we reformulate our analyses. (50)

But the dialogue goes in the other direction as well. Not only must I deal with Sylvia's interruptions of my professional conversations, but she and her colleagues must now deal with my presence in their conversations, too. Whether they like it or not, my notion that nuclear tests are like "primitive" rituals and my newspaper articles delineating the laboratory's response to the end of the cold war have now been absorbed into their discursive economy. And, even though I am no longer in the field, I sometimes get calls from journalists in Livermore hoping for a gnomic pronouncement on the laboratory's latest crisis—pronouncements that, if quoted, sometimes provoke correspondence from the laboratory.

If my fieldwork was a sort of dialogue, then, that dialogue is continuing, albeit in a new register. There is no stop button. And surely this is what we should ask of anthropology as we enter the twenty-first century—not that it settle conversations, but that it start them.

(1995)

2

Nuclear Weapons and the Other in the Western Imagination

> Think . . . what the world would be like if Saddam Hussein would have a nuclear weapon. First of all, it would change the balance of power. Second of all, he would use it. And that would be most disastrous.
> —Dan Quayle, U.S. vice president (1988–92)

> We cannot, to paraphrase Lincoln, have a world half nuclear and half nuclear free.
> —David McReynolds, War Resisters League

There is a common perception in the West that nuclear weapons are most dangerous when they are in the hands of Third World leaders. I first became interested in this perception while interviewing nuclear weapons designers for an ethnographic study of the Lawrence Livermore National Laboratory (LLNL)—one of three laboratories where U.S. nuclear weapons are designed.[1] I made a point of asking each scientist if he or she thought nuclear weapons would be used in my lifetime. Almost all said that they thought it unlikely that the United States or the Russians would initiate the use of nuclear weapons, but most thought that nuclear weapons would probably be used—by a Third World country.

The laboratory took a similar position as an institution. For example, using terminology with distinctly colonial overtones to argue for continued weapons research after the end of the cold war, an official laboratory pamphlet said:

> Political, diplomatic, and military experts believe that wars of the future will most likely be "tribal conflicts" between neighboring Third World countries or between ethnic groups in the same country. While the Cold War may be over, these small disputes may be more dangerous than a war between the superpowers, because smaller nations with deep-seated grievances against each other may lack the restraint that has been exercised by the US and the USSR. The existence of such potential conflicts and the continued danger of nuclear holocaust underscore the need for continued weapons research.[2]

It is not only nuclear weapons scientists who believe that nuclear weapons are much safer in the hands of the established nuclear powers than in those of Third World countries. There has long been a widespread perception among U.S. defense intellectuals, politicians, and pundits—leaders of opinion on nuclear weapons—that, while we can live with the nuclear weapons of the five official nuclear nations for the indefinite future, the proliferation of nuclear weapons to nuclear-threshold states in the Third World, especially the Islamic world, would be enormously dangerous. This orthodoxy is so much a part of our collective common sense that, like all common sense, it can usually be stated as simple fact without fear of contradiction.[3] It is widespread in the media and in learned journals,[4] and it is shared by liberals as well as conservatives. For example, just as Kenneth Adelman, a senior official in the Reagan administration, has said that "the real danger comes from some miserable Third World country which decides to use these weapons either out of desperation or incivility," at the same time Hans Bethe—a physicist revered by many for his work on behalf of disarmament over many decades—has said, "There have to be nuclear weapons in the hands of more responsible countries to deter such use" by Third World nations.[5]

Western alarmism about the dangers of nuclear weapons in Third World hands was particularly evident when India and Pakistan set off their salvos of nuclear tests in May 1998. Many analysts had already identified South Asia as the likeliest site in the world for a nuclear war. Soon after India's tests, Senator Daniel Patrick Moynihan (Democrat, New York) said on *The Charlie Rose Show*, "If Pakistan tests the bomb, we are on the edge of nuclear warfare." Three days later, following Pakistan's tests, Senator John McCain (Republican, Arizona) said that the world was "closer to nuclear war than we have been any time since the Cuban Missile Crisis."[6] Speaking to Reuters wire service on May 28, David Albright, president of the liberal Institute for Strategic and International Studies in Washington,

D.C., opined, "I don't think they [India and Pakistan] are up to the task of preventing a conventional conflict from accidentally slipping into a nuclear exchange." The *Washington Post* agreed: "Today, in the aftermath of a series of test explosions set off by the bitter rivals, there is no place on earth with greater potential for triggering a nuclear war."[7]

Eight years earlier there was a similar burst of alarmism over the prospect of an Iraqi nuclear weapon. In November 1990, when American opinion was still badly divided over the prospect of a war with Iraq, opinion polls suggested that more Americans were willing to go to war with Iraq to prevent it from acquiring nuclear weapons than to liberate Kuwait or to assure U.S. access to oil.[8] In the national debate leading up to the Gulf War, most American opinion makers agreed that Iraq should not be allowed to acquire nuclear weapons. Even those who accused the Bush administration of exaggerating the immediate danger in its search for a rationale for the U.S. military buildup in the Persian Gulf agreed that a line would eventually have to be drawn. For example, a *Christian Science Monitor* editorial for November 28, 1990, criticized the Bush administration's "scare-of-the-week campaign" but concluded apropos Iraq's nuclear program that "it may be . . . that ultimately force will be required to end it" (20). Many were not prepared to exercise even such short-term restraint. For example, in August 1990, former Reagan administration arms-control official Richard Perle advised the immediate bombing of Iraq in a *Wall Street Journal* op-ed piece; *New York Times* columnist William Safire was by November advocating preventive war; another *New York Times* columnist, A. M. Rosenthal, who has written that "unutterably many will die one day if we allow Saddam to hide and keep his weapons of mass murder," was recommending an American ultimatum to Iraq to dismantle its nuclear program or have it bombed; and Senator John McCain had called for a military attack on Iraq's nuclear facilities even before the invasion of Kuwait.[9] Whether they favored immediate military action or diplomatic efforts first, commentators across the political spectrum agreed that an Iraqi nuclear weapon would be intolerable; the only question was how to prevent it.

Nuclear Orientalism

According to the anthropological literature on risk, shared fears often reveal as much about the identities and solidarities of the fearful as about the actual dangers that are feared.[10] The immoderate reactions in the West to the nuclear tests conducted in 1998 by India and Pakistan, and to Iraq's nuclear weapons program earlier, are examples of an entrenched discourse on nuclear proliferation that has played an important role in structuring the Third World, and our relation to it, in the Western imagination.

This discourse, dividing the world into nations that can be trusted with nuclear weapons and those that cannot, dates back, at least, to the Non-Proliferation Treaty of 1970.

The Non-Proliferation Treaty embodied a bargain between the five countries that had nuclear weapons in 1970 and those countries that did not. According to the bargain, the five official nuclear states (the United States, the Soviet Union, the United Kingdom, France, and China)[11] promised to assist other signatories to the treaty in acquiring nuclear energy technology as long as they did not use that technology to produce nuclear weapons, submitting to international inspections when necessary to prove their compliance. Further, in article 6 of the treaty, the five nuclear powers agreed to "pursue negotiations in good faith on effective measures relating to cessation of the nuclear arms race at an early date and to nuclear disarmament."[12] One hundred eighty-seven countries have signed the treaty, but Israel, India, and Pakistan have refused, saying it enshrines a system of global "nuclear apartheid." Although the Non-Proliferation Treaty divided the countries of the world into nuclear and nonnuclear by means of a purely temporal metric[13]—designating only those who had tested nuclear weapons by 1970 as nuclear powers—the treaty has become the legal anchor for a global nuclear regime that is increasingly legitimated in Western public discourse in racialized terms. In view of recent developments in global politics—the collapse of the Soviet threat and the recent war against Iraq, a nuclear-threshold nation in the Third World—the importance of this discourse in organizing Western geopolitical understandings is only growing. It has become an increasingly important way of legitimating U.S. military programs in the post–cold war world since the early 1990s, when U.S. military leaders introduced the term *rogue states* into the American lexicon of fear, identifying a new source of danger just as the Soviet threat was declining.[14]

Thus in Western discourse nuclear weapons are represented so that "theirs" are a problem whereas "ours" are not. During the cold war the Western discourse on the dangers of "nuclear proliferation" defined the term in such a way as to sever the two senses of the word *proliferation*. This usage split off the "vertical" proliferation of the superpower arsenals (the development of new and improved weapons designs and the numerical expansion of the stockpiles) from the "horizontal" proliferation of nuclear weapons to other countries, presenting only the latter as the "proliferation problem." Following the end of the cold war, the American and Russian arsenals are being cut to a few thousand weapons on each side.[15] However, the United States and Russia have turned back appeals from various non-aligned nations, especially India, for the nuclear powers to open discussions on a global convention abolishing nuclear weapons. Article 6 of the Non-Proliferation Treaty notwithstanding, the Clinton and Bush administrations have declared that nuclear weapons will play a role in the defense of the United States for the indefinite future. Meanwhile, in a controversial move, the Clinton administration broke with the policy of previous administrations in basically formalizing a policy of using nuclear weapons against nonnuclear states to deter chemical and biological weapons.[16]

The dominant discourse that stabilizes this system of nuclear apartheid in Western ideology is a specialized variant within a broader system of colonial and postcolonial discourse that takes as its essentialist premise a profound Otherness separating Third World from Western countries.[17] This inscription of Third World (especially Asian and Middle Eastern) nations as ineradicably different from our own has, in a different context, been labeled "Orientalism" by Edward Said. Said argues that orientalist discourse constructs the world in terms of a series of binary oppositions that produce the Orient as the mirror image of the West: where "we" are rational and disciplined, "they" are impulsive and emotional; where "we" are modern and flexible, "they" are slaves to ancient passions and routines; where "we" are honest and compassionate, "they" are treacherous and uncultivated. While the blatantly racist orientalism of the high colonial period has softened, more subtle orientalist ideologies endure in contemporary politics. They can be found, as Akhil Gupta has argued, in discourses of economic development that represent Third World nations as child nations lagging behind Western nations in a uniform cycle of development or, as Catherine Lutz and Jane Collins suggest, in the imagery of popular magazines such as *National Geographic*.[18] I want to suggest here that another variant of contemporary orientalist ideology is also to be found in U.S. national security discourse.

Following Anthony Giddens in his *Central Problems in Social Theory*, I define *ideology* as a way of constructing political ideas, institutions, and behavior that (1) makes the political structures and institutions created by dominant social groups, classes, and nations appear to be naturally given and inescapable rather than socially constructed; (2) presents the interests of elites as if they were universally shared; (3) obscures the connections between different social and political antagonisms so as to inhibit massive, binary confrontations (i.e., revolutionary situations); and (4) legitimates domination. The Western discourse on nuclear proliferation is ideological in all four of these senses: (1) it makes the simultaneous ownership of nuclear weapons by the major powers and the absence of nuclear weapons in Third World countries seem natural and reasonable while problematizing attempts by such countries as India, Pakistan, and Iraq to acquire these

weapons; (2) it presents the security needs of the established nuclear powers as if they were everybody's; (3) it effaces the continuity between Third
World countries' nuclear deprivation and other systematic patterns of deprivation in the underdeveloped world in order to inhibit a massive north-
south confrontation; and (4) it legitimates the nuclear monopoly of the
recognized nuclear powers.

In the following pages I examine four popular arguments against horizontal nuclear proliferation and suggest that all four are ideological and orientalist. The arguments are that (1) Third World countries are too poor to
afford nuclear weapons; (2) deterrence will be unstable in the Third World;
(3) Third World regimes lack the technical maturity to be trusted with nuclear weapons; and (4) Third World regimes lack the political maturity to
be trusted with nuclear weapons.

Each of these four arguments could as easily be turned backward and
used to delegitimate Western nuclear weapons, as I show in the following
commentary. Sometimes, in the specialized literature of defense experts,
one finds frank discussion of near accidents, weaknesses, and anomalies in
deterrence as it has been practiced by the established nuclear powers, but
these admissions tend to be quarantined in specialized discursive spaces
where the general public has little access to them and where it is hard to
connect them to the broader public discourse on nuclear proliferation.[19] In
this chapter I retrieve some of these discussions of flaws in deterrence from
their quarantined spaces and juxtapose them with the dominant discourse
on the dangers of proliferation in order to destabilize its foundational assumption of a secure binary distinction between "the West" and "the Third
World." It is my argument that, in the production of this binary distinction, possible fears and ambivalences about Western nuclear weapons are
purged and recast as intolerable aspects of the Other. This purging and
recasting occurs in a discourse characterized by gaps and silences in its
representation of our own nuclear weapons and exaggerations in its representation of those of the Other. Our discourse on proliferation is a piece of
ideological machinery that transforms anxiety-provoking ambiguities into
secure dichotomies.

I should clarify two points here. First, I am not arguing that there are,
finally, no differences between countries in terms of their reliability as custodians of nuclear weapons. I am arguing that those differences are complex,
ambiguous, and crosscutting in ways that are not captured by a simple binary division between, on the one hand, a few countries that have nuclear
weapons and insist they are safe and, on the other hand, those countries
that do not have nuclear weapons and are told they cannot safely acquire
them. It is my goal here to demonstrate the ways in which this simple

binary distinction works as an ideological mechanism to impede a more nuanced and realistic assessment of the polymorphous dangers posed by nuclear weapons in all countries and to obscure recognition of the ways in which our own policies in the West have often exacerbated dangers in the Third World that, far from being simply the problems of the Other, are problems produced by a world system dominated by First World institutions and states.

Finally, while this chapter intervenes at the level of the way we talk about policy, it does not advocate a particular nuclear policy. My own politics are broadly antinuclear, and the logic of the issues discussed here leads me at least in the direction of nuclear abolition. Still, my critique of the nuclear double standard also draws on arguments advanced by some, such as Kenneth Waltz, who have advocated the further proliferation of nuclear weapons,[20] and I recognize that different nonorientalist constructions of the risks and benefits of nuclear weaponry are sustainable. As I will discuss in the conclusion, a nonorientalist discourse on proliferation could point in the direction of abolition, but it could also be compatible with quite different policy positions.

Four Common Arguments against Nuclear Proliferation

1. Third World Countries Are Too Poor to Afford Nuclear Weapons

It is often said that it is inappropriate for Third World countries to squander money on nuclear (or conventional) weapons when they have such pressing problems of poverty, hunger, and homelessness on which the money might more appropriately be spent. Western disapprobation of Third World military spending was particularly marked when India conducted its "peaceful nuclear explosion" on May 18, 1974. At the time one Washington official, condemning India for having the wrong priorities, was quoted as saying, "I don't see how this is going to grow more rice."[21] The next day the *New York Times* picked up the theme in an editorial titled "On to Armageddon":

> The more appropriate reaction [to the nuclear test] would be one of despair that such great talent and resources have been squandered on the vanity of power, while 600 million Indians slip deeper into poverty. The sixth member of the nuclear club may be passing the begging bowl before the year is out because Indian science and technology so far have failed to solve the country's fundamental problems of food and population. (1)

Similar comments were made after the Indian and Pakistani nuclear tests of 1998. Mary McGrory, for example, wrote in her column in the *Washington Post* that "two large, poor countries in desperate need of schools, hospitals, and education are strewing billions of dollars for nuclear development";

and Rupert Cornwell, writing in the British newspaper the *Independent,* said that "a country as poor as India should not be wasting resources on weapons that might only tempt a preemptive strike by an adversary; it is economic lunacy."[22]

Such statements are not necessarily wrong, but, read with a critical eye, they have a recursive effect that potentially undermines the rationale for military programs in the West as well. First, one can interrogate denunciations of profligate military spending in the Third World by pointing out that Western countries, despite their own extravagant levels of military spending, have by no means solved their own social and economic problems. The United States, for example, which in the mid-1990s allotted 4 percent of its GNP (over $250 billion per year) to military spending against India's 2.8 percent,[23] financed the arms race of the 1980s by accumulating debt—its own way of passing the begging bowl—at a rate of over $200 billion each year. Meanwhile in the United States advocates for the homeless estimate that two million Americans have nowhere to live, and another thirty-six million Americans live below the official poverty line.[24] The infant mortality rate is lower for black children in Botswana than for those in the United States.[25] As any observant pedestrian in the urban United States knows, it is not only Indians who need to beg.

Second, American taxpayers have consistently been told that nuclear weapons are a bargain compared with the cost of conventional weapons. They give "more bang for the buck." If this is true for "us," then surely it is also true for "them": if a developing nation has security concerns, then a nuclear weapon ought to be the cheapest way to take care of them.[26]

Third, critics of U.S. military spending have been told for years that military spending stimulates economic development and produces such beneficial economic spin-offs that it almost pays for itself. If military Keynesianism works for "us," it is hard to see why it should not also work for "them." And indeed, "Indian decision-makers have perceived high investments in nuclear research as a means to generate significant long-term industrial benefits in electronics, mining, metallurgy and other non-nuclear sectors of the economy."[27]

In other words, "they" may use the same legitimating arguments as "we" do on behalf of nuclear weapons. The arguments we use to defend our weapons could as easily be used to defend theirs. We can only argue otherwise by using a double standard.

2. Deterrence Will Be Unstable in the Third World

During the Cold War Americans were told that nuclear deterrence prevented the smoldering enmity between the superpowers from bursting into the full flame of war, saving millions of lives by making conventional war too dangerous. When the practice of deterrence was challenged by the antinuclear movement of the 1980s, Pentagon officials and defense intellectuals warned us that nuclear disarmament would just make the world safe for conventional war.[28] Surely, then, we should want countries such as Pakistan, India, Iraq, and Israel also to enjoy the stabilizing benefits of nuclear weapons.

This is, in fact, precisely the argument made by the father of the Pakistani bomb, Abdul Qadeer Khan. He said at a press conference in 1998, alluding to the fact that Pakistan had a nuclear capability for many years before its actual nuclear tests, "The nuclear weapon is a peace guarantor. It gave peace to Europe, it gave peace to us. . . . I believe my work has saved this country for the last twenty years from many wars."[29] Western security specialists and media pundits have argued, on the other hand, that deterrence as practiced by the superpowers during the Cold War may not work in Third World settings because Third World adversaries tend to share borders and because they lack the resources to develop secure second-strike capabilities. On closer examination these arguments, plausible enough at first, turn out to be deeply problematic, especially in their silences about the risks of deterrence as practiced by the superpowers. I shall take them in turn.

First, there is the argument that deterrence may not work for countries, such as India and Pakistan, that share a border and can therefore attack one another quickly.[30] As Michael Lev put it:

> In the heating conflict between India and Pakistan, one of the many dangers to be reckoned with is there would be no time for caution.
>
> While it would have taken more than a half-hour for a Soviet-based nuclear missile to reach the United States—time at least for America to double-check its computer screen or use the hotline—the striking distance between India and Pakistan is no more than five minutes.
>
> That is not enough time to confirm a threat or even think twice before giving the order to return fire, and perhaps mistakenly incinerate an entire nation.[31]

This formulation focuses only on the difference in missile flight times while ignoring other countervailing differences in missile configurations that would make deterrence in South Asia look more stable than deterrence as practiced by the superpowers. Such a view overlooks the fact that the missiles deployed by the two superpowers were, by the end of the cold war, MIRVed and extraordinarily accurate. MIRVed missiles—those equipped with multiple independently targetable reentry vehicles—carry several warheads, each capable of striking a different target. The MX, for example, was designed to carry ten warheads, each capable of landing within one hundred feet of a separate target. The unprecedented accuracy of the MX, together with the fact that one MX missile could—in theory at least—destroy ten Soviet missiles made it, as some arms controllers worried at the time, a destabilizing weapon that, together with its Russian counterparts, put each superpower in a "use it or lose it" situation whereby it would have to launch its missiles immediately if it believed itself under attack. Thus, once one adds accuracy and MIRVing to the strategic equation, the putative contrast between stable deterrence in the West and unstable deterrence in South Asia looks upside down, even if we were to grant the difference in flight times between the cold war superpowers and between the main adversaries in South Asia.

But there is no reason to grant the alleged difference in flight times. Lev says that it would have taken "more than a half-hour" for American and Russian missiles to reach their targets during the Cold War. While this is more or less true for intercontinental ballistic missiles (ICBMs), it was not true for the submarine-launched ballistic missiles (SLBMs) the superpowers moved in against each other's coasts; these were about ten minutes of flight time from their targets. Nor was it true of the American Jupiter missiles stationed in Turkey, right up against the Soviet border, in the early 1960s. Nor was it true of the Pershing IIs deployed in Germany in the 1980s. When the antinuclear movement claimed that it was destabilizing to move the Pershings to within less than ten minutes of flight time of Moscow, the U.S. government insisted that anything that strengthened NATO's attack capability strengthened nuclear deterrence. Here again one sees a double standard in the arguments made to legitimate "our" nuclear weapons.

Finally, even if we were to accept that the superpowers would have thirty minutes warning against five minutes for countries in South Asia, to think that this matters is to be incited to a discourse based on the absurd premise that there is any meaningful difference between half an hour and five minutes for a country that believes itself under nuclear attack.[32] While half an hour does leave more time to verify warnings of an attack, would any sane national leadership feel any safer irrevocably launching nuclear weapons against an adversary in thirty rather than five minutes? In either case, the time frame for decision making is too compressed.

In other words, the argument about missile flight times, quite apart from the fact that it misrepresents the realities of deterrence between the superpowers, is a red herring. What really matters is not the geographical proximity of the adversarial nations but, rather, their confidence that each could survive an attack by the other with some sort of retaliatory capability. Many analysts have argued that newly nuclear nations with small arsenals would lack a secure second-strike capability. Their nuclear weapons would therefore invite rather than deter a preemptive or preventive attack, especially in a crisis. Thus the *New York Times* editorialized on May 25, 1998, that "unlike the superpowers, India and Pakistan will have small, poorly protected nuclear stocks. No nation in that situation can be sure that its weapons could survive a nuclear attack" (14). Similarly, British defense analyst Jonathan Power has written that "superpower theorists have long argued that stability is not possible unless there is an assured second-strike capability. . . . Neither India and [sic] Pakistan have the capability, as the superpowers did, to develop and build such a second-strike capability."[33]

This argument has been rebutted by Kenneth Waltz, a leading political scientist seen as a maverick for his views on nuclear proliferation.[34] Waltz, refusing the binary distinction at the heart of the dominant discourse, suggests that horizontal nuclear proliferation could bring about what he calls "nuclear peace" in troubled regions of the globe just as, in his view, it stabilized the superpower relationship. Waltz argues that, although the numbers of weapons are different, the general mathematical principle of deterrence—the appalling asymmetry of risk and reward—remains the same and may even, perversely, work more effectively in new nuclear nations. Waltz points out in "More May Be Better" that it would take very few surviving nuclear weapons to inflict "unacceptable damage" on a Third World adversary: "Do we expect to lose one city or two, two cities or ten? When these are the pertinent questions, we stop thinking about running risks and start thinking about how to avoid them" (8). He argues that, while a first strike would be fraught with terrifying uncertainties in any circumstances, the discussion of building secure retaliatory capabilities in the West has tended, ethnocentrically, to focus on the strategies the superpowers employed to do so: building vast arsenals at huge expense on land, at sea, and in the air. But Third World countries have cheaper, more low-tech options at their disposal too: "Nuclear warheads can be fairly small and light, and they are easy to hide and to move. People worry about terrorists stealing nuclear warheads because various states have so many of them. Everybody seems to believe that terrorists are capable of hiding bombs. Why should states be unable to do what terrorist gangs are thought to be capable of?" (19). Waltz also points out that Third World states could easily and cheaply confuse adversaries by deploying dummy nuclear weapons, and he reminds readers that the current nuclear powers (with the exception of the United States) all passed through and survived phases in their own nuclear infancy when their nuclear arsenals were similarly small and vulnerable.[35]

The discourse on proliferation assumes that the superpowers' massive interlocking arsenals of highly accurate, MIRVed missiles deployed on hair-trigger alert and designed with first-strike capability backed by global satellite capability were stable and that the small, crude arsenals of new nuclear nations would be unstable, but one could quite plausibly argue the reverse. Indeed, as mentioned earlier, by the 1980s a number of analysts in the West were concerned that the MIRVing of missiles and the accuracy of new guidance systems were generating increasing pressure to strike first in a crisis. Although the strategic logic might be a little different, they saw temptations to preempt at the high end of the nuclear social system as well as at the low end.[36] There were also concerns (explored in more detail later in this chapter) that the complex computerized early-warning systems with which each superpower protected its weapons were generating false alarms that might lead to accidental war.[37] Thus one could argue—as former Secretary of Defense Robert McNamara (1986) and a number of others have—that deterrence between the United States and Russia would be safer and more stable if each side replaced its current massive strategic arsenals with a small force of about one hundred nuclear weapons—about the size India's nuclear stockpile is believed to be, as it happens. Further, Bruce Blair, a former missile control officer turned strategic analyst, and Stansfield Turner, a former CIA director, have suggested that the readiness posture of American and Russian nuclear forces makes them an accident waiting to happen.[38] The United States and Russia, they argue, would be safer if they stored their warheads separate from their delivery vehicles—as, it so happens, India and Pakistan do.[39] In the words of Scott Sagan, a political scientist and former Pentagon official concerned about U.S. nuclear weapons safety:

> The United States should not try to make new nuclear nations become like the superpowers during the Cold War, with large arsenals ready to launch at a moment's notice for the sake of deterrence; instead, for the sake of safety, the United States and Russia should try to become more like some of the nascent nuclear states, maintaining very small nuclear capabilities, with weapons components separated and located apart from the delivery systems, and with civilian organizations controlling the warheads.[40]

Given, as I have shown, that the crisis stability of large nuclear arsenals can also be questioned and that it is not immediately self-evident why the leader of, say, India today should feel any more confident that he would not lose a city or two in a preemptive strike on Pakistan than his U.S. counterpart would in attacking Russia, I want to suggest that an argument that appears on the surface to be about numbers and configurations of weapons is really, when one looks more closely, about the psychology and culture of people. Put simply, the dominant discourse assumes that leaders in the

Third World make decisions differently than their counterparts in the West: that they are more likely to take risks, gambling millions of lives, or to make rash and irresponsible calculations.

3. Third World Governments Lack the Technical Maturity to Handle Nuclear Weapons

The third argument against horizontal proliferation is that Third World nations may lack the technical maturity to be trusted with nuclear weapons. Brito and Intriligator, for example, tell us that "the new nuclear nations are likely to be less sophisticated technically and thus less able to develop safeguards against accident or unauthorized action."[41] And the *Washington Post* quotes an unnamed Western diplomat stationed in Pakistan, who, worrying that India and Pakistan lack the technology to detect an incoming attack on their weapons, said the United States has "expensive space-based surveillance that could pick up the launches, but Pakistan and India have no warning systems. I don't know what their doctrine will be. Launch when the wind blows?"[42]

In terms of safety technologies, U.S. weapons scientists have over the years developed insensitive high explosive (IHE), which will not detonate if a weapon is—as has happened with U.S. nuclear weapons—accidentally dropped. U.S. weapons scientists have also developed permissive action links (PALs), electronic devices that block the arming of nuclear weapons until the correct code is entered so that the weapons cannot be used if stolen and will not go off if there is an accident during routine transportation or storage of the weapons. Obviously the United States could, if it were deeply concerned about safety problems in new nuclear nations, share such safety technologies, as it offered to do with the Soviets during the cold war.[43]

Quite aside from the question of whether the United States itself could discreetly do more to improve the safety of nuclear arsenals in new nuclear nations, if one reviews the U.S. nuclear safety record, the comforting dichotomy between a high-tech, safe "us" and low-tech, unsafe "them" begins to look distinctly dubious. First, the United States has not always made use of the safety technologies at its disposal. Over the protests of some weapons designers, for example, the navy decided not to incorporate state-of-the-art safety technologies into one of its newest weapons: the Trident II. The Trident II does not contain insensitive high explosive because IHE is heavier than ordinary high explosive and would, therefore, have reduced the number of warheads each missile could carry. The Trident II designers also decided to use 1.1 class propellant fuel rather than the less combustible, hence safer, 1.3 class fuel, because the former would give the missile a longer range. After the Trident II was deployed, a high-level review panel appointed by President Bush recommended recalling and redesigning it for safety reasons, but was overruled partly because of the expense this would have involved.[44]

Second, turning to the surveillance and early-warning systems that the United States has but threshold nuclear nations lack, one finds that these systems bring with them special problems as well as benefits. For example, it was the high-technology Aegis radar system, misread by a navy operator, that was directly responsible for the tragically mistaken U.S. decision to shoot down an Iranian commercial jetliner on July 3, 1988, a blunder that cost innocent lives and could have triggered a war. Similarly, and potentially more seriously,

> At 8:50 a.m., on November 9, 1979, the operational duty officers at NORAD—as well as in the SAC command post, at the Pentagon's National Military Command Center (NMCC), and the alternate National Military Command Center (ANMCC) at Fort Richie, Maryland—were suddenly confronted with a realistic display of a Soviet nuclear attack apparently designed to decapitate the American command system and destroy U.S. nuclear forces: a large number of Soviet missiles appeared to have been launched, both SLBMs and ICBMs, in a full-scale attack on the United States.[45]

American interceptor planes were scrambled, the presidential "doomsday plane" took off (without the president) to coordinate a possible nuclear war, and air traffic controllers were told to bring down commercial planes before U.S. military commanders found that a training tape had mistakenly been inserted into the system.[46]

More seriously still, on October 28, 1962, at the height of the Cuban Missile Crisis when the United States was at a high level of alert and had its nuclear weapons cocked at the ready, another accident with a training tape caused U.S. radar operators to believe that a missile had been launched at Florida from Cuba. When there was no nuclear detonation, they realized they had mistaken a satellite for a missile.[47] Also during the Cuban Missile Crisis, at a time when sentries at U.S. military bases had been told to be alert to Soviet saboteurs, a bear climbing a fence at a base in Duluth was mistaken for a saboteur, and the alarm set off throughout the region was, in Wisconsin, mistaken for the nuclear war alarm. An officer had to drive onto the runway to block the nuclear-armed F-106As, already taxiing, from taking off.[48]

Looking next at the U.S. safety record in transporting and handling nuclear weapons, again there is more cause for relief than for complacency. There have, for example, been at least twenty-four occasions when U.S. aircraft have accidentally released nuclear weapons and at least eight incidents in which U.S. nuclear weapons were involved in plane crashes or fires.[49] In 1980, during routine maintenance of a Titan II missile in Arkansas, an accident with a wrench caused a conventional explosion that sent the nuclear warhead six hundred feet through the air.[50] In another incident an H-bomb was accidentally dropped over North Carolina; only one safety switch worked, preventing the bomb from detonating.[51] In 1966 two U.S. planes collided over Palomares, Spain, and four nuclear weapons fell to the ground, causing a conventional explosion that contaminated a large, populated area with plutonium. One hydrogen bomb was lost for three months. In 1968 a U.S. plane carrying four H-bombs caught fire over Greenland. The crew ejected, and there was a conventional explosion that scattered plutonium over a wide area.[52]

None of these accidents produced *nuclear* explosions, but recent safety studies have concluded that this must partly be attributed to good luck. These studies revealed that the W-79 nuclear artillery shell contained a previously unsuspected design flaw that could lead to an unintended nuclear explosion in certain circumstances. In consequence, the artillery shells had to be secretly withdrawn from Europe in 1989.[53]

In other words, the U.S. nuclear arsenal has its own safety problems related to its dependence on highly computerized warning and detection systems, its cold war practice of patrolling oceans and skies with live nuclear weapons, and its large stockpile size. Even where U.S. scientists have developed special safety technologies, they are not always used. The presumption that Third World countries lack the technical competence to be trusted with nuclear weapons fits our stereotypes about those countries' backwardness, but it distracts us from asking whether we ourselves have the technical infallibility the weapons ideally require.

4. Third World Regimes Lack the Political Maturity to Be Trusted with Nuclear Weapons

The fourth argument concerns the supposed political instability or irrationality of Third World countries. Security specialists and media pundits worry that Third World dictators free from democratic constraints are more likely to develop and use nuclear weapons, that military officers in such countries will be more likely to take possession of the weapons or use them on their own initiative, or that Third World countries are more vulnerable to the kinds of ancient hatred and religious fanaticism that could lead to the use of nuclear weapons in anger. These concerns bring us to the heart of orientalist ideology.

The presumed contrast between the West, where leaders are disciplined by democracy, and the Third World, where they are not, is nicely laid out by nonproliferation expert William Potter:

> Adverse domestic opinion may also serve as a constraint on the acquisition of nuclear weapons by some nations. Japan, West Germany, Sweden, and Canada are examples of democracies where public opposition could have a decided effect on nuclear weapons decisions. . . . The fear of adverse public opinion, on the other hand, might be expected to be marginal for many developing nations without a strong democratic tradition.[54]

This contrast does not hold up so well under examination. In 1983 Western European leaders ignored huge grassroots protests against the deployment of the cruise and Pershing II missiles. President Reagan, likewise, pressed ahead vigorously with nuclear weapons testing and deployment in the face of one million people—probably the largest American protest ever—at the U.N. Disarmament Rally in New York on June 12, 1982, despite opinion polls that consistently showed strong support for a bilateral nuclear weapons freeze.[55] And the governments of Britain, France, and Israel, not to mention the United States, all made their initial decisions to acquire nuclear weapons without any public debate or knowledge.[56] Ironically, of all the countries that have nuclear weapons, only in India was the question of whether or not to cross the nuclear threshold an election issue, with the Bharatiya Janata Party campaigning for office successfully in 1998 on a pledge to conduct nuclear tests. Pakistan also had a period of public debate before conducting its first nuclear test. Far from being constrained by public opinion on nuclear weapons, the Western democracies have felt quite free to ignore it.[57] Yet the idea that Western democracies live with their nuclear arms half tied behind their backs recurs over and over in the discourse on nuclear proliferation.

By contrast, Third World countries are often represented in the discourse on proliferation as countries lacking impulse control and led by fanatical, brutal, or narcissistic leaders who might misuse nuclear weapons. Defense Secretary William Cohen, for example, referred to India and Pakistan as countries "engaging in chauvinistic chest-pounding about their nuclear manhood."[58] Richard Perle, a leading arms-control official in the Reagan administration, said:

> Nuclear weapons, once thought of as the "great equalizer," must now be seen differently. They are one thing in the hands of governments animated by rational policies to protect national interests and a normal regard for human life. They are quite another in the hands of a brutal megalo-

maniac like Saddam who wouldn't blink at the mass destruction of his "enemies." . . . The most formidable threat to our well-being would be a Saddam in possession of true weapons of mass destruction. . . . In any contest in which one side is bound by the norms of civilized behavior and the other is not, history is, alas, on the side of the barbarians.[59]

Similarly, Senator Edward Kennedy (Democrat, Massachusetts) warned that "nuclear weapons in the arsenals of unstable Third World regimes are a clear and present danger to all humanity. . . . Dictators threatened with attack along their borders or revolutions from within may not pause before pressing the button. The scenarios are terrifying."[60]

It is often also assumed in the discourse on proliferation that Third World nuclear weapons exist to serve the ends of despotic vanity or religious fanaticism and may be used without restraint. In the public discussion of India's nuclear tests in 1998, for example, it was a recurrent theme that India conducted its nuclear tests out of a narcissistic desire for self-aggrandizement rather than for legitimate national security reasons. This image persists in spite of the fact that India, with a declared nuclear power (China) on one border and an undeclared nuclear power (Pakistan) on the other, might be thought to have reasons every bit as compelling as the five official nuclear powers to test nuclear weapons. Strategic analyst Michael Krepon said on *The News Hour with Jim Lehrer* for May 29, 1990: "These tests weren't done for security purposes. . . . They were done for reasons of domestic politics and national pride. . . . We have street demonstrations to protest nuclear weapons. They have them to celebrate them." Meanwhile, in an article titled "Nuclear Fear and Narcissism Shake South Asia," *New York Times* reporter Steve Weisman, speaking of India as if it were a spoiled child, wrote that India, "tired of what it considers to be its own second-class status in world affairs . . . has gotten the attention it wanted." Similarly, Senator Richard Lugar (Republican, Indiana) said that India tested in part because "there was a lot of indifference, under-appreciation of India. . . . We were not spending quality time in the Administration or Congress on India."[61] And Edward Teller, the so-called father of the hydrogen bomb, when asked if India and Pakistan were following his motto that "knowledge is good," replied: "These explosions have not been performed for knowledge. It may be to impress people. It may be a form of boasting."[62]

The Western discourse on nuclear proliferation is also permeated by a recurrent anxiety that Third World nations will use nuclear weapons to pursue religious squabbles and crusades. Commentators particularly fear an "Islamic bomb" and a Muslim holy war. Said identified the fear of a Muslim holy war as one of the cornerstones of orientalist ideology. Senator

Edward Kennedy worries about a scenario in which "Libya, determined to acquire nuclear weapons, receives a gift of the Bomb from Pakistan as an act of Islamic solidarity." Senator Daniel Patrick Moynihan warns that "you could have an Islamic bomb in no time, and God have mercy on us." Mary McGrory believes that "nothing is more important than keeping the 'Islamic bomb' out of the hands of Iran. Let it be introduced into the Middle East and you can kiss the world we know goodbye." Norman Kempster, in the *San Francisco Examiner,* quotes an analyst who explained Saddam Hussein's willingness to forgo $100 billion in oil revenues rather than end his nuclear weapons program by saying, "The single most important reason is Saddam's vision of his role in history as a saviour of the Arab world. He is comparing himself with Saladin."[63] Finally, syndicated columnist Morton Kondracke speculates about a despot "like the Shah of Iran" who "secretly builds an arsenal to increase his prestige":

> Then he is overthrown by a religious fanatic resembling the Ayatollah Ruhol-
> lah Khomeini, who then uses some of the Shah's bombs to intimidate or
> destroy neighboring countries. And other bombs he passes on to terrorists
> that will use them to wage holy wars.
>
> Be glad that it didn't happen in real life. But something like it could.[64]

The Western discourse on proliferation also stresses the supposedly ancient quality of feuds and hatreds in South Asia and the Middle East. As
the British journalist Nigel Calder puts it in *Nuclear Nightmares,* "In that
troubled part of the world, where modern technology serves ancient bitterness and nuclear explosions seem like a just expression of the wrath of
God, imagining sequences of events that could lead to a regional nuclear
conflict is not difficult" (83).

Explaining on *The Charlie Rose Show* for May 28, 1998, why Pakistan
named its new missile the Ghauri, Senator Moynihan said: "Ghauri was
a Muslim prince who invaded India in the twelfth century. These things
don't go away." "Nuclear missiles named for ancient warriors will probably be deployed by two nations with a history of warfare, religious strife,
and a simmering border dispute," said an ABC News reporter.[65] In this
vein it was widely reported in the U.S. media that the Indian Prithvi missile was named after an ancient warrior-king and that India's Agni missile
was named for the god of fire.[66] This claim is particularly striking because,
while it resonates with our stereotypes of Hindus enslaved to religion and
tradition, it is quite untrue. The word *Prithvi* means "world" or "earth,"
and *Agni* means fire itself and does not refer to a god. The Indians are naming their missiles after elements, not after warriors or gods.[67] Of course, if
Western commentators were looking for a country that names its nuclear

weapons after ancient gods and dead warriors, they need have looked no further than the United States, with its Jupiter, Thor, Poseidon, Atlas, Minuteman, and Pershing missiles.

After dictators and religious fanatics, the Western imagination is most afraid of Third World military officers. The academics Brito and Intriligator, for example, tell us that Third World governments might acquire nuclear weapons "mainly for deterrence purposes but might not be able to control such weapons once they were available. . . . Unilateral initiatives by junior officers could lead to these weapons going off."[68] One finds the same presumption in Nigel Calder's *Nuclear Nightmares,* where Calder expresses a concern about Third World military officers: "An American or Russian general in Europe is not going to let off the first nuclear weapon on his own initiative, even in the heat of battle, but will the same discipline apply to . . . a Pakistani general who has a private nuclear theory about how to liberate Kashmir?" (77).

Oliver North notwithstanding, it is taken as so obvious it does not need explaining that Third World junior officers, unlike our own, are prone to take dangerous unilateral initiatives. The passage from Calder makes sense only if one accepts the contrast it expresses as unquestionably natural. It is the kind of ideological statement that the French theorist Roland Barthes characterized in *Mythologies* as "falsely obvious" (11). As Edward Said says, once a group has been orientalized, "virtually anything can be written or said about it, without challenge or demurral."[69] This presumption that the Third World body politic cannot control its military loins is, I believe, a coded or metaphorical way of discussing a more general inability to control impulses, a pervasive lack of discipline assumed to afflict people of color.

But what if one tries to turn these contrasts inside out and asks whether the historical behavior of the Western nuclear powers might also give rise to concerns about undemocratic nuclear bullying, religious fanaticism, and unilateral initiatives by military officers? Because of its contradictions, gaps, and silences, the discourse on proliferation can always be read backward so that our gaze is directed not toward the Other but toward the author. Then the flaws and double standards of the discourse are illuminated. Thus, instead of asking whether Third World countries can be trusted with nuclear weapons, one can ask, how safe are the official nuclear powers from coups d'état, renegade officers, or reckless leaders?

Pursuing this line of inquiry, one notices that France came perilously close to revolution as recently as 1968 and that in 1961 a group of renegade French military officers took control of a nuclear weapon at France's nuclear test site in the Sahara desert.[70] Britain, struggling to repress IRA bombing campaigns, has been engaged in low-level civil war for most of the time it has possessed nuclear weapons. The United States has, since it acquired nuclear weapons, seen Presidents John F. Kennedy assassinated, Gerald Ford threatened with an empty gun by a member of the Manson family, and Ronald Reagan wounded by a gunman.

There have been problems with the U.S. military also. During the Cuban Missile Crisis, a group of military officers at Malmstrom Air Force Base rigged their missiles so that they could launch their nuclear weapons independently of the national command and control structure and outside of normal procedures requiring multiple officers to enable a launch.[71] In January 1963 a U.S. Air Force officer admitted to having tampered with the safety devices on a bomber's nuclear weapons, illegally disabling them.[72] During the 1950s, although this conflicted with presidential policy, "preventive nuclear attacks [against the Soviets] were clearly imagined, actively planned and vigorously advocated by senior U.S. military leaders."[73] One of these leaders was General Curtis LeMay, who, by 1954, had "begun raising the ante with the Soviet Union on his own, covertly and extralegally,"[74] by sending U.S. reconnaissance flights over the USSR—technically an act of war—despite President Truman's orders not to do so. And General Horace Wade had this to say about a successor to LeMay as head of the Strategic Air Command, General Thomas Power, in the early 1960s: "He was . . . a hard, cruel individual . . . I would like to say this. I used to worry about General Power. I used to worry that General Power was not stable. I used to worry about the fact that he had control over so many weapons and weapons systems and could, under certain conditions, launch the force."[75]

Although the United States is not a theocracy, the American people have their own sense of manifest destiny and divine calling that is not always so different from that of the Islamic fundamentalists whose nuclear ambitions they so fear. Major General Orvil Anderson was an officer who, in distinctly Manichaean terms, publicly advocated a nuclear attack on the Soviet Union (and lost his job for it): "Give me the order to do it and I can break up Russia's A-bomb nests in a week. . . . And when I went up to Christ—I think I could explain to him that I had saved Civilization."[76] Nor is Anderson's sense that the use of nuclear weapons would be sanctioned by God unique: in the course of my own research I have interviewed American nuclear weapons scientists who believe that Christ would have pushed the button to bomb Hiroshima and that nuclear weapons are part of God's plan to end the world as a prelude to the Day of Judgment and the Second Coming.[77] One can easily imagine the Western media's response if Indian or Pakistani generals or weapons scientists were to say such things.

Finally, U.S. leaders have sometimes treated nuclear weapons not as the ultimate weapons of self-defense and last resort but as weapons that can be used to threaten adversaries in the pursuit of America's interests and values abroad. The Cuban Missile Crisis of 1962 (during which President Kennedy put the chance of nuclear war "somewhere between one out of three and even") is only the best known of these gambles.[78] Other examples include the following: President Eisenhower threatened to use nuclear weapons against the Chinese, who did not then possess nuclear weapons of their own, in Korea in 1953, and in Quemoy-Matsu in 1954–55; Truman and Eisenhower sent military signals that the use of nuclear weapons was a possibility during the first Berlin Crisis, in 1949, and the second Quemoy-Matsu crisis, in 1958; and Henry Kissinger repeatedly conveyed President Nixon's threats of nuclear escalation to the North Vietnamese between 1969 and 1972.[79] During the Vietnam War, Barry Goldwater ran for president as the Republican nominee advocating consideration of the use of low-yield tactical nuclear weapons to defoliate the jungles of Vietnam.

The Orientialist Underworld: A Tour of Images

These falsely obvious arguments about the political unreliability of Third World nuclear powers are part of a broader orientalist rhetoric that seeks to bury disturbing similarities between "us" and "them" in a discourse that systematically produces the Third World as Other. In the process, we also produce ourselves, for the Orient, one of the West's "deepest and most recurring images of the other," is essential in defining the West "as its contrasting image, idea, personality, experience."[80]

The particular images and metaphors that recur in the discourse on proliferation represent Third World nations as criminals, women, and children. But these recurrent images and metaphors, all of which pertain in some way to disorder, can also be read as telling hints about the facets of our own psychology and culture that we find especially troubling in regard to our custodianship over nuclear weapons. The metaphors and images are part of the ideological armor the West wears in the nuclear age, but they are also clues that suggest buried, denied, and troubling parts of ourselves that have mysteriously surfaced in our distorted representations of the Other. As Akhil Gupta has argued in *Postcolonial Developments,* his analysis of a different orientalist discourse, the discourse on development, "within development discourse . . . lies its shadowy double . . . a virtual presence, inappropriate objects that serve to open up the 'developed world' itself as an inappropriate object" (4).

In the era of so-called rogue states, one recurrent theme in this system of representations is that of the thief, liar, and criminal: the very attempt to come into possession of nuclear weapons is often cast in terms of racketeering and crime. After the Indian and Pakistani nuclear tests, one newspaper headline characterized the two countries as "nuclear outlaws,"[81] even though neither had signed—and hence violated—either the Non-Proliferation Treaty or the Comprehensive Test Ban Treaty. When British customs officers intercepted a shipment of krytrons destined for Iraq's nuclear weapons program, one newspaper account said that Saddam Hussein was "caught red-handed trying to *steal* atomic detonators"[82]—a curious choice of words given that Iraq had paid good money to buy the krytrons from the company EG&G. (In fact, if any nation can be accused of theft here, surely it is the United States, which took $650 million from Pakistan for a shipment of F-16s, canceled the shipment when the Bush administration determined that Pakistan was seeking to acquire nuclear weapons, but never refunded the money.) According to an article in the *New York Times,* "it required more than three decades, a global network of theft and espionage, and uncounted millions for Pakistan, one of the world's poorest countries, to explode that bomb."[83] Meanwhile the same paper's editorial page lamented that "for years Pakistan has lied to the U.S. about not having a nuclear weapons program" and insists that the United States "punish Pakistan's perfidy on the bomb."[84] And Representative Steven Solarz (Democrat, New York) warns us that the bomb will give Pakistan "the nuclear equivalent of a Saturday Night Special."[85] The image of the Saturday night special assimilates Pakistan symbolically to the disorderly underworld of ghetto hoodlums who rob corner stores and fight gang wars. U.S. nuclear weapons are, presumably, more like the "legitimate" weapons carried by the police to maintain order and keep the peace.[86]

Reacting angrily to this system of representations, the scientist in charge of Pakistan's nuclear weapons program, Abdul Qadeer Khan, said, "Anything which we do is claimed by the West as stolen and we are never given credit except for the things like heroin. . . . You think that we people who also got education are stupid, ignorant. Things which you could do fifty years ago, don't you think that we cannot do them now."[87]

Third World nations acquiring nuclear weapons are also described in terms of passions escaping control. In Western discourse the passionate, or instinctual, has long been identified with women and animals and implicitly contrasted with male human rationality.[88] Thus certain recurrent figures of speech in the Western discourse on proliferation cast Third World proliferant nations in imagery that carries a subtle feminine or subhuman connotation. Whereas the United States is spoken of as having "vital interests" and "legitimate security needs," Third World nations have "passions," "longings," and "yearnings" for nuclear weapons that must be controlled and contained by the strong male and adult hand of America. Pakistan has "an evident ardor for the Bomb," says a 1987 *New York Times* editorial. Peter Rosenfeld, writing in the *Washington Post,* worries that the United States cannot forever "stifle [Pakistan's] nuclear longings." Representative Ed Markey (Democrat, Massachusetts), agreeing, warns in a letter to the *Washington Post* that U.S. weakness in its relationship with Pakistan means that the Pakistanis "can feed nuclear passions at home and still receive massive military aid from America." The image is of the unfaithful wife sponging off her cuckolded husband.[89]

But throwing the woman out may cause even more disorder: the *Washington Post* editorial page, having described Pakistan's nuclear weapons program—in an allusion to the ultimate symbol of Muslim femininity—as concealed "behind a veil of secrecy," goes on to warn that there are "advantages to . . . having Pakistan stay in a close and constraining security relationship with the United States rather than be cast out by an aid cutoff into a loneliness in which its passion could only grow."[90] Thus, even though American intelligence had by 1986 concluded that the Pakistani uranium-enrichment plant at Kahuta "had gone all the way,"[91] and even though the president can no longer, as he is required by law, "certify Pakistan's nuclear purity,"[92] the disobedient, emotive femininity of Pakistan is likely to be less disruptive if it is kept within the bounds of its uneasy relationship with the United States.

Third World nations are also often portrayed as children and the United States, as a parental figure. The message is succinctly conveyed by one *San Francisco Chronicle* headline: "India, Pakistan Told to Put Weapons Away." Ben Sanders praises the Non-Proliferation Treaty as a means to "protect the atomically innocent." But what about when innocence is lost? Steve Chapman, speaking of India and Pakistan, argues that "it's fine to counsel teenagers against having sex. But once they have produced a baby, another approach is in order." A *New York Times* editorial speaks of U.S. "scoldings" of Pakistan and "U.S. demands for good Pakistani behavior from now on." Hedrick Smith reports fears that the U.S. parental style is too permissive and will encourage misbehavior by Pakistan's naughty siblings: "those who advocated an aid cutoff said the time had come for the United States to set an example for other would-be nuclear nations." Warning that American parental credibility is on the line, the *New York Times* says that "all manner of reason and arguments have been tried with Pakistani leaders. It's time for stronger steps."[93]

These metaphorical representations of threshold nuclear nations as criminals, women, and children assimilate the relationship between the West and the Third World to other hierarchies of dominance within Western culture. They use the symbolic force of domestic hierarchies—police over criminals, men over women, and adults over children—to buttress and construct the global hierarchy of nations, telling us that, like women, children, and criminals, Third World nations have their proper place. The sense in the West that Third World nations had their proper place at the bottom of a global order in which nuclear weapons are the status symbols of the powerful alone—that nuclear proliferation was transgressing important symbolic hierarchies—is nicely conveyed by the condescending reactions in the Western media to India's and Pakistan's nuclear tests of 1998. Here many commentators sounded like secretaries of exclusive members-only clubs blackballing nouveau riche applicants. "With scant regard for the admonitions of other members of the [nuclear] group, India has abruptly and loudly elbowed itself from the bottom into the top tier of this privileged elite," said one commentator.[94] Putting the upstarts back in their place, U.S. Secretary of State Madeleine Albright said that it was "clear that what the Indians and Pakistanis did was unacceptable and that they are not now members of the nuclear club."[95] The same sentiment was expressed in stronger terms on the op-ed page of the New York Times by former national security adviser Robert McFarlane, whose characterization of India draws on classic orientalist imagery to make its point that the Indians are not "our" kind of people: "We must make clear to the Indian government that it is today what it was two weeks ago, an arrogant, overreaching cabal that, by its devotion to the caste system, the political and economic disenfranchisement of its people and its religious intolerance, is unworthy of membership in any club."[96] Mary McGrory, an alleged liberal, writing for the Washington Post op-ed page, expressed the same reaction against people rising above their proper station in life. In a comment extraordinary for its simple erasure of the great literary and cultural achievements made by persons of the Indian subcontinent over many centuries, she said, "People who cannot read, write or feed their children are forgetting these lamentable circumstances in the ghastly glory of being able to burn the planet or their enemies to a crisp."[97]

Nuclear Colonialism and the Return of the Repressed

Noam Chomsky has suggested that the arms race between the superpowers was not really "about" the U.S.-Soviet rivalry at all, but was a convenient way to assure the subjugation of smaller countries in the Third World under the guise of superpower competition.[98] One does not have to swallow whole the simple reductionism of this argument to accept that there is obviously some connection between the nuclear stockpiles of some developed nations on the one hand and the political clientship and economic underdevelopment of Third World nations on the other. Just as some nations have abundant access to capital while others do not, so some nations are allowed plentiful supplies of the ultimate weapon while others are prevented by elaborate treaties and international police activities from obtaining it. Without devising rigidly deterministic models connecting economic power and nuclear weapons—models that such states as Japan and Germany obviously would not fit—one can at least sketch the broad contours of this generalization: the nuclear underdevelopment of the developing world is one fragment in a wider and systematic pattern of global disempowerment that ensures the subordination of the south.[99]

The discourse on nuclear proliferation legitimates this system of domination while presenting the interests the established nuclear powers have in maintaining their nuclear monopoly as if they were equally beneficial to all nations. And, ironically, the discourse on nonproliferation presents these subordinate nations as the principal source of danger in the world. This is another case of blaming the victim.

The discourse on nuclear proliferation is structured around a rigid segregation of "their" problems from "ours." In fact, however, we are linked to developing nations by a world system, and many of the problems that, we claim, render other nations ineligible to own nuclear weapons have a lot to do with the West and the system it dominates. For example, the regional conflict between India and Pakistan is, in part at least, a direct consequence of the divide-and-rule policies adopted by the British raj; and the dispute over Kashmir, identified by Western commentators as a possible flashpoint for nuclear war, has its origins not so much in ancient hatreds as in Britain's decision in 1846 to install a Hindu maharajah as leader of a Muslim territory.[100] The hostility between Arabs and Israelis has been exacerbated by British, French, and American intervention in the Middle East dating back to the Balfour Declaration of 1917. More recently, as Stephen Green points out, "Congress has voted over $36.5 billion in economic and military aid to Israel, including rockets, planes, and other technology which has directly advanced Israel's nuclear weapons capabilities. It is precisely this nuclear arsenal, which the U.S. Congress has been so instrumental in building up, that is driving the Arab state to attain countervailing strategic weapons of various kinds."[101]

Finally, the precariousness of many Third World regimes is not at all unconnected with the activities of the World Bank, the International Monetary Fund, the CIA, and various multinational corporations based in the West. And if U.S. sanctions against India and Pakistan after their 1998 tests destabilize these countries, Western commentators will point to this instability as a further reason why these countries cannot be trusted with the bomb. "Our" coresponsibility for "their" problems and the origin of some of those problems in a continuing system of global domination that benefits the West is an integral part of ordinary political discourse in the Third World itself; it is, however, denied by an orientalist discourse in the West that disavows that we and the Other are ultimately one.

Conclusion

This chapter has examined policy talk grounded in an unsustainable binary opposition between nations that can be trusted with nuclear weapons and nations that cannot—an opposition that can be found in some antinuclear as well as establishment discourse in the West. I do not want to minimize the potential dangers of nuclear proliferation, which are, surely, clear enough. I do want to argue that these dangers, such as they are, should not be spoken about in terms that demean the peoples of the Third World. Nor should they be represented in ways that obscure both the dangers inherent in the continued maintenance of our own nuclear arsenals and the fact our own actions are often a source of the instabilities we so fear in Third World nations.

So, where does this leave us? This chapter has set out to critique not a particular policy but the way our conversations about policy choices on the nuclear issue may unthinkingly incorporate certain neocolonial hierarchies and assumptions that, when drawn to our attention, many of us would disown. Nor is this just a matter of policing language, since the embedded orientalist assumptions I have been looking at here underpin a global security regime that sanctifies a particular kind of Western military dominance in the world. Because I have set out to criticize a particular kind of policy talk rather than a specific policy, I will conclude not with a prescribed policy but by suggesting that there are three different discursive positions on proliferation, each pointing in the direction of a very different global security regime, that do not embody the double standard I have been concerned with here. I call them "exclusion," "participation," and "renunciation."

The strategy of *exclusion* is based pragmatically in the conventions of realpolitik. It involves the candid declaration that, while nuclear weapons may be no more dangerous in the hands of Muslims or Hindus than in those of Christians, they are a prerogative of power, and the powerful have no intention of allowing the powerless to acquire them. This is a position that, in its rejection of easy racism and phony moralism, is at least honorable in its frankness. It is the position of New York Times columnist Flora Lewis in her remark that "the 'rights' of nations are limited, and the limits must be imposed by those who can. They may not be more virtuous, but they must strive for it. That is the reason to keep insisting on nonproliferation."[102]

The second position, *participation,* is based on Kenneth Waltz's argument that all countries benefit from acquiring nuclear weapons. This position may have more appeal in certain parts of the Third World than in the West. It is the position of India, Israel, and Pakistan, for example, who have, like the older nuclear nations, sought to maximize their power and freedom by acquiring a nuclear capability. These countries pursued nuclear weapons in search of greater security vis-à-vis regional rivals and out of a desire to shift the balance of power in their client relationships with the superpowers.

The third strategy, *renunciation,* breaks down the distinctions we have constructed between "us" and "them" and asks whether nuclear weapons are safe in anyone's hands. "What-must-on-no-account-be-known," says Salman Rushdie, is the "impossible verity that savagery could be concealed beneath decency's well-pressed shirt."[103] Our orientalist discourse on nuclear proliferation is one of our ways not to know this. By breaking down the discourse, confronting those parts of our own personality and culture that appear as the childish, irrational, lawless, or feminine aspects of the Other, we could address our doubts about ourselves instead of harping continually on our doubts about others. Then we might accept that "the fact that we urge other nations not to depend on nuclear weapons in this way—and urge very strenuously—suggests that we have mixed feelings about how safe they make us."[104] This acceptance would lead us to the same conclusion reached by George Kennan, former ambassador to the Soviet Union and the originator of the policy of containment in the cold war:

> I see the danger not in the number or quality of the weapons or in the intentions of those who hold them but in the very existence of weapons of this nature, regardless of whose hands they are in. I believe that unless we consent to recognize that the nuclear weapons we hold in our hands are as much a danger to us as those that repose in the hands of our supposed adversaries there will be no escape from the confusions and dilemmas to which such weapons have brought us, and must bring us increasingly as time goes on. For this reason, I see no solution to the problem other than the complete elimination of these and all other weapons of mass destruction from national arsenals; and the sooner we move toward that solution, and the greater courage we show in doing so, the safer we will be.[105]

(1999)

Part II

Militarism and the Media

3

Short Circuit: Watching Television with a Nuclear Weapons Scientist

Cyborgs, Weapons Scientists, and Anthropologists

As an anthropologist I spend more time watching people than watching television. When I was doing my fieldwork, however, I sometimes combined the two pursuits, watching some quite lowbrow popular films on television with one of my "informants," Ray,[1] who loved nothing more than to spread out on the couch with the remote control and a pizza, chatting intermittently with me as we watched a movie or surfed the channels. I was a former antinuclear activist, now turned anthropologist, doing an ethnographic study of a nuclear weapons laboratory where Ray worked as an engineer. After he befriended me at a church social event, I ended up spending a fair amount of time with him and his television.

At first I was annoyed by Ray's fondness for television. I shared the perception, common among academics and humanists, that watching television is often a waste of precious time and an evasion of real human communication. I was trying to understand Ray's cultural world, and I saw the television, which Ray rarely turned off when I came to visit, as an electronic barrier against my attempts to understand him—a Maginot Line in his living room for me to transgress.

In fact, however, it was by watching television with Ray that I came to some of my subtler and most counterintuitive insights into his world. I eventually realized that television, especially science fiction fantasies on television, offered all kinds of commentaries, both oblique and direct, on Ray's world—a social world in which, as in much science fiction, the star character was often either technology itself or the sort of cyborg characters that achieved mass marketability in the decade of *The Terminator*, *Blade Runner*, and *Robocop*. In this context watching television with Ray was,

51

far from being an impediment to our relationship, a low-key but effective way of getting to know him, since the playful flow of images, stories, and fantasies on television catalyzed casual but revealing conversations about problematic issues in his life that could be discussed more freely in relation to the dreamworld of television than in the context of a formal ethnographic interview where, relentlessly searching for structure and consistency, I might make overzealous and reductionist attempts to pin down the underlying logic of Ray's life. That life, like most human lives and despite my academic attempts to make it otherwise, was obstinately complex and contradictory. The informal conversations and confidences evoked by the fantasy world of television helped me to see that complexity in a way that no formal interview could have, making me realize that the contradictions and inconsistencies in Ray's discourse were not "noise" that I had to filter out in distilling the essence of his world but were, in fact, an integral part of that essence.

In this chapter I want to briefly describe Ray's world, and then explain how watching television with him helped illuminate that world. My account will focus principally on one film we watched together, *Short Circuit*. Although the film at the time seemed a little silly to me, and although my conversation about the film with Ray was comparatively brief, that conversation was like an intellectual electric shock for me—a vital moment of recognition in my fieldwork that disrupted many of my presuppositions about both nuclear weapons scientists and a Hollywood film that had seemed so transparently simple before we got to discussing it. Ever since that conversation both nuclear weapons scientists and the cultural products of Hollywood have seemed more interesting and more complex to me.

The star character, and in many ways the most interesting character, of the film *Short Circuit* is a cyborg: the robot called "Number Five," which (who?) acquires human consciousness and becomes a pacifist. The machine that transcends its programming and becomes autonomous is a common figure in contemporary science fiction, although it usually appears as frightening and dangerous, like Hal, the computer that turns on the spaceship crew in *2001: A Space Odyssey,* the replicants that menace humanity in *Blade Runner,* and the artificial intelligence, Wintermute, that ruthlessly manipulates and kills in order to secure its autonomy in William Gibson's cyberpunk novel *Neuromancer.* These are all retellings of Mary Shelley's *Frankenstein,* and, as Langdon Winner has observed in *Autonomous Technology,* this recurring story is about our profound anxiety that we have lost control of, and may even be destroyed by, the technology we have created in the modern age. *Short Circuit* recasts this cyborg story yet again, but this time as comedy rather than as tragedy.

We are clearly quite fascinated by cyborgs at this moment in our history. Donna Haraway, who in "A Manifesto for Cyborgs" put the concept on the map of cultural criticism, defines a cyborg as "a hybrid of machine and organism, a creature of social reality as well as a creature of fiction" and "a kind of disassembled and reassembled, postmodern collective and personal self" (191, 205). Calling cyborgs "the illegitimate offspring of militarism and patriarchal capitalism, not to mention state socialism" (193), Haraway declares that "by the late twentieth century, our time, a mythic time, we are all chimeras, theorized and fabricated hybrids of machine and organism; in short, we are cyborgs. The cyborg is our ontology; it gives us our politics" (191).

One of the key characteristics of the cyborg for Haraway is its fundamental ambiguity. The cyborg has a dark side, but it also has utopian possibilities:

> From one perspective, a cyborg world is about the final imposition of a grid of control on the planet, about the final abstraction embodied in a Star Wars apocalypse waged in the name of defense, about the final appropriation of women's bodies in a masculinist orgy of war. From another perspective, a cyborg world might be about lived social and bodily realities in which people are not afraid of their joint kinship with animals and machines, not afraid of permanently partial identities and contradictory standpoints. (196)

My conversations with Ray emphasized that the cyborg is indeed an ambiguous figure, more ambiguous than I had realized. In this chapter I want to show how that ambiguity became manifest in our conversations, and how the ambiguous, shape-shifting figure of the cyborg helped me see more clearly the ambivalence and complexity at the heart of Ray's worldview. My approach here is strongly, if obliquely, influenced by *Reading the Romance: Women, Patriarchy, and Popular Literature,* Janice Radway's beautiful 1991 study of a group of suburban American women devoted to reading romance novels. Adopting Stanley Fish's (1980) notion of "interpretive communities,"[2] Radway argues that the same text may mean quite different things to different readers bringing different identities and social locations to the act of reading. She quotes Dorothy Hobson's argument that a text "comes alive and communicates when the viewers add their own interpretation and understanding" and that "there can be as many interpretations of a programme as the individual readers bring to it."[3] Radway argues that we cannot understand the meaning of a text simply by analyzing its plot by ourselves. Instead, she calls for ethnographies of reading—sociological studies of the multiple ways particular individuals and communities read particular texts.[4] In this chapter, which is focused on television rather than print, I show how the film *Short Circuit*, and in particular the cyborg character at the heart of it, signified quite different things to Ray and me because we viewed the film from different social and political standpoints, and I show how the cinematic cyborg can function as a Rorschach to provoke and focus debates on the politics of technology at the end of the second millennium.

Ray's World

Ray worked at the Lawrence Livermore National Laboratory, one of two nuclear weapons design laboratories in the United States (the other is the Los Alamos National Laboratory in New Mexico). The Livermore Laboratory, set amidst vineyards and rolling hills about forty miles east of San Francisco, was founded in 1952.[5] Since then its scientists have designed eighteen nuclear weapons, including the neutron bomb and the warheads for the MX, Minuteman, and Poseidon missiles. They have also worked on such technologies as the X-ray laser and Brilliant Pebbles as part of the Strategic Defense Initiative ("Star Wars"). With about eight thousand employees and an annual budget of a little over $1 billion, the laboratory devoted roughly two-thirds of its resources to weapons work throughout the 1980s, though it also sponsored research in such areas as new energy technologies, environmental cleanup, and the Human Genome Project.[6]

The 1980s were difficult years for the laboratory. In the early years of that decade, as the Nuclear Freeze movement swept across the country, Livermore became the local target of mass demonstrations organized by an antinuclear movement that was exceptionally strong in northern California.[7] Meanwhile, America's mainstream churches, especially the Roman Catholic Church, for the first time became vocally critical of the nuclear arms race: Livermore scientists, many of whom are committed Christians, had to contend with the spectacle of priests, nuns, even a bishop, getting arrested for civil disobedience at the Laboratory gates.[8] Then, in the late 1980s, the new Soviet government headed by Mikhail Gorbachev made increasingly strenuous efforts to end the cold war, which, for nearly forty years, had provided the laboratory's principal raison d'être. It was in this conflictual historical context that, in 1988, I met Ray.

Ray had a master's degree in electrical engineering, and his job was to maintain and reconfigure some of the immensely expensive and delicate experimental equipment at the laboratory. He was not directly involved in nuclear weapons research, but he was quite candid that his work contributed to nuclear weapons development. In the course of my research I found that many Livermore scientists believed they thought much more than their colleagues about the ethics of working at a nuclear weapons laboratory, and Ray was no exception.[9] "They [his coworkers] don't think very much about the ethics of what we do," he told me, adding that many of his colleagues even persuaded themselves that, since they were not participating directly in nuclear weapons design, there was no ethical issue to confront. "I have no illusions about my work," he said tersely.

I once commented to Ray that some of his colleagues seemed so wrapped up in the technical problems they were trying to solve that they had lost sight of what nuclear weapons could do to human beings. He surprised me by nodding and saying that was why some of them came up with some "really sick ideas" for new nuclear weapons, for example, the neutron bomb—a weapon that excited considerable controversy when it was produced in the 1970s because it was designed to kill human beings with an intense burst of radiation while doing relatively little damage to buildings.

At the time that I met him Ray had been forced to look again at the ethics of his work because of his membership in the Catholic Church, which he took seriously. The National Conference of Catholic Bishops had in 1983 issued *The Challenge of Peace,* a much publicized pastoral letter criticizing the nuclear arms race and appealing for its prompt cessation. Ray had even had the experience when he went to worship at a church in a nearby town, where the priest knew nothing about his work, of being asked why he was not helping to plan a protest against the laboratory. When he explained to the priest that he was employed at the laboratory there was, he said, "an uncomfortable silence." He added, "I had the feeling he really wished he could throw me out."

When I first knew Ray, from 1988 to 1989, he was quite sure that his work was ethical. He believed that the development of American nuclear weapons was, on balance, still more likely to stabilize than to endanger the world. This conclusion derived largely from his deeply held belief that the Communist regime in the Soviet Union was historically a ruthless, aggressive threat to world peace that was being contained by a democratic United States forced to arm in defense of itself and allied nations. He worried that the Gorbachev regime was essentially no different from its predecessors except in its aptitude for public relations, and one evening, when a news clip about Soviet arms-control policy came on television, he told me that if I thought Gorbachev had unilaterally suspended Soviet nuclear testing for eighteen months "because he's a nice guy, then I've got some real estate for you in the Arizona desert." At one point he even articulated a concern that the Soviets might be pursuing global nuclear disarmament because they had designed a secret nonnuclear weapon with which they would be able to seek global domination in a nonnuclear world. Still, he told me, "if

Gorbachev's sincere—which I doubt because it's all been too slick—but if he's sincere, then five years from now there won't be any need for this lab and I'll quit. I'm not saying that the government will see that there's no need for the lab. I'm saying I'll quit because the work will no longer be justifiable."

In Ray's discursive world, if the Soviets were dangerous and malevolent, antinuclear activists at home were naive. He did not dispute their good intentions, but he was quite adamant that, whether they knew it or not, much of their funding came surreptitiously from the KGB, whose goals they unwittingly furthered. "I'm not saying that antinuclear protestors are all bad. But they're naive about where their money comes from and whose interests they're serving. You'd be surprised how much of their money comes from the KGB."[10]

Ray's belief that his nuclear weapons work was ethical and appropriate was grounded, however, not just in his fearful mistrust of the Soviets but also in a positive faith in technology, particularly American technology, as a solution to human problems. It was this faith in technology, more than his anti-Sovietism (which, in any case, was far from universally shared by scientists at the laboratory, many of whom were political liberals), that bonded Ray with his colleagues. Ray's house was full of gadgets, and he loved to tell me about the amazing things Livermore machines were capable of doing. He was impatient with people who opposed nuclear power plants and genetic engineering, since he strongly believed that technology under rational and beneficent human control made the world a better and safer place. His attitude to gun control, which he and I often disagreed about, illustrates the point: where I saw guns as a menace to everyone's safety, he believed that people had the right to own guns and were safer with than without guns, but only if they had been properly trained so that they did not, for example, point them at people or keep them loaded in the house. I worried about guns, I worried about nuclear weapons, and I worried about the plutonium facility only two miles from my house. Ray said he just worried about the wrong people having guns and nuclear weapons, and the only time he worried about the plutonium facility was when they found one of the operators there was smoking marijuana. As long as technology was in the hands of reliable experts—a category of person of whose existence I was skeptical—Ray felt safe.

Watching Television with Ray

In Ray I had met someone profoundly different from me. In the rest of this chapter I want to outline how the differences between us were made clearer by watching television together, as well as give some sense of the ideological ambiguities and conflicts built into Ray's world—a world that can too easily be reduced to a set of linear consistencies by a thumbnail sketch such as the one above.

The otherness of Ray's world became dramatically clear to me one evening in the spring of 1989 when I was visiting him and we ended up watching *Short Circuit* on television. In view of the conversation that ensued I hesitate even to describe the movie, since it was obvious that the film I saw and the film Ray saw were not the same, even though we sat in front of the same television. Still, as I saw it, the story goes as follows.

It concerns a brilliant but naive young scientist called Dr. Newton Crosby, who, working for the Nova Laboratory,[11] invents a new kind of robot capable of going behind enemy lines with nuclear weapons and prosecuting a nuclear war. During a demonstration of the new robots to the top Pentagon brass, one robot, Number Five, in a scene that recapitulates *Frankenstein* as comedy, gets struck by lightning and somehow acquires consciousness and free will. Number Five escapes from the laboratory, and the military, afraid of an armed, superintelligent robot it cannot control, spends most of the rest of the film chasing it and trying to blow it up. Number Five, terrified of being "disassembled," befriends Stephanie, a young and beautiful animal rights activist, who becomes his (the robot is clearly male) protector. Stephanie contacts the laboratory ("Can I speak to your head warmonger, please?") and tries to convince the army and the scientists that Number Five is harmless and is a life-form rather than a robot, but the military, which tricks Stephanie into revealing Number Five's whereabouts, is intent on one thing only: blowing up its robot. Meanwhile, Dr. Crosby, who also has befriended Stephanie, refuses to believe what has happened, saying: "It's a machine. It doesn't get happy. It doesn't get sad. It just runs programs . . . It's malfunctioning and needs to be repaired." "Life," replies Stephanie, "is not a malfunction." Number Five, who has been reading the encyclopedia, learning to cook, and watching television, also becomes a pacifist, and, when Crosby asks who told him it was wrong to kill, he replies, "I told me. Newton Crosby, Ph.D., not know killing is wrong?" "Are all geniuses as stupid as you?" Stephanie asks Crosby not too long before they fall in love and, having outwitted the military, disappear into the sunset with Number Five in their van to live as a happy cyborg family in the Edenic wilderness of Montana.

As I watched the film its moral seemed transparently clear: the military just seeks to destroy and cannot be trusted; brilliant scientists are often naive and allow their work to be misused by an unscrupulous military; an enjoyment of love and life is antithetical to military and scientific life; and scientists and military men need to be brought to their senses by strong, activist women with big hearts. In short, the film seemed to me a searing indictment of Ray's life. Only one thing puzzled me: why was Ray enjoying it so much that he almost fell off the sofa laughing at one point?

"You enjoyed that film?" I asked, bemused.

"Wasn't it great? I've seen it before, but I love it," he answered, grinning from ear to ear.

I felt the way the first Newton must have felt when the apple fell on his head, but before he had any idea why. I was sure I was onto something important here, but I was not sure what. I told Ray my interpretation of the film, emphasizing what I took to be its critique of the military and of weapons scientists. There was a moment of silence as Ray looked first perplexed, then tired. I had taken him by surprise. He told me that the film, as far as he was concerned, may have poked some good-natured fun at the military and at scientists, but its central theme had to do with the fact that machines are enchanted and magical, and that people are unnecessarily afraid of them. "People are afraid of what they don't understand," he said. "That's what the film was about. It was making fun of people's fear of technology."

I realized that Ray and I had been watching different movies. *Short Circuit* revealed in stark relief the disparate cultural worlds Ray and I inhabited. If ever I had been inclined to doubt the palpable force of culture in human affairs, here was my evidence of its determinative influence. Where I had read the film as a transparent (almost embarrassingly so) warning about the evils of scientific militarism, and had been unable to see any other possible interpretation, Ray had seen it as a technological fantasy mocking popular fears of technology and celebrating the possibility that machines might be alive, magical, and essentially harmless. Separated by our initial attitude to technology, we had understood the film in fundamentally different ways. Ray's reading of the film was completely invisible to me as a possibility until our conversation.

Ideology and Popular Culture

An incident such as this prompts important questions about the relationship between hegemony and popular culture. One way of reading the event I have described would be to say that, in a situation where (as Janice Radway and Stanley Fish tell us) texts are susceptible to multiple interpretations whereas dominant discourses and ideologies are (as Foucault tells us) overwhelmingly powerful, then texts and films that appear from one perspective to be counterhegemonic can easily be recuperated and their message disarmed by the dominant discourse. Here the internal fissures and ambiguities of texts so celebrated by the deconstructionists become just one more means enabling webs of power to maintain themselves.

Although this is a plausible interpretation of this single instance, it is one that we should treat with caution—and not only because it would seem, in the world of political practice where human beings endeavor to persuade each other about right and wrong, to lead to the bleak conclusion that hegemonic systems are hopelessly immovable once established. It seems to me, instead, that ambiguity and internal contradictoriness cut both ways, affecting dominant discourses as well as counterhegemonic texts and artifacts. Thus I want to add an account of another conversation I had with Ray, this one provoked by a different film he and I watched together on television—a film that apparently caught him in a different mood than *Short Circuit* did.

The film in question is *Splash,* which like *Short Circuit,* stars a boundary-confusing creature persecuted by the military, only in this case a mermaid rather than a (male) robot. The mermaid in *Splash* falls in love with a man but is then found and captured by Pentagon researchers, who keep her imprisoned in a tank so that they can experiment on her. Her lover spends much of the film trying to rescue her. *Splash,* initiating a chain reaction of associations, prompted Ray to tell me about yet another movie he had seen with a similar theme: *Starman,* which, as Ray described it, is about an alien who accepts an invitation to visit Earth and is captured and dissected by the authorities. "There are governments in the world that would do that sort of thing, you know," Ray commented knowingly to me. I expected him to follow up this pronouncement with a commentary on Soviet human rights abuses, but to my surprise he said, "I wouldn't even put it past some people in the U.S. government . . . The scientists in the film remind me of the attitude of some scientists you see at the lab, doing things without being alive to the human consequences." He even likened these to German scientists in World War II who did experiments in the concentration camps and mused that he wondered how history would judge the laboratory's scientists if nuclear weapons were ever used.

What are we to make of this? Ray's response to *Splash* and *Starman* clearly fits with his perception, mentioned earlier, that some of his colleagues at the laboratory were less concerned about ethics than he. It also suggests that critical popular films about militarism are sometimes able to penetrate the dominant discourse, opening up fissures and enabling the articulation of doubts and queries that might otherwise remain unvoiced. While these doubts may only overwhelm a particular subject in unusual circumstances, that does not mean they can easily be put to rest. Thus, if I have a quarrel with Janice Radway's approach to the ethnography of reading, it is that articulating a fundamentally post-structuralist insight about the multipleness of the world with a structuralist sensibility, she assigns too much stability to her readers' responses, discerning in them a clearly consistent set of beliefs about the world that ultimately correlates with the social position of the readers. As I have tried to suggest here by exploring Ray's contradictory responses to different films we watched together, people's ideology may be unstable and fissured in its own way, just like the texts through which we strive to discern that ideology. After all, as Raymond Williams remarks in *Marxism and Literature,* hegemony is never finally stable but "has continually to be renewed, recreated, defended, and modified" (112).

Conclusion

I have sought here to probe the fractal multipleness of human social and cultural life by analyzing a scene from my fieldwork at a nuclear weapons laboratory. In this scene I thought I understood a film I saw and I thought I understood an informant I had come to know quite well, but once the film and the informant were combined I found myself in a situation where I could no longer be sure of my understanding of either—though both now seemed much more interesting to me than before. The fact that it does not all fit together neatly in the end, that systems electrical and hermeneutic are always vulnerable to short circuit, is what makes cultural analysis an impossible but vitally important and exciting project. Films may have more than one meaning, depending on the viewer and the context of viewing; informants may articulate fragments of different ideologies, depending on the situation that evokes their speech; cyborgs may be utopian or dystopian, tragic or comedic, depending on whether they appear in *Blade Runner* or *Short Circuit.*

I have tried here to weave my story about the fractal quality of texts, ideologies, and people around the enigmatic, liminal, shape-shifting, tricksterish figure of the cyborg. In doing so, I have taken my cue from Donna Haraway herself, who, arguing against the totalizing discourses of Marxism and ecofeminism, insists in her "Manifesto for Cyborgs" that the cyborg's only true politics lies in its opposition to disambiguating closure: "the cyborg . . . has no truck with . . . seductions to wholeness through a final appropriation of all the powers of the parts into a higher unity" (192). In her final paragraph Haraway claims that "cyborg imagery can suggest a way out of the maze of dualisms in which we have explained our bodies and our tools to ourselves. This is a dream not of a common language but of a powerful infidel heteroglossia" (223). Taking these ideas a little further and refracting them back on Haraway's own work, I want to conclude with a warning against an overromantic view of the cyborg among some contemporary writers that threatens to turn into a fatal attraction.

Paradoxically, and problematically, in insisting so vocally that the cyborg's politics are antiessentialist, Haraway herself essentializes the cyborg, in the process denying it the full extent of its shape-shifting ability. Thus, for example, Haraway tells us that the cyborg is "oppositional, utopian, and completely without innocence" (192). She goes on to say that

> the cyborg does not expect its father to save it through a restoration of the garden, that is, through the fabrication of a heterosexual mate, through its completion in a finished whole, a city and cosmos. The cyborg does not dream of community on the model of the organic family, this time without the Oedipal project. The cyborg would not recognize the Garden of Eden; it is not made of mud and cannot dream of returning to dust. (192)

I am struck by this passage because almost every clause of it is belied by the particular cyborg that is Number Five in *Short Circuit*. Number Five appeals to audiences precisely because of his quality of childlike innocence; he does expect his "father" (Newton Crosby) to save him, and the process of salvation involves a heterosexual union between Crosby and Stephanie that consummates Number Five's own romance with Stephanie and suggests a new covenant between science, society, and technology; Number Five *does* dream of returning to dust—he is haunted by the fear of being "disassembled"; finally, Number Five *does* indeed "dream of community on the model of the organic family, this time without the Oedipal project": in the final scene Number Five, Newton Crosby, and Stephanie escape to the Eden (Montana) that supposedly holds no appeal for cyborgs as a single family in which Number Five is a sort of robot-child that, by virtue of its mechanical inability to couple with humans, is freed from the Oedipal hex and able to complete a seamless, conflict-free family.

I offer this slightly heavy-handed exposition of both the film *Short Circuit* and Donna Haraway's prose in order to emphasize that, despite its liminality, the cyborg can easily be worked into the "maze of dualisms" that is so powerful in structuring Western thought. We can have unabashedly military cyborgs, liberal cyborgs, and feminist cyborgs just as easily as we can have cyborgs that undermine such categories. To think otherwise is to underestimate the power of the grand narratives of Western thought and to substitute a romanticized vision of the cyborg (based, paradoxically, on its supposed immunity to romance) for older romantic salvation narratives organized around either a return to nature or a surrender to technology.

Just as nature cannot save us, technology cannot save us, and the working class cannot save us, so also the cyborg cannot save us. We created the cyborg, just as we created nature, technology, and the working class, and only we can save ourselves.

(1995)

4

Hiroshima, the Gulf War, and the Disappearing Body

The Body in War

The suffering of the human body in war has a double aspect. When the body is the enemy's, its suffering may be a source of pleasure and power for those who have inflicted it; on the other hand bodily suffering—on occasion, even if it is endured by the enemy—may excite the kind of sympathy or empathic fear that fuels peace movements. As Elaine Scarry and Michel Foucault observe, the human body can be treated as an object to be tortured, wounded, dismembered, and destroyed—in other words engraved by the powerful with the marks of their power.[1] The very limit of this power is the ability of the powerful to make the human bodies of the Other completely disappear. However, the human body is also a place where pain, desire, and personhood are experienced as subjectively real.

Foucault and Talal Asad, writing about ritual torture and execution in premodern Europe, have argued that the inscription of pain upon the body produces political effects of truth, either by producing confessions or by transforming bodies into texts marked by power.[2] Scarry has made a similar argument in discussing torture and extrajudicial killings in the "dirty wars" of the Third World in the twentieth century. According to Foucault, however, Western societies in the past two centuries have, partly out of sensitivity to popular opinion at a time of increasing democratization, become much more circumspect about state torture or the public display of executed bodies. With the notable exceptions of such gory anachronisms as lynchings in the American South not so long ago, gone are the heads on pikes, the guillotinings in front of baying crowds, and the state-sponsored public hangings we associate with earlier periods of Western history. According to Foucault, the Western state replaced such spectacular but clumsy displays of its power with the more totalizing but discreet methods of disciplinary surveillance, internalized obedience, and bodily confinement.

Making an analogous argument about war, rather than domestic social discipline, we can say that contemporary war is becoming both more totalizing and, in a certain way, more discreet. Scarry argues that war has traditionally functioned as a kind of spectacular contest in which two teams seek to injure and destroy each other, and to achieve effects of truth thereby. We see this not only in the history of Western warfare but also in anthropological accounts of "primitive war" in which the human body was the focal resource, target, and visual center of fighting. Descriptions of fighting among the Iroquois, the Yanomamo, the Dani of New Guinea, and the Ilongots of the Philippines, for example, emphasize that the point of fighting was to jubilantly kill, wound, or torture the bodies of enemy men and, in some cases, to rape or capture the bodies of enemy women.[3] Both victory and heroism were judged in terms of damage done to bodies.

In recent years a shift has taken place in the public culture of war whereby, even as the destructive power of weaponry has increased, there has emerged a sudden public discretion about the effects of these weapons on the human body. Modern weapons, especially nuclear weapons, afford an unprecedented power to produce political effects of truth and domination by marking docile human bodies. Yet the mutilated war victims, as well as the fearful bodies of those who have yet to be annihilated, have an inflammatory potential that also makes them dangerous and requires circumspection. Nuclear weapons were invented and used during World War II, and this war marks a key turning point in the historical evolution I am suggesting here. With a death toll estimated at fifty million civilians and combatants,[4] World War II marked the apogee of war's destructiveness so far, and we associate the war visually with, for example, images of piled-up corpses at such places as Auschwitz and Buchenwald. At the same time, the United States went to great lengths to suppress images of bodily suffering in Hiroshima and Nagasaki.

Recent technological advances have multiplied the volume of damage that can be done to human bodies in war, but, ironically, the importance of bodies as targets has become increasingly marginal to an American military that often scores success mainly in terms of territory captured, enemy weapons destroyed, industrial infrastructure disabled, or morale undermined. In our contemporary postmodern era of nuclear and smart weapons, the unprecedented ability of commanders to destroy entire bodies of bodies is matched by a partial preemptive disappearance of the body from representations of war.

Thus while the contemporary U.S. military has an unprecedented capability to destroy human bodies on a massive scale, public discourse on this capability is increasingly euphemistic. This discourse, whether found in government statements, scientific documents, or media accounts, emphasizes the disembodied rationalism of American military decision making while drawing a cloak of invisibility over not only dead and maimed enemy bodies but over the very desire or intent to harm them. The American discourse on war is thus at odds with the very essence of war: that victory is inevitably achieved by damaging and destroying the bodies of the enemy.

In this chapter I explore American representations of Hiroshima and of the 1991 Gulf War, highlighting the twin features of the contemporary American discourse on war: an emphasis on the expert rationalism of military decision makers and the marginalization of the suffering enemy body. I start with a discussion of the American discourse on Hiroshima, which became of particular interest to me when I was doing anthropological field-work at the Lawrence Livermore National Laboratory.

Hiroshima

In the United States in recent years the remembrance of Hiroshima has become increasingly contested. In the 1960s and 1970s, although their work was little known outside the academy, a school of "revisionist" historians began to question the "official story" about Hiroshima first put forward in 1947 by Truman's secretary of war, Henry Stimson, in *Harper's* magazine. Where Stimson claimed that American war planners made a cool, rational decision that dropping the bomb was the only way to force Japanese surrender and thus save lives in the long run, the revisionists have argued, variously, that the Japanese would have surrendered without the use of the atomic bomb; that far fewer Americans would have died in an invasion of Japan than Stimson and others have claimed; that Hiroshima was really bombed to send a warning to the rest of the world, particularly the Soviets, as the postwar order was being formulated; that General Leslie Groves pushed for use of the bomb to secure his reputation as the military leader of the Manhattan Project; or that the bomb was dropped out of bureaucratic inertia, with casual indifference to the massive loss of civilian life in Japan.[5]

In 1994–95, as Americans prepared to commemorate the fiftieth anniversary of the bombing, disputes over the memory and meaning of Hiroshima ceased to be purely academic as senators, veterans, newspaper columnists, and peace activists clashed in what became an increasingly acrimonious public debate. The disputes focused largely on plans by the Smithsonian Institution's National Air and Space Museum in Washington, D.C., to mount a major exhibit around the refurbished *Enola Gay,* the plane that dropped the bomb on Hiroshima on August 6, 1945.[6] There was also a controversy about plans by the U.S. Postal Service to issue a commemorative stamp bearing a picture of a mushroom cloud and the caption, "Atomic bombs hasten war's end, August 1945." (The stamp was never issued.) During several months of conflict veterans' groups and some congressional representatives complained that the text of the planned Smithsonian exhibit gave too much ground to the "revisionists." Their noisy complaints led to changes that, in turn, provoked an outcry from many professional historians and peace groups who accused the Smithsonian of complicity in "historical cleansing." Caught in an increasingly impossible situation, the Smithsonian's curators finally canceled the whole exhibit except for the display of the *Enola Gay* itself, which in the words of conservative commentator Charles Krauthammer, would now be displayed "like Lindbergh's plane, with silent reverence."[7]

At the heart of these disputes were two concerns, the first being with the representation of bodies. Critics of the exhibit complained that the curators were planning to mount graphic, heartrending displays of the devastation caused by the bomb—including, for example, photographs of charred corpses and the display of a schoolchild's shredded uniform and melted lunch box. They were also upset that the exhibit's text challenged the popular assumption that as many as a million lives would have been lost in an invasion of Japan in 1945. The critics wanted the focus of the exhibit to be on the American soldiers saved by the bomb, not on the Japanese lost to it, and they wanted those people to be represented more as numbers than as sentient beings.

The second focus of the debate concerned the rationality of the decision to bomb Hiroshima. According to the "official story," first enunciated by Stimson, the bombing was rational because it saved lives, Japanese as well as American, by shortening the war and sparing the need for an invasion. The Smithsonian exhibit touched a nerve because it asked whether racism and a lust for vengeance, not just pure reason, influenced the decision to bomb Hiroshima, and because it questioned the accuracy of the arithmetic upon which the decision to drop the bomb was supposedly based. By thus questioning the first act of the nuclear age—the American creation myth of the nuclear age—the Smithsonian exhibit raised questions about the popular assumption in the United States, a society whose politics are broadly permeated by the rhetoric of technocracy, that Americans have a special role as rational and moral custodians of nuclear weaponry.

When I did fieldwork at the Livermore Laboratory, I found that Hiroshima and Nagasaki are not much discussed there, but, when they are, the hallmark of the dominant discourse is its tonal quality of distance and abstraction. Central to this discourse is the claim that the atom bombing of Japan was rational, even merciful, in that it brought the war to a swift end. This claim tends to be treated as self-evident common sense by laboratory scientists, and it has served as a historical anchor for the cold war ideology of nuclear deterrence, according to which nuclear weapons, despite their terrible destructive power, save lives: they saved lives in 1945 by ending World War II, say lab employees, just as they did after 1945 by deterring World War III.

Here is an example of Livermore's dominant discourse on Hiroshima from the autobiography of Herbert York, a physicist who worked on the Hiroshima bomb and went on to become the first director of the Livermore Laboratory:

> [In 1945,] the suffering and the misery caused by the war in Asia and the Western Pacific continued unabated. War-related deaths in China already numbered in the neighborhood of 20 million, and that number continued to grow as the Japanese expanded their holdings in that unfortunate country even while they were falling back in the Pacific. The goal of the [Manhattan] Project thus narrowed simply to ending the war at the earliest possible moment.[8]

What is remarkable about this statement is the location of the speaker. Although York was participating in the military effort of one of the most powerful of the warring nations, he writes about the war as if he were observing its misery from a lofty and compassionate distance; and he speaks not of beating an enemy but of ending a war. The putative objectivity of this discourse is the source of its strength. Claiming to transcend the dichotomy between victims and executioners, it invokes the aura of universal common sense to legitimate the bombing of Hiroshima and Nagasaki as acts that were in everyone's interest.

We find a striking instance of the ideological power of this discourse in a story run by a Livermore newspaper, the *Tri-Valley Herald*, on the forty-seventh anniversary of the bombing. The story profiles Miyako Matson, a survivor of the Nagasaki bomb who married an American dentist and settled in the Livermore Valley, where, we are told, she owns a hot tub and volunteers for the local Cub Scout group. She remembers vividly that day in August 1945 when she saw thousands of people staggering around like zombies in the ruins of Nagasaki, some with their eyes melted out of their sockets. She spent hours brushing maggots off people and putting white paint on their radiation burns. In the years after the bombing, her father, her uncle, and her aunt all died of cancer. Now Miyako suffers from a burning stomach, malfunctioning kidneys, and constant fatigue. She fears she also is about to die of cancer. However, in the words of the journalist who wrote about her, Miyako says, "The two atomic bombs prevented an even greater loss of lives. She believes nuclear weapons designed by the Lawrence Livermore National Laboratory are a necessary evil."[9] Miyako has, in this journalist's account, accepted the laboratory's narrative about Hiroshima and Nagasaki, together with its representation of the meaning of her suffering.

Although most Livermore scientists would surely have compassion for Miyako's story if they read it, the suffering of the people at ground zero tends to be absent, repressed even, in laboratory discourse about Hiroshima and Nagasaki. This discourse, in keeping with the broader impersonal discursive norms of Western science itself, represents the victims of the atomic bomb from a distance as numerical aggregates rather than in terms of their individualized suffering.[10] This is true whether the scientists are discussing the politics of the bombing or, in a more explicitly technical frame, its physical consequences. It can be seen most clearly in the remote, disciplined, and unemotional ways in which nuclear weapons scientists learn to talk about Hiroshima and Nagasaki as sources of scientific information about the effects of nuclear explosions. Today's scientists at Livermore are heirs to information gathered by Manhattan Project scientists who visited Hiroshima and Nagasaki almost as soon as the bombs had been dropped. At the same time that American officials were confiscating photographs and censoring news reports that might tell the outside world about the human effects of the bomb, these scientists went to Hiroshima and Nagasaki to turn the dead and injured bodies of the Japanese into bodies of data.[11] For example, they used measurements of the shadows of people, burned into buildings and into the ground by the bomb's flash, to calculate the altitude at which the bomb had exploded. They also used Japanese casualty figures, together with a mathematical formula called "the Standardized Casualty Rate," to calculate that "Little Boy," the bomb dropped on Hiroshima, had killed and wounded people 6,500 times more efficiently per pound delivered than conventional high-explosive bombs would have done.[12] American scientists spent subsequent years keeping careful track of Japanese casualties, trying to document the exact numbers killed and wounded by the initial flash, blast effects, the fireball, instantaneous radiation effects, and subsequent cancers.[13]

We now know that, in addition to studying Japanese bodies affected by the first two atomic bombs, after World War II American scientists experimented with radioactive substances on hundreds of Americans—usually sick, poor, incarcerated, conscripted, or mentally retarded Americans. To give just a few examples: terminally ill hospital patients were injected with plutonium, uranium, and other radioactive compounds; mentally retarded children were fed radioactive breakfast cereal; prisoners' testicles were irradiated; and American soldiers were positioned close to atomic explosions at the Nevada Nuclear Test Site, where they were forced to march into the mushroom clouds to evaluate their physical and psychological reactions.[14]

Needing still more bodies on which to experiment, scientists turned to animals. For example, scientists at the Nevada Test Site experimented with pigs—picked because their skin most closely resembles that of humans. The pigs were strapped into position at precisely selected distances from a nuclear detonation, and their skin carefully photographed as it was charred by the nuclear fireball and flash. Each pig wore a protective garment over about 80 percent of its body so that the protective capability of these garments and the effects of nuclear explosions upon exposed flesh could be studied from the burns on the pigs' bodies.[15] Scientists even went to the extreme of implanting plastic portholes in the sides of cows that grazed on the Nevada Test site so that the radioactive contents of the cows' stomachs could be monitored.[16]

These mammalian bodies have served as texts from which to read, calculate, and project the precise nature of the bomb's power, and have thus been indispensable in constructing the regime of simulations that has grown up around nuclear weapons. Scientists have methodically metamorphosed the mutilated and suffering bodies of these people and animals into tidy bodies of data used in myriad strategic calculations, for example, to help determine the efficiency of radiation and other nuclear weapons effects in killing and injuring the enemy and to devise measures aimed at protecting friendly populations against an enemy's nuclear weapons. Although nuclear war planners are principally interested in destroying enemy missiles, command and control facilities, and factories rather than in killing people per se, a nuclear war would inevitably involve enormous human casualties, and these casualties are integrated into the calculations made by war planners.

Foucault and Scarry have both argued that mutilated bodies, bodies spectacularly inscribed with marks of power, possess a unique ability to produce "effects of truth."[17] The corpses of prisoners display the power of the sovereign who executed them and reinforce the authority of the laws they transgressed; diviners often use animal entrails in proclaiming the unknown known; oaths are frequently solemnized across sacrificed animals; and wars settle contested national truth claims with the blood of the dead and the wounded. In a similar way, American (and other) scientists use mutilated human and animal bodies, reincarnated as bodies of data, to help display the military power of those who control nuclear weapons and to certify the realism of elaborate scenarios about hypothetical nuclear attacks—attacks that have not yet happened, and may never happen, but whose outcome is believed to be predictable despite strong historical evidence that the course of war is rarely predictable. These elaborate scenarios about the effects of "nuclear exchanges" form the basis for national arms-procurement policies, arms-control negotiation policies, and civil defense policies, as well as for national leaders' stratagems of threat and bluff in international crises. Such scenarios have been important in the regulation and replication of hierarchies of dominance in the international power structure.

But these bodies are booby-trapped. Even as injured bodies transmogrified into data are necessary in order to make real the bomb's power and to construct stable regimes of truth around that power, still the suffering bodies of atomic bomb victims have an incendiary, subversive potential that makes them dangerous. Mishandled, these bodies can excite feelings of sympathy and terror that work to undermine the nuclear state. The discourse on the effects of nuclear weapons is perched on a razor's edge between the bomb's need for bodies to display its power and the laboratory's need to conceal those bodies if that power is not to be inflammatory. Thus, in nuclear scientists' representations of Hiroshima, the body, even in its presence, has an absent quality.

Take, for example, nuclear scientists' photographs of Hiroshima and Nagasaki survivors. These photographs feature close-ups of burns, mangled limbs, and exposed tissue that are often taken from the back or focus so closely on ravaged flesh that the race, age, and sex of the victim are unclear. In these photographs, bodies metamorphose into pieces of human matter— fragments of bodies that have been reduced to pieces by the weapons but also, in the act of documentation, by the photographers whose cameras separate limbs from bodies as definitively as the bomb itself did. Although the images are of damaged human bodies, these bodies are seen from so close up that the effect is distancing. In laboratory culture, the disciplined, unemotional attention to detail is crucial. For example, one older scientist who had worked on the Manhattan Project showed me a photograph of a Hiroshima victim's burned back. "You see the spotty burns on this woman's back," he said. "When the bomb went off, she was wearing a white dress with black flowers on it. Each burn on her arm and back is where there was a black flower. The black absorbs the heat, and the white reflects it." This scientist had learned to read this woman's damaged body as a text, to translate the marks of her pain into the laws of physics.

The same scientist later became annoyed with me when I showed him a paper in which I had written that many people in Hiroshima were "vaporized" by the bomb. He pointed out that the correct term was "carbonized."

"That's the problem with nonscientists: you are so sloppy with detail," he added.

This scrupulous attention to detail is vital to the successful execution of scientific experiments and scientific analysis. It is surely one of the marks of a good scientist. Still, it has collateral effects. When one is focused on being precise about whether a body was vaporized or carbonized, when one's gaze is studying the pattern of the burns across the back, when the shadows on the wall become signatures of the bomb, then the body—the person in the body, the pain in the body, the subjectivity of the body—has begun to disappear. It is not impossible to combine these ways of seeing: to hold together in one's consciousness at the same time a dispassionate interest in the origins of burn patterns and an awareness of the pain that radiates through another person's being from each of those marks—and indeed, doctors in the physicians' movement against nuclear weapons in the 1980s sought to combine these two modes of awareness in exactly this way, allying their expertise as medics with the empathic compassion of the professional healer.[18] Still, at Livermore, operating outside the context of a healing mission or a critique of nuclear weapons policy, this way of representing victims' bodies has a more distancing, dismembering effect.

Such detached ways of representing the injured body are nicely illustrated by this passage from *The Effects of Nuclear Weapons,* a Pentagon book widely used by nuclear weapons scientists and defense planners:

> The general interactions of a human body with a blast wave are somewhat similar to that of a structure as described in Chapter IV. Because of the relatively small size of the body, the diffraction process is quickly over, the body being rapidly engulfed and subjected to severe compression. . . . The sudden compression of the body and the inward motion of the thoracic and abdominal walls cause rapid pressure oscillations to occur in the air-containing organs. These effects, together with the transmission of the shock wave through the body, produce damage mainly at the junctions of air-containing organs and at areas between tissues of different density, such as where cartilage and bone join soft tissue.[19]

In the same chapter of this book, the destroyed bodies of thousands of people are recomposed in the form of tables with such titles as "Average Distance for 50% Survival after 20 Days in Hiroshima," "Tentative Criteria for Direct (Primary) Blast Effects in Man from Fast-Rising, Long-Duration Pressure Pulses," and "Probability of Glass Fragments Penetrating Abdominal Wall." The latest edition of the book features a pouch at the back containing the "nuclear bomb effects computer"—a circular slide rule that enables the reader to calculate "1–99% probability of eardrum rupture" and "probability of a glass fragment penetrating 1-cm of soft tissue," if they know the strength and distance of a nuclear explosion.

This portrayal, abstracted from the experiences of Hiroshima and Nagasaki victims, has a generic quality. It is not about any particular body, but about the body in general. The observer is not located anywhere and has no acknowledged relationship with the disassembled body. And the body we see here is presented not as a person but as a set of components that undergo mechanical interactions with blast waves and glass fragments. Instead of wounds, we have damage, a word usually reserved for inanimate objects such as buildings and machines. These are words that dismember.

The Gulf War

The representation of the 1991 Gulf War to the American public, both by the media and the U.S. government, brings many of these themes into sharper focus. This representation was remarkable for the way in which it treated bodies as objects for mechanical enhancement, weapons as surrogates for the bodies of warriors and, above all, for the extraordinary visual and thematic absence of dead, maimed, mutilated, strafed, charred, decapitated, pierced, or diseased human bodies in a heavily televised war that is now thought to have cost two hundred thousand Iraqi lives—by coincidence, about the same number killed at Hiroshima and Nagasaki.[20]

American supremacy in the Gulf War was often portrayed in terms of the U.S. ability, through technology, to transcend the limitations of the human body or to reengineer the human body. While the Iraqis' ability to fight was constrained by their need to sleep and their inability to see in the dark, American pilots were using amphetamines to suppress their body rhythms so they could bomb around the clock, and American pilots and ground forces were using night vision goggles and thermal sights to enable them to see targets in the dark that would not usually be visible to the human eye.[21] American soldiers were also inoculated and wore suits to protect them against chemical and biological weapons. The bodies of American warriors thus had a posthuman, cyborglike quality that was often foregrounded in television images of soldiers in chemical suits with masks or wearing night-vision goggles.

If humans in the Gulf War were invested with mechanical qualities and their bodies marginalized, machines were invested with human qualities and moved to the visual and thematic center of battle. "Anyone with a television set . . . must wonder: if these weapons were just a little more gee-whiz, couldn't the grunts and their ground assaults be dispensed with altogether? [And] who needs pilots when missiles have minds of their own?"

asked *Newsweek*.[22] It was repeatedly emphasized to American audiences that their military was using "smart weapons"—humane weapons that spared human lives by targeting buildings and the enemy's armaments so precisely. (In fact, only 8–10 percent of the weapons used in the Gulf War by U.S. forces were "smart.")[23] Meanwhile, in the media's representation of the war, machines became surrogates for bodies in combat, lending the war a surreal air of simulation. This was particularly clear in the battle of the Scuds and Patriots—two missiles fighting each other as proxies for national armies. The television footage of the war did not show people killing people, but tanks, planes, missiles, and helicopters destroying tanks, missiles, transport vehicles, and artillery pieces. It was impossible to tell from those images whether there were people inside the tanks being blown up and, consequently, the war began to look like a war between machines. Where American commanders in Vietnam were obsessed with "body counts," at the end of the Gulf War General Norman Schwarzkopf's charts in his final briefing concentrated on the number of destroyed Iraqi tanks, armored vehicles, and artillery pieces and gave no estimates of Iraqi dead.

These fetishized machines at the visual and tactical center of the war were invested with human, bodily qualities. We were repeatedly told that tanks, missiles, and planes could "see" targets and "make decisions." Meanwhile, although American leaders and many journalists did their best to use euphemisms for the word *kill* in regard to human casualties in the war, they repeatedly talked about tanks being "killed." In this vein, one ABC News reporter referred to a mass of charred, splintered metal as "a cemetery of twisted tanks."[24] And a *New York Times* reporter, conjuring an image of an Iraqi weapon as a naughty child (or making an allusion to sex-play?), even spoke of "spanking" an Iraqi tank with a two-thousand-pound bomb.[25]

If the dead and mutilated bodies of tanks were recurrent images in the media, the same cannot be said of the dead and mutilated bodies of human beings, which, American as well as Iraqi, largely disappeared. The disappearance of American bodies was partly accomplished by their semantic transformation into "human remains" that discreetly returned to the United States not, as in the Vietnam War, in "body bags" but in "human remains pouches." The Department of Defense, newly sensitive to the potency of broken bodies, changed its traditional rules for war coverage, refusing to allow media coverage of the return and processing of these pouches.[26]

But surely the most extraordinary feature of that war was the virtual absence of dead and wounded Iraqi bodies in public representations of a war in which an estimated two hundred thousand Iraqis died in close proximity to roughly one thousand journalists in search of a story. Fifty-six thousand of those were Iraqi soldiers, many of whom were killed by overwhelming U.S. airpower on the so-called highway of death in the last hours of the war.[27] However, not only did the American people see very few images of these ravaged bodies, but the American public discourse on the war made these bodies disappear conceptually before and after they were physically destroyed. If the dead Iraqis were civilians, their bodies were concealed within the term *collateral damage*. If they were soldiers, the bodies of Iraqis were collectively referred to as "forces," "units," "assets," and "targets"— anything but people. The systematic killing of these soldiers was referred to as "softening up," "pounding," "giving attention to," or "attriting"—as in General Schwarzkopf's statement, reframing mass killing as the completion of a bureaucratic task, that the Iraqi "front lines had been attrited to 25%."[28] The visual backdrop for Schwarzkopf's remark was a map of Iraq on which thousands of Iraqi soldiers were represented as a few green rectangles that, when sufficiently "attrited," were removed from the map and placed in one corner, as in a board game. After the war these corpses disappeared from the map in a further sense as some journalists stopped talking about "remarkably light American casualties" and simply spoke of "remarkably light casualties" in the war. The formulation "remarkably light casualties" has an aura of comprehensiveness about it, but it is this very pretense that the statement refers to all people which enables it to obliterate the obliteration of the Iraqis, creating a semantic space that feigns their inclusion while actually accomplishing their exclusion.

American leaders were also able to make Iraqi corpses disappear by personalizing the war as a war against Saddam Hussein rather than against the Iraqi people. Thus, submerging individual Iraqi soldiers into the single unloved figure of Saddam Hussein, American leaders spoke of "ejecting Saddam" from Kuwait and the need to "keep bombing Saddam."[29] Although "Saddam" was not being bombed or ejected, and his soldiers were, this rhetorical formulation reversed the terms of this reality and depersonalized the Iraqi soldiers and civilians who were Hussein's tokens in exact proportion to the degree Hussein himself was personalized.

On the rare occasions when American leaders were asked about the dead Iraqis, their corpses vanished in the middle of sentences. For example, Brent Scowcroft, President Bush's national security adviser, made the bizarrely incoherent statement to reporter Sam Donaldson that "our goal was not to kill people. Our goal was to destroy the Iraqi army."[30] Similarly, General Schwarzkopf at his triumphal briefing told a reporter who asked about Iraqi casualties, "We are not in the business of killing." Schwarzkopf was able to make the extraordinary and, on the face of it, absurd contention that he was fighting a war without being in the business of killing largely because of the power of a system of representations that marginalizes the presence of the body in war, fetishizes machines, and personalizes international conflicts while depersonalizing the people who die in them.

The official Iraqi discourse on the war was quite different, being as frankly violent as the American discourse was sanitized. Before the war broke out Saddam Hussein spoke explicitly about his intention to kill as many Americans as possible, and there was no pretense that the Scud attacks on Israel and Saudi Arabia were intended to do anything but terrorize and kill civilians. Later in the war Baghdad radio described American soldiers as "swimming in their own blood" and "wading in their own blood" and told American soldiers, "we will send you back to your families as lifeless corpses."[31] This is a discourse on war that did not banish the body, and, for this reason, although the Americans killed far more people than did the Iraqis, the Iraqis seemed more violent.

The contrast between the American and Iraqi discourses on war enabled the American media to construct the war as a clash not just between nations but between two modes of warfare, only one of which was presented as explicitly involving the mutilation of the body. Although the media eschewed grisly pictures or verbal depictions of dead Iraqi soldiers, they were not so discreet about Kuwaitis tortured and killed by the Iraqis. Thus, shortly after the liberation of Kuwait City, the front page of the *Boston Globe* carried an article with these passages:

> The corpse in drawer 12 of the Sabah Hospital had been burned with some flammable liquid. The body was curled like a shrimp and what remained of the head was barely recognizable as a skull.

> The corpse in drawer 3 had its hands tied behind its back with a strip of white rag. The body had been beaten from the soles of the feet to the crown of the head, which had been stove in by a club.

> [A doctor said], "We started getting mutilated and tortured bodies. Not simply shot, but eyeballs taken out, heads smashed, bones broken. . . . You would see heads that were completely unvaulted. . . . A woman I know personally was brought in. . . . The top of her head was gone and bullets were in her chest. She was—my God—she was completely mutilated. There was no brain inside her skull. Why should they take the brain?"[32]

The contrast between an American imaginary of war in which the body is largely absent and this representation of the Iraqis as people who mutilate bodies is central to the general American perception that U.S. victory in the war represented the triumph not of one form of violence over another but of decency over violence—a triumph not so much in war as over war.

Resistance

What are the hairline fractures in such a system of representations that are exploited by antiwar activists? Two strategies for resisting the contemporary American technocratic mode of warfare are to challenge the putatively omniscient rationalism of its discourse and to resurrect the suffering human bodies of its victims.

Taking the theme of rationalism first, we see that opponents of U.S. militarism have made their greatest inroads when they were able to produce counternarratives that challenged the technocratic rationalism of the warfare state. Thus, the original text for the Smithsonian exhibit on Hiroshima and Nagasaki upset veterans' groups and conservatives precisely because it deployed a different kind of expert rationalist rhetoric (that of historians and museum curators) to question whether the decision to drop the bomb on two Japanese cities was really as rational and measured as the official story suggested. The text for the exhibit, before it was censored in response to political pressure, introduced evidence that the decision to use the bomb was opposed by some military leaders and that it was in part a product of unthinking inertia, and of an American desire, inflected by racial prejudice, to hurt and kill the enemy.

Likewise, the antiwar movement was able to delegitimize the Vietnam War by opening a similar space between an official discourse proclaiming the rationality of American war making and a much uglier and messier reality. In that war, while Robert McNamara touted body counts and game theory as symbols of his search for perfect rationality in war, a disjuncture became increasingly apparent between the clean mathematical models of the Pentagon and the reality of meaningless and chaotic violence on the ground. One of the most memorably absurd catchphrases of the war—"We had to destroy the village in order to save it"—perfectly highlighted this disjuncture, and some of the most successful films about that thoroughly discredited war—*Apocalypse Now* and *The Deer Hunter,* for example— portray young American soldiers in danger of losing their minds.

The antinuclear movement of the 1980s similarly sought to encircle or subvert the self-proclaimed rationality of the nuclear warfare state. One strategy was to mobilize a discourse of expert rationality as strong as or stronger than that of nuclear war planners. Hence the prominence given to the members of such groups as Physicians for Social Responsibility and International Physicians for the Prevention of Nuclear War. These doctors cracked apart the nuclear state's hyperrational scenarios for limited and survivable nuclear wars by showing the absurdity of allegedly rational plans to evacuate entire cities under threat of imminent nuclear attack, to have people survive nuclear war by hiding in holes covered with doors, and to treat the survivors of a nuclear war with existing medical resources.[33]

Another strategy used by the antinuclear movement of the 1980s was to suggest that, while state spokesmen claimed that the arms race was the product of a rational pursuit of security in a dangerous world, it was in fact driven by dark unconscious forces that were being rationalized. One of the most powerful academic voices raised against the arms race in the United States was that of the psychologist Robert Jay Lifton who, suggesting that war planners were "rationalizing" rather than being rational, argued that America's weapons scientists and war planners were afflicted with "psychic numbness," "denial," and an unconscious love of the bomb. Meanwhile, the women's groups who mobilized against the arms race in the 1980s recast the U.S. accumulation of thousands of nuclear weapons not as a rational pursuit of national advantage but as a testosterone-driven obsessive-compulsive disorder—an indulgence of what the feminist activist Helen Caldicott called "missile envy."[34]

A brief vignette from my fieldwork in Livermore may illustrate both the importance of rationalist discourses of legitimation to the nuclear state and the possibilities for destabilizing those discourses. I met "Tom,"[35] a weapons scientist at the laboratory, at a 1988 protest outside the lab gates where he was trapped inside his car by protesters sitting in the road in front of him and by a long line of traffic behind him. As two women wearing "Another Dyke for Peace" buttons sauntered over to debate Tom through his car window, I watched the rage spread through his body, his arms trembling and his fists clenching and unclenching. A week later I interviewed Tom, an engineer and an active member of the local Church of Latter-Day Saints, in his home. He wanted to explain to me the irrationality of the protesters and the rationality of the nuclear state, saying: "You get back to what's the justification for ever having used or ever having nuclear weapons at any point. Do they cause less suffering or less destruction at the time they were used or not? And the whole justification would be that it could put an end to it quicker. And that's the justification in the original use of the bombs at Hiroshima and Nagasaki."

"So do you think," I asked, "that Jesus Christ would sanction the use of nuclear weapons in some instances?" Tom answered without hesitating: "In some instances, yes." He added: "Remember the kamikaze bombers? How do you deal with those people? The two bombs convinced the Japanese that further resistance would be fruitless, saving lots of lives on both sides."

Tom said that Jesus Christ came to earth to teach "fundamental truth." For Tom, Jesus Christ represents a transcendent fusion of perfect rationality and perfect morality that does not flinch from tough choices—a Christ who would, presumably, have no difficulty with Dostoyevsky's famous question: would it be permissible to torture a single child in order to end all human suffering? In Tom's words we see a classic example of the way in which the dominant discourse at Livermore rephrases moral questions in pragmatic and rationalist terms, turning them into problems to be solved by cost-benefit analysis.[36]

My interview with Tom was an unusual one, taking on overtones of therapeutic dialogue at times. Throughout the interview he was troubled by two things. First, he was upset that the U.S. government had, the previous day, bombed Iranian oil platforms in the Persian Gulf. He saw this as an irrational act of escalation. Second, he was upset at his own anger at the protest where I had met him. Four times in the interview he returned, almost obsessively, to this theme: "I had feelings like, doggone it, I want to drive right on through there and things like that, which I don't want to exercise again. I think that the better way to feel . . . is to keep in better control of what you want to do . . . Anger's a valid feeling, but I got angrier than I probably in retrospect feel like I should have done. I was more angry than I wanted to be."

Tom's reaction to the protest, in the context of an unexpected dialogue with an anthropologist a few days later, was forcing him to question his assumptions about the human capacity for rationality—assumptions that lay at the base of both deterrence theory and his own worldview as a deeply religious engineer. Tom was struggling with the issue raised by the psychologist John Mack in his article "Nuclear Weapons and the Dark Side of Humankind," where he says, "[N]ot far below the surface in each of us are impulses of hatred and violence which can be roused with a minimum of provocation" (225). Mack goes on to quote the novelist Salman Rushdie who observes our need to deny "that savagery could be concealed beneath decency's well-pressed shirt." Tom was wrestling with what lay under his own well-pressed shirt. He was struggling with the problem that we need nuclear weapons to fend off the irrational violence of others, but may not ourselves be rational enough to be trusted with them. The protest and our conversation about it a few days later did not make Tom give up his work on nuclear weapons, but it did open a fissure in his worldview, dramatizing at the level of a single individual both the vital importance of ideologies of technocratic rationalism in legitimating the warfare state and the possibilities for cracking apart that discourse in moments of crisis.

If questioning the rationality of war planners is one way of opening up such cracks, another is to exhume and resurrect the suffering bodies concealed by the discourses of the warfare state.

Elaine Scarry argues that it is hard for us to identify with the pain in another person's suffering body, but that the imaginative grasp of another's pain is an essential practice within the humane ideologies that counter war and torture. Thus antimilitary activists, disrupting the system of representations of war as a form of sport or as an international video game, often seek to make the disappearing body reappear by displaying images of corpses and wounded bodies, by connecting people with the fear that is apprehended through bodies, maybe even in civil disobedience by ringing military installations with bodies that refuse to disappear, bodies that insist on deploying their vulnerability as a means toward political power.

To return to the example of Hiroshima, it is no coincidence that U.S. military authorities strenuously censored reporting of the bombing, especially reporting that foregrounded the suffering of Japanese bodies, whereas activists have sought to highlight that suffering. In the immediate postwar years a series of articles on the bombing of Hiroshima by John Hersey in the *New Yorker* communicated to Americans in graphic but humane language what it was like to live through an atomic attack, and those articles (soon published as a book) became an early focal point for American unease about the bombing precisely because they portrayed so vividly the bodily and emotional suffering of Japanese civilians. Here is an example from Hersey's account selected because it serves as a nice counterpoint to the scientist mentioned earlier who lectured me on burn patterns on human skin:

> Mr. Tanimoto . . . was the only person making his way into the city; he met hundreds and hundreds who were fleeing, and every one of them seemed to be hurt in some way. The eyebrows of some were burned off and skin hung from their faces and hands. Others, because of pain, held up their arms as if carrying something in both hands. Some were vomiting as they walked. Many were naked or in shreds of clothing. On some undressed bodies, the burns had made patterns—of undershirt straps and suspenders and, on the skin of some women (since white repelled the heat from the bomb and dark clothes absorbed it and conducted it to the skin), the shapes of flowers they had had on their kimonos.[37]

At Hiroshima Day protests at the Livermore Laboratory activists have often sought to bring the bodies of the victims to Livermore by staging "die-ins" at the lab gates, by stenciling the shapes of dead bodies on the sidewalk outside the lab, or by wearing around their necks searing pictures of wounded Hiroshima survivors, especially women and children. Meanwhile, veterans' groups and conservatives partly objected to the planned Smithsonian exhibit because it was to contain photos of wounded Japanese civilians and, most poignantly and dangerously of all, the charred lunch box of a Japanese schoolgirl. Similarly, in the mid-1990s, scientists at the Los Alamos National Laboratory vigorously opposed an exhibit, staged by anti-nuclear activists at the local science museum, that featured comparable images.[38]

In the Vietnam War also the suffering human body proved a potent focus of critique and resistance. Perhaps the single most famous image of that war is of a naked prepubescent Vietnamese girl, covered in napalm, running. It is hard to imagine a more innocent victim, and the image was so widely disseminated precisely because it encapsulated, in the condensed way powerful images do, the horror of war and a sense of the havoc wreaked upon the innocent by indiscriminate and overwhelming American firepower.

One of the lessons the U.S. military learned in Vietnam was not to let reporters and television crews roam freely through war zones, where they could capture inflammatory stories and images that might give those on the home front too vivid a sense of the physical suffering of American soldiers, enemy civilians, or even enemy soldiers. In its first major conflict after Vietnam, the Gulf War of 1991, the U.S. military restricted the movements of reporters by forcing them into pools and selecting individual journalists to represent the pool in tours of the battlefield that were carefully controlled by the military. Thus the American people saw very little of the carnage in the last day or two of the war on the "highway of death" from Kuwait into Iraq. One reporter who notably stayed outside this system of surveillance and restraint was CNN's Peter Arnett, who reported on the war from Baghdad, where he was able to some degree to offset highly abstract images of smart bombs hitting buildings with pinpoint accuracy, taken from the bomb's point of view, by providing vivid narratives and images of life in a city under bombardment. For doing so, he was denounced as a traitor by Senator Alan Simpson (Republican, Wyoming).

But the main moment when the American government lost control over the public representation of the Gulf War occurred when a civilian air-raid shelter, misidentified by the Pentagon as a military target, was bombed and the American people saw the destroyed and suffering bodies of Iraqi civilians and heard the moans and wails of Iraqi women on television. In a war where the American people, despite living in a media-saturated society, saw very little uncontrolled footage of the conflict, this incident briefly liberated the resistant power of the body.

Conclusion

In this chapter, using Hiroshima and the Gulf War of 1991 as windows into the functioning of American militarism, I have emphasized its fondness for technocratic logic, its sanitization of war, and its concern to maintain the public legitimacy of its interventions. This legitimacy, I have suggested, depends in particular on the perceived technocratic rationality of Pentagon weapons programs and strategic decisions within war and on the Pentagon's ability to spare the public the unpleasant truth that war invariably inflicts terrible suffering on the human body, not infrequently the bodies of innocent civilians whom we have all now learned to refer to, internalizing the sanitized language of the bureaucrats of war, as collateral damage. It seems that the American people want to believe that its military has almost learned to fight wars without killing people and that they like their leaders to talk to them about their military interventions in foreign lands in a language that mixes the predictable patriotic talk of heroism and sacrifice with the idioms of bureaucratic rationality, so that they can believe that everything is under control.

As I have demonstrated here, the discourses of the American warfare state have tremendous ideological power, but they are not invulnerable. Indeed, the fevered attempts to police public remembrance of Hiroshima fifty years after the fact, even at the cost of destroying the Smithsonian exhibition, and the careful planning of media control in the 1991 Gulf War suggest a certain insecurity among guardians of the arsenals. As long as there are, in the ranks of civil society, expert communities willing to challenge the technocratic discourses of militarism and as long as the suffering bodies of war's victims call out for our attention in the writings of a John Hersey, in the images of war photographers, or in the iconography of antiwar activists, then peace will still have a chance.

(1991; 1997)

Part III

Ideological Frames

5

Presenting the Creation:
Dean Acheson and NATO

In 1939, the United States Senate approved the Neutrality Act, reinforcing an almost unbroken national tradition of isolationism. Only ten years later, by a margin of eighty-two to thirteen, the Senate ratified the North Atlantic Treaty whereby the United States finally, and definitively, broke with George Washington's declaration in his farewell address that "the great rule of conduct for us in regard to foreign nations is, in extending our commercial relations to have with them as little political connection as possible."[1]

The North Atlantic Treaty marked the start of "an American protectorate for Europe"[2] that, in less than five years, came to involve the permanent stationing of U.S. troops in Europe, an institutionalized European dependence on U.S. weapons and military leadership, and a complex interpenetration of U.S. and European defense bureaucracies. These arrangements in turn became the infrastructural and symbolic bedrock for an attempted Pax Americana based on encirclement of the Soviet bloc.

With the benefit of fifty years' hindsight, then, it is clear that, even if Lawrence Kaplan exaggerates by calling it a second American revolution, the North Atlantic Treaty was indeed a "radical transformation in American policy . . . [and] as sharp a break with isolationism as any diplomat could imagine."[3] There were critics at the time who warned as much, among them Senator Robert Taft (Republican, Ohio) and a former presidential candidate, Henry Wallace,[4] outside the administration, and George Kennan within. Given the magnitude of the break NATO represented as the end of the United States' proud isolation from a fallen Europe and the start of a bold lurch toward global hegemony, it is surprising that such critical views were not more prevalent and that ratification was so easily secured from the Senate. The low threshold of opposition was due partly to the fact that it was genuinely unclear how far the militarization of NATO would proceed and to what extent NATO would come to anchor a global projection of U.S. power.[5] Many also felt that Stalin's determined consolidation of Soviet control in Eastern Europe and the ineffectiveness of the United Nations left the United States with an obligation to assume more responsibility for European stability. However, the broad consensus on NATO was also the result of careful management of public opinion by the Truman administration. The administration in general, and Secretary of State Dean Acheson in particular, took pains to present the new treaty in the most conservative and unsensational light possible, and was deliberately discreet about requests for military aid being made by the Europeans even as the treaty was being unveiled in Washington.[6]

The manufacture of consensus in U.S. political life has been one of the hallmarks of the American political system's efficacy, especially in regard to foreign policy.[7] In 1949, the United States made a profound adjustment in its foreign policy with remarkably little dissent or rancor. In this chapter, in an attempt to use techniques of rhetorical analysis to shed some light not only on the decision to join NATO but also, more generally, on the discursive practices that have nourished this politics of consensus, I analyze closely a particular text in its historical context. The text is Secretary of State Dean Acheson's radio broadcast to the American people on March 18, 1949—the day the North Atlantic Treaty was made public in the capitals of the twelve signatories. "Never has a debutante been presented with such fanfare," Acheson would write later in his memoirs.[8] His own broadcast was a substantial part of the fanfare: screened carefully by Truman beforehand, the speech was reprinted in full in the next day's *New York Times,* and it was summarized and quoted extensively by other sectors of the press. (Truman's speech on the treaty was shorter, less thoroughly promoted, and given two weeks after Acheson's.) Acheson's speech was, in short, both the first and the principal means by which the American people came to know in detail about the alliance they were about to join and manage; and, as the first major statement about the alliance, it framed the terms of the subsequent debate in the United States.

The realist perspective that still predominates in international relations and security studies represents national interests as self-evident. Recent work in critical security studies, on the other hand, has emphasized the ways in which national interests and identities are socially constructed through the functioning of dominant discourses.[9] In the analysis that follows, I highlight the effectiveness of certain rhetorical devices and discursive formulas

Acheson used in his radio speech to enlist the American people in his construction of the Soviet threat and of a new Atlantic community. Lest there be any confusion, I am not claiming that secretaries of state can do whatever they please, as long as they make fine speeches as they do it. Clearly the general U.S. endorsement of the North Atlantic Treaty was due to a whole host of factors, including the rising temperature of the cold war; the smooth diplomacy of the Western European governments; the disappointing performance of the United Nations; and Acheson's carefully cultivated rapport with the Senate Foreign Relations Committee.[10] But the graceful execution of U.S. foreign-relations somersault from isolationist giant to emergent global hegemon was also facilitated by the rhetorical strengths of the texts through which this maneuver was declared, and Acheson's speech is both one of the most important and one of the most masterful of these. In his speech, Acheson brilliantly preempts and derails objections, and naturalizes the world he is constructing. This is the hallmark of the best ideological work: to define the terrain for everyone and to naturalize one's own construction of an ambiguous situation.[11]

Looking back at this moment in 1949 from the perspective of the world that Acheson helped to bring into being—a world whose security structure has been so deeply shaped by NATO—it is easy to lose sight of the situation as it looked in 1949, when NATO was still a strange concept to the citizens who were about to be joined in its novel community. If the NATO alliance has become a routine part of our own geopolitical landscape, the logic of the new alliance was by no means self-evident to Western publics in the fluid and turbulent international situation of the late 1940s. In the account that follows, I seek to "brush history against the grain," in Walter Benjamin's marvelous phrase,[12] to open up a sense of the alternative historical paths that were lost in 1949, and to show how a contingent outcome was made to seem foreordained. The contemporary relevance of the debates of 1949 is, of course, considerable, since today NATO stands again at a crossroads of decision as the West debates an enlargement of the NATO community in the face of renewed pleas (one of the most passionate coming, notably, again from George Kennan)[13] to resist the seductions of NATO and to build an alternative architecture of security.

Historical Background

Before we look at Acheson's speech in more detail, it is important to place it in its historical context.

The thinking of the U.S. government at the end of World War II was dominated by Roosevelt's internationalist liberalism. This viewpoint, reminiscent of the Wilsonian internationalism that had briefly followed World

War I, stressed the benefits of free trade in rebuilding decimated economies and free elections in reconstructing shattered and exhausted societies. In international relations, it placed high hopes in the United Nations (founded in 1945) to resolve conflicts by means other than war and, unlike the failed League of Nations, to keep Europe's old imperial powers constrained.[14]

At the time of Roosevelt's death, U.S. officials were thinking in terms of co-opting the Soviets into this internationalist world order. They wanted the Soviets to help stabilize the United Nations and to join with the United States, Britain, and France in guaranteeing a disarmed and democratic united Germany.[15] As we all know, this is not the way things worked out. Without rehearsing tired arguments as to whether the United States or the Soviet Union was more to blame for the cold war, we can say that events were not kind to those who were hoping for a robust internationalist order after World War II. The Soviet Union digested East Germany into its Eastern European sphere of influence; it refused an open-door trade policy for its new Eastern European satellites; it turned down the Baruch Plan, presented in the United Nations in 1946, to place atomic weapons under international control; and it nourished communist rebellions in Greece and Turkey while blocking U.S. complaints in the United Nations. Meanwhile, the United States implemented Marshall Aid for Western Europe and military aid for Greece, and issued a stern warning to the Soviet Union in the form of the Truman Doctrine that "it must be the policy of the United States to support free peoples who are resisting attempted subjugation by armed minorities or outside pressures."[16] As events unfolded, 1948 saw the first Berlin blockade; a coup in Czechoslovakia clumsily orchestrated by the Soviets; communist unrest in Italy and France that the Western powers attributed at least in part to Soviet mischief making; and complaints from Norway of Soviet pressure on its independence.

In 1947, the Truman administration, guided by Kennan's vision of containment, had seen the communist threat in Europe more in social and economic than in military terms. The Marshall Plan was the American strategy to inoculate the economies of Europe so that they could resist the communist virus within. Kennan thought that the Soviet Union was sufficiently absorbed with problems inside its own sphere of influence that, no matter how badly it behaved there, it could be deterred from further expansion relatively easily and cheaply.

Kennan himself advised against proceeding toward NATO. He believed that the militarization of containment would only divert money better spent on economic growth, and he feared the ossification of Europe into two armed blocs. He felt Europe would be stabler and more flexible if it could be returned to the balance-of-power politics it had enjoyed after 1815, before the rise of Germany skewed the balance. He also felt that Americans were temperamentally unsuited to assume the responsibility of a European protectorate.[17]

After the Berlin blockade and the 1948 coup in Czechoslovakia, European and U.S. leaders found Kennan's vision less convincing. They began to think in terms of militarizing containment. In this, the United States and each major European power had overlapping but separate motives that happened to mesh comfortably. The United States had now been sucked into two world wars originating in Europe's volatile balance-of-power politics. Not only did American planners want to find some way of stabilizing European internecine conflict so that this drama would not be played out a third time, they also shared with European elites a concern that Germany's defeat had left a power vacuum in Central Europe into which the Soviets might find it all too easy to move. American officials wanted to avoid a Europe dominated by a single, hostile Great Power, and the Europeans themselves, "confronted by what they perceived to be a malevolent challenge to the balance of power from the east . . . set about inviting in a more benign form of countervailing power from the west rather than undertake the costly, protracted and problematic process of building their own."[18]

In the process, each European country "sought to borrow American strength to further their individual national purposes."[19] The British, for example, had traditionally avoided too deep an involvement in continental Europe, and they saw NATO as an opportunity to use their special relationship with the United States to stabilize the European balance of power while they attended to urgent problems in the colonies. The French also needed someone to assure the containment of Germany and the Soviet Union while they took care of problems in North Africa and Indochina; and they were hoping that NATO might afford them the opportunity to infiltrate the "special relationship" between the United States and Britain. The Americans, for their part, saw the prospect of military bases in Europe as a quid pro quo.[20]

The Immediate Context of Acheson's Speech

Although the Vandenberg Resolution, passed by the U.S. Senate in June 1948, had cleared the way for the North Atlantic Treaty, Truman and Acheson still had good reason to fear resistance to the treaty. There were three principal foci of opposition: isolationism, concerns about the U.S. Constitution, and internationalist sentiment.

To take isolationism first: Lawrence Kaplan writes that in the hearings on the North Atlantic Treaty before the Senate Foreign Relations Committee, "the most persistent issue for hostile witnesses was isolationism and the damage to tradition that a military alliance would effect."[21] Although the East Coast elite was by now permeated by Ivy League anglophilia and Wall Street internationalism, and Pearl Harbor had dealt a body blow to old isolationist assumptions that the United States could hide behind vast oceans, nevertheless old traditions die hard, and it had been the fundamental orienting principle of U.S. foreign policy for 150 years to avoid "entangling alliances" in Europe. This principle embodied not merely a certain practical wisdom but also a core cultural myth of national identity constructed around a contrast between fallen, war-prone Europeans and the uncontaminated New Jerusalem in America.[22] Acheson's task was, first, to reorient a traditional feeling of distant superiority over Europeans toward a more direct sense of kinship and responsibility and, second, either to minimize the break with the isolation of the past or else justify it in the strongest terms. He also had to deal with the problem that fiscal conservatives, for example, the influential isolationist Senator Taft, were seeing invisible red ink between the lines of article 3 of the North Atlantic Treaty, at a time when the allies, who saw U.S. military aid as a key benefit of the pact, were submitting a request for $1 billion in military aid. This would make the end of American isolation as problematic financially as it was diplomatically and culturally.[23]

The second problem for Acheson was the U.S. Constitution and its relationship to article 5 of the North Atlantic Treaty, which reads:

> The Parties agree that an armed attack against one or more of them in Europe or North America shall be considered an attack against them all and consequently they agree that, if such an armed attack occurs, each of them, in exercise of the right of individual or collective self-defence recognised by article 51 of the Charter of the United Nations, will assist the Party or Parties so attacked by taking forthwith, individually and in concert with other Parties, such action as it deems necessary, including the use of armed force, to restore and maintain the security of the North Atlantic area.

This wording was the result of several months of delicate negotiations between European diplomats, the U.S. State Department, and the Senate Foreign Relations Committee. The problem, in a nutshell, was this: in order to give the treaty maximum deterrent force against the Soviets, the Europeans had to make the U.S. commitment to meet aggression in Europe with war as unambiguous and automatic as possible; the Truman administration, on the other hand, in order to secure popular support and Senate ratification, had to make sure that the treaty did not interfere with Congress's constitutional custody over the decision to go to war. "The negotiation of article 5 became a contest between our allies, seeking to impale the Senate on the specific, and the Senators, attempting to wriggle free," Acheson would later write.[24] The result was a Catch-22 situation that could only be finessed with difficulty. The treaty's promoters, confronted with a zero-sum logic that made European security inversely proportional to congressional freedom of maneuver, tried to have it both ways: they claimed that such a treaty would have deterred World Wars I and II by making the initiators of those wars fear U.S. retaliation, but they also claimed that the U.S. Congress's freedom of decision was not constrained since the commitment was ultimately a moral and not a legal one. The Truman administration wanted Europeans and Russians to see a commitment and Americans not to see one, except in the vaguest terms.

For the more literal-minded, such sophistry was unconvincing. For the most part, the Europeans decided that they now had an unambiguous commitment of U.S. retaliation against attack. The French foreign minister, Robert Schumann, for example, told the French people that the North Atlantic Treaty meant "the United States recognizes that there is neither peace nor security for America if Europe is in danger, and it offers us . . . a moral and juridical commitment sufficient to provide rapid, immediate and effective assistance."[25] Henry Wallace, sharing Schumann's interpretation but not his satisfaction, denounced the treaty on the grounds that "it effectively takes the power to declare war from the Congress and puts it in the hands of a military staff located on the continent of Europe."[26] Senator Taft worried that the treaty would shift the constitutional balance between the president and Congress by increasing the power of the president to declare war.[27] It was Acheson's task in his speech to head off these concerns, which in retrospect we must recognize as quite prescient, that the new treaty would subtly shift the balance of powers enshrined in the Constitution.

Acheson's third problem was the lingering strength of internationalist sentiment. The United Nations retained a hold on the U.S. political imagination, despite recent unhappy experiences in the Security Council. Senior officials at the State Department felt that NATO would be deeply unpopular if it was perceived as undermining the United Nations and returning the world to the sterile politics of spheres of influence that were associated in the popular mind with the old European empires and their wars.[28] Therefore it was crucial that NATO be perceived as in harmony with the United Nations. This was tricky both symbolically and substantively. It was tricky symbolically because the United Nations was created with the express purpose of obviating such military blocs and their ancillary arms races as a route to security; the whole point of the United Nations was to find other means of resolving disputes between nations and providing for collective security. It was tricky substantively because only the loosest read-ing of article 51 of the United Nations Charter, which the North Atlantic Treaty invokes for legitimacy, could be seen as allowing advance collective planning within the context of a military alliance. Such regional self-defense arrangements more properly came under article 53, which obligated their members to report regularly to the Security Council, where the Soviet Union had a seat—a procedure that would plainly have been intolerable to the NATO allies.[29] Thus Kaplan has concluded that "there was an inherent conflict between treaty and charter that could not be avoided."[30] Acheson's problem, then, was how to erase this conflict at the rhetorical level: how to move away from the United Nations security framework while giving the impression that, as Senator Arthur Vandenberg (Republican, Michigan) put it, "there is nothing in the North Atlantic pact which is not written inside the four corners of the United Nations charter."[31]

The Speech

Acheson's overall rhetorical strategy was to play down the break with the past represented by NATO while aggressively preempting possible attacks. Instead of presenting NATO as a departure from past U.S. policy or as a new security concept, he described it as a realization of past trends and an extension of existing approaches to security. Meanwhile, he preempted concerns that the treaty undercut the United Nations and made the United States vulnerable to another European war by repeatedly declaring the exact reverse to be true. We are familiar with this strategy of preemptive rhetorical reversal as a favorite of contemporary television commercials, which, for example, advertise Japanese cars by saying how roomy they are, cough medicines by how nice they taste, and cigarettes by how attrac-tive they make smokers. It is a classic move in the rhetoric of persuasion, which works by representing a perceived weakness as a definitive strength. Acheson used this ploy repeatedly, and he used it well.[32]

NATO and the United Nations

"A hasty reading of the [North Atlantic] treaty could leave the impression that the pact was actually a codicil of the [United Nations] charter itself, and this was precisely what was intended," says Kaplan.[33] Speaking the same day as the British foreign minister, Ernest Bevin, told the House of Commons that the United Nations "did not fulfill its purpose" but that NATO would now protect Europe, Acheson told the people of the United States that "the Pact is carefully and conscientiously designed to conform in every particular with the Charter of the United Nations" and that "it is an essential measure for strengthening the United Nations." Having pointed out that the Soviet Union's obstructive use of the veto had undermined the familial workings of the United Nations, Acheson argues not, as we might expect, that NATO was therefore necessary to assure Western security where a defective United Nations could not, but that NATO was itself the remedy that would restore the health of the United Nations. Although, as we have said, the United Nations was designed precisely to create peace and security by means other than military alliances, Acheson described NATO as if it were a conscientious implementation of the United Nations ideal:

> The Charter recognizes the importance of regional arrangements consistent with the purposes and principles of the Charter. Such arrangements can greatly strengthen it . . . [NATO] is designed to fit precisely into the framework of the United Nations and to assure practical measures for maintaining peace and security in harmony with the Charter.
>
> It is the firm intention of the parties to carry out the Pact in accordance with the provisions of the United Nations Charter and in a manner which will advance its purposes and provisions.

Acheson went on to say that the United States had already established "one such arrangement under the Charter"—the Rio Pact of 1947, which instituted a common defense agreement for the Americas. This lumping together of the Rio and North Atlantic pacts as two phases of one process "under the Charter" glossed over the important difference between the two agreements—a significant difference from the point of view of article 51 of the United Nations Charter—namely, that the Rio Pact did not provide for advance collective military planning and coordination where the North Atlantic Pact, of course, did.[34]

In presenting NATO as a way of strengthening the United Nations, not undercutting it, Acheson performs two subsidiary rhetorical maneuvers. First, he appropriates the United Nations ideal of a pluralistic world of peace and international tolerance on behalf of the Western powers in general and the United States in particular. Where Henry Wallace saw NATO as "a flagrant violation of the charter of the United Nations [which] would replace the United Nations concept of one world with two irreconcilable blocs of nations,"[35] Dean Acheson contrived to preserve the United Nations internationalist ideal by subtly shifting its symbolic location from a multinational United Nations to a U.S.-led NATO.[36] He did this in his speech by consistently fusing and juxtaposing the goals of the United States, NATO, and the United Nations. Take this passage:

> Peace and security require confidence in the future, based on the assurances that the peoples of the world will be permitted to improve their conditions

of life, free from the fear that the fruits of their labor may be taken from them by alien hands.

These are the goals of our own foreign policy which President Truman has emphasized many times, most recently in his inaugural address when he spoke of the hope that we could help create "the conditions that will lead eventually to personal freedom and happiness for all mankind." These are also the purposes of the United Nations, whose members are pledged "to maintain international peace and security" and to promote "the economic and social advancement of all peoples."

Here the United States and the United Nations become symbolically merged. The rhetorics of nationalism and internationalism fuse. Where before the United Nations was a supranational forum in which particular nations with parochial interests hammered out common goals, now the particular nation of the United States becomes the embodiment of the transcendent, universal ideal.

Second, Acheson succeeds in this speech in appropriating the United Nations ideal of common security to the concept of security through military deterrence. It is one of the principal purposes of Acheson's argument to create a textual world in which these two notions of security, distant cousins at best, are married. In one sentence, for example, he describes NATO as "an essential measure for strengthening the United Nations, deterring aggression, and establishing the sense of security necessary for the restoration of the economic and political health of the world." The structure of the sentence runs together the United Nations and deterrence as the two complementary sources of security, even though the whole purpose of the United Nations had been to oppose armed defense with a different approach to security. Meanwhile, it is no accident that, wherever possible, Acheson avoids the word *defense,* which carries too many connotations of Old World security thinking. He uses the word defense only six times, whereas he uses *security* twenty-five times and *peace* thirty-seven times. In short, he embeds his announcement of a return to armaments and military blocs in a Wilsonian internationalist vocabulary that fogs the critical listener's mind.

Constructing a Community

The attempt to root NATO in the traditions of the past is nowhere clearer than in Acheson's claim that the NATO alliance was not so much about creating a new community as discovering an old one. This is his stratagem to efface the discontinuity with the isolationism of the past. He announced the joining of such apparently diverse nations as Britain, Luxembourg, France, the Netherlands, Portugal, Italy, Iceland, Denmark, Belgium, Norway, Canada, and the United States with these words, which bear quoting at length:

> The really successful national and international institutions are those that recognize and express underlying realities. The North Atlantic community of nations is such a reality. It is based on the affinity and natural identity of interests of the North Atlantic powers.
>
> The North Atlantic Treaty which now unites them is the product of at least three hundred and fifty years of history, perhaps more. There developed on our Atlantic coast a community, which has spread across the continent, connected with Western Europe by common institutions and moral and ethical beliefs. Similarities of this kind are not superficial, but fundamental. They are the strongest kind of ties, because they are based on moral conviction, on acceptance of the same values in life.
>
> The very basis of western civilization, which we share with the other nations bordering the North Atlantic, and which all of us share with many other nations, is the ingrained spirit of restraint and tolerance. This is the opposite of the communist belief that coercion by force is a proper method of hastening the inevitable. . . .
>
> Added to this profoundly important basis of understanding is another unifying influence—the effect of living on the sea. The sea does not separate people as much as it joins them, through trade, travel, mutual understanding and common interests.

Acheson's rhetorical construction of the NATO community has four interesting features. First, like all the most convincing ideological work, it presents institutions created by people as naturally given, almost inescapable.[37] Although the countries being joined had fought one another a number of times during the 350 years of history uniting them, and although Italy had itself been at war with other members of this community only four years previously, the pact, Acheson tells us, "is not an improvisation"; it is "in *reality* one community," the result of a "*natural* identity of interests" produced by ineluctable historical processes (not human decisions) and embodied in the "simple *fact, proved by experience,* that an outside attack on one member of this community is an attack upon all its members" (my italics). Instead of presenting the North Atlantic Treaty as a decision made by leaders to solve recurrent problems and create a new kind of community, in this passage he legitimates the pact as the discovery of a fundamental reality beyond the control of leaders: history, not diplomats, had created NATO.

Second, Acheson again makes brilliant use of the tactic of preemptive rhetorical reversal, transforming an apparent weakness into a strength. I am referring here to his invocation of the sea, the ultimate symbol of U.S. isolation for two centuries, as the idiom of connection between the two halves of this community. In two simple sentences, Acheson manipulates the declaratory power of words to turn America's traditional historical geography on its head.

Third, Acheson's articulation of the basis of this community in Atlantic geography and democratic values cleverly finesses two anomalies: Italy and Portugal. For different reasons, neither nation fitted the character of the NATO community as Acheson defines it in this speech, but the rhetorical power of the speech is sufficient to obscure this. As Acheson wrote in his memoirs, using a different, more candid kind of language than he used in his speech:

> Italy presented a perplexing problem. She was most decidedly not a North Atlantic state in any geography. . . . Yet from a political point of view an unattached Italy was a source of danger. A former enemy state, without the connection with the United States such as Greece and Turkey had had since 1947 through our economic and military programs, without connections to Western Europe, except of the late, lamented one made between Mussolini and Franco, Italy might suffer from an isolation complex and, with its large communist party, fall victim to seduction from the East.[38]

That is to say, precisely because Italy was not a "natural" member of this community, it was vitally important to make out that "she" was. And, as for Portugal, despite the inconvenience of its fascist government for the "ingrained spirit of restraint and tolerance" at the heart of the NATO community, "the importance of Portugal, the possessor of the Azores [i.e., strategic bases], to western defense was clear enough," Acheson confided in his memoirs.[39] In other words, in this speech Acheson sets off some rhetorical fireworks—democracy and Atlantic community—that were powerful enough to distract attention from diplomatic maneuvers based on a realpolitik entirely at odds with the discursive legitimations defining the new alliance.

Fourth, and finally, Acheson, here and in other parts of his speech, uses communism in a very skillful way to help define the community of nations he is constructing. Throughout the speech communism is the evil Other against which the good self is defined. This use of communism as the contrastive Other that defines the boundaries of community helps to ensure, by focusing attention outside the community, that anomalies such as Italy and Portugal within the supposed community are less salient.[40]

Curiously, the word *Communist* is mentioned only once in the entire speech, and the Soviet Union is only mentioned twice by name. Yet the speech is saturated with the dangerous, inchoate, sinister presence of Stalin and communism, which, like some unspeakable sexual practice in Victorian discourse, can never be named but is always menacingly present. We are told that unspecified "alien hands" may take the fruits of our labor; that some unnamed source has made "allegations that aggressive designs lie behind this country's signature of the Atlantic Pact"; and that an unidentified "aggressor" wants to keep the NATO nations divided.[41] This reticence in naming the Other is a masterful rhetorical device that, first, makes the enemy seem all the more sinister—like the murderer seen only in shadow in Alfred Hitchcock's *Psycho*; second, leaves the listener's psychological projections of an enemy undisturbed by any specificity on the part of the speaker; and, third, incubates an ambiguous enemy identity where images of Nazis and Communists can converge in such a way that the communist threat attracts all the psychological energy that had been until recently collectively trained on the Nazis. In other words, the cold war is textualized in such a way as to maximize psychological and ideological continuity with World War II. The use of ambiguous constructions to effect the transference of hatred from Nazis onto Communists is particularly clear in this passage:

> We have also learned that if the free nations do not stand together, they will fall one by one. The stratagem of the aggressor is to keep his intended victims divided. . . . Then they can be picked off one by one. . . . We and the free nations of Europe are determined that history shall not repeat itself in that melancholy particular.

Although Acheson names no one, his language conjures a composite Hitler-Stalin figure—the symbolic totalitarian Other demanding the reconstitution of an imagined community of democratic Atlantic states to prevent the last war or fight the next one.

U.S. Obligations

Acheson is careful to defer until relatively late in his speech the subject of U.S. obligations to Europe signified by the new treaty. He first dwells at length on the consistency of NATO with the United Nations Charter and the fact that the new community being created already in fact existed. Only then, having embedded NATO as deeply as possible in established institutions and history, does he move on to discuss the possible cost, in money and lives, that NATO might entail. And throughout, he makes sure that, while he raises this issue, he leaves its resolution ambiguous. This was but the beginning of an ingrained pattern in NATO politics. As David Calleo puts it: "Ambiguity has been NATO's heritage from the very beginning. People have found in it whatever they were looking for. . . . NATO's ambiguity was heightened by the way it was sold to the American public."[42]

So, at a time when the British, French, and Belgian foreign ministers and prime ministers were hailing the treaty as the end of U.S. isolationism, Senators Taft and Harry Byrd (Democrat, Virginia) were worrying that the pact was inseparable from paying for weapons for Europe,[43] and the new allies—who saw military aid as "the keystone of the pact"[44]—were submitting a request for $1 billion, Acheson chose his words to the American people carefully. He strove to honor the symbolic link between the treaty and military aid even as he emphasized their formal legal separation: "The treaty does not bind the United States to any arms program," he began, only to add that, in view of the preponderant strength of the United States in military production, "we expect to ask the Congress to supply our European partners some of the weapons and equipment they need to be able to resist aggression."

He was equally circumspect about the precise nature of the U.S. military commitment in the case of an armed attack on a NATO member. Having more or less read aloud the torturously ambiguous language of article 5 itself, including the agreement that "an armed attack against one or more of them in Europe or North America shall be considered an attack against them all," he undermines the apparent force of this statement by adding that "this does not mean that the United States would be automatically at war if one of the nations covered by the Pact is subjected to armed attack. Under our Constitution, the Congress alone has the power to declare war." Then, the syntax growing as elusive as the trajectory of the argument, he says, "I should not suppose that we would decide any action other than the use of armed force" if confronted by another Hitler, but "that decision will rest where the Constitution has placed it."

The ambiguity in this part of Acheson's speech was an apt expression of the ambiguity at the heart of the bargain between the United States and Europe, a bargain that was phrased to reassure the Europeans, comfort the Americans, and deter the Russians all at once. Years later, Acheson wrote in his memoirs that the ambiguity "seemed inherent in the Constitution" and "was general and insoluble."[45]

Conclusion

I have set out to analyze what we might liken to one snapshot in the American transition, accomplished over many years, from isolationist giant to principal pillar of an Atlantic military and political community. The corollary of this transition was, for the duration of the cold war, the paralytic failure of international institutions in which some had, at the end of World War II, placed high hopes for a new world order.

In this chapter, I have taken one of many speeches that helped effect this global reconfiguration and used it as a sample specimen that, under the microscope of textual analysis, can reveal some of the rhetorical processes by which the new Atlantic community, and the new world of two blocs, was articulated into U.S. political consciousness.

The analysis shows that this community was incorporated into the American consciousness as a continuation of the past more than as a break with it; that it drew psychological and ideological force from the imagery of World War II polarizations reworked through a new enemy; that hard calculations of realpolitik were secreted in the soft folds of a rhetoric stressing historical community and democracy; that a turn toward military alliances was phrased in the vocabulary of a Wilsonian internationalism that has continued to saturate the self-image of NATO; and that NATO was presented as an embodiment of U.S. destiny even as the precise nature of the U.S. commitment toward it was left deliberately ambiguous.

And now the Soviet threat that provoked the alliance has disintegrated, while the cultural and political community sacralized by NATO is much more of a reality than it was when Acheson, claiming to see it already, in fact began its construction. As NATO ponders whether its recent victory in the cold war will lead to its decay or to an extension of the Atlantic community into Eastern Europe, this is a good moment to look back at the way NATO was represented at the moment of its birth. I have tried to suggest here that Acheson's rhetoric, borrowed from Wilson and Roosevelt, cleverly glossed the fact that the North Atlantic Treaty created one international community, NATO, even as it undermined another, the United Nations; and that it fused and confused two different senses of the word *security* and two different enemies. Now, as the future of NATO is debated, we stand at the crossroads again. Again voices in the U.S. State Department are telling us that we should feel kinship with nations whose armies, until just a few years ago, we were planning to destroy; again we are told that the best hope for peace and international friendship is to extend a military alliance; and again we are told that a community of democracies is properly a military community. In all of this, Acheson's legacy, both political and rhetorical, endures.

(1999)

6

Missing the End of the Cold War
in Security Studies

This chapter explores representations of superpower relations by American international security studies specialists in the journal *International Security* in the years and months immediately before the end of the cold war—an event that was largely unexpected, and certainly unpredicted, in mainstream international security circles.[1] Indeed, it is fair to say that readers who relied on that publication alone for their understanding of world politics would have been taken more or less completely by surprise by the end of the cold war in the fall of 1989.[2] In the words of two prominent international relations scholars, "Measured by its own standards, the profession's performance was embarrassing. There was little or no debate about the underlying causes of systemic change, the possibility that the Cold War could be peacefully resolved, or the likely consequences of the Soviet Union's visible decline. . . . Practitioners remained insensitive to the change after it was well underway."[3]

Little has been written about the culture and discursive logic of security studies intellectuals—a small epistemic community mediating the worlds of government and academia that has constructed an influential expert discourse on security issues.[4] Although I attend its seminars and interact with its members as part of my normal academic routine, I have not undertaken a formal anthropological study of this community. What follows is a constructivist reading of one of the community's key journals informed by my collegial knowledge of this community, by my training as an anthropologist specializing in security issues, and by my personal biography as an antinuclear activist turned academic.

Security Studies

Security studies developed in the kind of hybrid, interstitial intellectual space the historian of science Peter Galison (1997) has referred to as a "trading zone."[5] Located on the borderlands between more established fields, intellectual "trading zones" are developed by people from different disciplinary backgrounds who nonetheless share a set of thematic interests around which they interact from their different disciplinary vantage points. Classic contemporary examples would include chaos theory and cosmology in the physical sciences and cultural studies in the humanities. Galison argues that, faced with a need to communicate in the absence of a shared disciplinary vocabulary, the inhabitants of trading zones develop "pidgins" and "creoles" that evolve into mature discourses as the interstitial zones develop into recognized, institutionalized fields.

Security studies developed in an intellectual trading zone peopled by academics, military officers, think-tank staffers, weapons scientists, and government officials discussing security issues in an intellectual vocabulary drawn eclectically from physics, political science, history, and economics. Practiced in an archipelago of political science departments, think tanks, national laboratory adjunct centers, university arms-control centers,[6] and in the mazeways of the Pentagon, security studies had by the early 1980s achieved mature stability in terms of its basic vocabulary and concepts and its institutional infrastructure. Two leading practitioners of security studies, surveying the field in 1988, saw it as global in scope but focused principally on U.S.-Soviet relations, especially on the nuclear relationship between the superpowers and on the balance of power in Europe—issues largely discussed in the field from an American, or at least Western, vantage point.[7] We might add that, since the core interdisciplinary dialogue in security studies in the 1980s was between political scientists and physical scientists, the epistemology of security studies was deeply positivist, and its vocabulary was inflected by the idioms of physics (the international system was full of "forces," "vacuums," and "balances") and economics (targets were "lucrative," alliances were "bargains," and nuclear attacks had "payoff matrices"). Participants in security studies included self-identified liberals and conservatives.

My first entry into the orbit of security studies was as an antinuclear activist of European origin working for the Nuclear Freeze Campaign in the United States in the early and mid-1980s. At this time, the U.S. peace movement was campaigning for an end to the nuclear arms race as a prelude to a more complete, if vaguely formulated, restructuring of the relationship between the superpowers.[8] Meanwhile, the European peace movement, influenced particularly by the visionary British historian and intellectual E. P. Thompson, was less focused on arms-control proposals, arguing instead that it was time to dismantle the cold war itself and to move beyond a mode of civilization Thompson dubbed "exterminist." At a time when the governments of the Western alliance were arguing that it would be a sign of weakness to forgo new deployments of nuclear weapons, the European peace movement saw the rejection of new U.S. nuclear weapons slated for deployment in Europe in the 1980s as a vital first step in the direction of ending the arms race, transcending the cold war, and demilitarizing Western society.[9]

As I moved from the antinuclear movement to the academy in the mid-1980s, deciding to focus my graduate study on the political culture of nuclear weapons, I became more familiar with, and frustrated by, the field of academic security studies. Where the antinuclear movement was exploring scenarios to reverse the arms race and transform the cold war system of antagonistic blocs, such possibilities were off the agenda in mainstream security studies.[10] The dominant discourse in security studies seemed to me, even in its liberal versions, to broadly legitimate the status quo, evincing an ahistorical and conservative (with a small *c*) aversion to discussions of fundamental political change. This manifested itself in a predilection for "technostrategic discourse"[11] and game theory as the preferred way of discussing nuclear weapons; in an unquestioned assumption that the relationship between the United States and the Soviet Union would be one of insurmountable rivalry that could at best be carefully managed; and in an insistence, influenced by (neo)realism in academic international relations theory, that the international sphere was to some degree anarchic and that there were therefore limits to the scope of agreements and cooperation that could be negotiated.[12]

By the late 1980s, in the waning years of the cold war, security studies, although it was full of energetic debates about new weapons systems and international relations theories, had for this reader an increasingly "ancien régime" quality.[13] Its practitioners, persisting in their search for the alchemical formulas of strategic stability, insisted, in the face of mass movements to end the arms race and Mikhail Gorbachev's calls for "new thinking," that it was naive to believe that the cold war or the arms race could be transcended. For example, Albert Carnesale and Richard Haass, a Democrat and a Republican at Harvard's Kennedy School of Government, concluded in 1987 in their collaborative evaluation of the scope of arms control that "what emerges above all is the modesty of what arms control has wrought. . . . Proponents and critics, liberals and conservatives, hawks and doves—all seem to exaggerate the potential and actual impact of arms control."[14] At about the same time, Stanley Hoffman, a member of the field's liberal wing, concluded in the midst of Gorbachev's reforms: "The very nature of international reality rules it [disarmament] out. . . . They [security studies specialists] see the contest between Washington and Moscow . . . [and] they believe that it . . . cannot be transcended . . . because it is the very essence of international politics that the two biggest actors must be rivals, that the growth of the power of one must cause fear in the other."[15] Comments such as these made many of those in the peace movement who followed academic security studies decide that it was part of the problem, not the solution.

In this chapter, writing as an antinuclear activist turned constructivist academic, I explore the literature on U.S.-Soviet relations in *International Security* in the three years immediately preceding the end of the cold war to see how the journal sustained views such as Hoffman's. Focusing on the treatment of two crucial themes—the nuclear arms race and the implications of Gorbachev's reforms—I examine the ways in which authors in the journal constructed a discursive world within which the indefinite continuation of the cold war was plausibly presumed and what we would in retrospect narrate as signs of the impending end of the cold war were rendered dubious or invisible.

George Marcus asks how we can exploit fissures in the master discourse of security studies in order to deconstruct it and allow new discourses to emerge.[16] Surely, the end of the cold war, unpredicted in mainstream security studies circles, presents us with a large fissure to probe. In this context, it is tempting, especially given the emphasis on positivist modes of argumentation, deterministic analysis, and predictive accuracy within mainstream security studies, to play security studies specialists at their own epistemological game and to portray the 1980s as a giant scientific experiment whose outcome the security studies specialists ought to have predicted the way we expect astronomers to predict comets. This would, however, be to fall back into a variant of the very discourse I am critiquing. If at times I seem to be making a positivist argument of this kind, it is only in an occasional spirit of irony—temporarily borrowing another's discourse in order to shake it apart from within. My mode of argument here, then, in accordance with Marcus's admonition to exploit fissures in the master discourse, is to expose the gaps and weaknesses in empiricist security studies at the end of the cold war by means of a constructivist argument that nevertheless highlights the fact that mainstream security studies failed in its own positivist terms.

The final years of the cold war were, in retrospect, marked by great historical fluidity and contradiction. In such circumstances, we should expect from analysts a complex grasp of possibilities rather than the precise prediction of events so emphasized by positivist traditions of policy analysis. It is the essence of the kind of constructivist approach taken here to argue not for inevitable patterns of events but for the decisive importance of human agency and understanding in shaping history and for the plausibility of multiple representations of the world—in other words, for a certain contingency and openness in the path of history and in its interpretation. Constructivist scholars in security studies, arguing against the grain of positivism, make the point that international affairs are sufficiently ambiguous that they can be plausibly constructed in multiple ways by political analysts and actors. This is not just an academic exercise but an attempt to ground the argument that, at key junctures in history, important state actors might have behaved differently than they did. Jutta Weldes and Jennifer Milliken, for example, argue that we have retroactively reified as self-evident security crises two events (the invasion of Korea in 1950 and the stationing of nuclear missiles in Cuba in 1962) that need not have been so.[17] In a complementary but converse way, I show here that the international system of the 1980s was sufficiently susceptible to multiple constructions that it was quite possible for America's most prestigious international security specialists to fail to see a "crisis" (the end of the cold war) that did in fact materialize.[18] Ken Booth, speaking of the final years of the cold war, has said that we cannot "say that the story we heard from the professors did not contain elements of reality, only that the story we did *not* hear also contained elements of reality."[19] The problem with the dominant discourse in security studies in the 1980s therefore was not that its construction of the international system was wrong—it was, in fact, perfectly plausible—but that it so marginalized discussion of competing constructions.

In the end, the telling failure here is not that the international security studies community did not predict what actually happened, but that its members were to a striking degree unable even to entertain the possibility of its happening.[20] As Lebow and Risse-Kappen state in *International Relations Theory and the End of the Cold War*, "Political scientists and their theories failed not only to anticipate any of the dramatic events of the last several years but also to recognize the possibility that such changes could take place" (1). What interests me here about the dominant discourse in security studies, then, is not a failure in prediction that, within the framework of conventional social science, would be mortally discrediting, but a failure in vision that suggests a massive blind spot in the discourse. The unpredicted end of the cold war then becomes important as a symptom that helps diagnose that blind spot.

International Security

Rather than analyze the entire international security studies literature since the mid-1980s, this essay focuses for purposes of parsimony and coherence on one segment of the broader discourse community, following the evolution of debate in the journal *International Security*. In the 1980s and 1990s, this publication served as a salon for an international security elite straddling the worlds of academia and policy. I have chosen it for analysis here because of the stature of many of its contributors[21] and because, unlike other journals in the field (e.g., *International Organization, International Studies Quarterly,* and *World Politics*), it mixes theoretical and policy-oriented articles in such a way as to create a discussion where the theoretical and policy issues entailed in security studies are densely interwoven with one another. In the 1980s, *International Security* provided a forum for debates about such matters as the Reagan defense buildup, the Strategic Defense Initiative (SDI), the case for and against the B-2 bomber, the feasibility of nuclear war-fighting strategies, the balance of conventional forces in Europe, the prospects for peace in the Middle East, and the dynamics of the U.S. relationship with Japan and other allies. *International Security* has also provided a consistent forum for theoretical debates about, for example, the merits of neoliberal institutionalism, the contested relationship between democracy and international peace, and the stability of different kinds of alliance structures in the international system.

International Security was founded in the mid-1970s by a young group of scholars in the Cambridge, Massachusetts, area. Reacting against the style of established journals in the field, such as *Foreign Policy,* the editors sought out well-footnoted, refereed articles on policy-relevant issues rather than "ex cathedra" pronouncements on policy issues by leading figures. *International Security* soon developed a unique identity as a journal that dealt with policy issues in a more scholarly way than did other journals in the field, even though it did not limit itself to articles by academics.

Edited at Harvard and published by MIT Press, *International Security* and its editorial board have a strong Cambridge and East Coast establishment tilt. The board has included Harvard University's Joseph Nye and Ashton Carter (both of whom served in the first Clinton administration), and Albert Carnesale (an arms-control negotiator for the Carter administration who went on to become provost of Harvard and then president of UCLA). The board has also included Herb York and Michael May, two former directors of the nuclear weapons laboratory in Livermore, California; Thomas Schelling, one of the originators of game theory in security studies; Brent Scowcroft, national security adviser to the first President Bush; Richard Betts of the Brookings Institute; and such acclaimed masters of international relations and deterrence theory as Alexander George, John Mearsheimer, Barry Posen, Robert Jervis, Stanley Hoffman, and Lawrence Freedman. Under the guidance of people such as these, *International Security* provides a forum where academics, think-tank analysts, government officials, and would-be government officials can come together to debate security issues. In these debates, the contributors to *International Security* have by no means spoken with one voice, and some have used the journal as a platform from which to attack major U.S. weapons programs such as SDI, the MX missile, and the B-2 bomber. Still, discourse within the journal has functioned within certain parameters, and it is to the definition of these parameters that I now turn.

The International Security Discourse Community

Commitments to particular constructions of the world crystallize within discourse communities.[22] Members of discourse communities are bound together both by shared allegiance to explicitly formulated propositions about the world (that the existence of nuclear weapons during the cold war made the international system more stable, for example) and also by common consumption of aspects of discourse that exist on the edge of awareness (figures of speech that identify nuclear weapons with male virility or international relations theory with the solidity of Newtonian physics, for example). Michel Foucault, in *Power/Knowledge,* points out that discourses inevitably draw boundaries around themselves by celebrating certain kinds of statements while excommunicating others, which then take on the status of what he calls "subjugated knowledges." (Thus, in the defense community in the 1980s, for example, one could not have continued to belong to that community if one had said that nuclear weapons were immoral and that the United States should unilaterally disarm.)

Foucault also pointed out that discourses do not meld people into community by enforcing complete agreement or conformity. On the contrary, discourses thrive on debate and controversy—this is how they elaborate themselves—but in ways that are channeled and contained. In *The History of Sexuality,* Foucault argued that discourses construct community and reality most subtly and effectively by means of what he called "incitement to discourse"—by channeling disagreements into certain frameworks within which the act of disagreement obscures actors' shared allegiance to deeper structures of thought that contain their disagreements. Thus, in the act of debating, members of a discourse community unthinkingly reproduce the categories, taken for granted, that make disagreement possible. As an example, in the discursive world of security studies in the 1980s, actors were incited by the Reagan administration's SDI proposal to a discourse on the feasibility of strategic defense in which, although the debate was never consensually resolved, the conduct of the debate reinforced axiomatic beliefs in the defense community that stationary land-based multiple-warhead missiles were destabilizing, that game theoretic models of nuclear "exchanges" were an important tool in discussing the pros and cons of defenses, and that the abolition of nuclear weapons by treaty was not feasible. As I will show, a debate on the abolition of ballistic missiles that took place in the pages of *International Security* in the final years of the cold war similarly reinforced certain foundational precepts of strategic discourse, even as participants in the debate disagreed about the best path forward in terms of strategic weapons deployments.

Finally, as Donna Haraway has argued, academic discourses consist of more than systems of facts, beliefs, and propositions.[23] Academic discourses become compelling in part because they implicitly embody, often at the edge of awareness, narratives to which listeners are drawn. Haraway contends that primatologists, in constructing laws of primate behavior, implicitly told stories about primate gender, sexuality, and violence that had human resonance in an era of patriarchy, capitalism, and colonialism and that primatology should be seen as an epic displaced narrative of humanity, not just as a set of observational claims about primates. In a similar vein, I have made the case that the dominant discourse in security studies embodied a "Cold War narrative" in which drama and meaning derived from an unending, but constantly shifting, clash between two global empires, and from the repeated introduction of new technological possibilities and threats into the story line.[24] Despite efforts on the part of the antinuclear movement to substitute different stories (ending either in global extinction or transcendence of the arms race), this story remained compelling in the pages of *International Security* to the very end of the cold war, as I will now show.

Missing the End of the Cold War I: Nuclear Weapons

In the last three years of the cold war, *International Security* published twenty articles on nuclear weapons issues. Although many of these discussed some quite dramatic possible reconfigurations of the superpower arsenals—abolishing ballistic missiles, scrapping the B-2 bomber, 50 percent cuts in weapons, and deploying SDI—not one discussed the possibility that the arms race, let alone the cold war, might end. In fact, all more or less explicitly assumed that it would continue, whatever the fate of individual weapons systems.

In a winter 1986–87 article, for example, Barry Blechman and Victor Utgoff discussed future spending projections for SDI. Assuming that the U.S. defense budget would continue to rise and using various graphic curves to plot this, their low projection was for a 54 percent increase in defense spending by 2010 and their high projection was for a 100 percent increase—both enough to pay for an SDI system. They discussed whether this should be paid for by an 11 percent increase in income tax or, more probably, by a mix of tax increases, cuts in social programs, and deficit spending. At only one point in the article did they ask whether the relationship between the United States and the Soviet Union might fundamentally shift in the next fifteen years: "Deployment of strategic defenses conceivably could lead to a breakthrough in relations with the Soviet Union and far-reaching arms-control agreements—perhaps specifying a transition to a defense-dominated strategic regime involving much smaller forces, as well as reductions in forces in Europe."[25] Here, the only transformation in U.S.-Soviet relations the authors could imagine is presented as a consequence of breakthroughs in weapons technologies, not politics.

In the summer of 1987, incited by Gorbachev's suggestion at Reykjavik the previous year that both superpowers abolish ballistic missiles, *International Security* published four articles on ballistic missile abolition. Richard Perle argued that a world without ballistic missiles would be a world in which Soviet superiority in strategic bombers and conventional forces would become more important unless the United States continued to develop SDI and modernize its remaining nuclear forces.[26] Leon Sloss argued that the abolition of ballistic missiles would save the most money for the Soviets, who would "almost certainly" invest it in modernizing other nuclear weapons; he worried that it would also lead to "a relaxation in U.S. defense efforts based on the belief that tensions with the Soviet Union had declined." Thomas Schelling favored the abolition of land-based intercontinental ballistic missiles (ICBMs), but warned that "in years to come," U.S. submarines might become vulnerable to a Soviet attack and that the United States should therefore phase out submarine-launched ballistic missiles (SLBMs) in favor of cruise missiles "over the next decade or two."[27] Randall Forsberg, the furthest to the left of the contributors, argued that the abolition of ballistic missiles was of peripheral importance as long as the United States continued to rely on the threat of nuclear war to protect its allies in Europe and Asia, recommending a switch from extended to existential deterrence.[28]

The following summer, in 1988, a little over one year before the end of the cold war, *International Security* published an article by Michael May, George Bing, and John Steinbruner on the possible consequences of 50 percent cuts in the superpower arsenals. They concluded that 50 percent cuts were quite safe since they would have little effect either on casualty rates in a nuclear war or on strategic stability. If cuts went deeper, they did worry about the "reaction of the major U.S. allies to a situation where the U.S. would no longer be so obviously the military and strategically dominant partner. National considerations might come to receive more priority relative to alliance considerations than they do now. Such an effect would not be expected in the case of the Soviet Union and the Warsaw pact."[29] The last sentence, as it turned out, got the course of events over the next decade exactly back to front.

Two issues later, *International Security* sponsored a debate on the possible abolition of sea-launched cruise missiles (SLCMs). Henry Mustin and Linton Brooks both argued that the Intermediate-Range Nuclear Forces (INF) Treaty of 1987 had weakened the credibility of American nuclear threats by removing one rung (land-based intermediate missiles) of the escalatory ladder, and that SLCMs were vital in replacing the missing rung. Rose Gottemoeller and Theodore Postol, on the other hand, argued that it would be better to restrict SLCMs now before—as they surely would otherwise— the Soviets perfected them over the next decade.[30]

Finally, in the fall of 1989, *International Security* published three articles on stealth technologies, especially the B-2 bomber. Of the three, I will discuss only Michael Brown's "The U.S. Manned Bomber and Strategic Deterrence in the 1990s."[31] In the very season that saw the end of the cold war, fall 1989, just as the Soviets were initiating their second unilateral moratorium on nuclear testing in a decade, Brown argued: "Given that the Soviet Union began to deploy accurate ICBMs approximately ten years after the United States did so, it is not unreasonable to assume that the Soviet Union will deploy highly accurate SLBMs by the end of the 1990s, roughly ten years after the D-5 [missile on the Trident II submarine] comes on line" (10). Worrying about a future crisis in which the Soviets might launch a disarming first strike against a United States reliant mainly on stationary ICBMs and unscrambled bombers for its deterrent, he called for the United States to scrap the B-2 bomber and the MX missile and to invest substantial resources in a "large Trident [submarine] force" and a new mobile land-based single-warhead ICBM.

If this panoramic overview of three years' articles gives some sense of the scope and depth of the assumption that the cold war would continue, we need to look in more detail at a particular debate in order to analyze the particular discursive mechanisms that anchored this presumption and made it real. These discursive mechanisms, and the power of the ontological assumption that the arms race and the cold war would continue indefinitely, are nicely dramatized by a debate on ICBM "modernization" that took place in the pages of *International Security* in 1987–88.

There are two ways to view the context of this debate, one in terms of a slowly shifting calculus of military hardware capabilities, the other in terms of a rapidly evolving drama of political change. In the minds of most defense intellectuals, the context for this debate consisted only of the shifting nuclear hardware capabilities of the two superpowers. Since both countries had learned to MIRV[32] their missiles and greatly increase their accuracy in the 1970s, it had become possible (in the abstract world of strategic theory, at least) that one side could use its multiwarhead missiles to knock out the land-based missile force of its opponent in a preemptive bolt from the blue. The Carter administration had proposed to close this "window of vulnerability" by deploying a new ICBM, the MX, that would routinely circulate between shelters on thousands of miles of railway in Utah and Nevada, in an elaborate nuclear shell game. This plan collapsed in the face of political opposition, especially in Utah and Nevada, where the MX was to be based.[33] In 1983, the Scowcroft Commission, appointed to resolve the ICBM problem, proposed a two-track plan: deploying fifty "rail-garrison" MX missiles in such a way that they could be dispersed rapidly by train in the event of a crisis, and also building a new small intercontinental ballistic missile (SICBM) that would have only one warhead and would, therefore, be a less "lucrative" target for Soviet ICBMs than the ten-warhead MX. The Scowcroft Commission's solution generated as much controversy as it resolved, however, and defense intellectuals were still arguing over the wisdom of its recommendations at the time of the *International Security* debates in 1987.

The other way one might contextualize this debate on ICBM modernization is to embed it in the rapidly unfolding drama of U.S.-Soviet relations in the years of perestroika. Gorbachev had ascended to power as the Soviet general secretary in March 1985 and, by 1987, had made substantial progress in implementing his policies of glasnost and perestroika and in reshaping Soviet foreign policy. In August 1985, in what he declared was a bid to end the nuclear arms race completely, he had unilaterally suspended Soviet nuclear testing, and he maintained this moratorium for eighteen months despite continued U.S. nuclear testing. At Reykjavik in 1986, Gorbachev had proposed not only a ban on SDI but also the complete elimination of all ballistic missiles and, eventually, the complete elimination of nuclear weapons of all kinds. In 1987, he accepted the INF Treaty, even though its terms were widely seen as more advantageous to the United States than to the Soviet Union. At the same time, Gorbachev was articulating new ideas of mutual security and, with respect to conventional weapons, defensive defense—the reconfiguration of military forces in such a way that they would be appropriate for defense but not offense. By the summer of 1987, he had made substantial reforms in Soviet domestic politics as well, including the relaxation of the state's central control of economic enterprise and the abolition of the Communist Party's monopoly in politics. This monopoly had been the keystone of Soviet politics since Lenin.

It is striking that, in no less than seven different articles on ICBM modernization in *International Security,* none of the political changes summarized in the preceding paragraph are explored or even mentioned—with the exception of Jack Ruina, who does briefly mention in the final paragraph of "More Is Not Better" that "the Soviets under Gorbachev seem readier than ever to be accommodating and to agree to acceptable limits on nuclear arms" (192).[34] Only Ruina questioned whether the United States needed a new ICBM at all. The context in which the U.S. ICBM force is situated in these articles is not the political relationship between the superpowers but the interlocking configuration of their nuclear hardware.[35] In other words, the narrative that underlies these analysts' discussions is one that brackets and freezes politics while finding its dynamism in the evolution of technology.

Attention to Soviet politics and even to arms-control proposals and agreements might have produced a perception of diminishing threat, but the focus on hardware did not. Thus, Donald Hicks, for example, despite the Soviet testing moratorium, the INF Treaty, and the internal reforms, concluded unambiguously that the Soviet threat was increasing: "although the Soviet threat has continued to increase, the strength of the U.S. bomber and submarine legs of the strategic triad is sound and improving."[36]

It is characteristic of recent security studies discourse to marginalize possible intentions of adversaries and instead to privilege analysis of their technical capabilities and worst-case scenarios for their employment. Thus, in "Strategic Forces Rationale," John Toomay argues:

> Our approach emphasizes Soviet potential capability rather than intent, because intent is qualitative and transitory. . . . We are not satisfied to make the probability of a Soviet attack low; we must make that probability vanishingly small. . . . No matter that these attacks [scenarios for Soviet preemptive attacks on U.S. ICBMs] are complex and stylized, requiring an order of precision not likely within Soviet capability, because even low likelihoods are too high. (194–95)

This analytic convention of assuming the worst and focusing only on hardware capabilities enacts a bias toward the status quo and ensures that an adversary's policy changes or emergent transformations in the structural relationship between the superpowers will lie largely outside even the peripheral vision of the analyst. It also focuses the analyst's intellectual energy on elaborate hyperreal scenarios of how nuclear wars might be fought rather than scenarios (which, in the end, turned out to be more realistic) of how the cold war might be ended. Only a year before the end of the cold war, Barry Fridling and John Harvey published "On the Wrong Track?" in which they anguished over the possibility that a rail garrison MX missile force might not be able to disperse quickly enough to avoid obliteration by a Soviet first strike. They also worried that the dispersal of MX missiles by rail might be sabotaged by "covert Soviet agents in train control facilities scattered throughout the nation" who might have secretly installed weight sensors on railroad tracks or hidden transmitters on the missile trains themselves (134).

With the benefit of hindsight, from the other side of the great divide constituted by the end of the cold war, it is easy to mock such scenarios as paranoid and unreal. However, they made eminent sense within the frame of reference of a discourse—technostrategic discourse—that took it as given that the arms race was a fact of life and would continue indefinitely. This assumption was, as is so often the case with the most powerful structuring assumptions in any discourse, rarely articulated explicitly, but its functioning can clearly be seen in the discourse nonetheless. It is present, for example, in Fridling and Harvey's concern that the MX "does not provide a hedge against future vulnerability of submarines" and in their recommendation that "increased funds for ICBM basing research and development (R&D) need to be appropriated at the earliest opportunity in order to provide the next administration with feasible alternatives for Peacekeeper or alternate approaches to retaining the viability of ICBMs" (140). The assumption is more explicit in Toomay's "Strategic Forces Rationale":

> After 35 years of successful deterrence, is our vigilance waning? Are we becoming complacent? Have we lost interest in the details? . . . Perhaps we should remind ourselves that the men and women in our strategic forces have been faithfully adhering to a discipline of technical and operational standards, requiring a monastic dedication—every hour of every day for ten thousand days; that we have sunk billions into every facet of the nuclear umbrella, keeping it intact; and that our deterrence posture is a bulwark of strength throughout the free world. (201)

We even find the assumption of an indefinite arms race in the most liberal of the seven articles, Ruina's "More Is Not Better," in which he states that "there is some possibility that, in the future, new technologies might threaten a second leg of the triad" (189) and that "if the political climate either deteriorates badly so that strategic force enhancement is in order, or improves substantially so that there is a real interest in deep reductions, a new and different strategic weapons system may be needed with characteristics we cannot now specify" (192). While arguing that no new ICBM needed to be deployed at all and criticizing "conflict scenarios that are truly surrealistic and depend upon assumptions of perverse and suicidal reasoning by the adversary," Ruina does not articulate the possibility that the arms race might completely end or that freezing ICBM deployments might be a means of bringing it to an end (187–88). Instead, he can only cast his argument as an appeal for deferral in the face of the shifting dynamics of an endless superpower competition. This is a perfect example of what Foucault meant by "incitement to discourse."

Missing the End of the Cold War II: Soviet Reform

In the two years preceding the end of the cold war, the only authors in *International Security* who came anywhere close to sensing what was about to happen were three Soviet specialists: Jack Snyder, Stephen Meyer, and Mark Kramer. It is significant that, while the nuclear strategists and international relations grand theorists were continuing about their business as usual, it was Soviet specialists—more attuned to domestic politics and well aware of the transformative scope of Gorbachev's reforms—who caught glimpses of the potential transformation of an entire order, though they could not discern the shape of this transformation to come. It is also no coincidence that the titles of two of their three articles end with question marks: in all three articles there is a pervasive tone of disorientation and uncertainty. In Stephen Meyer's words, "Gorbachev's effort to recast Soviet military doctrine has created a great deal of confusion and uncertainty in what was a very stable policy environment" (132).

Snyder, Meyer, and Kramer all take Gorbachev's reforms seriously and, unlike the nuclear specialists who discount statements about intentions and focus solely on hardware, they pay considerable attention to Soviet doctrinal discussions and statements. Thus, Meyer says in "Sources and Prospects," "I reject immediately the argument that the ongoing doctrinal dialogue in the Soviet Union is mere propaganda" (125), and Snyder, highlighting the unprecedented scope of Gorbachev's initiatives in his article "The Gorbachev Revolution," says:

Even Kruschchev understood that superficial concessions could demobilize the West, buying time and preparing the ground for a strategy of offensive detente. But the articulation of the correlation of forces theory by Khrushchev and Brezhnev clearly signaled their intentions from the outset of their detente diplomacy. There is nothing analogous to the correlation of forces theory in Gorbachev's strategic arguments. On the contrary, he insists that this kind of a one-way approach to security constitutes a "world of illusions." (120)

Snyder and Meyer agree that Gorbachev, faced with the need to divert resources from the military sector to economic development, had established an alliance with the intelligentsia against the military-industrial complex and was aiming for a profound restructuring of Soviet society. In Snyder's words: "Gorbachev is aiming for nothing less than smashing the power of the entrenched Stalinist interest groups. . . . The military-industrial complex, old-style ideologues, and autarkic industrial interests are in eclipse. Civilian defense intellectuals, reformist ideologues, and supporters of liberalized trade policies among the intelligentsia are gaining influence and trying to force changes" (109–10). Snyder and Meyer also agree in taking "new thinking" seriously and believing that Gorbachev genuinely aimed to move toward a relationship with the United States based on mutual security.

When it came to taking the next step, however, and proposing explicitly that the cold war might end, Snyder, Meyer, and Kramer squinted into the darkness and drew back at the last moment. Reading these articles, one has a strong sense of authors stumbling in unknown terrain, wrestling with the unthinkable. All three recall Khrushchev's failure, a generation earlier, to make his liberalization of the Soviet Union enduring and self-sustaining. The narrative of Khrushchev's failure haunts their attempts to make sense of Gorbachev's reformism so that, perceiving Gorbachev through the lens of this failure, they worried that the reforms of the 1980s were, like those of the Khrushchev era, a prelude to a backlash and to a reintensification of cold war.

Snyder begins his article elliptically circling the unthinkable: "Many Americans have long believed that Soviet expansionism stems from pathological domestic institutions, and that the expansionist impulse will diminish only when those institutions undergo a fundamental change. The Gorbachev revolution in Soviet domestic and foreign policy has raised the question of whether that time is close at hand" (93). Later, drawing back a little, Snyder sets limits on the opening he created with these words. One way in which he does this is to say that if the reforms do succeed, then Gorbachev will be able "to seek structural changes in Soviet military posture that would stabilize the military competition" (116–17). In other words, the cold war would be scaled back but not closed down. The second way Snyder sets limits on the degree of change to be expected is by articulating circumstances that would bring about a domestic backlash and a reintensification of cold war. Thus, he says that the reformers might well be defeated in a situation where "SDI was being deployed, Eastern Europe was asserting its autonomy, and Soviet clients were losing their counter-insurgency wars in Afghanistan, Angola, and Ethiopia" (128). As it turned out, of course, this is almost exactly what happened, but the reform process intensified and the cold war ended.[37]

Meyer's argument follows a comparable trajectory. Opening with a similarly expansive gesture, he says in his first paragraph: "some of the ideas being articulated are doctrinally and ideologically revolutionary in the context of Soviet security policy. Indeed, the ongoing doctrinal dialogue, if carried to its logical extreme, could imply even greater changes in Soviet military policy than those associated with Khrushchev's doctrinal initiatives of the late 1950s and early 1960s" (124). In his conclusion, however, Meyer says:

> Should they [the reforms] spawn new problems, then more traditional elements in the leadership would have an opening to attack the full spectrum of new political thinking—including new thinking on security. The turmoil in Azerbaijan during 1987–88 is one case in point. Equally ominous—and perhaps more directly connected with external security—would be another burst of political self-assertion, tinged with anti-Soviet behavior, in Eastern Europe. Powerful members of the Politburo seeking to contain the power and authority of the general secretary could use such events to create a consensus against the new political thinking. (156–57)

Meyer concludes by adding that "looking beyond Gorbachev, there is no reason to expect that future general secretaries—or other members of the Politburo—will be 'new thinkers'" (157).

Mark Kramer, writing for an issue of *International Security* that was on the newsstands after the Berlin Wall came down, was equally concerned that events in Eastern Europe would cause a crackdown and equally perplexed by Gorbachev's policies. After all, it was an axiom in security studies in the 1980s that, as one international relations theorist paraphrased it, "hegemons are expected to make every possible effort to retain their principal sphere of influence."[38] Although noting that "the precise limits of the Soviet Union's willingness to accept internal change in Eastern Europe are still unclear," Kramer is confident that those limits excluded the possibility of what in fact did eventually happen:

[A] major problem with Gorbachev's approach is that it may eventually result in such ambiguity about the limits of Soviet tolerance that East bloc countries will be overwhelmingly tempted to test those limits. Already an impression has spread in Eastern Europe that the "threshold" needed to provoke Soviet military intervention has been raised so high that almost anything short of a renunciation of socialism or withdrawal from the Warsaw Pact is now feasible. (26)

Although all three authors took Gorbachev's reforms seriously and were well aware that they held out the possibility of fundamentally transforming Soviet society, none of them could finally countenance the possibility that, as eventually transpired, the Soviet Union could allow Eastern Europe to go free, and, although all three are careful to eschew predictions of the future in favor of menus of scenarios, none of them speculated that the cold war could end. If this was unthinkable for the nuclear specialists discussed earlier because of their decontextualized reduction of the arms race to a matter of technical rationality, it was unthinkable to the Soviet specialists, one suspects, for a different reason: not because they could not think politically, but because the cold war was the containing structure within which they had learned to constitute the Soviet Union as an object of study, the context within which they had learned their analytical reflexes. Without the cold war, the Soviet Union would no longer exist as the familiar object of their expertise. It would become another country—as indeed it did.

A New Security Studies?

In "Dare Not to Know," Ken Booth has asked the rhetorical question: "If academic international relations theory could not adequately describe, explain or predict such a turning point in history [as the end of the cold war], should it not be discarded as another of the failed projects buried by the Wall?" (329). I hoped in the early 1990s that practitioners of conventional security studies would be chastened by their spectacular failure to foresee the end of the Cold War and that this failure would trigger an internal critique of the dominant discourse and the efflorescence of new discourses.[39] To what degree did this happen in the pages of *International Security*?

In the winter of 1992–93, *International Security* did publish a major critique of the prevailing wisdom in security studies: John Lewis Gaddis's "International Relations Theory and the End of the Cold War." This article used the unexpected end of the cold war as a battering ram against the dominant discourse in security studies and international relations theory, particularly its traditional focus on positivism and prediction. Gaddis opened his article by saying:

Historians, political scientists, economists, psychologists, and even mathe-maticians have claimed the power to detect patterns in the behavior of nations and the individuals who lead them; an awareness of these, they have assured us, will better equip statesmen—and states—to deal with the uncertainties that lie ahead.

The end of the Cold War provides an unusual opportunity to test these claims. That event was of such importance that no approach to the study of international relations claiming both foresight and competence should have failed to see it coming. None actually did so, though, and that fact ought to raise questions about the methods we have developed for trying to understand world politics. (5–6)

Gaddis attacked the dominant international security studies paradigm on three grounds. First, he questioned the very notion of deterministic predict-ability that anchors international relations theory's aspirations to become a Newtonian science of international affairs. Second, he criticized the denial of learning, agency, and human will central to the dominant international security studies paradigm, taking issue with the presumption that humans are like molecules that repetitively obey grand laws of motion. Third, he challenged the common privileging of structure over process in security studies and its fundamental presumption that, like the basic laws of phys-ics, the laws of the international system remain static and do not evolve over time.

Gaddis's view has not been unopposed, however, and there have been at-tempts to recuperate the rupture opened by the unexpected end of the Cold War, particularly by (neo)realists in security studies.[40] The first of these, pub-lished before Gaddis's article, was John Mearsheimer's controversial "Back to the Future: Instability in Europe after the Cold War." Mearsheimer begins by stating that "the world can be used as a laboratory to decide which theories best explain world politics" (9) and by asking which theory in security studies has proved most reliable in understanding the past so that we can use the same theory to orient our expectations and behavior in the future. One might expect neorealism to fare poorly in such a contest, given the neorealists' failure to foresee the end of the cold war, but Mearsheimer ignores this issue. Picking his test case carefully, he takes as his acid test not the ability of a theory to explain the end of the cold war but its ability to account for the "long peace" of the cold war itself.[41] He argues that neo-realism, which took as a core axiom that bipolar systems are more stable than multipolar ones, was best able to explain this abnormally long period of stability and is therefore the most reliable theory to guide our actions in the future.[42] Mearsheimer then argues that, far from being a cause for celebration, the end of the cold war is a dangerous development that, by introducing multipolarity, threatens to make Europe war-prone again unless a strong Germany emerges as a balancing power within Europe. Warning of the danger that Europe will be revisited by war, he concludes by advocating "managed nuclear proliferation" to Germany as a way of creating a new strategic stability anchored by nuclear deterrence within Europe.

A second realist article, Kenneth Waltz's "The Emerging Structure of International Politics," follows a broadly similar strategy of ignoring the failure of security studies to foresee the end of the cold war and insisting that, the peaceful end of the cold war notwithstanding, the international system remains anarchic and (neo)realism remains the best theory for understanding it. Slyly treating the end of the cold war as if it were anticipated all along, Waltz says: "in a 1964 essay, I predicted that bipolarity would last through the century. On the brow of the next millennium, we must prepare to bid bipolarity adieu and begin to live without its stark simplicities and comforting symmetry" (44). After making the case that (neo)realism perfectly explained the superpowers' behavior throughout the cold war, he goes on to argue that the cold war ended because the underlying structure of the international system itself changed. He concludes, like Mearsheimer, by warning that the new multipolar order will be less stable than the old one.[43]

A third realist article, this one explicitly rebutting Gaddis's stinging attack on international relations theory, is William Wohlforth's "Realism and the End of the Cold War." Where Mearsheimer and Waltz avoid the topic of this chapter—the failure of international relations specialists to foresee the end of the cold war—Wohlforth confronts it head-on. He opens by saying: "a central question faces students and practitioners of international politics. Do the rapid decline and comparatively peaceful collapse of the Soviet state, and with it the entire postwar international order, discredit the realist approach?" (91). His answer: "A thoroughly realist explanation of the Cold War's end and the relatively peaceful nature of the Soviet Union's decline that relies entirely on the propositions of pre-1989 theory is in many ways superior to rich explanations based on other theoretical traditions" (92).

Wohlforth argues that the realist failure to foresee the end of the cold war is in fact unproblematic for two reasons. First, realists never said the end of the cold war was impossible: "No particular finding about the Cold War's end will suffice to falsify an entire research program, such as realism. For a single series of events to constitute a critical test of a theory, it must not only be inconsistent with the theory but be unambiguously ruled out by it" (95). Second, realists made few predictions anyway: "Such criticisms miss Waltz's main contention: that a theory of international politics cannot predict state behavior or explain international change. Waltz and his followers often employed the theory to discuss Cold War statecraft, but its core predictions are only two: balances will form; and bipolar systems are less war-prone than multipolar ones" (101–2). Wohlforth argues that, in retrospect, the peaceful end of the cold war makes sense within the framework of realism since "declining challengers" (such as the Soviet Union in the 1980s) behave differently from "declining hegemons," being less likely to respond to their decline by launching preventive war. He concludes that, "although it appeared to require an intellectual revolution in Moscow, a policy of careful appeasement and retrenchment is a historically common response to relative decline. The Roman, Byzantine, and Venetian empires attempted such strategies when they confronted the dilemma of decline" (115).

Conclusion

As Richard Ned Lebow and Thomas Risse-Kappen have written, in the 1980s "most theorists and policy analysts assumed that bipolarity and its associated Soviet-American rivalry would endure for the foreseeable future. In the unlikely event of a system transformation, the catalyst for it would be superpower war."[44] As I have sketched out here, many security studies specialists have refused to be chastened by the fact that their assumptions were so spectacularly contradicted by events. Lebow and Risse-Kappen report that, at the conference that generated their edited volume, one prominent international relations theorist argued that the end of the cold war proved nothing since it was only a single "data point." Meanwhile, Wohlforth argues that realism was not discredited by the end of the cold war because it never explicitly ruled out the possibility that the cold war might end. This leads one to wonder, with Lebow, whether it is "impossible for realists to predict much of anything before the fact but all too easy for them to explain anything once it has occurred."[45] If the unforeseen end of the cold war does not discredit the theories and assumptions of this variant of realism, what would have, or what might yet? Would a U.S.-Soviet nuclear war have been seen as discrediting their theories? Would fifty years of stable multilateralism now? Or bandwagoning in the new Europe? Or could ex post facto explanations be found for all of these phenomena, too?

Finally, the dominant discourse in security studies reminds this writer of the famous case of Azande witchcraft in the anthropological literature.[46] Among the Azande of Africa, witchcraft was a system for explaining the provenance of misfortune: if something bad happened, it was a witch's fault, and magic had to be used to fend off the witchcraft. The anthropologist Edward Evans-Pritchard found that witchcraft theories could never be empirically falsified because the system always contained plausible explanations for its own failure to predict events or cure ills (this particular witch doctor was incompetent, the witch's magic was stronger than the curer's, the ritual had been enacted improperly, etc.). The dominant discourse in security studies bears an uncanny resemblance to witchcraft among the Azande in that, although its practitioners boast about their predictive successes, there is apparently no kind of event that would enable us to falsify the discourse. It is a discourse that gives interpretive meaning to events but cannot be tested by them. Whether the cold war continued or ended, security studies could account for it. Whether the cold war ended violently or peacefully, security studies had an explanation for it. Whether the Soviets attempted to repress the East Europeans or gave them their freedom as the cold war ended, security studies could explain it. If war breaks out in the post–cold war international system, it will prove the realist presumption of anarchy; and if war does not break out, it will demonstrate the functioning of the balance of power or will be a lull before the next war. As E. P. Thompson, the most incisive critic of the cold war, wrote in *Beyond the Cold War*: "the practitioners [of cold war discourse] are trapped within the enclosed circularity of their own self-validating logic. Every conclusion is entailed within the theory's premises, although a finely wrought filigree of logic may be spun between one and the other." In such a situation, as Thomas Kuhn argued long ago, the way to change people's minds may not be to argue with old paradigms but to build new ones.

(1999)

7

Cultures as Strategic Hamlets: An Anthropologist Reads Samuel Huntington

There is an old saying that, when the gods want to punish us, they make our wishes come true. As an anthropologist working in the field of security studies, I have for many years complained that mainstream international relations theorists do not take culture seriously, writing instead as if states and their leaders are impelled in their actions by "interests" existing in some sort of pure, cultureless vacuum, and as if the social movements that arise within and across state boundaries are of scant relevance to international relations.[1] My punishment has taken the form of international relations theorist Samuel P. Huntington's *The Clash of Civilizations and the Remaking of World Order*—a book that replaces the flat determinism of realism with an equally crude cultural determinism, which, if it is informed by any reading of anthropology at all, is, as the anthropologist Ulf Hannerz has noted, indebted to "what is largely a mid-century way of thinking about culture" in anthropology (the century in question being the twentieth, in case there is any doubt).[2] The eminent international relations scholar Robert Jervis, noting that Huntington's book marks a break with the dominant realist school in international relations, has suggested that the perspective in *The Clash of Civilizations* "has much in common with [that of] constructivist scholars who stress the importance of identity and culture."[3] Huntington's argument does indeed clash with realism—sometimes in interesting and productive ways, which I explore here. However, any resemblance between Huntington's and the constructivists' perspective is superficial indeed, and the treatment of culture in Huntington's analysis would appall most constructivist scholars in the social sciences. As I will argue, while Huntington puts his finger on some interesting anomalies in the realist picture of the world, his best-selling book stands as an object lesson in how not to bring culture back into international relations theory.

Published first as an article in *Foreign Affairs* in 1993 and then as a full-length book in 1996, *The Clash of Civilizations* argues that the international system is evolving from the bipolar structure of the cold war years to a new multipolar structure organized around different historical civilizations. Saying that, in the world following the end of the cold war, "the rivalry of the superpowers is replaced by the clash of civilizations" (28), Huntington argues that "in a world where culture counts, the platoons are tribes and ethnic groups, the regiments are nations, and the armies are civilizations" (128). Insisting that "a civilization is a culture writ large" (41), he cites Adda Bozeman's argument that civilizations coalesce around "values, norms, institutions, and modes of thinking to which successive generations in a given society have attached primary importance."[4] He argues that seven distinct civilizations have formed and endured over many centuries and have deep psychological power in the subjective worlds of their inhabitants. According to Huntington, globalization may actually strengthen these civilizational identities, as intrusions from without provoke local cultural backlashes around the world.

Huntington's seven civilizations, in the order in which he lists them, are Sinic (i.e., Chinese), Japanese, Hindu, Islamic, Orthodox, Western, and Latin American (though he seems of two minds as to whether Latin America might not, after all, be part of Western civilization). He also lists Africa as "possibly" a civilization, thus prompting Hannerz to observe wryly that, despite his emphasis on the clear distinctness of civilizations, Huntington "appears not quite sure how many civilizations there are" (394).[5] He argues that "cleft states" (those, such as India and Indonesia, where a single government presides over a population drawn from more than one civilization) will be the most unstable in the coming era. In the absence of the discipline imposed by the old superpower struggle of the cold war, Huntington expects wars in the future to occur at the fraught interface between civilizations (the "fault line," as he calls it, drawing on the geologic imagery of tectonic plates grinding against one another). He sees the conflict in the former Yugoslavia between representatives of three different civilizations—Orthodox Serbs, Catholic Croats, and Bosnian Muslims— as paradigmatic of the kinds of wars we can increasingly expect. Fault line wars are often protracted and exceptionally vicious, tending in the direction of genocide, because it is not easy to separate the warring constituencies, because each side can enlist support from civilizational kin outside the country, and because "fundamental issues of identity are at stake" (252).

These issues often involve religion since "millennia of human history have shown that religion is not a 'small difference' but possibly the most profound difference that can exist between people" (254).

Huntington is particularly concerned with three of these seven civilizations and the potential for combustible interactions between them. They are the Western, Islamic, and Sinic civilizations. The West is defined for Huntington by its modernizing dynamism over several centuries and by its historic commitment to Enlightenment values of rationality and universal rights. In a generalization many will find dubious, he says:

> The great ideologies of the twentieth century include liberalism, socialism, anarchism, corporatism, Marxism, communism, social democracy, conservatism, nationalism, fascism, and Christian democracy. They all share one thing in common: they are products of Western civilization. No other civilization has generated a significant political ideology. The West, however, has never generated a major religion. (53–54)

Huntington sees the West today as a great civilization probably entering into decline as its economic and population growth rates level off, while crime and drug abuse rates rise, the family erodes, and the Protestant work ethic weakens. In Stephen Walt's words, "he is clearly worried that the hedonistic, individualistic culture of the West is no longer up to the challenges it faces."[6] But he is also worried that the West's liberal concern to promote human rights and democracy around the world and its tendency to see Enlightenment values as universal rather than simply Western will drag it into conflicts with other civilizations in which it will lack the economic, political, and military power to prevail.

Huntington views Islam, another civilization with a universalist orientation, as an expansive, unstable, and dangerous force. Pointing to conflicts in Bosnia, Kosovo, Turkey, Chechnya, Malaysia, Indonesia, and a plethora of other places around the world, he says, "wherever one looks along the perimeter of Islam, Muslims have problems living peacefully with their neighbors" (256). He attributes this Islamic pugnaciousness to rapid population growth in the Islamic world, to a supposed Islamic affinity for militarism ("Islam has from the start been a religion of the sword" [263]), to the fact that "even more than Christianity, Islam is an absolutist faith" (264), and to the lack of a clear core state to exert discipline within the Islamic world. Pointing to the leadership role exercised by Russia in the Orthodox world and the United States in the West, Huntington is concerned that, absent such a core state, Islam is an anarchic force that cannot be restrained and directed. He suggests that, given the insistent drumbeat of Islamic-sponsored terrorist attacks on American embassies, airliners, and military facilities, the United States has since the Iranian Revolution been in a "quasi war" with Islamic civilization (216–17).

Huntington also sees Chinese civilization as an expansive force. With high rates of economic growth, a large population, and a social discipline now lacking in the West, Sinic civilization is bound to challenge the West for hegemony in Asia sooner or later, Huntington argues. While Western states have traditionally sought to prevent the emergence of a single hegemon by practicing balance-of-power politics in their international relations, Huntington argues that Asian cultures have "had little room for social or political pluralism and the division of power" (234), taking "international politics as hierarchical because their domestic politics are" (237). Thus Japan is likely to desert its alliance with the United States in the long run as Asian countries "bandwagon" against the West behind the dominant Asian power—China. Huntington fears that this Sinic-led bloc may forge an alliance against the West with the Islamic world.

Warning that "the dangerous clashes of the future are likely to arise from the interaction of Western arrogance, Islamic intolerance, and Sinic assertiveness" (183), Huntington is concerned that, unless the core states of different civilizations exercise restraint in their relations with one another, respecting regional spheres of influence, local conflicts along the fault lines between different civilizations could flare into wider, even global, wars. He ends the book with a narrative, which he describes as possible but not likely, of an imagined world war in which the United States comes to the aid of a Vietnam that has been attacked by China and the conflict ripples across the globe as India and Russia get drawn into fighting China, and Japan comes to China's aid, while Muslims all over the world attack the West. Latin America sits out the war and claims the radioactive spoils at the end, its fifth column of immigrants taking over the United States at the same time. In a policy prescription for what Mary Kaldor aptly characterizes as "a kind of global apartheid,"[7] Huntington suggests that the only way to evade such a global conflagration is for each civilization to stay out of the affairs of the others, thus partitioning the world into seven regions stabilized, if possible, by local core states. Arguing that "countries tend to bandwagon with countries of similar culture and to balance against countries with which they lack cultural commonalty" (155), he says, "the world will be ordered on the basis of civilizations or not at all. In this world the core states of civilizations are sources of order within civilizations and, through negotiations with other core states, between civilizations" (156).

The public reception of *The Clash of Civilizations* has been akin to that of some Hollywood blockbusters: panned by the critics but a box office success. While the academic international relations theorists have quarreled with the schema laid out by Huntington, the book has been, for an academic book, a best-seller, and it has been enthusiastically endorsed by such celebrity alumni of the national security apparatus as Henry Kissinger and Zbigniew Brzezinski.

We cannot know for sure why Huntington's book—despite the striking deficiencies cataloged by the critics—sold so many copies and provoked such animated debate in the West.[8] However, it is presumably not unrelated to the fact that Huntington was writing at a moment when the bipolar system of the cold war had collapsed and people were wondering what would replace it. In his review of *The Clash of Civilizations,* M. E. Ahrari observed that "with the dismantlement of the Soviet Union, the Western democratic paradigm won. Now this confident paradigm or, more precisely, its believers, are looking for other enemies to fight."[9] Huntington, trying to define a new security framework for the post–cold war period in the way that George Kennan did for the cold war world shortly after World War II,[10] told people where to look for those enemies, how to interpret their enmity, and how to contain them. More precisely, he provided an explanation for the diffuse but evident hostility toward the United States from the Arab world that did not require Americans to confront their sins of complicity with the Israeli national security state, and he gave shape and texture to an inchoate sense shared by many Americans that China was stepping into the shoes of the former Soviet Union as a threat with which future confrontations loomed. The downside of his compelling narrative about future threats is that, as Walt has observed, "the more we believe it and make it the basis for action, the more likely it is to come true" (189).

We might add that Huntington's book provided a useful intellectual position from which to attack the rhetoric and policies associated with the Clinton administration in the mid-1990s. That administration talked copiously about universal human rights and about its mission to spread liberal democracy around the globe and, in Haiti, Bosnia, and Kosovo, invoked democracy and human rights to legitimate military intervention. While Huntington warned that members of different civilizations would mix as well as oil and water, the Clinton administration preached the virtues of multiculturalism everywhere from Arkansas to Bosnia. More than a little influenced by Francis Fukuyama's controversial claim that history had ended and liberal democracy would now diffuse around the world, as well as claims by liberal international relations theorists that democracies do not go to war with one another and that economic globalization would make war less likely between interdependent nations,[11] senior policy makers in the Clinton administration talked about remaking the world in America's image as a pluralistic community of liberal democracies. Taking aim at such talk and observing that "societies that assume their history has ended . . . are usually societies whose history is about to decline" (301), Huntington warns against confusing global consumption of Western commodities with genuine Westernization:

> Somewhere in the Middle East a half-dozen young men could well be dressed in jeans, drinking coke, listening to rap, and, between their bows to Mecca, putting together a bomb to blow up an American airliner. During the 1970s and 1980s Americans consumed millions of Japanese cars, TV sets, cameras, and electronic gadgets without being "Japanized" and indeed while becoming considerably more antagonistic toward Japan. Only naïve arrogance can lead Westerners to assume that non-Westerners will become "Westernized" by acquiring Western goods. What, indeed, does it tell the world about the West when Westerners identify their civilization with fizzy liquids, faded pants, and fatty foods? (58)

Pointing out that "what is universalism to the West is imperialism to the rest" (184), he counsels Western leaders not to undertake the Sisyphean task of imposing their way of life on others and not to confuse an appetite for Western goods around the world with a desire to embrace Western institutions and values, arguing in particular that post-Soviet Russia is, despite the best fantasies of the Clinton administration, unlikely to evolve into a Western democracy.[12]

In the end, while Huntington's analysis may have been panned by the academic critics, its diffuse influence is suggested by the fact that many of Huntington's policy prescriptions have become policy positions of the Republican administration of George W. Bush. In the first presidential debate candidate Bush said he would not play the role of "ugly American" telling people in other countries to behave like his own people. In office, George W. Bush has sought to expand the Atlantic alliance to include the Baltic Republics and other East European states (as Huntington recommended in his book), identified the Islamic world as a major source of popular hostility and terrorist violence against the United States, treated China as an emerging rival that must be isolated and contained, sought to befriend Russia and delegate it a sphere of influence between Asia and Europe, and refrained from lecturing the rest of the world on human rights.

Empirical Problems with the Argument

Before discussing the realist critique of Huntington's work and developing my own more anthropological line of critique, it is worth taking note of some of the obvious empirical weaknesses of the schema Huntington lays out in *The Clash of Civilizations*. The regional and national examples he cites are not always well matched to the generalizations he claims they support. Thus the book, read closely, is full of fissures between the overarching argument and the details from which the argument is constructed, and these fissures offer the critical reader an opportunity to prise apart important parts of the entire thesis and, rereading Huntington's narrative for a new story line, to reassemble them in a different shape. The most striking fissures and anomalies concern the exact locations where Huntington chooses to draw the dividing line between supposedly distinct civilizations; the degree to which his civilizations really are unified; the ease with which his argument can or cannot accommodate cross-civilizational alliances; and his typological characterization of Western civilization. Let's take these points one by one.

Dividing Lines

One could quibble with many of the boundaries Huntington claims to discern around the edges of his civilizations, and indeed with the very notion that civilizations have clear boundaries, but the most strikingly problematic dividing line is the one Huntington notes at the Eastern edge of the West, separating the Christian West from what he calls Orthodox civilization. This boundary "is provided by the great historical line that has existed for centuries separating Western Christian peoples from Muslim and Orthodox peoples. This line dates back to the Roman Empire in the fourth century and to the creation of the Holy Roman Empire in the tenth century" (158). This selective invocation of history leaves out the fact that ancient Greece is often portrayed as the fount of the democratic tradition that Huntington later identifies as the very essence of Western civilization; the fact that the philosophical thinking that Huntington defines as unique to Western civilization derives from such ancient Greeks as Plato and Aristotle; and the fact that, during World War II, the Greek people rallied against fascism in support of the Enlightenment values Huntington identifies with Western civilization.[13] In other words, one could make a very good argument that Greece, and maybe other parts of what Huntington terms "Orthodox civilization" as well, are part of the Western tradition, and that Huntington's distinction between the two is much flimsier than he would have us believe—as he himself lets slip in his confused and confusing aside that "Greece is not part of Western civilization, but it was the home of Classical civilization, which was an important source of Western civilization" (162). The ancient Greek philosophers, who taught us syllogistic reasoning, would surely be unimpressed by this mangling of the form they perfected.

Civilizational Unity

Huntington makes much of wars between groups from different civilizations, citing them as precedents for a dangerous future, but his treatment of
some intracivilizational conflicts verges on erasure. For example, he scarce-
ly mentions that the two most devastating wars in human history—World
Wars I and II—started as conflicts within a single civilization, Western
civilization, where most of their destructive force was focused. Other
intracivilizational conflicts, just to name the recent ones, that barely figure
in Huntington's narrative are those between China and Taiwan, Iraq and
Iran, Vietnam and Cambodia, North Korea and South Korea, and, in the
West, between Catholics and Protestants in Northern Ireland.[14] Meanwhile,
as Jervis has observed, Huntington "loads the dice" (308) by discerning so
many separate civilizations in Asia that it becomes more likely that any conflict in that region can be characterized as intercivilizational. In the Islamic
world Huntington cites the war of the 1980s between Afghanistan and the
Soviet Union as the first truly civilizational war (246–48), but ignores the
fact that this struggle mutated into a "war within Islam, between Sunnis and
Shiites, city Muslims and rural ones, with at least four regional powers—
Pakistan, Iran, Tajikstan, Uzbekistan—fighting for hegemony there."[15] He
cites the Gulf War of 1991 as the second truly civilizational war, saying that
popular sentiment throughout the Middle East was anti-Western, but his
characterization of this war as civilizational is surely made problematic by
the fact that many Muslim states, most notably Saudi Arabia and Turkey,
allied themselves with the West against their Muslim brethren in Iraq.

In other words, while it is not hard to find examples of wars that straddle
civilizations, and it is these kinds of wars (in Bosnia, for example) that
Huntington mostly discusses, neither is it hard to find abundant examples of
intracivilizational conflicts, or to renarrate some of the conflicts Huntington
cites as intercivilizational as at least partly intracivilizational. This undermines both Huntington's claim that civilizations function as relatively coherent units and his prediction that the great flashpoints for future war will
be on the fault lines between civilizations.

Cross-Civilizational Alliances

Huntington maintains that "relations between groups from different civilizations . . . will be almost never close, usually cool, and often hostile. Connections between states of different civilizations inherited from the past,
such as cold war military alliances, are likely to attenuate or evaporate"
(207). The wars he fears in the future will start as local conflicts between
groups from different civilizations and escalate as each group recruits al-

lies from its civilizational bloc. Yet one could point to many examples of people from different civilizations coexisting reasonably equably within a single state—the Chinese diaspora in Asia for example has, for the most part, got along with Buddhist and Muslim compatriots[16]—and, as Richard Rosencrance points out in his review of Huntington's book, the ASEAN alliance unites Buddhists, Christians, and Muslims (980). There are other, more glaring, anomalies. Although the war in Bosnia is one of Huntington's favorite examples of intercivilizational warfare, it should, at least partly, be a major embarrassment to him: whereas the Germans did aid their Croat Christian brethren and the Russians did side with the Orthodox Serbs, the United States, and in the end the whole Western alliance, came to the aid of the Bosnian Muslims, and, finally, did more for them than their Muslim allies abroad.[17] This is a stunning departure from Huntington's script. Meanwhile, farther afield, we might point out that, Huntington's model notwithstanding, two of the United States' strongest alliances are intercivilizational: with Taiwan and with Israel. The United States has been willing to drop hints that it would consider using nuclear weapons in defense of Taiwan,[18] and, despite Huntington's prediction that intercivilizational alliances will weaken in the post–cold war era, the administration of George W. Bush has made statements escalating its solidarity with Taiwan. As for Israel, as Stephen Walt has pointed out, according to Huntington's own criteria, Israel cannot be part of Western civilization, and yet the United States continues to pour more military and foreign aid into Israel than any other country and to hitch its own vital interests to the Israeli star—a policy that has strong support on both sides of the aisle in U.S. politics. Perhaps it is because this situation is so hard to explain from within Huntington's schema that his book is, in Walt's words, "strangely silent about Israel" (186).

The Nature of the West

Huntington characterizes Western civilization, particularly its core state, the United States, as one that is uniquely defined by its attachment to human rights and democracy and one that, if it causes global conflict, will do so by refusing to compromise its promotion of human rights and democracy in its dealings with other civilizations since "imperialism is the necessary logical consequence of universalism" (310). Without belaboring the point, the claim that the United States intervenes abroad in order to spread democracy and human rights would come as a surprise to the victims of the CIA-backed coup in Chile in 1973, the victims of the CIA-backed coup in Guatemala in 1956, and the victims of U.S.-backed death squads in El Salvador and Guatemala in the 1980s—to name just a few of the many possible examples. At another point in the book, in a lucid passage that is hard to reconcile with his repeated warnings that Western countries may start a war by seeking to impose liberal democratic culture where it does not belong, Huntington surely comes closer to the truth about American foreign policy:

> Hypocrisy, double standards, and "but nots" are the price of universalist pretensions. Democracy is promoted, but not if it brings Islamic fundamentalists to power; nonproliferation is preached for Iran and Iraq but not for Israel; free trade is the elixir of economic growth, but not for agriculture; human rights are an issue with China but not with Saudi Arabia; aggression against oil-owning Kuwaitis is massively repulsed but not against non-oil-owning Bosnians. (184)

This atypical quote, accenting the disjuncture between cultural values and actual behavior driven by considerations of realpolitik, is a good segue into a discussion of the realist critique of Huntington's book.

The Realist Critique

In his first chapter Huntington makes it clear that his book is intended as a break with what Michael Ignatieff in his review called "the grindingly narrow emphasis among 'realists' on state interests" (13). In a passage that converges with recent neo-Weberian thinking in international relations by, for example, Peter Katzenstein, Richard Price, and Elizabeth Kier,[19] a passage with which this reader finds himself in substantial agreement, Huntington says of "realist" theory:

> It assumes all states perceive their interests in the same way and act in the same way. Its simple assumption that power is all is a starting point for understanding state behavior that does not get one very far. States define their interests in terms of power but also in terms of much else besides. States often, of course, attempt to balance power, but if that is all they did Western European countries would have coalesced with the Soviet Union against the United States in the 1940s. States respond primarily to perceived threats, and the Western European states then saw a political, ideological, and military threat from the East. They saw their interests in a way that would not have been predicted by classical realist theory. Values, culture, and institutions pervasively influence how states define their interests. The interests of states are also shaped not only by their domestic values and institutions but by international norms and institutions. (34)

Huntington follows this general attack on realists' inability to explain state behavior with an argument about the declining relevance of the state in international relations today. Blending neoliberal institutionalist theory in international relations with recent arguments about the effects of globalization,[20] he asserts:

> While states remain the primary actors in world affairs, they are also suffering losses of sovereignty, functions, and power. International institutions now assert the right to judge and constrain what states do in their own territory. In some cases, most notably in Europe, international institutions have assumed important functions previously performed by states, and powerful international bureaucracies have been created which operate directly on individual citizens . . . State governments have in considerable measure lost the ability to control the flow of money in and out of their country and are having increasing difficulty controlling the flow of ideas, technology, goods and people. State borders, in short, have become increasingly permeable. All these developments have led many to see the gradual end of the hard "billiard ball" state, which purportedly has been the norm since the Treaty of Westphalia in 1648, and the emergence of a varied, complex, multilayered international order more closely resembling that of medieval times. (35)

Huntington argues, in other words, that as people decide whom they want to fight for and against, the important units of analysis are increasingly civilizations and regions rather than freestanding, self-contained states—entities that are being undermined by globalization and by the development of transnational institutions—and that, in any case, the interests of states have never been, nor are they now, as "realists" often make out, self-evident, since these interests can only be constructed by those who must act upon them through the prism of culture, and what might seem to an American international relations theorist to be in, say, China's interest might look rather different to a state bureaucrat in China reared within a different cultural system.

The task for Huntington's realist critics, then, is to recuperate the state as the central unit of analysis—and as a centered, unified category of analysis—and to recuperate a notion of "interests" that stands above culture. Thus most realist reviews of Huntington's book attempt to renarrate some of his case studies through a realist frame. Ahrari, for example, makes the realist argument that the building conflict between China and the United States has nothing to do with China being Confucian and everything to do with its being a rising power challenging the United States for regional hegemony in Asia; he also argues that the alliance between China and Pakistan has less to do with a civilizational bond between Islam and Confucianism than with the two countries' calculation of their interests vis-à-vis Russia and India (58–61).

The most thorough and aggressive rereading of Huntington's material is offered by Stephen Walt in a brilliant review article in *Foreign Policy*. Walt does not, as an anthropologist would, challenge Huntington's reification of civilization; instead, he treats them as an independent variable with far less explanatory power than the realists' preferred independent variable: the state and its interests. He starts, proclaiming at the outset the realist creed centered on self-evident interests, by stating that political units from tribes to states "have repeatedly ignored cultural affinities in order to pursue particular selfish interests. These political units have always been willing to fight other members of their own civilization and have been equally willing to ally with groups from different civilizations when it seemed advantageous to do so" (183). Making the distinction between rhetoric and action that is a prominent feature of realist thinking, Walt adds, "the question is not just what Lee Kuan Yew or Muammar Qadaffi say, because talk is cheap and political rhetoric serves many functions. The real issue is what these leaders (or their countries) will actually do, and how much blood and treasure they will devote to 'civilizational' interests" (185). Giving Huntington the benefit of the doubt that the international order may have changed since the end of the cold war, and looking only at the conflicts that have taken place in the post–cold war era—the period in which Huntington's model should be strongest—Walt points out that in the Gulf War and in Rwanda one sees people at war with others in their own civilizations, and that in Bosnia the United States—a Western, Christian power—came to the aid of the Bosnian Muslims. In other words, there is fighting within civilizations and an important alliance across civilizations. Then, in the most devastating move of all, Walt renarrates the imaginary war with which Huntington concludes *The Clash of Civilizations,* arguing that a realist interest-based analysis better explains the alliances between states than does Huntington's own civilizational framework—even in a scenario in which Huntington has made up the alliances. Finally, infiltrating Huntington's book through a sort of trapdoor in the argument, he points out that Huntington's fear is of war between the "core states" of different civilizations not between nonstate entities; this, Walt suggests, shows the "enduring relevance of the realist, statist paradigm" (188) rather than the power of an alternative civilizational paradigm. He concludes that "Huntington's central error is his belief that personal loyalties are increasingly centered on 'civilizations' rather than the nation-state. . . . It is not civilization that is thriving in the post–cold war world; it is nationalism" (187). The resurgence of nationalism also explains the large number of civil wars in states divided between two ethnic groups, each wanting its own nation-state, according to Walt.

The realist critique is more successful in critically wounding Huntington's model of the world than in restoring the status quo ante. If the realist critics succeed in collapsing large portions of Huntington's argument with their renarrations of his case studies, they are less successful at reinscribing the analytical centrality of the state and its supposedly self-evident interests. They do not, for example, take on Huntington's point, quoted earlier, that advanced industrial states have, in recent years, surrendered certain elements of their sovereignty—to the European Union and to the NATO alliance—entering into transnational, civilizational alliances that are increasingly important actors in the world in their own right. As Huntington correctly observes, this takes us into a different set of relationships between states, at least in some corners of the world, than the Westphalian state system produced. Huntington also makes an important argument, ignored in realist reviews of his book, that diaspora created by recent waves of transnational migration play an important role in international relations, both by funneling resources into home state conflicts from outside, adding fuel to the fire, and in shifting the balance of internal pressures on policy making in their host countries.

Meanwhile, the realist renarration of the Bosnian and Gulf War cases is only partly successful as an attempt to reinstantiate the central analytical importance of calculations based in traditional realpolitik. While U.S. military support for Bosnia at the end of the war is indeed a problem for Huntington's model of contemporary international conflict, nevertheless his explanation of the initial Russian tilt toward the Serbs and the initial German tilt toward the Croats probably works better than anything realism can offer. Similarly, in the case of the Gulf War, Huntington's culturalist approach captures something important in its analysis of the widespread grassroots hostility toward the allies in the Middle East. Realists will point out that, in Bosnia, the Russian and the German governments eventually ignored civilizational affinity and supported U.S. intervention on behalf of the Bosnian Muslims, whereas in the Gulf War, there was no shortage of Muslim governments on the U.S. side against Iraq, whatever the feelings of the proverbial (wo)man on the street. One's evaluation of such arguments will depend, in part, on what exactly one believes international relations theory is supposed to describe and explain. If we rephrase the core question of international relations theory, asking not (as realists do) "when and why do states go to war with one another?" but, instead, "what are the sources of conflict in the international system?" then we see that Huntington's analysis illuminates important phenomena that are largely left in shadow by the realist paradigm: the importance of memory, identity, religion, and culture in provoking conflict within and between states.

On the day I am writing these words, for example, I see from my newspaper that Christians in Egypt are rioting because of perceived slights against them in the local Islamic press; that fighting between Muslims and Orthodox Christians in Macedonia threatens to ignite a war that could draw in other countries in the region; that fighting continues in Israel, threatening the stability of an entire region, in a months-long spasm of violence provoked by a Jewish politician's (Ariel Sharon's) visit to an Islamic holy site; and that the pope on his visit to Ukraine is being greeted by large protests organized by the Orthodox church—protests that are harming a tottering Ukrainian government as well as relations between Ukraine and Russia. Allegiances that follow the lines of identity, religion, and culture exert a powerful force in the world today, then. Sometimes these allegiances fit snugly with state boundaries and with the calculus of interstate rivalry; sometimes they work more in the direction of breaking apart states or of creating transnational solidarities that work against Metternichian calculations of state interest. State leaders often ignore these cultural forces in their foreign policy calculations, but it may sometimes be hard to do so. Thus, to give three examples, we can argue that one cannot fully understand Jordan's abandonment of its traditional alliance with the United States in the Gulf War without understanding the role of the Palestinian diaspora and of transnational Islamic consciousness in Jordanian politics at that moment; that one cannot understand the Reagan administration's support for the UK in the Falklands/Malvinas War of the early 1980s, a conflict in which it had little strategic interest, without attending to the sense of civilizational affinity between the British and Americans; and that the Clinton administration's decision to expand NATO in violation of a pledge given to the Russians by the first President Bush was grounded not only in ruthless calculations of strategic advantage vis-à-vis the Russians but also in internal electoral calculations focused on securing the vote of Polish Americans in the United States.

In sum, Huntington's analysis is valuable because, whatever its flaws, it illuminates a disjuncture between the logic of culture and the logic of the state that is invisible in realist readings of the international system, yet is vitally important in understanding contemporary international relations. If Walt, going through that trapdoor in Huntington's book, argues that there is a flaw in Huntington's civilizational argument because of the key role played by "core states" within civilizations, we might argue that there is a symmetrical flaw in Walt's argument because he acknowledges the importance of nationalism in tearing apart states and starting conflicts that can spread internationally, and yet he and the realists have no model of culture and identity that can explain this phenomenon.

Cultures as Strategic Hamlets

As an anthropologist I have some sympathy for Huntington when he speaks up for the importance of culture against those international relations theorists, representing foreign policy decision makers as if they were culture-free computer programs, who are obsessed with rational-actor models, payoff matrices in decision making, and so on. (Is it possible, by the way, that a tendency to understand statecraft primarily in terms of rational actors calculating strategic advantage tells us as much about the profit-oriented American culture from which these models derive as it does about international relations?) I also sympathize with Huntington's critique of what he calls "Davos culture"[21]—a critique of our contemporary prophets of globalization that reprises the themes of an earlier anthropological literature arguing, against the grain of American modernization theory in the 1950s and 1960s, that economic development would not inevitably turn Third World countries into secular democracies with Western values. From an anthropologist's point of view, then, the problem with Huntington's book is not that he takes culture seriously but that his way of speaking about culture is so strange.[22]

Take the following exerpt from *The Clash of Civilizations*:

> The major differences in political and economic development among civilizations are clearly rooted in their different cultures. East Asian economic success has its source in East Asian culture, as do the difficulties East Asian societies have had in achieving stable democratic political systems. Islamic culture explains in large part the failure of democracy to emerge in much of the Muslim world. Developments in the postcommunist societies of Eastern Europe and the former Soviet Union are shaped by their civilizational identities. Those with Western Christian heritages are making progress toward economic development and democratic politics; the prospects for economic and political development in the Orthodox countries are uncertain; the prospects in the Muslim republics are bleak. (29)

This passage is noteworthy for a number of reasons (quite apart from its questionable accuracy). Each cultural tradition is spoken of as if it were self-contained and geographically separate. There is also no sense that, within the categories "East Asian societies" and "Muslim world" there might be considerable internal heterogeneity. Instead, each is construed as a coherent bundle of values that impels, as if for eternity, certain kinds of behaviors and outcomes. If for Freud biology was destiny, in Huntington's world culture is destiny, leaving the East Asians forever condemned to authoritarian prosperity, the Muslims condemned to authoritarian poverty, and so on.

Huntington's model of culture echoes—one might even say parodies—that of anthropologists at about the time the cold war began, when national character studies were in vogue. At that time anthropologists spoke of culture as if it existed in a timeless vacuum (what anthropologists call the "ethnographic present"), as if all people in a community shared the same set of rules and understandings (their "culture"), as if those rules and understandings were internally coherent, and as if they could be formally codified by anthropologists in what amounted to a cultural grammar book.[23] Nowadays, tempted to abandon use of the word *culture* altogether in some cases, anthropologists tend to emphasize that cultures are always shifting with their historical context, that cultural rules and meanings are constantly contested and remade, that cultures are always already hybrid phenomena, and that cultures are better thought of as elusive and ambiguous texts than as rules that can be written down.[24] Renato Rosaldo's metaphorization of culture as a "garage sale" captures this sense of culture as a field of organized chaos.[25]

In contrast to the prevailing practice in contemporary anthropology, Huntington treats civilizations as primordial, self-contained communities, each with its own deeply grounded values and practices. Hannerz characterizes this approach as a form of "cultural fundamentalism." It assumes, he says, that "cultures are distinct and incommensurable; relations between bearers of different cultures are intrinsically conflictive. . . . As they are incommensurable, they must be spatially segregated."[26] Writing against "an old habit of speaking about 'cultures,' in the plural form, as if it were self-evident that such entities exist side by side as neat packages, each of us identified with only one of them" (401–2), Hannerz points out that in reality "many people have biographies entailing various cross-cutting allegiances—they share different parts of their personal repertoires with different collections of people. And if there is an 'integrated whole,' it may be quite an individual thing" (402). Where Huntington presents the Western Christians, the Muslims, and the East Asians as following their own neatly separate paths, Hannerz concludes, "there are now surely many different ways of being more or less Christian, more or less Muslim, more or less Confucian" (402).

The critique Hannerz makes of Huntington's homogenizing approach to culture focuses, at a somewhat theoretical level, on the relationship between the individual and culture. It is Hannerz's concern to free culture from the Durkheimian straitjacket, simplistically equating culture with a shared set of norms, that has been passed down by many generations of social theorists.[27] Another anthropologist, Aihwa Ong, also accuses Huntington of falsely homogenizing culture, but Ong does so by focusing on the scale of his putative civilizations and on their relationship to local cultural traditions and class divisions. Anthropologists have discovered the hard way that it is difficult enough to make meaningful generalizations about meanings, beliefs, and values in the kinds of small-scale settings where anthropologists have conventionally done their fieldwork. The notion that one could make substantial generalizations about cultural units that, like Islam, span several continents, is deeply problematic. Still, Huntington writes as if all Muslims, from Bosnia to Saudi Arabia to Indonesia, share a single essence (including a propensity to violence and authoritarianism) even though in each case Islam fused with, incorporated, and was inflected by distinctly local patterns of culture.[28]

In fact, the civilizations of which Huntington writes are deeply complex and variegated cultural stews, often inwardly fragmented and layered by local variations of class, region, ethnic tradition, and religion. Ong, herself a specialist in Southeast Asian politics and culture, expresses "skepticism about whether any civilization can be anything but a blend of different ethnicities, cultures, and traditions." Quarreling with Huntington's arbitrary delineation of cultures, she says:

> Sinic civilization seems to have cut like a heavy smog through East Asia, but Japan, a country much influenced by Chinese Confucianism and culture, is a separate civilization. There is no mention in Huntington of the Southeast Asian civilizational complex that is a mélange of Hindu, Buddhist, Islamic, and Christian religions intermixed with animistic traditions. Instead, Indonesia, which is only nominally Muslim, is considered by Huntington to be a subdivision of Islamic civilization.[29]

It is precisely this sense that transnational migration, trade, and culture contact have irreversibly rearranged the global mosaic of culture and that cultures are, in any case, always a product of miscegenation and hybridity that Huntington's model denies. He warns repeatedly, almost obsessively, that multiculturalism threatens to destroy the United States from within, and he sees the boundaries where distinct civilizations come into contact with one another as dangerous spaces—"fault lines" that can release subterranean energies of destruction. While there can be no denying that certain borders (those separating India from Pakistan and Greece from Turkey, for example) are fraught spaces where conflict hangs in the air, still there is another way of looking at borders. Such analysts as Renato Rosaldo and Gloria Anzaldúa have recently suggested that "borderlands" can be, in Rosaldo's words, vibrant "sites of creative cultural production" or, as Ulf Hannerz puts it, "ludic spaces" where cultures mingle and mutate, and that we should see the cultural vibrancy of borderlands as metaphors for broader processes of cultural fusion throughout society.[30] In his analysis of

the U.S.-Mexico border, while acknowledging the deep political and economic divisions it marks, Rosaldo figures the border as a zone where Anglo
and Mexicano cultures can fuse and cross-fertilize, spawning new cuisines,
linguistic idioms, musical forms, religious practices, political understandings, and so on. He points out that the border is not just a way of dividing
the two communities but an incitement to interactions and "border cross-
ings." While Rosaldo celebrates the U.S.-Mexico border as a place where
American and Mexican cultures mingle to the benefit of both, Huntington
says there is a serious possibility that the United States will become a "cleft"
society "encompassing two distinct and largely separate communities from
two different civilizations" (204). He also fears that a "Mexican demographic invasion" now might eventually lead to a reversal of "the results of
American military expansion in the nineteenth century" (206) by allowing
the incubation of a sort of informal Mexican state within U.S. borders.
Since, in his way of understanding the relationship of migration to culture,
the migrants will still be Mexican, they will constitute a sort of fifth column within the United States for Mexican expansion.[31]

Instead of seeing cultural hybridity as a source of mongrel strength,
Huntington fears in it infection and defilement of purity. Look, for example, at the metaphors of disease in this passage where civilizational
contact is seen as causing a sort of cultural foot-and-mouth disease (non-
lethal but ineradicable): "the Western virus, once it is lodged in another
society, is difficult to expunge. The virus persists but is not fatal; the pa-
tient survives but is never whole. Political leaders . . . infect their country
with a cultural schizophrenia which becomes its continuing and defining
characteristic" (154).[32]

This powerful sense that migrants from one culture cannot be incorporated into another and that different civilizations should not, and ultimately
cannot, be mixed finds strongest expression in Huntington's jeremiads
against multiculturalism. If he fears that attempts to spread uniquely Western values to countries from other civilizations or to sustain multiciviliza-
tional nations (in the former Yugoslavia, for example) will create disasters
abroad, he is equally concerned that multiculturalism will wreak havoc
at home. In both cases, what is separate should be kept separate; cultures
become strategic hamlets. Thus he says:

> The clash between the multiculturalists and the defenders of Western
> civilization and the American Creed is, in James Kurth's phrase, "the *real*
> clash" within the American segment of Western civilization. Americans
> cannot avoid the issue: are we a Western people or are we something else?
> The futures of the United States and of the West depend upon Americans

reaffirming their commitment to Western civilization. Domestically this means rejecting the siren calls of multiculturalism. Internationally it means rejecting the elusive and illusory calls to identify the United States with Asia. Whatever economic connections may exist between them, the fundamental cultural gap between Asian and American societies precludes their joining together in a common home. Americans are culturally part of the Western family; multiculturalists may damage and even destroy that relationship but they cannot replace it. When Americans look for their roots, they find them in Europe. (307)[33]

Huntington wrote these words as, at home, the United States was in the midst of a protracted and acrimonious debate about speech codes to protect minorities and the reform of "Western civilization" curricula on campus and, abroad, the end of the cold war was followed by a slew of civil wars in multiethnic states from Yugoslavia to Rwanda. If many on the left wanted to intervene in at least some of those civil wars, whether by taking military action or sending in peacekeepers and mediators, conservatives argued that the United States lacked a vital interest in these struggles and that the conflicts derived from ancient and implacable hatreds that would hardly be ended by UN or U.S. diplomacy.[34] The view that such conflicts derive from centuries-deep and ineradicable hatreds, a view with which Huntington is clearly aligned, became a sort of common sense for many pundits and policy makers in the United States in the 1990s in spite of its evident weaknesses. In fact, however, in such places as Bosnia and Rwanda, members of different ethnic groups had for many years lived peacefully side by side. In many cases, the boundary between the groups that would turn on one another had been partly lost through intermarriage and cultural drift, and it required real work to sort out the ethnic group to which some people belonged so that they could be apportioned a side in those civil wars.

In Rwanda, for example, the division between Hutus and Tutsis was as much a product of colonial administrative policies that separated the two groups, according one preferential treatment over the other, as of ancient allegiances that would not die. The question about Muslims, Croats, and Serbs in Bosnia and about Hutus and Tutsis in Rwanda is not why old hatreds were impervious to change but how it was possible to excavate buried animosities and transform people who were successfully living together into people who were willing to kill one another. While memories of past conflicts between these groups were an important resource for the political leaders who instigated these conflicts, the political scientists, journalists, and anthropologists who tracked the conflicts as they burst into flame have emphasized that these civil wars embodied a break with the past and that it required ideological work on the part of political leaders and the media, in the context of a moment of broader political and economic distress, to bring them about.[35] While Huntington is right that such wars are hard to stop once started and that they often take on a genocidal logic, because the warring populations are spatially imbricated with one another, the historical and ethnographic record belies his presentation of these conflicts as ancient, continuous, and therefore predetermined. Theories, such as Huntington's, that portray such conflicts as timeless and inevitable deny the role of human agency and shifting circumstances in bringing about violence and falsely naturalize these conflicts.

The Clash of Civilizations is, however, premised on a deep denial that cultures can and do change.[36] Huntington's civilizations may rise and fall, but they do not change. Dieter Senghaas observes that Huntington

> assumes civilizations to be some kind of "beings" at the macro-level . . .
> He regards civilizations as not adaptable and changeable over centuries.
> Deep down, they remain constant, and they tend to process external influ-
> ences so as to guarantee continuity. The ahistorical assumptions concern-
> ing culture, especially about deep culture or the soul of culture, produce
> a view of variable events as always predestined by the deep structure of
> individual civilization.[37]

This "tendency to naturalize cultural immutability and persistence" is, according to Ulf Hannerz, in his analysis of culturespeak, another aspect of "cultural fundamentalism" (401). It underwrites Huntington's conviction that Western rights culture will not take root in other civilizations, that attempts to shift countries from one civilization to another (for example, moving Turkey from the Islamic civilization into Europe) are usually doomed to failure, that animosities between cultures cannot be transcended, and that it is best for civilizations to respect each other's discrete spheres of influence. It also, of course, ignores the immense plasticity of human civilizations over time. For example, Huntington uses evidence of high levels of violence between Muslims and others to argue that there is an essential "Muslim propensity toward violent conflict" (258). Of course, if one had collected evidence about Europeans' levels of violence in the nineteenth and early twentieth centuries, as Europe was at the height of its colonial period and in the midst of two world wars, one would conclude that they too were a terribly violent people. However, since 1945 they have built institutions that have brought them relative peace within their own community and in their relations with the outside world.

Cultures change with circumstances, not always of their own choosing. If the Islamic world's relations with the West are currently marred by violence, this is the consequence not only of its own cultural potential for conflict with heathens but also of the Western world's decision in the twentieth century to create and sustain a Jewish state in the middle of the Arab world and to sell large quantities of weaponry to states all over the region. If Vietnam and Cambodia are not democracies, this is the consequence not only of whatever authoritarian tradition may or may not exist in Asian cultures but also of the fact that the United States traumatized and destabilized these countries by dropping more bombs on them than they dropped in all of World War II.[38] Meanwhile, on the other side of the ledger, the rights cultures Huntington so celebrates as the essence of Western civilization did not spring full-blown from the brow of Zeus at the beginning of recorded Western history. A civil war had to be fought in the United States to establish that black people could not be owned as property. In Europe citizens struggled over many centuries against monarchs and aristocracies who saw appeals for wider voting rights and other civil liberties as dangerous fabulations that threatened to undermine Western culture. Similar struggles are under way today in many corners of the world, their outcomes as yet uncertain.

Conclusion: Cultural Realism and Real Culture

I began by suggesting that the field of international relations is sorely in need of scholars who, departing from the realist script, take culture more seriously. Samuel Huntington, however, is a false prophet. It is true, as he says, that many conflicts in the world today occur where people from different cultural backgrounds feel their identities threatened in their interactions with one another, and that social movements and conflicts grounded in identity exert their own gravitational pull on the policies of governments. However, the cultural identities that generate the most powerful expressions of solidarity and conflict in the international system seem to this anthropologist to derive more from national and subnational categories than from the civilizational units that are the primary building blocks of Huntington's world. Moreover, cultural identities and ideologies are more fluid and historically elastic than Huntington allows.

While it might superficially seem as if Huntington, by taking a cultural turn, has broken with realism, his model is best thought of as a form of "cultural realism." His analysis transposes realism into a cultural key, retaining in the process some of its defining and most insidious assumptions. Let me name four here. First, his civilizations are reified in the same way that states are reified in realist theory. If many conventional international relations theorists have been criticized for treating the state as a unitary actor, a sort of black box whose inner conflicts do not need to be probed too closely, Huntington, substituting "culture" for "state," reproduces the same basic error, treating civilizations also as unitary actors that, like nation-states in realist theory, have necessarily agonistic relations with one another.

Second, just as realists have debated endlessly whether and in what circumstances states will balance or bandwagon, Huntington discusses whether his civilizational units will balance or bandwagon, arguing that states from the same civilization will align against outsiders. And, just as realists believed that a balance of power between states preserved global stability during the cold war, so Huntington sees a balance of power between civilizations as essential to global stability in the post–cold war world. He even develops a new version of the old containment policy with his recommendations to protect American culture from foreign impurities (formerly communism, now multiculturalism) and to contain the Islamic-Sinic bloc through an alliance with Orthodox, Hindu, and Japanese cultures.

Third, just as realists during the cold war berated liberals and radicals for their naïveté in believing that the superpower conflict could be transcended, arguing that conflict between nations is the essential condition of the international system, so Huntington berates liberals and radicals for their naïveté in believing that ethnic, religious, and cultural conflicts might be transcended, maintaining that civilizational conflict is the essential condition of the international system. "Those who do not recognize fundamental divides . . . are doomed to be frustrated by them," he says (309).

Finally, preserving the epistemology of realism intact, Huntington treats culture as an independent variable. Realists, as positivists, assume that states, alliances, conflicts, interests, balances of power, and so on are relatively unproblematic categories whose interactions can be mapped through the modeling of relations between independent and dependent variables, the point of the game being to determine the independent variable and its mode of action in the system. Huntington preserves this basic worldview, adding to the system civilizational culture as the new master variable occupying the slot formerly belonging to "national interests."

But if there is anything anthropologists have learned about culture after writing about it for a century, it is that it is very hard to treat it simply as an independent variable. This is partly because culture is not only the object of our descriptions but also the means through which it is perceived, thus making it notoriously difficult to disentangle subject and object. More to the point in the current context, culture is not a sort of computer program that sits in the heads of all members of a society instructing them how to behave; it is a constantly shifting and evolving web of discourses, practices, symbols, and structures of feeling that acts recursively upon itself through feedback loops, gets tangled with other cultural webs so that the boundaries between them can be hard to discern, and looks a little different to all the people suspended within it.

What sorts of studies and inquiries would this more constructivist, actor-oriented and fluid understanding of culture produce in the field of international relations? One could imagine, to give a few random examples, the following kinds of projects: a study of elite transnational cultures—those of, say, defense intellectuals or bankers—and the role they play in shaping and restraining conflict;[39] a study of U.S. relations with Israel explaining how it was that a nation with a history of anti-Semitism came to forge such a deep alliance with Israel, and what role was played in the formation and consolidation of this alliance by popular discourses about the Holocaust and a sense of cultural kinship between two "Peoples of the Book" who established frontier societies in foreign lands after fleeing persecution and hardship in Europe; a study explaining the relevance of struggles to develop a sustainable postcolonial political identity to the pursuit by a country such as India of its own nuclear arsenal;[40] a study explaining how the United States, by making alliances with carefully selected fragments of society in Japan in the 1940s, was able to transform the expansionist scourge of Asia in the 1930s into a demilitarized democracy;[41] a study explaining how, only four years after World War II, U.S. leaders were able to persuade the American people that they shared a cultural bond with the Germans and Italians and should therefore enter the new NATO alliance with them;[42] or a study of the culture of American foreign correspondents explaining the ways in which this culture often works to legitimate U.S. intervention abroad.[43] Instead of treating cultural units from states to transnational civilizations as sealed black boxes whose relations, like those of atomic physics,[44] are governed by deterministic laws of attraction, repulsion, and fission, such studies would look at culture as a resource that is deployed and contested in struggles over foreign policy, and as an entity that operates at the level of professional groups and social movements, and not just on a national or "civilizational" scale.

If, instead of Huntington's cultural realism, we had a realistic model of culture, such a model would show the importance of culture in helping to determine policy choices without being deterministic. Instead of presenting culture as a sort of computer program blindly enacted by governments and populations, it would present culture as something more akin to a conversation that keeps referring back to itself but also keeps shifting as new people enter, sometimes misunderstanding what is being said and arguing noisily with others.[45] Then we could move away from cartoonish parodies of others—Muslims as angry and violent, Asians as hierarchical and hardworking—and continue the important business of talking across our differences, building new cultures, and understanding our common humanity.

(2001)

Part IV

Nuclear Testing

8

Nuclear Weapons Testing as Scientific Ritual

> Nuclear weapons are both symbols and pieces of hardware. Their role as symbols is what matters to most people, including scientists, most of the time.
>
> —Michael May, director, Livermore Laboratory (1965–71)

In the late 1980s, when I was doing fieldwork at the nuclear weapons laboratory in Livermore, California, the testing of nuclear weapons was a focal concern of both the Livermore Laboratory and the American antinuclear movement.[1] The Livermore Laboratory organized itself around the production of nuclear tests, and the antinuclear movement organized itself around ending them. Carrying out or ending nuclear tests, was, for each community, the mission that facilitated its integration as a community and connected it in contentious antipathy with the opposed community.

There have been periodic attempts to halt nuclear testing since at least the 1950s, and the American antinuclear movement has consistently seen a test ban as its first priority. In the mid-1950s, when the American public was increasingly concerned about the health effects of atmospheric nuclear testing, an antitesting campaign spearheaded by the Nobel Prize winner Linus Pauling gathered the signatures of ten thousand scientists and mobilized hundreds of thousands of other citizens in opposition to nuclear testing.[2] Public concern abated after the Limited Test Ban Treaty of 1963 pushed testing underground—although the rate of nuclear testing actually accelerated after the treaty went into effect. In the late 1970s, seeking to

147

rein in the arms race, Jimmy Carter attempted to negotiate a complete test ban but failed as détente collapsed after the Soviet invasion of Afghanistan. In the 1980s, however, the United States came under renewed pressure to end nuclear testing. This pressure came, at home, from the Nuclear Freeze movement of the 1980s and, abroad, from the Soviet Union, which under Gorbachev, initiated a series of unilateral moratoriums on testing in order to put pressure on the Reagan and Bush administrations to end the arms race. Throughout, America's nuclear weapons laboratories strenuously opposed all initiatives to ban testing.[3]

At Livermore, nuclear weapons testing has structured much of the organizational and symbolic life of the laboratory community. Diverse everyday tasks, throughout the laboratory and at the Nevada Nuclear Test Site five hundred miles away, have taken on organizational purpose and symbolic meaning because of their contributions to programs converging in the production of nuclear tests. In the 1980s there were about eighteen tests a year. In a test—an "event" in the parlance of weapons designers—a bomb consisting of about five thousand components must work perfectly in the fraction of an instant before the components are destroyed by the explosion they create. The preparation for such an experiment generates fantastically complex interactions over a period of years between thousands of physicists, engineers, computer scientists, chemists, administrators, technicians, secretaries, and security personnel. A single nuclear test is a kind of busy intersection where individual lives, bureaucratic organizations, scientific ideas, intricate machines, national policies, international rivalries, historical narratives, psychological conflicts, and symbolic meanings all come together. This chapter investigates the controversy over nuclear testing in the late 1980s as it involved the laboratory, and makes the case that nuclear tests can be seen as high-tech rituals that are as important for their cultural and psychological as for their technical significance. They have been vital not only in the production of nuclear weapons but also in the production of weapons scientists and in the social reproduction of the ideology of nuclear deterrence.

Deconstructing Testing

Although many Livermore scientists in the 1980s supported arms control treaties such as SALT I, SALT II, and the INF agreement, they were almost unanimous in their opposition to a nuclear test ban. Why is this? Critics of the laboratory say that it is simply a matter of self-interest. In the words of Hugh DeWitt, an internal critic at Livermore, "the laboratories oppose a comprehensive test ban because they want to continue nuclear weapons development—to refine existing designs and do research in exciting new areas such as the X-ray laser."[4]

Livermore scientists have explained their opposition to a test ban differently. In the 1980s, the main reason for continued testing given by both laboratory officials and many warhead designers was that the reliability of the nuclear stockpile could not be assured without continued nuclear testing. One experienced warhead designer, Jack, put it like this: "I think a lot of people think a bomb is a bomb; build it once and it's there forever. It's not true. If you bought a Cadillac, you wouldn't just stick it in your garage and stake your life that you could start it ten years later if you didn't do anything other than put air in the tires and charge the battery. I wouldn't bet on it." Jack added that, as well as assuring the reliability of weapons, tests assured the reliability of the scientists who must ultimately make judgments about weapons reliability.

These arguments about reliability have twice entered the national political debate on nuclear testing. In 1978, when President Carter was attempting to negotiate a test ban treaty, the directors of Livermore and Los Alamos met with him to warn him that the reliability of the U.S. arsenal would degrade without nuclear testing and that teams of weapons scientists would disperse in such a way that it might be impossible to reassemble them if they were needed again.[5]

Meanwhile Jimmy Carter received a two-page letter from Norris Bradbury, a former director of Los Alamos; Carson Mark, former head of the theoretical physics division at Los Alamos; and Richard Garwin, a nationally known consultant on nuclear weapons physics who played a major role in developing the hydrogen bomb.[6] Bradbury, Mark, and Garwin assured Carter that, in their technical judgment, the laboratory directors were mistaken and that the continued reliability of the U.S. nuclear stockpile could be assured without further nuclear tests. Herb York, Carter's lead negotiator and a former Livermore director, says in his memoirs that "the nuclear establishment's fears were exaggerated. . . . We concluded that regular inspections and non-nuclear tests of stockpiled bombs would uncover most such problems and provide solutions to them" (286). The issue became moot when the test ban negotiations fell victim to the collapse of détente in the late 1970s.

The issue resurfaced in 1987, however. In response to congressional hearings on a test ban, the Livermore Laboratory provided the U.S. Congress with a report on weapons' reliability prepared by three of its leading weapons designers.[7] The report gave details of fourteen warhead designs that required postdeployment retesting to detect and rectify flaws. In the case of the Polaris missile the problem was serious enough that, some years after deployment, about one-half of the warheads were found to be "lemons."[8]

Meanwhile, Les Aspin (Democrat, Wisconsin), chair of the House Armed Services Committee, made a highly unusual move by asking Ray Kidder, a well-regarded Livermore scientist known to sympathize with the test ban cause, to reanalyze the information in the Livermore report. Kidder was allowed full access to all the relevant classified information. In his own report, issued in 1987, he argued that the laboratory's position was unconvincing. He claimed that all the weapons with problems were inadequately tested in the design process, mostly because they were rushed into the stockpile without full testing just before the 1958–61 testing moratorium, so that the subsequent tests that revealed problems after those weapons had been added to the stockpile should more properly be thought of as deferred design tests than as postdeployment reliability tests. He also argued that it was possible to remanufacture warheads in proven ways that rendered reliability testing redundant, saying that, if the laboratories were concerned about reliability, it would be easy for them to design more robust and reliable warheads. We might also add that the number of tests assigned to verification of stockpile reliability has been a small fraction of the total number of tests—probably no more than one test a year.[9]

What are we to make of this arcane but hardly trivial dispute? We could plausibly argue that the technical judgment of the weapons scientists has been compromised by their vested interests; or we could just as plausibly argue that the weapons scientists are uniquely placed to know about the mechanical reliability of nuclear weapons, and that their opponents are technically less informed or have allowed their own politics to color their technical assessments. As one probes the debate, one has a vertiginous sense of standing on shifting ground as the distinction between political and technical judgments—a distinction anchoring the expert case both for and against a test ban—melts into air.

My goal here is neither to evaluate the honesty of the participants in this debate nor to provide a definitive judgment of the technical concerns at issue—a task that would clearly be beyond my competence in any case. Instead, addressing this debate more obliquely than directly, I shall follow the lead of a young physicist at Livermore who reminded me that I was an anthropologist and not a physicist. Having read some of the literature in the sociology of science, he advised me to stop thinking of these technical judgments as right or wrong answers to a question and to start thinking of them as interpretations of highly complex and ambiguous information. Instead of seeking a definitive technical assessment, then, we should ask about the processes by which such assessments come to be considered definitive and their authors authoritative. After all, part of the argument made by the designers is that Ray Kidder was not in a position, despite his knowledge of thermonuclear physics, to make the technical pronouncements he made. By what processes, then, social as well as technical, does one acquire the authority to render such judgments?

Furthermore, what is reliability?[10] How much weapons reliability is enough, and why is reliability so important? We have been incited to a discourse here in which weapons reliability is taken for granted as an indispensable asset.[11] The proponents of testing maintain that one's enemies are less likely to attack if they are sure, and you are sure, that you have reliable nuclear weapons. We might plausibly argue, on the contrary, that if neither side is particularly sure that its nuclear weapons work, then neither side will have the confidence to attack or pressure the other, so that a test ban might result in low confidence in weapons reliability, which, in turn, would enhance deterrence. We must ask, then, how a social world comes to be constructed such that deterrence depends on the hyperreliability, not on the soft reliability, of nuclear weapons.

In the remainder of this chapter, asking why and how reliability matters, rather than whether the nuclear arsenal is in fact demonstrably reliable, I offer a cultural explanation as to how and why weapons scientists come to care about weapons reliability; how nuclear scientists become authorized to make expert judgments; and how a ban on nuclear testing strikes at the heart of the collective culture of Livermore's weapons scientists who must therefore, whatever the merits of the respective technical arguments, feel placed in much greater jeopardy by a comprehensive test ban treaty than by any other possible arms control measure.

But first we must understand the testing process itself.

How to Design and Test a Nuclear Weapon

Nuclear tests are conducted for a variety of purposes: to explore the basic physics of nuclear explosions, to test a new warhead design approach, to recertify the reliability of an old warhead, to test the effects of nuclear explosions on military hardware, to adapt an old warhead design to a new delivery vehicle, or to validate the finished version of a new design. Any individual test may serve more than one of these purposes.

As William Broad describes in *Teller's War*, the nuclear weapons design process consists of three phases (128). In phase 1, *concept study*, designers review the results of earlier tests, looking for ways to push the limits of the basic physics while satisfying the military requirements articulated by the Department of Defense and the Department of Energy.

In phase 2, *scientific feasibility*, weapons designers turn their ideas into specific design proposals that are evaluated by the bureaucracies in the laboratory, in the Department of Defense, and in the Department of Energy. This evaluation process may involve some nuclear testing. It also involves meetings, often lasting as long as three hours, at which reviewing scientists try to poke holes in the proposals. "These are not nice reviews," said the weapons designer Lester:[12] "They're very critical. I've seen men all in tears. The big reward in our division is to do an experiment, to get your idea tested. It's highly competitive. For every twenty things people propose, maybe one is going to make it onto that shot schedule."

For phase 3, *engineering development,* scientists validate the performance of a finished prototype warhead ready for deployment in the national nuclear stockpile. It is phase 3 that involves the most nuclear testing. Broad quotes one Livermore designer who described the climax of the engineering development phase: "I have never seen people work so hard. They would sleep in assembly rooms for days, not seeing their families. Many times I saw people with tears running down their face because they had worked so hard."[13] The designers, who are often working sixty to eighty hours a week at this point, are under constant pressure because other members of the team are waiting for their calculations. They must consult with engineers on the choice of materials for the bomb; with chemists as they choose how to fit the bomb with tracer elements for diagnostic purposes; and with the technicians who, often working with highly toxic materials in glove boxes, must machine the device's components with extraordinary precision. Since parts of the device are machined at Rocky Flats in Colorado, and the device is assembled at the Nevada Test Site rather than at the laboratory, this phase can also involve a lot of travel. Barry recalls traveling to Rocky Flats to watch the technicians machine the plutonium "pit" for his device:

> I looked at the plutonium in its glass case. It was black, with an oxide skin. It's like coal, except that it's hot to the touch because it's constantly emitting radiation. You know plutonium is pyrophoric. The technician scraped the skin off with his gloves, and white sparks flew out. I remember thinking, "Holy shit! This lump of rock is going to go in *my* bomb. *That's* going to be that powerful."

Gradually the test date approaches. Clark remembers his test nearing completion:

> Here was an experiment I had been working on for three years with a cast of hundreds, and watching this thing as it gets all put together laboriously at a couple different places around the country. . . . So you see this whole thing coming together, gee, it's almost like having a baby or something.

It's a comparable length of time and many more people involved in the process. . . . One of my big fears was that pieces would get misplaced somehow and the wrong end was facing forward. It was a complex thing. It had lots of parts. . . . By the time you're done this is at least a $5 million deal, and yet I'm thinking this whole thing rests on a few of my late-night computer calculations.

As the device and the diagnostic equipment are being assembled, the test site workers drill the shaft into which the device and its diagnostic canister will be placed. This cylindrical canister, crammed full of sensitive instruments and cables, can weigh hundreds of tons. When the canister is ready for final assembly, the nuclear device is transported with an escort of armored vehicles to its rendezvous with the diagnostic equipment. There the device and canister are bolted together ("married" or "mated," in the parlance of weapons scientists) within a portable building, known as a bogey tower, which sits astride the test shaft to shield it from both the weather and the gaze of enemy satellites. Once the device and canister have been lowered into the shaft, they are connected to nearby trailers on the desert surface by thick cables that will transmit a chorus of measurements from the exploding bomb under ground to the scientists above ground. They are then covered with hundreds of feet of sand and gravel as well as coal and tar epoxy plugs designed to keep all the radiation from the blast below ground. Over the past three decades, as they have become more complex, underground nuclear tests have grown more expensive. According to Broad, by the late 1980s they cost $30 million to $60 million each (91).

Lester remembers finally seeing his device ready to be lowered into its shaft. "You go out to the test site, and there's this huge two-hundred-foot canister filled with all this beautiful equipment and they're about to put it down. That's a real gut-wrencher."

Before dawn a party goes out to arm the device. Broad describes one instance of this process:

A small group of scientists and security guards . . . drove out to a trailer known as the "red shack" to electronically arm the weapon, which had earlier been placed at the bottom of a 1,050-foot-deep hole and covered with dirt. At the red shack, security was tight as usual. Two of the scientists carried a special briefcase and a bag of tiny cubes that had numbers painted on their sides. They alternately took cubes out of the bag and punched the numbers into an "arm enable" device in the briefcase, generating a random code that was sent to the buried weapon on a special electrical cable. The scientists then drove across the desert to the control point in a mountain pass overlooking the test site. . . . There, in a high-technology complex surrounded by armed guards and barbed wire, they again opened their briefcase and sent the same random code to the weapon. It was now armed. (87)

When the detonation takes place, the scientists see it in two ways: on video monitors relaying the picture from a helicopter hovering over the test shaft and also as a set of flickering needles on seismographs and oscilloscopes registering in the control room what the diagnostic equipment has picked up from the transitory flare beneath the surface of the earth just miles away.

Here is Clark describing his test:

> We got up at 3:30 or 4:00 in the morning. Drive out. Stars are out. Go out to this remote outpost. Standing around going through the what-ifs. "God, what if this happens, what are you going to do then? . . ."
>
> And everything went smooth and it went off and they show a picture on the TV screens there of a helicopter hovering above the site and you could actually see dust rising. I mean, it's not like you're watching the old atmospheric tests. I mean, it's pretty benign really. You can see a shock wave ripple through the earth. . . . You're not allowed out to the site until the crater is actually formed, and that can happen in thirty seconds, it can happen in ten hours. Turned out with mine that it happened in about an hour. . . . And that was really awesome, standing there with this thing which was at least a hundred yards across, and see what I had been looking at on my computer screen for years all of a sudden show up in this gigantic movement of the earth. It was as close as I've had to personal contact with what the force of the nuclear weapon is like. And then eventually some of the data starts to come in and by the end of the day it was clear that—we didn't have all the data, but it was clear it was going to be a success and it was a very complicated shot. So I knew that would be good for my career.

As the day progresses, the data through which the bomb's performance will be interpreted are retrieved from the diagnostic devices. "We bury these things half a mile underground and you get some electricity out of a wire and some melted glass that's radioactive and go out and analyze those, and you can tell somebody all about what happened," said Jack, marveling at the almost magical nature of the diagnostic technology.

A Ritual Analysis

Nuclear tests, as well as being scientific experiments, are cultural processes that produce weapons scientists as persons and enable them to play with, maybe even resolve, core issues in their ideological world. In this regard, it is heuristically helpful to think of nuclear tests as sharing some of the characteristics of rituals. Since the comparison of nuclear tests to rituals may seem improbable, even offensive, to some, particularly the scientists who carry them out, it bears a word of explanation. My intention in making the analogy is not to be cute; nor is it to satirize nuclear weapons scientists by comparing them to tribal "savages," nor yet to deny that nuclear tests are rigorously executed scientific experiments. I make the guarded analogy between ritual and nuclear testing because it seems to me to genuinely illuminate the significance of testing for Livermore scientists in a way that affords a new vantage point, not only on the vexed debate over nuclear testing, but also, more broadly, on the cultural and psychological significance of scientific experimentation in general. After all, it is not for nothing that, when I asked the weapons designer Barry who he considered a real designer, he replied, "Anyone who's been through the ritual all the way." Obviously there are many ways in which nuclear tests are not at all like, say, the Catholic mass or African adolescent circumcision rituals. Still, as Sally Falk Moore and Barbara Myerhoff argue in their book *Secular Rituals,* while we should avoid the temptation to mechanically label almost every social process a ritual, nonetheless ritual analysis can profitably be applied to many events that are not, formally speaking, religious or sacred. In the case of nuclear weapons testing, if we bracket the obvious differences between a scientific experiment and a sacred ceremony, then the comparison to ritual processes brings into focus certain kinds of intense symbolic meaning nuclear tests carry for scientists that might otherwise go unnoticed.[14]

Anthropologists have theorized ritual in a number of different ways. Émile Durkheim and his intellectual descendants have stressed the power of ritual to heal social conflicts. They maintain that ritual allows the symbolic expression and transcendence of conflicts, facilitating the intersubjective production of a sense of community.[15] This sense of community may be experienced most deeply within ritual in moments of mystical transport that Durkheim labeled "collective effervescence" and Victor Turner called "communitas." Another school of thought, influential in Britain and articulating a more psychological function for ritual, has presented ritual as a means of allaying anxiety by simulating human control over that which ultimately cannot be controlled—death, disease, crop failure, and so on.[16] Still others have focused on the ability of certain kinds of rituals, "rites of passage," to transform those who participate in them. In rites of passage, the social status of initiates is irrevocably changed as they are indoctrinated with the special, or even secret, knowledge of the initiatory group.[17] Finally, the U.S. school of cultural anthropology has portrayed ritual as a text—as a means of celebrating, performing, displaying, and transmitting the ethos, symbols, and norms of the particular cultural community that uses ritual to clarify and speak to itself about its values and identity.[18] In the analysis that follows I draw eclectically on all these traditions in order to illuminate the significance of nuclear testing for Livermore scientists.

I explored the meaning of nuclear testing for nuclear weapons scientists by collecting tape-recorded narratives of nuclear tests. The first thing one notices about these narratives is that, unlike official laboratory statements about the importance of nuclear testing, they say nothing about reliability testing of old weapons. In fact, Clark went so far as to preface his test narrative with the statement, "Stockpile maintenance is boring, so I don't do that." The main themes in these narratives have to do with the fulfillment of personal ambition, the struggle to master a challenging new technology, the scientific drama of bringing something fundamentally new into the world, and the experience of community and communitas in the deeply competitive world of nuclear physics.

Nevertheless, although the reliability testing of old weapons is absent from this narrative world, that world is still saturated with a more broadly and diffusely expressed anxiety about the reliability of the weapons. The narratives are largely about reliability, but they frame that concern very differently than the laboratory's official policy statements do.

Overtly, these narratives are about a purely technical process and have nothing to say about the broader political purposes of these weapons or about the system of international relations and international meanings into which the weapons are inserted. It is, however, my contention that these physics experiments as they are narrated do embody a kind of politics, that the technopolitical worldview of the weapons scientists is embedded in, experienced through, and simulated by these experiments—that it is in the design and testing of a nuclear device that the abstract clichés comprising the ideology of deterrence become experientially real to the scientists who must live deterrence as a truth.

Initiation

Nuclear tests are not only a means of testing weapons designs. They are also a means of testing and producing weapons designers—the elite within the laboratory. To become a fully fledged member of the weapons design community new scientists must master an arduous, esoteric knowledge, subject themselves to tests of intelligence and endurance, and finally prove themselves in a display of the secret knowledge's power. If a test goes well, and it is a designer's first test, the designer's social status is changed. In the words of the senior designer Seymour Sack, testing is a way of "punching your ticket by having your name associated with a particular test."[19] One designer, Martin, remembers the day after his first test—a particularly challenging one: "It was extraordinary. I was walking around the lab and people were coming up to me, I mean, just all over the place, people I didn't even know were coming up to me and shaking my hand, congratulating me on this tremendous achievement." Martin's experience speaks to the fact that nuclear tests not only test technology, they also test people.[20]

Tests are also the socially legitimated means of producing knowledge about nuclear weapons. This knowledge takes the form both of a socially attributed knack for judgment and, more concretely, the view graphs summarizing the results of tests, which scientists display in post-test briefings in the laboratory's Poseidon Room. Thus participation in nuclear tests confers a kind of symbolic capital that can be traded as power or as knowledge.[21] The more tests scientists participate in, the more authority they acquire as they move toward the status of senior scientists, whose judgment about nuclear weapons is particularly respected and sought after.

It is partly in this context that we should understand the debate about weapons reliability. This debate is as much about the authorization of knowledge and the hierarchical authority of knowers as it is about the reliability of weapons. The laboratory argues that there is only one way to know for sure whether a weapon will work; only one way to train people to know this; and only a very select group who can certify the continuing reliability of old weapons whose parts are decaying, have been replaced, or have been slightly redesigned without another test. Scientists stress the mysterious uniqueness of knowledge about nuclear weapons—knowledge that cannot be learned entirely from textbooks or briefings, knowledge whose uniqueness is marked by its very nontransferability and ultimate nontradeability.

This throws new light on the significance of Ray Kidder's intervention in the weapons reliability debate. He was not only attacking the central mission of the laboratory in saying that the reliability of nuclear weapons could be assured without continued testing, and assenting to the prohibition of the ritual by which membership in the laboratory elite is regulated. Kidder was also a physicist intimately acquainted with thermonuclear physics who attacked the whole system of power/knowledge that organizes the status hierarchies and cosmology of the laboratory. This system is based upon nuclear testing as the means of production of both knowledge and power. By suggesting that knowledge could be separated from its local production in nuclear tests, Kidder threatened to tear the social and political fabric of the laboratory world.

We can bring the power/knowledge stakes in the conflict between Kidder and the weapons establishment into still sharper focus if we consider the conflict in the context of Kidder's own scientific biography. Earlier in his career, Kidder had weapons experience and served on a number of weapons design review committees. From there he went on to found and run the laboratory's Inertial Confinement Fusion (ICF) program, which created microscopic thermonuclear explosions by firing enormously powerful lasers at pellets smaller than a pinhead. In so doing he developed a different technology, one that did not involve the nuclear weapons design process or the use of the Nevada Test Site, to simulate within the laboratory itself the basic product of the weapons designers. More recently it has been suggested that, if there were a nuclear test ban, the laboratory should rely much more heavily on its fusion laser to explore the physics of thermonuclear explosions. Seen in this light, Kidder was not just a critic of nuclear testing, he was also the author of a different social-technological system for producing thermonuclear power/knowledge, and his intervention in the debate on reliability represented a deep challenge to the power/knowledge system of the laboratory's weapons community.

Mastery

As the psychologist Robert Jay Lifton and Richard Falk point out in *Indefensible Weapons,* the very existence of nuclear weapons inevitably raises the question of whether the weapons are under our control or whether we are at their mercy. The issue here is not only whether humans can be relied upon not to use the weapons deliberately but also whether we are capable of devising fail-safe systems to prevent the weapons from exploding accidentally. Lest the latter be thought a far-fetched concern, there have been a number of unfortunate accidents involving U.S. nuclear weapons. In one incident, in 1961, a B-52 accidentally dropped two multimegaton hydrogen bombs on a farm in North Carolina. Nuclear weapons were again lost in accidents involving B-52s in 1966 and 1968, in Spain and Greenland, respectively. In both cases the conventional explosive in the weapons detonated, and although there was no nuclear explosion, plutonium was dispersed over wide areas. In 1955, a B-47 accidentally dropped a nuclear weapon as it was landing at Kirtland Air Force Base near Albuquerque, and, in North Dakota in 1980, a B-52 with nuclear weapons on board caught fire. Recent computer simulations of the latter incident have suggested that, if the wind had blown the fire in a different direction, there might have been at least a conventional explosion dispersing plutonium as widely as at Chernobyl. Other simulations have suggested that the W-79 nuclear artillery shell, formerly deployed in Europe, might, in certain circumstances, have detonated if accidentally struck by a bullet.[22]

Despite these mishaps, nuclear weapons scientists have been reasonably confident that nuclear weapons would not explode as a result of human or mechanical error. I want to argue here that, for scientists at Livermore, the lived experience of nuclear testing is important in fostering this confidence. Just as, according to classical anthropological theory, the performance of rituals can alleviate anxiety and create a sense of power over, say, crop failure and disease, so too can nuclear tests in an analogous way create a space where participants are able to play with the issue of human mastery over weapons of mass destruction and symbolically resolve it. Since the stability that nuclear weapons are supposed to ensure—nuclear deterrence—exists so much in the realm of simulations, and since the reliability of deterrence involves the absence of a catastrophe more than the active, direct, positive experience of reliability, nuclear tests play a vital role in making the abstract real in scientists' lives. They give scientists direct experience of what can only otherwise be known as an absence, bridging the gulf between a regime of simulations and the realm of firsthand experience.

The issue of human control over nuclear technology is a recurrent theme in nuclear test narratives. Many test narratives involve a sequence of events in which scientists fear that their machines will not behave as predicted but, after a period of painful anxiety, learn that humans can predict and control the behavior of technology. The most exciting narratives are those, as in any story, where the outcome seems in doubt for a while. For example, the scientist Eric told me this story when I asked which tests stood out in his mind as the most memorable:

> The most exciting tests were the ones . . . where we were in great danger . . . of losing the test altogether . . . and through some enormous heroic development of solutions to problems, we were able to save the test.
>
> There was one test in which we finally solved the problem, and it was an electrical problem, by deciding to do what I should call a lobotomy. We had to destroy a component. And so we finally decided that we could, by sending a powerful pulse of electricity down a pair of wires, burn that component out into the condition that it would allow the rest of the system to function. And so then finally we talked this out and we rehearsed it and we practiced it with cables of the right length and components of the right sort and so forth. And, if it had failed, the experiment would have been completely lost, and it was buried. We couldn't have pulled it back to the surface. It would have been just a piece of garbage at the bottom of the hole. . . .
>
> And that particular test, I felt we had to do something to commemorate it, and so within a few weeks I had invited all of the principals here, and we had a party and set up pictures in the backyard of all of the trials and tribulations we had gone through.

Many of the test narratives have complex emotional rhythms in which control over the technology and helplessness before it alternate with one another. If the final point of the story is that humans can control nuclear technology, the scientists often learn, on the way, that they must also trust the technology and let go of their concerns. This happens particularly in the period between the placement of the device in the test shaft and the actual test. "This is a hard period for the designer, especially the younger designers," says Lester. "You go through a period where you have a lot of doubts because the computer codes don't cover everything." As Clark put it: "You're kind of helpless after a time. You've got to just take your hands away and hope everything works out all right." This confidence that we can make the weapons do our bidding mixed together with a trusting helplessness before them is, of course, the basic psychology required by deterrence.

Where many of us worry that a nuclear explosion will occur at some point in our lives, Livermore scientists worry that one won't. Over and over again, scientists have the experience of fearing that something will go wrong with the bomb only to learn—in most instances—that it does not. By means of this lived journey from anxiety to confidence, structured by the rhythms of the testing process itself, scientists learn that the weapons behave, more or less, predictably, and they learn to associate safety and well-being with the performed proof of technical predictability. Then, like Lester, they can say: "When you're a device physicist, [the bomb] is no more strange than a vacuum cleaner. You don't feel a fear for it at all, and it's not an alien thing. And I understand that to the people that don't do it, it is an alien thing. I felt the same way before I went to the lab."

Lester is explaining that, before he went to the laboratory, he too was nervous about the bomb; but participation in the practices of nuclear weapons design and testing has restructured his subjective world so that he now feels in his bones that nuclear weapons are as benign as vacuum cleaners. For many of us, understanding the engineering of a hydrogen bomb will in no way allay our fear that a mad president, general, or admiral will misuse it. If anything, it may magnify that fear. Lester's remark, which implicitly equates safety from nuclear annihilation with technical mastery over the bomb, only makes sense in the context of the practical consciousness embodied in and engendered by nuclear testing.

To put it a little differently: as well as assuring the technical reliability of nuclear weapons, nuclear tests provide in an elusive way a symbolic simulation of the reliability of the system of deterrence itself. Each time a nuclear test is successfully carried off, the scientists' faith in human control over nuclear technology is further reinforced. Seen in this light, the "reliability" the tests demonstrate has an expandable meaning, extending out from the reliability of the particular device being tested to the entire regime of nuclear deterrence.

Life and Death

Rituals in general are often marked by particular kinds of language: an abundance of birth and death metaphors, allusions to mythic or divine entities, and so on. U.S. nuclear weapons culture is full of mythical allusions. Thus we have the Excalibur weapon, the Polaris and Poseidon missiles, and experimental chambers named kivas—the name given to sacred ceremonial structures by the Pueblo Indians who live around Los Alamos.

But more striking than the use of explicitly sacred language in U.S. nuclear weapons culture is the absence of metaphors of death and the superabundance of birth metaphors. The pattern is startling, and it goes back to the beginning of the nuclear age, when scientists at Los Alamos, where the nuclear reactor was named "Lady Godiva," wondered aloud whether the bomb they were about to test would be a "boy" or a "girl" (i.e., a dud). They called the prototype tested in New Mexico "Robert's [Oppenheimer's] baby"; the bomb dropped on Hiroshima was named "Little Boy." Secretary of State Henry Lewis Stimson informed Winston Churchill of the first successful nuclear test by passing him a sheet of paper saying, simply, "Babies satisfactorily born," and Teller cabled Los Alamos the message, "It's a boy," after the first successful hydrogen bomb test.[23] In subsequent years there were debates as to whether Teller was really the "father" of the hydrogen bomb or had in fact been "inseminated" with the breakthrough idea by the mathematician Stanislav Ulam, and had merely "carried" it.

And now we have bombs that are constructed around fissile "pits." The production of these "pits" may involve the use of "breeding blankets" and "breeder reactors" to produce plutonium—an artificial substance that does not exist in nature. After the bomb has been "married" or "mated" to the diagnostic canister, it explodes and "couples" with the ground, producing "daughter fission products" that go through "generations." Clark referred to the process of bringing this about as "like having a baby," and talked about the tense decision at the moment of the test as being whether to "push" or not. Another designer told me he has "postpartum depression" after his tests. When the first nuclear weapon was tested, the Manhattan Project scientists referred to the apparatus from which it was suspended as a "cradle." Subsequently, the steel shells in which ICBMs sit in their silos became known as "cribs," and missile officers refer to the ICBMs as being connected to control panels by "umbilical cords."

What is going on here? Brian Easlea in *Fathering the Unthinkable* has that nuclear scientists are men who are impelled to their work by womb envy—an overpowering jealousy that women can create life and a determination, inflamed by the distance from women and from birth enforced upon men in modern society, to themselves do something as awesome as birth.

There are problems with Easlea's interpretation. The first is that, since birth imagery is applied to so many activities in our society (from writing term papers to growing gardens), we would, following Easlea's logic, have to argue that all these activities are animated by womb envy. The second problem is that a few of the weapons scientists—including at least one who used these birth metaphors quite inventively—are women. Where most cultural feminist theories can fairly easily account for a few women who behave like stereotypical men, Easlea's theory is so closely tied to female reproductivity as an absolute index of difference that this is more problematic for him.

While there can be no doubt that the culture of nuclear testing is a scientific celebration of masculine values, I would argue against using a broadly Freudian strategy of reading these birth metaphors as clues or "slips" that enable the determined investigator to uncover preexisting unconscious motives at the individual level. I prefer to see a shared language as the symptom of a political ideology, rather than individual psychology, and as a means of shaping individual subjectivities so that people can work together.[24]

The physicists themselves, when I pointed out the abundance of birth metaphors in their discourse, either insisted that I had found a fact without significance or pointed out that all sorts of people apart from weapons scientists make abundant use of such metaphors. Still, while the use of birth metaphors might seem unremarkable enough in many situations, it is surely more noteworthy to find birth metaphors applied to the process of creating weapons that can end the lives of millions of people than to find them used to describe the process of, say, writing a book or a computer program. All metaphors achieve their effect because of the gulf between the literal and the figurative, but in the case of applying birth metaphors to nuclear weapons development the gulf between the literal and the figurative is great enough that the metaphor is as dissonant as it is evocative. But this is the point. Thus I take the recurrence of images of fertility and birth in weapons scientists' discourse about weapons of destruction as an attempt to cast the meaning of this technology in an affirmative key. In metaphorically assimilating weapons and components of weapons to a world of babies, births, and breeding, weapons scientists use the connotative power of words to produce—and be produced by—a cosmological world where nuclear weapons tests symbolize not despair, destruction, and death but hope, renewal, and life. In this semantic world, the transformation of a mass of metals and chemicals into a transient star under the surface of the earth is phrased in images of life and birth. And, after all, in the context of these scientists' practices and beliefs about deterrence, we can see how each nuclear explosion might symbolize for them the fertility of the scientific imagination, the birth of community, and the guarantee of further life. A weapon is destroyed, and a community is born.

The scientists' use of such images is also part of a wider laboratory discourse that exchanges and mingles the attributes of humans and machines. This way of speaking in general, and the birth images in particular, create a discursive world where nuclear weapons appear to be "natural." This happens because the discourse fuses, or confuses, the spheres of production and reproduction, depicting machines made by humans as fruits or babies, as if they grew on trees or inside human bodies instead of being assembled in laboratories and factories. Karl Marx argued well over a century ago that, in presenting interest and profit as something that naturally accrue to invested capital, as if by breeding, capitalist ideology obscures the way profit is produced in social relationships that extract some of the value of a worker's labor and convert it into the investor's profit. In the same vein, the scientists' metaphorical cosmology, by assimilating the world of mechanical production to the world of natural reproduction, obscures the social relationships and political choices underlying the design of new nuclear weapons. This semantic system constructs nuclear weapons by metaphorical implication as part of the natural order, and it gives metaphorical vigor to the "realist" assumption that the arms race and the development of new nuclear weapons have a momentum of their own, that "you can't stop technology."

Conclusion

I have argued that, as well as testing the reliability of particular weapons designs, nuclear tests are a means of testing and initiating the designers themselves. Tests also play a crucial role in structuring the hierarchies of knowledge and power at the laboratory and in inducting new scientists into the laboratory social and ideological system. Whereas laboratory officials have argued that nuclear tests are necessary to maintain the technical reliability of the arsenal, and their critics have denied this and accused them of dishonesty, I have suggested that, if one looks at reliability figuratively as well as literally, then testing is vital to reliability as a felt reality.

Many anthropologists have argued that the myths and rituals of nonliterate peoples often contain what we might call, in our own terms, "scientific knowledge" about the world.[25] I have here been arguing the complementary converse—that some of our most expensive scientific experiments are saturated with elements of myth and ritual. This is not to say that they are not really scientific experiments. It is to say that there is more to scientific experiments than meets the eye.

These experiments are ritual furnaces in which the abstract clichés that comprise the ideology of nuclear deterrence are forged into subjective truths in the lives of the scientists who design the weapons. Although the clichés legitimating the scientists' work are often transmitted verbally, through discourse, it is in the practical experience of these rituals that they take on the incandescent quality of truth.

(1996)

9

The Virtual Nuclear Weapons Laboratory in the New World Order

Anthropologists have had little to say about nuclear weapons.[1] Yet the complexes that design, produce, and control these weapons are powerful institutions in the modern world, and the weapons themselves play a central role in regulating hierarchies and relationships between nation-states in the global order. In this chapter, I join the anthropology of science with perspectives from political economy and critical security studies[2] and use a fine-grained ethnographic analysis of a current dispute over U.S. nuclear weapons policy to explore the shifting processes by which knowledge and power are constructed within the contemporary nuclear weapons complex. I also map the implications of these processes for the evolving structure of military power in the post–cold war global order. I base this chapter on multisited research[3] in the defense bureaucracy in Washington, D.C., and at two of the three nuclear weapons laboratories in the United States: the Los Alamos National Laboratory in New Mexico and the Lawrence Livermore National Laboratory in California.[4] The secrecy of these institutions makes them problematic sites for ethnographic observation; however, I have been interviewing and observing scientists at the Livermore Laboratory since 1987 and, after 1992, at Los Alamos. I have supplemented insights from this long-term research program with interviews of key players in Washington's national security bureaucracy, including retired members of the first Clinton cabinet.

The emergent literature on global processes and structures in anthropology and cultural studies has tended to ignore military institutions and the relationships between nation-states with which they are imbricated.[5] Focusing on global flows of migrant workers, refugees, capital, and popular culture, this literature has accented those processes and relationships that cut against the grain of the nation-state: the development of transnational diasporas, the growth of multinational corporate cultures, and the hybridization of popular cultures in the era of global communications. Indeed, some contributors to this literature have suggested that the nation-state may be withering in the face of these new transnational flows, with national allegiances being superseded and undermined by new postnational forms of identity.[6] While the nation-state may appear to be withering from the point of view of those who follow the voyages of ethnic migrants and electronic capital, it looks less fragile to one who studies the militarization of scientific institutions, the accumulation of weapons, and the promulgation of nationalist-military ideology by state apparatuses. From this position an important, if understudied, dimension of the emergent global structure consists of what—in a supplement to Appadurai's schema in *Modernity at Large* of "ethnoscapes," "technoscapes," "financescapes," "mediascapes," and "ideoscapes"—I call "securityscapes": asymmetrical distributions of weaponry, military force, and military-scientific resources among nation-states and the local and global imaginaries of identity, power, and vulnerability that accompany these distributions. These imaginaries are mediated by expert communities of defense intellectuals that are becoming increasingly globally networked and by global media spectacles of war that take the form of both news and entertainment.[7] As Virilio and Lotringer argue in *Pure War,* war can be an important starting point from which to theorize the social.

In this chapter, I explore the emergent securityscape of the world in the first decade after the end of the Cold War by means of an analysis of a new strategy for nuclear weapons science adopted by the United States in the 1990s—a strategy that, in replacing nuclear testing in the Nevada desert with new virtual testing technologies, was crafted to stabilize U.S. global superiority in nuclear weaponry while stemming the ability of other countries to develop nuclear weapons. This new approach paired negotiation of a global nuclear test ban treaty with a transition to increasingly virtual techniques in nuclear weapons science that are beyond the reach of most national science establishments. The precise limits and capabilities of these virtual techniques are at present a matter of some scientific and political controversy within the United States and abroad. Indeed, one way to read this chapter is as a case study demonstrating that, contrary to naive accounts of science as an eternally stable set of procedures for adjudicating truth, the political environment within which scientists work may redefine what counts as knowledge and which procedures are accepted as valid in adjudicating knowledge claims.[8] Arguing that scientific knowledge based heavily on simulation techniques is hyperconstructible, so that disputes about the validity of such knowledge may be particularly difficult to resolve, I explore the controversy about virtual nuclear weapons science both in order to extend the anthropology of science into contemporary debates about simulations in science and to shed light on the shifting securityscape at the end of the twentieth century.[9]

Virtual Weapons Science and a New Securityscape

Remarkably, nuclear weapons scientists at the Livermore and Los Alamos National Laboratories find themselves almost a decade after the end of the cold war with more money for nuclear weapons research and development than they had enjoyed, on average, during the cold war.[10] They have accomplished this by reinventing nuclear weapons science to adapt it to new models of the international securityscape in the national security bureaucracy.

In the early 1990s, as the cold war was succeeded by the Gulf War, officials of the U.S. national security state began to worry less about the United States' traditional nuclear rivalry with Russia and more about the rise of so-called rogue states (such as Iraq, Iran, Libya, and North Korea) and about the possibility that a collapsing post-Soviet nuclear complex might hemorrhage bomb materials and scientists to such states.[11] Third World countries seeking First World weapons,[12] formerly present only in the peripheral vision of the national security state, became a major object of concern. Under these circumstances, U.S. weapons designers who had worked on bombs targeted against the Russian military complex were now sent to Russian nuclear facilities to work with their former adversaries in ensuring that Russian weapons materials and scientists did not leave the country. They also began to draft designs for a "mininuke" especially designed for use against a rogue state.[13] Meanwhile, the national security bureaucracy in Washington began to revise and reemphasize its strategy for preventing nuclear proliferation.

The principal bulwark against nuclear proliferation was the Non-Proliferation Treaty of 1968, which granted ready access to nuclear energy technology for nonnuclear signatories on condition that they pledged never to acquire nuclear weapons and submitted to United Nations inspections to verify their compliance with this pledge. By the 1990s, however, many Third World countries were complaining that the Non-Proliferation Treaty had established a system of international "nuclear apartheid" according to which the five permanent members of the United Nations Security Council (the United States, Russia, the United Kingdom, France, and China) had publicly acknowledged and legitimated nuclear arsenals while no one else did.[14] Many Third World countries complained that the established nuclear powers had for too long violated article 6 of the treaty that, more than two decades earlier, had committed them to "pursue negotiations in good faith on effective measures relating to cessation of the arms race at an early date and to nuclear disarmament."[15] A well-organized group of nonaligned nations threatened to block indefinite extension of the Non-Proliferation Treaty at the 1995 review conference if the established nuclear powers did not at least end nuclear testing.[16]

When the Clinton administration took office in 1993, the directors of the weapons labs were determined to beat back attempts by arms controllers to end all nuclear testing. Arguing that the long-term integrity of the arsenal could not be assured without continued nuclear testing, they proposed that, if there was to be a test ban treaty, it should at least allow small nuclear tests of maybe half a kiloton[17] and that, in the meantime, the labs should conduct a series of fifteen full-scale nuclear tests to check the safety and reliability of weapons in the nuclear stockpile.

Directors of the weapons labs made their case for a series of fifteen nuclear tests at a secret meeting at the Department of Energy in May 1993. The meeting did not go well for them. Present at the meeting were Hazel O'Leary, the new secretary of energy; James Schlesinger, a former secretary of energy; the directors of the three weapons laboratories; the directors of the weapons programs at the laboratories; and three prominent physicists who had been invited by Secretary O'Leary to provide independent advice, much to the consternation of the lab directors. (These physicists were Sid Drell of Stanford University, Frank von Hippel of Princeton University, and Ray Kidder, an internal critic at the Livermore Laboratory.) The lab officials made the case for a vigorous series of tests, while the independent physicists argued against them. One of these independent physicists told me that, by the second day of the two-day meeting, it was clear that O'Leary was unconvinced by the case for resuming nuclear testing. At this point, one of the lab directors volunteered that the managers of the weapons labs would feel more comfortable certifying to Congress the continued safety and reliability of the nuclear stockpile in the absence of nuclear testing if the labs could at least monitor the stockpile through a generously funded program of simulated testing. According to this physicist, the lab directors proposed what all present understood to be a bargain: their gracious acquiescence in the end of testing in exchange for the weapons labs' ticket to the twenty-first century—the program of simulation technologies that became known as "science-based stockpile stewardship."[18]

Hazel O'Leary remembers the meeting a little differently. In a 1997 interview, she told me:

I'm amused now to recall that some of the people at that meeting had the clear expectation that they would just be listened to. There would be some nods, and they would leave the room, and the truth as they saw it would be the answer. And I think they were shocked and dismayed. . . . After they'd done all their little models, and we'd talked and pushed and pulled . . . I simply looked down at the table in the SCIF [secure compartmented information facility] where the three lab directors were sitting almost ringed around the table, and I said, "You know you guys have got to look me dead in the eye. Is there anybody among you who will say that you cannot certify the safety and reliability of the nuclear stockpile [without testing]?" And the room was deadly silent. And finally [one lab director] said, "I believe we don't need the tests. We can certify without them." And then I just kept staring. . . . And they all pulled in line. . . . I understand James Schlesinger has said publicly that I sort of held the labs up by threatening to close down Livermore and then asked, "How about a little stockpile stewardship?" I don't think it worked that way at all.

In the end, the weapons labs lost nuclear testing because, in the post–cold war securityscape, the Clinton administration calculated the costs and benefits of nuclear testing differently than its predecessors did. Given that the United States already had a substantial and well-tested nuclear arsenal and there was no longer an arms race with the Soviet Union, the Clinton administration was most concerned about the possible proliferation of nuclear weapons to new countries. In this situation, the end of testing was a quid pro quo to the international community to secure the strengthening of the international regime against nuclear proliferation (albeit one that failed spectacularly when India and Pakistan conducted their nuclear tests in 1998), and it is widely believed in Washington that the stockpile stewardship program was a quid pro quo to the weapons labs to secure their cooperation in the end of testing.[19]

In any case, by the mid-1990s the directors of the weapons labs found themselves with no nuclear tests, but with a handsomely funded program of stockpile stewardship. This innocuously named program—stewardship, after all, sounds vaguely environmental—is slated to cost $5 billion over the next ten years.[20] It will include these principal components:

1. The National Ignition Facility at Livermore—a laser the size of a football stadium that will create tiny thermonuclear explosions when fired at pellets of tritium and deuterium. It is expected to be the most powerful laser in the world.[21]

2. The Dual Axis Radiographic Hydrotest (DARHT) Facility at Los Alamos. This will use accelerators to take X-ray snapshots of imploding

atomic bombs from which the plutonium or uranium has been removed, so that there is no nuclear explosion.

3. Subcritical tests at the Nevada Nuclear Test Site. In these underground tests, small amounts of plutonium are shocked by high-explosive detonations in order to explore their behavior. The first two subcriticals conducted cost $50 million each, making them more expensive than many full-scale nuclear tests during the latter years of the cold war.[22]

4. The Accelerated Strategic Computing Initiative (ASCI), a $3 billion program aiming to produce computers with one thousand times the speed and memory of today's supercomputers. Weapons scientists plan to use these computers to integrate data from stockpile stewardship experiments with data from past nuclear tests so that they can generate three-dimensional computer simulations of nuclear explosions vastly superior in their complexity and fidelity to those in use today.[23]

Three Narratives

In recent years, public discussion of U.S. nuclear weapons policy has been dominated by three quite incommensurable narratives about this massive program of simulations. I call them "the official story," "the antinuclear critique," and "the revolt against the hyperreal," the hyperreal being Baudrillard's term for a simulation that displaces the real itself. (Everyday examples of the hyperreal would include the food used in television commercials that is painted to look fresh or celebrities' bodies that have been altered by cosmetic surgery—alterations of originals that set new standards for, and in a sense, become more real than "real" food and "real" bodies.)

The Official Story

Over the past seven years, scientists and bureaucrats in the nuclear weapons complex have developed a script—elaborated at public hearings, press conferences, and in a proliferating mass of official reports and brochures—that explains the need for stockpile stewardship. My formal interviews with weapons scientists usually generate versions of this script, and I have watched scientists' ability to reproduce and elaborate on the script progress through the 1990s as the official story has consolidated its discursive grip within the weapons complex. According to the official story, the stockpile stewardship program strengthens the test ban treaty by making it possible for the United States to maintain its deterrence without nuclear testing. It does this in three ways.

First, stockpile stewardship will help weapons scientists refine their understanding of the underlying physics of nuclear weapons and, thus, improve the supercomputer codes they use to simulate the weapons' behaviors. As one senior manager at Livermore explained it to me: "Before, we were able to ignore many of the scientific details and work our way around them because we had the empiricism of nuclear tests. . . . It sort of didn't matter why you were right as long as you were right. . . . If you had a problem, you did something whether you understood it or not as long as it made it work."

Second, experts at the weapons labs argue that, in the absence of nuclear testing, stockpile stewardship is essential to verify the continued integrity of aging nuclear weapons and to validate minor design changes in the process of routine maintenance, forced by the obsolescence of old manufacturing technologies. U.S. nuclear weapons, originally designed with an anticipated shelf life of fifteen to twenty years, are already fourteen years old on average, and some are more than twenty years old, though there are no plans to retire them soon. As particular components wear out, as helium bubbles appear in the aging plutonium cores, as corrosion and cracking appear within the weapons, scientists need to know whether parts need to be replaced and how their replacement with differently manufactured components will affect the explosive yield of the bombs. Carefully designed stockpile stewardship experiments, they say, will help answer these questions.

Finally, managers at the weapons labs say that a vigorous program of stockpile stewardship will help them attract first-rate scientists, evaluate these scientists' skills, and keep them at the top of their form in case another arms race should occur. As they see it, the purpose of stockpile stewardship is not just to maintain the weapons but, by providing experiments related to nuclear weapons design, to maintain the ultimate guarantee of the weapons' reliability: the scientific intuition and technical judgment of the weapons designers themselves. As one weapons scientist explained it when I asked about the rationale for Livermore's National Ignition Facility (NIF):

> It's an exercise machine for designers. . . . A good analogy might be supposing that I'm a professional tennis player. Well, if I sit on my butt and don't do anything, pretty soon I'm not going to win any games. But if I go to a gym . . . The people that used to run down to Nevada and make all these difficult measurements aren't making them anymore, so what are they going to do? Well, they're going to stay out of the tennis court and go to the gym. . . . The NIF is an exercise facility for not fully employed weapons people that you don't want to simply get rid of.

The Antinuclear Critique

Many antinuclear activists see stockpile stewardship in a much more sinister light. Groups such as Greenpeace, the Natural Resources Defense Council,

Peace Action, the Western States Legal Foundation, the Los Alamos Study Group, and the umbrella coalition Abolition 2000 see stockpile stewardship as an end run around the Comprehensive Test Ban Treaty of 1996.[24] Activists argue that the United States was willing to sign the treaty only because it had developed simulation technologies that enabled it to develop new nuclear weapons without nuclear testing. Many activists refused to celebrate the signing of the test ban treaty, saying that the stockpile stewardship program put the United States in violation of the spirit of the treaty, the goal of which was, as stated in the preamble, "ending the development of advanced new types of nuclear weapons."[25] For example, a flyer put out by the Western States Legal Foundation in Oakland states:

> The CTBT [Comprehensive Test Ban Treaty] will ban large explosions. But it will not cap the "development" of new nuclear weapons by the U.S. or—to greater or lesser extents—the other nuclear weapons states. . . . Research and development activities . . . are continuing, unabated, at the weapons labs and will be greatly enhanced by stockpile stewardship.

The Clinton administration vehemently denied such charges. Thus, for example, John Holum, the head of the Arms Control and Disarmament Agency, said in a 1996 speech:

> The safe maintenance of existing weapons is a far cry from the confident development of new ones. The latter requires nuclear explosive tests, which the CTB would preclude. . . . Let me repeat: U.S. stockpile stewardship activities will not give us the means in the absence of nuclear testing to frustrate the CTB, to discover technological alternatives, or to build new types of nuclear weapons.[26]

Activists in turn rebut such denials by pointing to statements they have hunted down, with forensic care, in government reports and in the congressional testimony of managers from the weapons labs. They contend that statements culled from the internal communiqués of the government bureaucracy reveal the true intent behind stockpile stewardship and that the more modest rationale presented to foreign governments and to the U.S. public is only a cover story. For example, they quote a statement by John Immele, associate director for Nuclear Weapons Technology at Los Alamos, that stockpile stewardship aims to achieve "the full integration of the kind of capabilities that we've always been able to achieve in developing nuclear warheads and in our nuclear testing program"; or from Sandia Laboratory's Institutional Plan, which says that Sandia is seeking "the development of rapid prototyping and agile manufacturing . . . so advanced that they enable virtual prototyping and processing and, ultimately, computational design of entire systems."[27] Above all, they point to the Clinton administration's 1994 Nuclear Posture Review, an internal Pentagon review of nuclear weapons programs, which said that stockpile stewardship should afford the United States the "capability to design, fabricate and certify new weapons without underground testing."[28]

As further evidence that new weapons might be designed and deployed without nuclear testing, activists point to the B61 mod 11, a modified version of the B61 nuclear gravity bomb that, unlike the other versions of the B61, burrows before exploding. This capability makes it ideal for destroying underground targets such as command and control centers—or buried weapons factories. And indeed the new version of the B61 first came to activists' attention when Harold Smith, a Pentagon official trying to telegraph U.S. displeasure at reports that Libya was building an underground chemical weapons factory at Tarhunah, told reporters at a breakfast meeting in April 1996 that the United States was about to deploy a new weapon that could destroy the factory without damaging nearby Tripoli—unlike the B53 bomb it would replace. The weapon in question was the B61 mod 11, deployment of which began at the end of 1996—without the benefit of nuclear testing.

When I asked nuclear weapons scientists about the B61 mod 11, they insisted that it was not a new weapon. They pointed out that what weapons designers call "the physics package"—the nuclear device within the weapon—was unchanged from previous models in the B61 family and that the novel earth-penetrating capability of the mod 11 derived from a new casing—a mere engineering modification that required flight testing but no nuclear testing. While it might look like a new weapon from the point of view of Libya, since it conferred on the United States a new military capability, to a nuclear weapons designer it was an old weapon in a new wrapping.

Next, I asked weapons designers about the statements in government documents cited by activists that seemed to suggest it would be possible to design entirely new weapons under the stockpile stewardship program. Most weapons scientists insisted they would never feel comfortable certifying new weapons designs without nuclear testing. Especially if I turned off my tape recorder, or if we were talking informally over a beer, a number of weapons designers confided to me that they feared lab managers and Department of Energy officials were exaggerating the weapons applications of stockpile stewardship in their statements to Congress and to the Pentagon. According to them, these officials were securing funds for a program designed not to develop new weapons but to give the weapons labs something to do in the absence of nuclear testing. In 1994, putting on paper what others were saying more discreetly, Hugh DeWitt, a dissident physicist at

Livermore who often sides with its antinuclear critics, wrote to Secretary O'Leary and to Mike Campbell, Livermore's associate director for lasers, complaining that Livermore's National Ignition Facility was being misrepresented to Congress and to the Pentagon. In these letters, which DeWitt has given me permission to quote, he says:

> To critics outside the weapons labs it is easy to perceive it [NIF] as an important ongoing weapons program since its purpose is often described as doing "weapons physics" in a laboratory. [NIF] can certainly yield some very useful physics information for weapons designers . . . but in fact it is not in any way a weapon development program. . . . [Its] applications to maintenance of the stockpile are very indirect. . . . The promotion of the NIF by LLNL [Lawrence Livermore National Laboratory] because of its weapons connections is likely to backfire. [letters to Hazel O'Leary (September 2, 1994) and Mike Campbell (September 16, 1994)]

So I began to ask weapons designers how much one could redesign a nuclear weapon without nuclear testing. Fairly typical was one senior weapons designer who told me:

> It is simply a matter of experience that, when we do things that are close to what we've done in the past, the answers tend to be pretty good. When we do things that are different, you know, really different, the number of times we've been surprised is sobering. And it's not that, when something fails, you'd want to stand next to it, but it isn't doing the job that you set out to make it do.

One of the senior managers at the Livermore Laboratory, Jim,[29] himself an experienced weapons scientist, made the same point in more technical terms:

> Nobody in their right mind would design a sophisticated technological object and rely on it without testing. . . . In a physicist's language, we want to always be in the situation where we're interpolating. You have an answer here, which was all the old nuclear test data, and you're going to develop a new set of experiments from DARHT [the Dual Axis Radiographic Hydrotest Facility at Los Alamos] and NIF and everything, and then you're going to use the new computer codes to connect those two. So we think we will be able to do that—that in and of itself is a major challenge. If you take this [test data on a specific design] away and you don't have the nuclear test base, that's called extrapolation, and we don't think we will be able to extrapolate. We think we'll be able to interpolate between old nuclear test data and much higher quality nonnuclear test data

with advanced simulations. So that means we're basically stuck with the kinds of military characteristics that are in the weapons we have.

Rather than assume that the activists are mistaken and that, as Jim says, the weapons laboratories can use the new simulation technologies only to make minor modifications to existing designs based on interpolation, let me frost the glass one more time. By coincidence, just after I interviewed Jim, I interviewed another senior manager at Livermore, Harry, also a veteran of the testing program. Telling me that stockpile stewardship promised to finally give weapons scientists the capability to extrapolate, not merely interpolate, he said:

> Well, let me speak a little bit of heresy. . . . If you went over and talked to [Jim] . . . he would tell you, oh, we'll never have perfect understanding and all we're doing is to try to improve the intuition of our designers by having them exercise their tools in a wide variety of cases. He would say [we could never design a new weapon without a test]. . . . I have tackled very complex physics phenomena that people said, you'll never understand it. And we have understood it. So, I'm an optimist. I think it's a grand challenge. I think . . . it's ten years away. It's going to take NIFs and advanced hydros and pedaflop computers and a lot of that stuff, but there is a grand challenge that potentially, we could understand it.

The Revolt against the Hyperreal

While activists and weapons scientists debate whether the new simulation technologies will allow the labs to perfect new weapons without nuclear testing, a second critique of stockpile stewardship professes a profound skepticism about even very limited use of simulation technologies. There are left and right versions of this critique. The left version is associated with Ray Kidder, an internal critic at the Livermore Laboratory who has proposed an alternative stockpile stewardship plan that would confine the labs to reproducing identical copies of old nuclear weapons when they wear out. This proposal, which would effectively demote physicists to engineers, is not well liked at Livermore or Los Alamos. Kidder published an article in *Nature* in 1997 attacking the government's stockpile stewardship program on the grounds that, by encouraging weapons designers to make even minor design modifications unproved by nuclear testing, it would actually compromise the integrity of the nuclear stockpile. He said: "A decline in competence concerning nuclear weapons is virtually inevitable. . . . With less competent designers and engineers, a program of continuing modification of the physics package—believed necessary by the DOE [Department of Energy] to maintain competence—would in fact pose an unnecessary risk to the safety and reliability of the stockpile."[30] The same argument was made to a U.S. Senate subcommittee in 1997 with a very different political spin by Robert Barker, a senior manager at the Livermore Laboratory allied with prominent conservatives in Washington, and by Republican Congressman Floyd Spence (South Carolina) and Republican Senator Robert Kyl (Arizona), both ardent opponents of the nuclear test ban treaty.[31] In his testimony Barker stated:

> As a nuclear weapon designer, I learned the limitations of simulations and the humility that comes with the failure of a nuclear test. Computer calculations, regardless of how good or fast the computer is, are only as good as the data and models you give them and the knowledge and experience of the individual doing the calculations. Even today, no computers are big enough or fast enough to simulate all that goes on when a nuclear weapon explodes. The true knowledge of and experience with the limitations of calculations came from understanding the differences between calculations and experiments, including nuclear tests.

What to Believe?

Most, but not quite all, weapons scientists say the new simulation technologies will enable them to make minor modifications in the design of old weapons, but no more than that; antinuclear analysts argue—citing some statements issued by the weapons labs' own experts—that the new technologies will allow the labs to field new designs; and conservative Republicans, together with a few scientists within the labs, argue, conversely, that the new technologies will undermine weapons reliability and threaten national security. One can, with a little effort, find examples of weapons scientists who have taken each of the three positions. What is one to make of these discrepancies? What, dare one ask, is the truth?

It has become axiomatic in science studies in recent years that scientific knowledge is, in some sense, socially constructed. Proponents of this view do not mean—as, unfortunately, some of their critics have recently alleged—that gravity, for example, exists only if you want it to.[32] They mean that, within the moment of scientific controversy, evidence is often ambiguous, that it can be interpreted differently by differently positioned actors and that, as Thomas Kuhn explained over three decades ago, the process of bringing scientific debates to closure involves social and political, as well as purely logical, processes.[33]

Peter Galison has recently noted that science "is more like a quilt than a pyramid,"[34] and that different standards of evidence and modes of argument prevail in different territories within the empire of science—that there is, to bend a familiar anthropological phrase, such a thing as local scientific knowledge. Unfortunately, in their eagerness to debunk naive empiricism, constructivists within science studies are tempted to adopt a one-size-fits-all approach to the analysis of knowledge production. By contrast, taking up Galison's invitation to think about different logics within science, I would like to suggest here that, in those scientific neighborhoods where knowledge production is heavily dependent on complex models and simulations of events that cannot be wholly observed—recent work on global warming and nuclear winter come to mind as good examples—scientific disputation may show distinct characteristics: debate over the correspondence between models and the natural world may be especially pronounced and the process of bringing closure to scientific debates may be more problematic than usual. In such situations, I argue, knowledge becomes hyperconstructible: the remoteness of empirical experience aggravates the difficulty of striking the winning blow in scientists' "trials of strength"[35] by depriving them of the kinds of evidence generated by physical experiment or measurement that have conventionally been understood as decisive in the settlement of well-managed scientific disputes. In introducing the notion of hyperconstructibility here, I am not arguing that there is an absolute categorical distinction between hyperconstructible and other kinds of knowledge—a position that would run the risk of undermining the notion in the preceding paragraph that all knowledge is in some sense socially constructed—but I do want to suggest that there is a difference of degree at stake: that it can be more difficult to effect closure in scientific disputes as the conduct of those disputes becomes more dependent on simulations as evidence.

Conventionally, weapons scientists' disputes about the performance of a hypothetical weapon have been settled by building a prototype to see whether, and how, it explodes—what the manager Jim referred to as "the empiricism of nuclear testing." But this is now a forbidden experiment. In the absence of the forbidden experiment, which in the past was consensually accepted as decisive in weapons designers' duels to define truth, how is Ray Kidder to be persuaded that minor design changes will not affect the weapons' performance? And how is Harry to be persuaded that major design changes, even though validated by computer codes, may make the weapons unreliable?

The debate on stockpile stewardship affords a fine example of a contest to define hyperconstructible terrain. In this contest, the different cognitive frames, experiential histories, and political ideologies inhabited by various actors generate incommensurable narratives about the new simulation technologies that spiral within their own logics. Political conservatives, such as Roger Barker and Congressman Floyd Spence, are inclined to see the Comprehensive Test Ban Treaty (1996) as the culmination of a series of treaty restrictions, enforced by liberals at home and foreigners abroad, that constrain the United States' full autonomy in its development of military strength. Such conservatives are suspicious of any substitute for the ultimate proof of U.S. military strength: nuclear tests.

Antinuclear activists, on the other hand, read stockpile stewardship through the lens of a different narrative—a narrative not of the national security state's progressive enfeeblement but of its enduring resilience. The key event in this narrative is the signing of the Limited Test Ban Treaty of 1963, which banned atmospheric nuclear testing by the superpowers. The activists' sense of elation at the time was soon undercut by the realization that the treaty had not ended the arms race but merely moved it underground, where its pace actually intensified. This sense of betrayal was only reinforced by subsequent arms control treaties, from the Non-Proliferation Treaty to SALT and beyond, which all failed to end the development and deployment of new weapons.[36] For these activists, stockpile stewardship represents another iteration of the familiar story line in which the national security state only agrees to arms control treaties that pacify public opinion without impeding the development of new weapons.

And what of the scientists? Most weapons scientists tend to see the state as, in part at least, a labyrinthine bargaining arena, and they assume that, whatever its technical rationale, the stockpile stewardship program was the price their leaders exacted for surrendering testing in the complex bartering process of Washington politics. In terms of their scientific practice most, but not all, weapons scientists have over their careers been socialized into a craft science[37] that has increasingly emphasized a conservative incrementalism in approaches to nuclear weapons design and that has traditionally insisted that all design changes except the most minor be proof-tested underground. As I have argued in *Nuclear Rites* and in chapter 8 of this book, nuclear tests were traditionally the ultimate means of producing knowledge and power among U.S. nuclear weapons scientists. It is not surprising, then, that some of these scientists would insist that there is absolutely no substitute for testing while the majority would, on the whole, profess to be skeptical about departing too far from established and well-tested designs, even with the benefit of the new simulation technologies.

Because the overwhelming majority of nuclear weapons scientists say that it would be scientifically irresponsible to deploy new weapons designs in the absence of nuclear testing, it would seem logical to rule against the activists and defer to the judgment of those who are, presumably, best placed to understand the intricacies of the science. I want to suggest, however, that this would be premature since these scientists' criteria for the reliability of weapons designs are based on experimental conventions that can shift over time. Current experimental conventions were developed over the course of fifty years within institutions that naturalized nuclear tests as the definitive and decisive experiments, but, as Peter Galison and Stefan Helmreich have shown in their recent writings on modeling of neutron scattering and artificial life, respectively, the increasing turn toward computer simulations promises to redefine, at least partially, what counts as an experiment in science.[38] Indeed, a cursory glance at the technical history of nuclear weapons development itself shows that experimental conventions have not remained static. In his work on the early history of Los Alamos, Galison has shown that development of the hydrogen bomb was only possible after the introduction of the Monte Carlo method, which used computer-generated sequences of pseudorandom numbers to model neutron scattering.[39] Assuming that there was a symmetry between the stochastic processes of nature and those in the computer models, and in the absence of any way to measure actual fusion processes, Los Alamos scientists, despite the skepticism of some, treated the resulting "measurements" as if they were experimental data that should guide weapons designers. Referring to the Monte Carlo runs as "experiments" in "artificial reality," Galison comments:

> The Monte Carlo ushered physics into a place dislocated from the traditional sociointellectual poles of experiment and theory. Monte Carlos formed a tertium quid, a simulated reality that borrowed from both experimental and theoretical domains, fused these borrowings together, and used the resulting amalgam to stake out a netherland at once nowhere and everywhere on the methodological map.[40]

Another example of a shift in favor of the simulated came in 1975 when the Threshold Test Ban Treaty came into force. This treaty forbade nuclear tests larger than 150 kilotons, even though many weapons in the U.S. arsenal were much larger than that. Henceforth, weapons scientists doctored devices exploded in nuclear tests to keep the yield below 150 kilotons and extrapolated the yield of the weapons actually deployed to the stockpile on the basis of theoretical models.

In the future, then, it is not impossible to imagine weapons designers, over a period of decades, making progressively greater modifications to existing designs. Indeed, this is precisely what older designers will sometimes say they fear. Some of these designers have occasionally told me that their younger colleagues put too much faith in computer models and that this makes them nervous. As one designer said to me: "A young designer with a code is like a drunk driver. Just as the driver thinks he's driving better the more he has to drink, so a reckless designer may think they're doing better the more they're relying on the code."

If simulations do become increasingly accepted as a basis for weapons modification, however, it will not be the scheduled unfolding of a carefully designed plan superintended by the directors of the weapons labs as the activists expect; it will be the result of a contingent and contested process that will involve painful struggles, dislocations, and realignments between different groupings of weapons scientists—fission specialists and fusion specialists, computational physicists and laser physicists, scientists and engineers—struggling to preserve their craft in the face of new theories and new tools.

Emergent Securityscapes

By way of conclusion, let me return to the broader political relevance of this somewhat arcane scientific debate. What does it tell us about the future role of nuclear weapons, and of nuclear weapons laboratories, in the emergent order of a global society still reconfiguring its alliances, its norms, its hierarchies, and its structures of violence after the sudden collapse of the cold war? Let me sketch three conceivable scenarios for the future so as to indicate the underlying structure of possibility and, perhaps, the space still open for political action.

The first scenario has been suggested by Hisham Zerriffi and Arjun Makhijani in a report deeply critical of the stockpile stewardship program.[41] It is what I would like to call the "breakout" scenario. Zerriffi and Makhijani fear that the stockpile stewardship program will enable the weapons labs to preserve intact their vast social and technical infrastructure for weapons design and to do considerable preliminary work on new weapons designs that, like fertilized eggs awaiting implantation, would be ready for birthing if the test ban treaty collapsed or if the United States decided, for whatever reason, to withdraw from the treaty. If the United States resumed testing, then the new simulation technologies, already built, would be used not to supplant testing but to supplement it and to suggest shortcuts in the design of new weapons. The nuclear weapons Leviathan might emerge stronger than ever from the hiatus in testing.

A second scenario is that of a "virtual arms race." In this scenario, the nuclear powers, each nervous of falling behind the others, could begin to compete in stockpiling supercomputer facilities, lasers, pulsed power experiments, and hydrodynamic tests in an effort to signal national will and credibility. The old race to accumulate ever more capable and versatile nuclear weapons would then be sublimated into a new race to accumulate better and better simulation technologies, either for their own sake or in case the test ban treaty collapsed.

In a sense, this would be a second-order sublimation, since the arms race of the cold war period was itself, at least partly, a contest that sublimated and substituted for the actual clash of armies, displacing this clash into the simulated space known as deterrence, where war was endlessly gamed and rehearsed but never finally waged. It is this that has led Jacques Derrida to refer to nuclear war as "fabulously textual"[42] and Jean Baudrillard to declare in *Simulations*: "War has become a celibate machine. . . . Just as wealth is no longer measured by the ostentation of wealth but by the secret circulation of speculative capital, so war is not measured by being waged but by its speculative unfolding in an abstract, electronic, and informational space, the same space in which capital moves" (36, 56).

I profoundly disagree with Baudrillard's totalizing insistence that nuclear deterrence *"excludes the real atomic clash*—excludes it beforehand like the eventuality of the real in a system of signs" (59–60; emphasis in the original). His understatement of the gross physical menace of nuclear weapons backhandedly legitimates the system of deterrence he claims to oppose. Nevertheless, there is an important evolutionary insight in his writings on war, namely, that, in an international system partly organized around what Timothy Luke calls "postwarring," the use value of nuclear weapons has been superseded by their exchange value such that "strategic nuclear forces can be seen as elements of a code, texts enscribed with meanings. . . . Nuclear weapons have not been, and are not, called upon for use as weapons. Instead, they are made operational to be continually exchanged . . . in 'shows of force,' 'displays of capability,' 'proofs of credibility,' or 'displays of determination.'"[43]

Of course, "postwarring" is a luxury not everyone can afford.[44] Against Baudrillard's tendency to speak of the hyperreal as a blanket condition that has fallen uniformly upon the world, I would counterpose the insight of James Der Derian and Arthur Kroker that virtual spaces are spaces of power not accessible to all alike. Just as within nations, some spaces on the side of the road (to use Kathleen Stewart's evocative phrase) are left behind by the information superhighway, so within the international system, some nations cannot afford the massive simulacra of death the nuclear powers have used to sublimate their contests for precedence.[45] And now, just at the moment when rogue states threaten to upset the stratification of the international system by acquiring nuclear weapons (the ultimate symbols of upward mobility in global society), a new zone of stratification has been added. Whether one sees stockpile stewardship as a way to develop new nuclear weapons or just as a way to keep the old ones in good order, this new development in the international nuclear potlatch opens a space where India, Pakistan, Iraq, Iran, and North Korea cannot easily follow. A privileged few will have expensively maintained, highly simulated advanced nuclear weapons supported by a massive infrastructure of weapons scientists kept in top shape by their nuclear exercise machines, while the rest will—unless willing to risk the opprobrium of their betters by engaging in the vulgar practice of nuclear testing—be left to cobble together crude devices too large and clumsy to fit on missiles.

There is a third scenario for the future, which I will call "virtual disarmament." This scenario has been mapped out in a provocative article by the sociologists of science Donald MacKenzie and Graham Spinardi. Drawing a distinction between explicit knowledge, which can be codified in written texts, and tacit knowledge, which can only be learned by doing, usually in the context of apprenticeship, MacKenzie and Spinardi argue that the successful design and production of properly functioning nuclear weapons depends critically on skills that can only be learned in apprenticeship, especially in the context of nuclear testing.[46] They say further:

> Suppose . . . that specific, local, tacit knowledge was vital to [nuclear weapons] design and production. Then there would be a sense in which relevant knowledge could be unlearned and in which these weapons COULD be uninvented. If there were a sufficiently long hiatus in their design and production (say a couple of generations), then that tacit knowledge might indeed vanish. . . . An accidental uninvention, in which current tacit knowledge is lost, seems quite plausible. (217)

MacKenzie and Spinardi are aware that it is now easy to design crude nuclear weapons like the one dropped on Hiroshima and be confident of their reliability without testing them. They are intrigued, however, by a hypothetical situation decades in the future where the ability to design advanced nuclear weapons, especially hydrogen bombs, would be lost. Perhaps the budgets of the weapons labs would have dwindled as the weapons they superintended faded further into the background of international affairs. And there might be no one alive who had designed a weapon and seen it tested in Nevada; all the stockpiled weapons would literally be simulacra— copies of copies for which no originals exist—their use value increasingly uncertain. The weapons would still exist but their capability would be increasingly virtual. A sort of disarmament would have taken place.

Conclusion

I am not attempting to predict the future but to make the point that anthropology has a special contribution to make to the kinds of policy debates on nuclear proliferation and the international system analyzed here, and that their discussion by anthropologists will enrich anthropology. The past decade in anthropology has seen the emergence of both the anthropology of science and the anthropology of the global system as energetic new fields of inquiry. In this chapter, located at the confluence of these two fields, I seek to show new kinds of questions that anthropologists might now investigate.

If there is a danger in the current rash of interest in globalization, it is that anthropologists will enact their new interest in studying global society in a way that subtly reinforces old disciplinary divisions of labor in the academy while producing a skewed vision of global society. Although the current global system is, as Arjun Appadurai has pointed out in *Modernity at Large,* characterized by flows of migrants, capital, and culture that undermine the integrity of the nation-state and produce intriguing new forms of global hybridity, there are also processes at work that are increasing the power and reach of state apparatuses, expanding the military firepower of national governments, and deepening the psychic hold of nationalist ideologies. The emergent neoliberal world order will surely be characterized not only by unprecedented mobility of capital, culture, and people, but also by new arms races, wars, and militaristic ideologies. By coining the new term (adapted from Appadurai's own neologistic vocabulary on globalization) *securityscape,* I have explored this second set of processes and joined those who caution against prematurely hailing the supposed withering away of the state in the era of globalization. For too long, anthropologists have conceded the study of security to political scientists, with unfortunate consequences for both anthropology and discussions of security. This disciplinary division of labor emerged in the academy after World War II and was reinforced by the painful fiasco of anthropology's secret involvement in Vietnam—a fiasco that, once revealed, produced an allergic response to security issues in many anthropologists. But armies, weapons, wars, and military ideologies are also important facets of the new global system taking shape as Fordism and the cold war security structure collapse and are remade by scientists, military officers, national bureaucrats, and NGOs. Until anthropologists make the evolution of post–cold war military institutions and ideologies integral to their narratives of globalization, they are not getting the whole story.

(2001)

Part V

Life around the Barbed Wire Fence

10

The Death of the Authors of Death: Prestige and Creativity among Nuclear Weapons Scientists

> We must locate the space left empty by the author's dis-
> appearance, follow the distribution of gaps and breaches,
> and watch for the openings that this disappearance uncovers.
> —Michel Foucault, "What Is an Author?"

In a 1996 talk at MIT the chemist and "science in fiction" novelist Carl Djerassi pointed out that, whereas novelists often eschew personal fame by writing under pseudonyms, it is usually vitally important to scientists to win recognition for their work under their own names.[1] In the words of the narrator of Djerassi's novel *The Bourbaki Gambit*:

> There is one character trait . . . which is an intrinsic part of a scientist's culture, and which the public image doesn't often include: his extreme egocentricity, expressed chiefly in his overmastering desire for recognition by his peers. No other recognition matters. And that recognition comes in only one way. It doesn't really matter who you are or whom you know. You may not even know those other scientists personally, but *they* know *you*—through your publications. (18–19)

Djerassi was intrigued by a group of distinguished French mathematicians who, playing the exception to the rule, refused science's cult of individual fame by publishing, starting in 1934, under the collective nom de plume Nicolas Bourbaki. (Their aim was, in part, to demonstrate that the truth status of knowledge was independent of the authority of its authors—though, ironically, as "Bourbaki" acquired his own reputation as a mathematician, the experiment fell victim to its own success.) The identities of the mathematicians who made up Bourbaki were kept secret and, in Djerassi's narrator's words, "now people refer to *him,* not *them*" (18). In Djerassi's novel the "Bourbaki gambit"—the melding of individual scientists into a collective disguised as a pseudonymous individual—is repeated by an international group of contemporary scientists at the age of retirement who, in Djerassi's fictional narrative, develop the revolutionary biotechnological technique of polymerase chain reaction (PCR). At the moment of success the group fractures as individuals seek to step forward and claim their success.

I want to suggest here that the conditions of bureaucratic secrecy under which American nuclear weapons research has been conducted have created what we might refer to as the "Bourbakification" of science. This phenomenon is by no means unique to the world of nuclear weapons science: indeed, corporate secrecy in, for example, the biotech industry and the practice, common to Big Science and engineering projects, of assembling large teams to generate new knowledge and develop new technologies is making the discernment of individual contributions to knowledge progressively more difficult in a wide range of science and engineering contexts. However, the world of nuclear weapons science provides a particularly stark instance of a Bourbakified mode of scientific production that is becoming more widely dispersed. In the process of Bourbakification, the distinctive contributions of individual scientists have been repressed or gathered together under the sign of sacralized individuals standing for groups. Unlike the original Bourbaki experiment, this has not been a ruse entered into voluntarily, nor does it derive from an idealistic impulse to show that knowledge can survive independently of the public reputation of its originators. It has been enforced by the conjoint workings of military secrecy and Big Science,[2] both working together to produce the phenomenological death of the scientific author in a way that lends weight to Foucault's cryptic observation in "What Is an Author?" that creative "work, which once had the duty of providing immortality, now possesses the right to kill, to be its author's murderer" (142).

Early and crude examples of Bourbakification in the first heroic decade of American nuclear weapons science are well known. In 1945, for example, after the revelation of the atomic bomb, it was Robert Oppenheimer, the director of the Los Alamos Laboratory and *Life*'s Man of the Year, who received the credit for the bomb—even though the possibility of building such a bomb was first seen by Leo Szilard and the implosion mechanism, crucial in making the plutonium bomb work, was conceived by Seth Neddermeyer (a scientist whose name is hardly well known today), possibly in response to an earlier variant of the idea articulated in Robert Serber's lectures, and was then refined and reshaped with the input of numerous other Manhattan Project scientists, including John von Neumann and George Kistiakowsky, over a period of two years.[3]

Seven years later, after the first hydrogen bomb was tested, the media erroneously gave the credit to Edward Teller's new laboratory at Livermore, and scientists at Los Alamos, furious to find their entire institution stripped of credit for its work, were prevented by national security regulations from correcting the error.[4]

Edward Teller himself has been known for years as "the father of the H-bomb," even though the key design breakthrough is now widely credited to Stanislav Ulam,[5] and Teller largely withdrew from the project as it entered the engineering phase. Disquiet among former colleagues at Teller's popular identification as *the* inventor of the hydrogen bomb eventually impelled him, in 1955, to publish his *Science* article, "The Work of Many People," in which he described the H-bomb as "the work of many excellent people who had to give their best abilities for years and who were all essential for the final outcome." He protested that "the story that is often presented to the public is quite different. One hears of a brilliant idea and only too often the name of a single individual is mentioned" (267). That individual was, of course, Teller himself and, although in his article he named the other people who were vital to the project, he was not permitted by security regulations to say what any of them actually did. Thus the article, paradoxically, reinforces the appearance of Teller's singularity since, as lone author, he is arbiter and custodian of others' unknown contributions, which he authorizes.

We see in these examples how secrecy and a mode of production based on teamwork, both characteristic of nuclear weapons research, make it difficult to certify the distinctive contributions of individuals. This murkiness can create a situation in which credit tends to gravitate toward those, such as Teller and Oppenheimer, who already have established scientific reputations or bureaucratic positions of authority. Thus, in large hierarchical research institutions like nuclear weapons laboratories, intellectual value, or capital, tends to behave in the same way as material value in large capitalist institutions: it is extracted from those on the bottom, who create it through labor, accruing as wealth to those on the top, so that the labor of a Neddermeyer is transmuted into the reputation of an Oppenheimer.

Nuclear Salvage History

The past ten years have seen accelerating attempts to undo the Bourbakification of the inventors of the atomic and hydrogen bombs and to bestow

secure identities and lines of credit on those scientists who, as their generation dies, stand between anonymity and immortality. I call this "nuclear
salvage history." Nuclear salvage history seeks to reverse the phenomenological death of the scientific authors of the first decade of the nuclear era
just at the moment when their physical bodies are expiring. This project
has been aided by the progressive declassification of basic weapons design
information and by the increasingly urgent desire of the pioneers of nuclear
weapons science, now in their twilight years, to record their labors.

The leading practitioner of nuclear salvage history is the indefatigable
Richard Rhodes, whose books *The Making of the Atomic Bomb* and *Dark
Sun: The Making of the Hydrogen Bomb* have cataloged, in encyclopedic
fashion, the personalities and contributions of the principal scientists in
the first decade of nuclear weapons science. Rhodes's history is resolutely
middlebrow in the sense that it is the story, vividly told, of great men, each
a miniature portrait in his own right, acting on the world to change history.[6]
Rhodes's books about weapons scientists are epics of invention in which he
is deeply concerned with the documentation and demarcation of individual
originality and creativity. Martha Woodmansee points out in "On the Author Effect," that the modern conception of authorship is "a by-product of
the Romantic notion that significant writers break altogether with tradition
to create something utterly new, unique—in a word, 'original.'" (16). This
essentially Romantic trope of originality as an individual gift that strikes
in world-changing flashes of inspiration is common in middlebrow science
writing, where it resonates with high school textbook accounts of Archime-
des' and Newton's discoveries, and it figures prominently in Rhodes's accounts. Some of the most compelling passages in his books describe the
exact moment of creative inspiration, which he hunts down with extraordinary determination. Take the cinematically vivid opening paragraph of
The Making of the Atomic Bomb, in which he describes Szilard's sudden
realization that it might be possible to construct an atomic bomb powered
by a nuclear chain reaction:

> In London, where Southampton Row passes Russell Square, across from
> the British Museum in Bloomsbury, Leo Szilard waited irritably one gray
> Depression morning for the stoplight to change. A trace of rain had fallen
> during the night; Tuesday, September 12, 1933, dawned cool, humid and
> dull. Drizzling rain would begin again in early afternoon. When Szilard
> told the story later he never mentioned his destination that morning. He
> may have had none; he often walked to think. In any case another desti-
> nation intervened. The stoplight changed to green. Szilard stepped off the
> curb. As he crossed the street time cracked open before him and he saw

a way to the future, death unto the world and all our woe, the shape of things to come. (13)[7]

The same trope recurs in *Dark Sun: The Making of the Hydrogen Bomb*, where Rhodes records Françoise Ulam's memory of her husband's breakthrough in the design of the hydrogen bomb with the same dramatic emphasis on one man's destiny to change history:

> Engraved on my memory is the day when I found him at noon staring intensely out of a window in our living room with a very strange expression on his face. Peering unseeing into the garden, he said, "I found a way to make it work." "What work?" I asked. "The Super," he replied. "It is a totally different scheme and it will change the course of history." (463)[8]

Michel Foucault has observed in "What Is an Author?" that the modern individualist idea of the author has a "classificatory function," since the author's "name permits one to group together a certain number of texts, define them, differentiate them from and contrast them with others" (147). We see this classificatory function clearly in Rhodes's books, as well as other accounts of the Manhattan Project,[9] which seek to demarcate the exact contribution made by each of the leading weapons scientists and to rank them. (Rhodes spends several pages, for example, discussing whether Ulam or Teller should get more credit for the hydrogen bomb.) In the process of this enormous accounting operation, Rhodes salvages the contributions, formerly known to few, of less well known scientists working on the Manhattan Project, saving them from their own premature authorial deaths, and he redefines the contributions of the manager-scientists, of whom Oppenheimer is the obvious exemplar. Oppenheimer's brilliance is displaced in Rhodes's account from scientific invention to recruitment, synthesis, and leadership. For example, Oppenheimer may not have thought of implosion, but he had, in Hans Bethe's words, "created the greatest school of theoretical physics the United States has ever known,"[10] where many of those who made the bomb work were trained. But above all, Oppenheimer—described by historian Lillian Hoddeson in "Mission Change" as "empowered to function like a general in moving his scientific troops around" (266)—was a man who managed and led. Rhodes summarizes his contribution to the Manhattan Project thus:

> Robert Oppenheimer oversaw all this activity with self-evident competence and an outward composure that almost everyone came to depend upon. "Oppenheimer was probably the best lab director I have ever seen," Teller repeats, "because of the great mobility of his mind, because of his successful effort to know about practically everything important invented

in the laboratory, and also because of his unusual psychological insight into other people which, in the company of physicists was very much the exception." "He knew and understood everything that went on in the laboratory," Bethe concurs, "whether it was chemistry or theoretical physics or machine shop. He could keep it all in his head and coordinate it. It was clear also at Los Alamos that he was intellectually superior to us."[11]

This evocation of the role of the manager in the big physics laboratories that emerged in midcentury is, incidentally, echoed in Yakov Zel'dovich's comment about Oppenheimer's Soviet counterpart, Yuli Khariton, who oversaw the construction of his country's first atomic bomb. Zel'dovich told the young Andrei Sakharov, "There are secrets everywhere, and the less you know that doesn't concern you, the better off you'll be. Khariton has taken on the burden of knowing it all."[12]

The Soviet bomb project has produced its own nuclear salvage history, the finest example of which is David Holloway's *Stalin and the Bomb*. Holloway's writing is less novelistic in style than Rhodes's, and it is more deeply informed by an academic grasp of the connections between the unfolding of nuclear science and geopolitical history. Still, like Rhodes, taking an approach that emphasizes the "classificatory function" of authorship, Holloway seeks to discern the contributions made by specific individuals, to rank and compare them, and to mark what was original—though this turns out to be a troubling category.

In producing this history, Holloway faced two special problems. The first was the intense secretiveness of the Soviet state, which had rendered its own nuclear scientists even more anonymous and mysterious, more Bourbakified, than their counterparts in the United States. Thus, if Rhodes's writing derives much of its power from his ability to show us vivid individual characters and richly textured narratives of scientific work behind Los Alamos's veil of secrecy—to salvage the details of authorship from the well of anonymity—Holloway's accomplishment in salvaging the details of the Russian nuclear story in a much more closed society must be judged still more extraordinary.[13]

Holloway's second difficulty was, in writing his own version of the nuclear epic, to establish the authority of scientists condemned to a repetition. The Soviet scientists were, after all, not only doing something that had already been done; they were, in the case of the atomic bomb at least, doing it with the aid of design information purloined from Los Alamos by the spies Klaus Fuchs and Ted Hall, among others.[14] As Martha Woodmansee argues in "On the Author Effect," while copying and embellishing the work of others used to be seen as a form of authorship in its own right in medieval Europe, in the context of contemporary copyright law and current ideologies of authorial individualism, copying is now seen as a highly degraded form of creativity. This is especially so in the world of science. Thus, the enterprise of establishing scientific authority in Holloway's nuclear salvage history is enacted in circumstances that call for different, at times more defensive, narrative strategies than Rhodes's. In Holloway's account it is also clear that, given the fusion of technoscientific achievement and nation-building in Soviet nationalist ideology, from nuclear weapons to *Sputnik,* what is at stake in establishing the authorship of these weapons is not only the reputation of individual scientists but also the reputation of the nation these scientists represent.

As far as the atomic bomb is concerned, Holloway's strategy is to remind us that Khariton could not be sure the purloined information was accurate, so that "Soviet scientists and engineers had to do all the same calculations and experiments" as their American counterparts (199). Holloway then details who did what here. In his narrative, in terms of creativity, the difference between going first (as the Americans did) and going second (as the Soviets did) is minimized and, given the acutely scarce resources of the postwar Soviet state, the obstacles surmounted by the Soviet nuclear weapons scientists were in many respects more formidable than those faced by their American counterparts. As regards the hydrogen bomb, Holloway shows that the information Fuchs gave the Soviets about design efforts in the United States would have misled them since Los Alamos at this time was, under Teller's guidance, pursuing a design strategy that turned out to be a blind alley. Holloway demonstrates that Sakharov and Zel'dovich followed their own design path, in many ways making quicker progress than their American counterparts and that, although the Americans were slightly ahead of the Soviets in creating a full-blown thermonuclear explosion, the Soviets were ahead in learning to use lithium deuteride—the key in making a deliverable bomb rather than an enormously unwieldy thermonuclear firecracker.[15]

The stakes attached to originality (even if only the originality of a repetition) here are high, for individuals and nations. When Daniel Hirsh and William Mathews published an article in 1990 in a fairly obscure American journal alleging that the Soviets had used fallout from the first American H-bomb test in 1952 to deduce the design breakthrough made by Teller and Ulam, Holloway explains that

> it caused some consternation among scientists who had taken part in the Soviet project. Khariton asked that a search be done of the files of those scientists who had been engaged in the detection and analysis of foreign

nuclear tests. Nothing was found in those files to indicate that that useful information had been obtained from analysis of the Mike test. This was not because of self-denial. Sakharov and Viktor Davidenko collected cardboard boxes of new snow several days after the Mike test in the hope of analyzing the radioactive isotopes it contained for clues about the nature of the Mike test. One of the chemists at Arzamas-16 unfortunately poured the concentrate down the drain by mistake, before it could be analyzed. (312)

Thus did the carelessness of a chemist save the honor of a nation.

The nuclear salvage history of Holloway and others has given names to the scientists behind the Soviet bomb, bestowed epic status on their labors, and enabled them to take their place as individuals in the pantheon of science. In other words, it has saved them from Bourbakification in a way that is nicely evoked by the English physicist Stephen Hawking's quip when he finally met Zel'dovich: "I'm surprised to see that you are one man, and not like Bourbaki."[16]

It is worth noting here that the fate of these American and Russian nuclear weapons scientists has, in their eventual emergence into the pantheon of history, been different from that of, for example, the engineers responsible for ICBMs, the Apollo Program, or the Boeing 747. Anonymity has been the norm for those working on large-scale military-industrial engineering projects, even those in leadership positions, in a way that has not been the case in large team-based physics projects. In receiving credit for their work as scientific authors, nuclear weapons physicists have finally been treated in accordance with the conventions of the academic science community from which the rules of secrecy had partly severed them.[17]

Interlude

Recent developments in literary theory have destabilized traditional notions of the author. Almost thirty years ago Roland Barthes declared "the death of the author," saying that "the author is never more than the instance writing, just as *I* is nothing more than the instance saying *I*" (155; emphasis in the original). Retheorizing the author not as a centered, willful point of origination for the text but as a medium in some ways created by the text itself, Barthes exploded the Romantic individualist trope of authorship ("the modern scriptor is born simultaneously with the text itself" [156]); turned the author's work into a plural text ("we know that a text is not a line of words releasing a single 'theological' meaning [the 'message' of the author-God] but a multi-dimensional space in which a variety of writing, none of them original, blend and clash" [156]); and, as a corollary, promoted reading to a form of authorship in its own right ("the birth of the reader must be at the cost of the death of the author" [157]).

In the same year Michel Foucault's article "What Is an Author?" deconstructed the author in a more historical mode. While echoing Barthes's claim that the unity and coherence of texts is illusory, Foucault was also interested in the historical origins of the author entity itself. He argued that "the coming into being of the notion of 'author' constitutes the privileged moment of *individualization* in the history of ideas, knowledge, literature, philosophy and the sciences" (141; emphasis in the original). More recently, Martha Woodmansee and Peter Jaszi, building on Foucault's archaeology of the author, have argued that, in reality, creativity is as often collaborative as individualized and that modern notions of authorship tend to misrecognize "a collaborative process as a solitary, originary one."[18] Pointing to collaborative forms of writing and to avowedly derivative forms of artistic creativity of the kind that Henry Jenkins refers to as "textual poaching," Woodmansee and Jaszi protest that "most writing today—in business, government, industry, the law, the sciences—is collaborative, yet it is still being taught as if it were a solitary, originary activity" (9).

The Death of the Authors of Death

The Livermore Laboratory, which I have been studying as an anthropologist since 1987, was founded in 1952 in order to intensify work on atomic and hydrogen bombs as the cold war escalated. Most parts of the laboratory are off limits to the public, and access to spaces and to information for its eight thousand employees (almost three thousand of them scientists and engineers with Ph.D.'s) is regulated by an elaborate system of rules and taboos. The laboratory is divided into zones of greater or lesser exclusion related to the system for classifying information and people. A few areas on the perimeter of the laboratory are "white areas" accessible to the public. (These areas include two cafeterias, the Public Affairs Office, and the Visitors' Center.) Large parts of the laboratory are "red areas," which are off limits to the public, although only open research is done there. These red areas serve as a buffer zone around the "green areas" where secret research is done. The green areas constituted roughly half of the laboratory during the 1980s, but they have shrunk a little after the end of the cold war. Only those with green badges (bestowed at the end of a lengthy investigation by the federal government) can enter these areas unescorted. They are protected not only by armed guards but also by mechanical barriers such as automated doors that will only open for those with appropriate badges. (As an extra precaution, the badges are magnetically encoded with the weight of their owner, and the access doors to green areas are set within booths that weigh the person seeking entry.) Within the green areas, there are also special exclusion areas, set apart by barbed wire fences and guard booths, accessible only to a few. The plutonium facility, for example, is in an exclusion area, as is the facility where intelligence reports are handled within vaultlike rooms that have built-in countersurveillance features such as copper mesh in the walls, to disrupt attempts to intercept electronic activities inside. The laboratory, then, is a grid of taboo spaces and knowledges segregated not only from the outside world but, to some degree, from each other as well. Red areas, for example, although they are located inside the laboratory's perimeter fence are, in terms of informational flow, functionally a part of the outside world that is separated by informational shielding from the laboratory's green areas—some of which are, in turn, shielded from others.[19]

Unlike academic scientists, Livermore scientists in the green areas are not under pressure to publish in order to keep their jobs. The system of a multiyear probationary period followed by either ejection or permanent tenure that organizes scientific careers in the academy does not apply at the Livermore Laboratory. Here scientists have had near-guaranteed job security as long as they worked conscientiously and kept their security clearances in order, and the laboratory's work ethic, especially in comparison with that of research universities, emphasized teamwork over individual distinction.[20]

Up to the end of the cold war at least, nuclear weapons science was principally organized around the design and production of prototype devices for nuclear tests at the Nevada Nuclear Test Site and around the measurement of these tests. (Measurement was a challenge, since the devices, buried underground with the measuring instruments, destroyed the measuring equipment a few nanoseconds after the commencement of the experiment.) This design and production work was undertaken by enormous multidisciplinary teams of physicists, engineers, chemists, and technicians, with small teams of physicists playing the lead design role and overseeing the tests. The laboratory had various divisions, each of which was responsible for a different part of the nuclear weapons design and testing program. The physicists of B Division, for example, designed the atomic bombs (known as "primaries") that use processes of nuclear fission to produce an atomic explosion. These components serve as triggers for a thermonuclear explosion in a hydrogen bomb. The physicists of A Division designed the part of a nuclear device (known as the "secondary") that, harnessing energy from the primary, uses processes of nuclear fusion to generate a thermonuclear explosion. Within each of these divisions, some physicists primarily focused on the generation of the enormous supercomputer codes that simulated the behavior of different weapons designs, while others took the lead role in designing and troubleshooting devices for testing. Meanwhile, engineers in the laboratory's W Division were responsible for developing prototype devices, in consultation with the physicists of A and B Divisions, whereas L Division took charge of preparing the enormously complex and subtle diagnostic equipment that measured weapons performance in nuclear tests. Scientists from all of these divisions were assembled through the laboratory's matrix system into large multidisciplinary teams that prepared particular nuclear tests.[21]

Within these teams, and indeed within the laboratory as a whole, the physicists tended to be the elite.[22] The work of these physicists involved calculating the expected performance of the device, often by refining the enormous supercomputer codes used to model nuclear explosions; checking predictions against data from previous tests and, in the process, flagging anomalies that might be resolved by further research; making serial presentations to design review committees; consulting with colleagues whose expertise might improve the experiment; consulting with representatives of the Department of Energy and the armed forces about military requirements; and overseeing the machining of parts and the final assembly of the device and the diagnostic equipment. One weapons scientist, Peter,[23] mentioned in an e-mail message to me that "while the design activity is genuinely a group effort, neither the contribution to the effort nor the acknowledged credit for the result is evenly distributed. One person may be thought of as the principal architect, while others are given credit for significant components." In particular, the lead designer would get special credit. In the localized face-to-face community of weapons designers, this credit would be established and circulated as much by word of mouth—in gossip and in formal presentations—as through the written documentation of individual contributions and achievements, though there were formal shot reports and supervisors did write evaluations of their subordinates' job performance. The final product of the weapons scientists' labor was as much the test itself as any written distillation of it. It was the test that ultimately clarified the validity of the designers' theories and design approaches, and if we ask what it is that nuclear weapons designers were authoring all those years, we might have to say that it was not ultimately written texts so much as devices and "events"—the weapons scientists' term for nuclear tests.

The world of nuclear weapons science behind the fence is, though not completely informationally impervious to the outside world, fundamentally autarkic. (One weapons designer told me that her first few years at the laboratory felt like the equivalent of a second physics Ph.D. in fields not taught at the university.) Thus, although it is sometimes possible to transform information produced in the laboratory's weapons programs into knowledge that can be traded on the open market outside the laboratory, often this is not the case. Peter described one end of the spectrum in his e-mail message:

> As you know, the people involved in weapons work range from someone like Forest Rogers[24] (who calculates wonderful opacities, but would have little practical understanding of a W or B anything [finished nuclear weapons]), to Dan Patterson (who lives and breathes weapons). People at Forest's end of the spectrum can publish the bulk of their work in regular scientific journals. As an example, the first publications of OPAL opacities (OPAL is the code that calculates the opacity) resulted in a paper that for some years was the most cited in astrophysics (fortunately uranium is not important in calculating astrophysical mixtures).

At the other extreme are scientists the very titles of whose publications are secret, so that their résumés are, to the outside world, surrealistically blank after years of labor. One of these joked during a layoff scare, "If I made a résumé, there'd be nothing on it." Another physicist, reflecting on current fears of downsizing with some bitterness, characterized the government's attitude to its scientists as: "Thanks for defending the country. It's too bad you don't have a résumé, but we don't need you now." And, indeed, when scientists retire, they are not allowed even to keep copies of their own work if it is classified—a "death of the author" of a particularly poignant kind, as a lifetime's creative work is confiscated and swallowed up by the state at the exact moment it releases the person's aged body. This reminds us that weapons designers do not own the knowledge they produce—do not even have a guaranteed right of access to it after they have produced it—since it belongs to the state and the bureaucratic organizations that have commissioned it. In other words, weapons scientists, despite their Ph.D.'s, are wage laborers for the state—albeit well-paid ones—and, in the final analysis, they have little control over the knowledge they build.[25]

This knowledge is often well shielded from the knowledge markets of the outside world. "There was this complete disconnect with the outside world," one scientist told me. Peter's e-mail message says:

> Many [weapons designers] have given up outside publication entirely. Any good academic paper begins by offering a context to show why the particular detail being investigated is of interest. For example, the detailed processes of lithium production in a particular class of stars are pretty boring to most astronomers who are not nucleosynthesis aficionados. It becomes of interest when framed in the context of determining the original baryon

density of the universe. The context for much weapons work cannot be provided, and thank the gods that there is no suitable academic journal for the material that they investigate.

Another scientist recalled a colleague who told him he had not been to the library in years because the outside world knew nothing of him and therefore probably had nothing of interest to say to him in its publications. This can induce a twofold sense of erasure: first, one's achievements and hence one's professional person may be completely invisible to the larger scientific community (or even to one's colleagues within the laboratory: one scientist told me that one of his colleagues won the prestigious Lawrence Award for his work, but he was never able to find out what his colleague had done). Second, one's work may be literally written over by the scientific community outside the fence, which, in an inversion of the Soviet nuclear scientists' repetition that established itself as original, publishes original work that is unknowingly a replication. Peter's e-mail message describes the predicament of Livermore researchers in inertial confinement fusion—until recently a highly classified technology because of its applications to thermonuclear design: "I went to a conference in 1983 at which an academic researcher was discussing hohlraums as a means of smoothing the laser pulse and converting it to X rays. The lab people had to sit in silence as a colleague re-discovered territory that they had crossed years before."[26] Until much of the laboratory's work on inertial confinement fusion was declassified and published after the end of the cold war, it did not publicly exist.

But the predicament of nuclear weapons scientists as authors extends beyond their inability to trade their knowledge, and thus to establish their reputations, outside the laboratory. Even within the laboratory, establishing their reputations via written authorship can be complicated. As John Sutton explains in his own study of Livermore's organizational culture, "Communication within the laboratory is highly compartmentalized—that is, major projects are divided into a number of smaller research tasks, and communication outside the immediate group is only occasional."[27] The laboratory's internal knowledge economy mixes the characteristics of a common market with those of a premodern economy having many separate zones of barter, currency, and taxation. In some ways the national security state has created an intellectual economy analogous to the traditional nonmonetarized African economies described by the anthropologist Paul Bohannon, in which there were separate spheres of exchange that could not be integrated so that, for example, the beads of one family could be exchanged for the cloth but not the food of another family, since beads and food, circulating in different spheres, were untradeable and nonconvertible.[28] Thus, nuclear weapons knowledge was recorded not so much in standardized and refereed articles, as it would be in conventional academic settings, but rather in reports detailing the results of nuclear tests, new ways of calculating opacities, and so on. These reports, instead of being codified into a uniformly accessible grid of knowledge, were often stored eccentrically. Although a classified library was eventually established at Livermore, the internal compartmentalization of the laboratory's knowledge economy on the one hand and its self-contained informality on the other led to a situation in which, as much by accident as by design, knowledge circulated and was stored in less formal, centralized ways. One scientist described the situation this way:

> There was a mill for publishing the results of test shots, the latest methods for calculating opacities and so on. But there was no serious library for these reports in the early days. The reports would get thrown in a room, then someone would take one and hold on to it and that article would now be officially "misplaced." (That's why the GAO found that 10,000 secret documents were missing at Livermore. They're not exactly lost. They're not floating around outside the lab. They're in people's offices somewhere.) Old-timers would have safes full of documents inherited from someone else who retired ten years earlier. So, when they retired, you'd get those documents transferred to you, and that was a sort of library.

In other words, even within the laboratory, knowledge could be stored and exchanged in highly localized ways. The circulation of knowledge might be restricted by the semiforgotten nature of a written report, languishing in a colleague's safe, by networks of friendship, or by the assumption that weapons scientists, for national security reasons, should not have access to too much secret information unless it was directly relevant to their work.

This system has its own potential for abuse and manipulation. For example, it was widely believed in the 1980s by weapons designers in A and B Divisions, the two main weapons design divisions, that O Group, a breakaway group of designers ultimately protected by Edward Teller's patronage, manipulated secrecy regulations to protect its work from peer review. O Group was working on, among other things, a nuclear bomb–pumped X-ray laser that was highly controversial both technically and politically and was ultimately canceled.[29] Many weapons scientists complained that they suspected O Group's science was not rigorous, but they could not evaluate it because of special levels of classification placed on O Group's reports and briefings.

At its most extreme, the laboratory environment can unmake the very form of writing itself as a means of storing information, creating within one of the most high-tech environments in the world a partial return to the orality that preceded literacy and hence the very possibility of authorship in the modern writing-based conception of the term. Many scientists' reputations rest not on written reports[30] but rather on oral presentations they have given; on insightful questions in design review meetings, on an inventive idea they are locally remembered to have suggested and worked through, on a beautiful component they designed, which was instantly vaporized by the very test whose success it enabled, on huge craters their devices have inscribed upon the surface of the Nevada Desert, and on a socially recognized knack for judgment—a feeling for the devices and how they will behave. Because so much weapons design knowledge is practical knowledge that is unwritten or is thought to be hermeneutic rather than purely factual in nature, it is seen as residing in the designers themselves. (For this reason the laboratory prohibits groups of designers from traveling together on the same plane, in case it crashes.) One of the older designers, Seymour Sack, was described to me as "a walking repository of five hundred experiments [nuclear tests]."

This unusual emphasis on the oral circulation of knowledge and credit has endured for a number of reasons. First, there is comparatively little need to share knowledge with outsiders—even those at the rival weapons laboratory at Los Alamos. Second, the funding and promotion of individual scientists are not tied to their literary production since, at Livermore, "in contrast to an academic setting, money is awarded to a programme rather than an individual."[31] Third, the small face-to-face settings within which weapons work is largely done at the laboratory have diminished the need to formalize knowledge, creating a system in which knowledge tended to be transmitted as much through apprenticeship and oral instruction as through solitary reading. And, fourth, there are advantages to orality in a situation where every classified document that is created requires special measures to store and protect it and cannot be freely copied.

Still, such heavy reliance on oral knowledge entails liabilities, especially as the older scientists with the most extensive knowledge retire. As Peter put it:

> There are so few people genuinely involved in design, you efficiently communicated by other means [than formal writing]. . . . And the formal record suffers from this deficiency. While we have vaults containing the measured results of tests [as well as cutaways of nuclear devices showing their internal "anatomy"], the reason that certain choices were made is

not obvious from the materials stored there. This information still exists as oral histories, but the content of this reservoir diminishes as the experience base drops.

The end of the cold war, and the end of nuclear testing in particular, are bringing about changes in the knowledge economy at the laboratory. Managers at the laboratory and at the Department of Energy are worried that, as the most experienced designers retire en masse, they will take with them much of the knowledge, so inadequately recorded, that they have accumulated over the years and that, if the United States needs to again design advanced nuclear weapons at some date in the future, it may find that it has forgotten how to do so. This danger is particularly acute in the absence, now that the testing ranges of the world have fallen silent, of the nuclear tests that, more than written documentation, have enabled the reproduction and transmission of the weapons designers' science. This science has been passed on by means that, in some ways, have more in common with medieval craft apprenticeships than the computerized bibliocentric mazeways of most scientific disciplines at the end of the twentieth century.[32]

Thus the years since the end of the cold war have seen increasing attempts to codify and document what the weapons scientists know and to bring the means by which their information is recorded into greater conformity with the practices of the outside world. This is a form of nuclear salvage work, thought it differs from the efforts of Rhodes and Holloway in that it is more interested in the formal codification of knowledge than in the individualization of its authors. Thus, in recent years, Livermore scientists have invested time in cataloging reports and installing them in a central library, and in making written or videotaped records of the reasons for specific design decisions. Meanwhile the Los Alamos Laboratory has initiated a formal program of instruction in nuclear weapons science for new designers at the laboratory.

In a further attempt to formalize their knowledge, in 1989 the weapons laboratories also started a peer-reviewed classified journal, modeled on those published by university scientists. This journal has not, however, done very well, partly because it runs counter to the comfortable orality of knowledge circulation long established among the weapons scientists. One scientist said the journal was "of little consequence." Another described it as "a strung-out, thin sort of a thing, not conveniently available." He said: "I never tried to publish in the journal because I thought it was pointless. Three people would read it, and then it would disappear forever." He added (echoing the sentiments in the Djerassi quotation with which this chapter began) that the point of publishing is to have people who have not met you read about your work, but, since his research can only be discussed within a small face-to-face community that already knows about his work, publication would be a futile waste of time.

Conclusion

Michel Foucault and Roland Barthes have both argued that what we recognize as authorship is a social institution that emerged at a particular historical moment defined by social individualism, scientific rationalism, and, we might add, commodification. Over the past two centuries the ideology of authorship has tended to privilege written texts. These have been construed, through the lens of Romantic assumptions about individual creativity, as the products of unique individuals. Especially in the sciences, which Robert Merton long ago defined precisely in terms of their commitment to the universal circulation and accessibility of texts,[33] these texts have circulated freely and have been collected in libraries that facilitated widespread access to them.

The Livermore Laboratory has developed a mode of scientific production partly at odds with these conventional notions of authorship. Although some knowledge circulates in formally authored texts, much of it circulates orally or via informal publications such as memos and reports. This knowledge is often produced in collaborative teams, so that individual intellectual production is not so highly fetishized as it is in academic circles, where lead authorship and quantity of authorship is so vital a metric in tenure and promotion decisions. And, far from circulating freely, the written knowledge produced within the laboratory often cannot leave the laboratory (unless it is going to Los Alamos) and, even within the laboratory, may lie dormant in safes or travel eccentric routes of exchange marked by chains of friendship rather than universal availability.

What are we to make of this? Martha Woodmansee has argued in *The Author and the Market* that the conventional ideology of authorship, which fetishizes the individual and commodifies texts through copyright laws, is a prison house that inhibits collaborative creativity and forces us to misrecognize the degree to which all intellectual production is, no matter what the copyright lawyers say, inherently social and collaborative. In some ways scientists at Livermore might be said to have escaped this prison house, liberated by the barbed wire fence around them. The knowledge they have produced largely circulates outside the commodified sphere of exchange regulated and constrained by copyright laws and the academic promotions treadmill. And many Livermore scientists, in a critique of academic culture that is increasingly resonant for this author, find fault with the cult of individual assessment in the university and the emphasis in academia on stockpiling refereed articles as commodities, even if hardly anyone reads many of them. Many scientists told me they were attracted to Livermore precisely because it emphasized collaborative teamwork and did not force its scientists to publish or perish.

As one weapons designer put it:

> I find writing hard, and I don't like the publish or perish business. It's not that I don't like pressure or hard work; I just like to impose my own deadlines rather than jump through other people's hoops. The university is like the military the way it confines you and arranges everyone in hierarchies. . . . I have more freedom at the lab.[34]

On the other hand, this freedom from the grants and publications treadmill comes at a price, since weapons scientists may lose individual control over the products of their intellectual labor. These scientists may not be allowed to own copies of their own writings once they retire, may not be allowed to circulate their papers—even to name them—to friends, family, and colleagues beyond the confines of the lab. Indeed, they could be prosecuted for discussing their own ideas with the wrong people, since their ideas belong to the state. Hence they cannot use their writings to build a public persona as authors conventionally do. Nor, until recently, could they earn royalties if they designed something patentable, since the patent was awarded to the Department of Energy.

There are now signs, however, that the end of the cold war is forcing a revision of authorship practices at the Livermore Laboratory. Just at the moment when it has lost nuclear testing, traditionally a means of consolidating and transmitting weapons design knowledge, the laboratory is increasingly moving to formalize and codify its knowledge, cataloging and centralizing reports, trying to transcribe oral knowledge, and establishing a peer-reviewed journal for weapons designers. In some ways the laboratory seems to be trying to bring about the (re)birth of the author. It is ironic that weapons scientists should be moving toward the norms of formal, commodified authorship that have prevailed in the wider society just at the moment when, according to many commentators, those norms are increasingly being eroded by corporate practices of secrecy in the increasingly powerful centers of commercial science.[35]

But what are the limits of the (re)birth of the author at Livermore? Can it rupture the isolation of the laboratory and restore its weapons scientists to history, as Rhodes and Holloway have done for Stanislav Ulam, Seth Neddermeyer, Yakov Zel'dovich, and Lev Altschuler? It may be that, unlike the contributions of Neddermeyer and Ulam, the work of today's American weapons scientists lies beyond the retrieval techniques of nuclear salvage history. Working in teams on design tasks seen as routine rather than charismatic, their work shrouded in secrecy and only partly documented, these scientists, known as unique individuals by one another, may be condemned in the knowledge of the outside world to live outside middlebrow history, to always work in what Foucault calls "the anonymity of a murmur."

Foucault finished his interrogation of the author by saying:

> I think that, as our society changes . . . the author-function will disappear. . . . All discourses, whatever their status, form, value and whatever the treatment to which they will be subjected, would then develop in the anonymity of a murmur. We would no longer hear the questions that have been rehashed for so long: "Who really spoke? Is it really he and not someone else? With what authenticity and originality? And what part of his deepest self did he express in his discourse?" Instead . . . we would hear hardly anything but the stirring of an indifference: "What difference does it make who is speaking?" (160)

(2003)

11

How Not to Construct an Incinerator

In his book *The Risk Society*, Ulrich Beck writes that "in advanced modernity the social production of wealth is systematically accompanied by the social production of risks" (19). Commenting that the powerful industrial technologies of the late twentieth century inevitably produce health and environmental risks together with wealth, Beck argues that the political struggles of late modernity will increasingly be struggles not over the distribution of wealth (as in Marx's theory of the first wave of capitalism) but over the definition and distribution of risk.

In this chapter I analyze one such struggle. The struggle took place from 1988 to 1990 in the northern California city of Livermore. Located forty miles east of San Francisco, Livermore is home to the Lawrence Livermore National Laboratory (LLNL), where nuclear weapons have been designed since the laboratory was founded in 1952 by the physicists Ernest Lawrence and Edward Teller.[1] Since then, the lab's scientists have designed eighteen different nuclear weapons, most notably the neutron bomb and the warheads for the Polaris, Minuteman, and MX strategic missiles. In the late 1980s, when I arrived to study the laboratory and the surrounding community as an anthropologist, the lab employed eight thousand people and had an annual budget of $1 billion, of which roughly two-thirds was weapons related.[2]

Livermore had about fifty-six thousand inhabitants in the late 1980s.[3] Insulated from the San Francisco Bay Area by a greenbelt of undeveloped land, it had a small-town suburban feel. Although the antinuclear movement of the early 1980s had staged large protests at the laboratory, drawing thousands of people, most of the protesters came from the more radical urban communities of Berkeley and San Francisco.[4] The Livermore lab had traditionally enjoyed great deference in its own local community, where its scientists sat on the council and on church and school boards and were estimated to pump $450 million a year into the local economy.[5] City residents seemed at ease with the main business in town, putting a whirling atom on their city logo and patronizing stores with such names as Atom Appliance. There was a small antinuclear group in Livermore called Tri-Valley Citizens Against a Radioactive Environment (CAREs).[6] Originally founded in 1983 as a local affinity group in support of the protests at the lab, when I began my study in 1987 Tri-Valley CAREs was a marginal group with almost no budget and little local support. That was to change quite dramatically after the laboratory's plans to build a hazardous and radioactive waste incinerator became known in 1988. Tri-Valley CAREs' campaign against the incinerator enabled it to metamorphose from an informal affinity group into a more formal community-based organization.

The laboratory's incinerator plans set the stage for a David and Goliath struggle between Tri-Valley CAREs and the lab that dramatically divided the city of Livermore while boosting support for the citizens' group. Unlike the antinuclear movement that had protested the lab's work in previous years, very few supporters of Tri-Valley CAREs criticized the ethics or politics of the laboratory's central mission—nuclear weapons design—during this dispute; instead, many complained bitterly about the unfair risks they believed this mission imposed on them in the form of the proposed incinerator. Laboratory managers were blindsided by this outcry from their neighbors. In retrospect, this dispute served notice that Livermore was no longer the simple company town it had been since 1952. The following account dissects the anatomy of that moment of transition in Livermore, using a single fine-grained case study to cast light on suburban middle-class environmentalism as a social form and on the complex dynamics of environmental controversy in what Beck calls "the risk society." Because the account that follows takes no position on the final merits of the incinerator proposal, the chapter can be read, according to the taste of the individual reader, either as a sad description of a not-in-my-backyard movement's obstruction of a technically sound project or an analysis of the heroic mobilization of resistance against a powerful institution's dirty technology.

Theoretical Framework

This chapter analyzes the struggle between the Livermore laboratory and Tri-Valley CAREs by examining the successes and failures of the two sides' rhetorical and organizational strategies. It places these successes and failures in the context of background changes in U.S. public discourse on nuclear weapons and the environment and underlying shifts in the political economic structure of Livermore itself. My analytical strategy here draws heavily on the broadly Gramscian model Ernesto Laclau and Chantal Mouffe put forward in *Hegemony and Socialist Strategy* for understanding political struggles in late-capitalist societies. Taking note of the conservatism of the working class under Ronald Reagan and Margaret Thatcher and the emergence of new social movements (such as the peace and environmental movements) often supported by what David Parkin has called "middle class radicals," and the puzzle this poses for conventional political sociology, Laclau and Mouffe argue that we should attend less to predetermined positions we expect particular social classes and categories of people to adopt, focusing more on the rhetorical and organizational strategies of political actors who build political blocs and coalitions by reframing the way others perceive their own interests in changing historical circumstances. Laclau and Mouffe present politics as a "battle for position" between actors trying—in the context of the particular political, economic, and ideological landscape they inhabit—to recruit the uncommitted middle of society to their own interpretation of such powerful terms as *democracy, rights, peace,* and *environmentalism.*[7]

This processual, actor-oriented strategy of analysis for understanding the incinerator struggle in Livermore represents a break from most conventional academic models seeking to interpret struggles between government or corporate institutions on the one hand and lay communities on the other over plans to build waste sites, nuclear reactors, incinerators, and so on.[8] These models, usually based on analysis from a distance, tend to embody explanatory schemas that, generalizing across many cases, emphasize the importance of social or cognitive structures in predetermining actors' risk perceptions. They tend not to accent the fluidity of risk perceptions and the contingent nature of many struggles over risk; and when they do emphasize the importance of human agency in shaping risk perceptions (as in the literature on the rhetorical strategies of risk communicators), it is the agency of the risk presenters, not the risk consumers, that is foregrounded.[9] Thus, for example, Mary Douglas and Aaron Wildavsky argue in *Risk and Culture* that the risks people fear correlate well with three broader complexes of social roles, institutional affiliations, and ideologies, which they label *entrepreneurial, hierarchical,* and *egalitarian.* According to their theory, those positioned in a hierarchical orientation to society (e.g., members of the military) tend to accept risks posed by government and corporate projects, whereas those positioned in an egalitarian orientation to society (e.g., members of Greenpeace and other groups that emphasize loose, egalitarian principles of social organization) will oppose them.[10] Other models are more cognitive in orientation and emphasize the incommensurability of different cognitive frames that experts and laypeople bring to calculating risk. Spencer Weart, also foregrounding the divide between experts and the public, sees popular fear of nuclear power (to Weart, irrational) as a psychological displacement of a healthier fear of nuclear weapons.[11]

The analysis here, by contrast, foregrounds the potential fluidity of public reactions (within limits) and the importance of organizational and rhetorical strategies in bending public perception of potentially controversial projects. Rather than simply correlating perceptions of risk with structures, whether cognitive or sociological, it asks why social movements contesting particular risks can be brought into being at some moments and not others, and in particular communities but not others.[12] It finds the answer to this question in a conjuncture between propitious shifts in the underlying political economic structure, capable political entrepreneurship by social movement leaders, and strategic blunders by the opponents of those social movement leaders.[13] Also, rather than assuming that there is a unitary community of experts that sees environmental risks differently than do laypeople (as do those who tend to see expert judgments as simply correct and public fears as irrational),[14] I assume that there is often more disagreement within expert communities than the public realizes and that the public mobilization of oppositional experts is an important component in the mobilization of social movements against perceived risks.[15]

The Incinerator

In the late 1980s, the Livermore laboratory was shipping about 90 percent of its hazardous, radioactive, and mixed (hazardous and radioactive combined) waste off-site, mostly to other states, for treatment, storage, and disposal.[16] The lab had purchased an incinerator in 1978, but, thanks to legislation passed in 1984, it was operating under an interim permit that would expire on November 8, 1989, unless it could pass a U.S. Environmental Protection Agency (EPA)–administered trial burn before then.[17] In any case, the old incinerator—described to me by one Livermore scientist as "barely better than a fireplace"—was allowed to burn less than 10 percent of the waste generated by the laboratory because it lacked air filters or pollution control devices.[18] By the mid- and late 1980s, the exportation of waste for treatment from Livermore was becoming more expensive; it was also becoming an increasingly volatile political issue in states such as Nevada and Idaho that received Livermore's waste—so much so that Governor Cecil Andrus of Idaho had at one point ordered waste-bearing trucks from the Rocky Flats nuclear facility in Colorado turned back at the borders of Idaho, and the Nevada Nuclear Test Site had returned a small amount of waste sent from Livermore. Facility managers were increasingly concerned by their dependence on out-of-state disposal sites and on an existing incinerator that might soon be obsolete. Thus, they proposed a $41 million decontamination and waste treatment facility (DWTF), half the size of a football field, that would include a state-of-the-art incinerator. According to the official pamphlet, the facility was "designed to be secure, all-enclosed, aesthetically pleasing, logistically and operationally functional, and able to accommodate a staff of 50." The new facility would enable the laboratory to treat 90 percent of its waste on-site before shipping the residue elsewhere. Lab management promised that the incinerator, which would be fitted with high-efficiency particulate air (HEPA) filters to trap escaping particles, would burn hazardous, radioactive, and mixed waste with an efficiency of 99.99 percent.

The laboratory presented a strong environmentalist rationale for its proposed facility, arguing that it had a responsibility to take care of its own waste, that the waste treatment facility was designed with the most modern features to protect the environment, and that interstate transportation of waste posed a greater hazard to public safety and to the environment than incineration. The pamphlet *DWTF—Meeting the Environmental Challenge* put it this way:

> Because DWTF will be able to treat a wider variety of wastes than currently possible, about 90 percent of LLNL's wastes will be able to be treated on site. This results in benefits to the public and the environment. A modern and centralized hazardous waste operation facility, such as DWTF, is safer and consistent with LLNL environmental goals. Treating more wastes on site will lead to less wastes being transported on public roads. And, in the long term, a lower volume of wastes means fewer wastes in off-site disposal sites, and a cleaner environment.

Both sides—the scientists who designed the DWTF and their opponents in Tri-Valley CAREs—strongly believed that they were protecting the environment, and the struggle that developed between LLNL and Tri-Valley CAREs was, in part, a struggle for ownership of the term *environmentalist*—a word whose symbolic power no one wants to be on the wrong side of in the contemporary United States.

In this battle for position, the motives of Tri-Valley CAREs' core members extended far beyond stopping the incinerator. These core activists opposed the entire nuclear weapons design mission of the lab and the international arms race that lent it legitimacy. They realized that the new environmental laws of the 1970s and 1980s offered them a new angle of attack on the arms race and that, denied properly licensed procedures for the disposal of waste, the lab might be forced to curtail its nuclear weapons activities.

However, while they sensed the possibility of substantial local support for a campaign against the incinerator, especially in the context of the revitalized national and international environmental movements of the late 1980s, activists knew their neighbors well enough to recognize that there would be much less support for a full frontal attack on the core mission of the largest employer in town. Thus, making a savvy tactical choice, they mostly restricted their campaign in the years 1988–90 to the incinerator and other environmental concerns (such as groundwater contamination), keeping more of a distance from the kinds of issues raised and the kinds of protest tactics (such as civil disobedience) used by antinuclear groups from Berkeley and San Francisco when they came to Livermore.

Background Shifts

Tri-Valley CAREs' campaign would not have progressed very far were it not for important shifts that had recently taken place at the international, national, and local levels.

At the international level, Mikhail Gorbachev's reform program within the Soviet Union and his diplomatic initiatives to roll back the arms race opened a new space for public debate in the United States and the Soviet Union about the wisdom and costs of the arms race. In the atmosphere of crisis that prevailed when the cold war was in full swing, such debate had been tainted with the odor of disloyalty. Especially after the Reykjavik summit in 1986, where Reagan and Gorbachev discussed abolishing all nuclear ballistic missiles, and the INF Treaty of 1987, which abolished all intermediate-range nuclear weapons, it became more plausible to imagine an end to the arms race and to reassess the costs of the cold war. High among these costs was the damage inflicted on public health and the environment by facilities in the nuclear weapons complexes of the United States and the Soviet Union.[19]

But maybe the most important shifts were in the local political economy of Livermore itself. It is often assumed that, in the United States at least, capitalism and militarism are interlocking systems and mutually supportive structures, which is why it is so hard to reduce the military budget, cancel weapons systems, and so on.[20] While this is doubtless true in a general sense, particular conjunctural configurations at the local level may offer interesting variations on the general story. Thus, in Livermore the interests of local capital in the 1980s developed in such a way that those interests partly came into conflict with the laboratory, and this conflict created an opening for local antinuclear activists with a very different set of goals in opposing the lab.

There had been a social divide between lab employees and other residents in the 1950s, but this division had been contained by the stable dominance of LLNL within the community.[21] Between 1960 and 1990, the population of Livermore had more than tripled, increasing from 16,000 to 56,000, largely in response to regional development pressures in the San Francisco Bay Area. Livermore was growing at a rate of 3 percent a year during the development boom of the late 1980s. In 1989, house prices rose 30 percent in Livermore—although they remained lower than in most other parts of the Bay Area. Young families were moving to Livermore, commuting to work elsewhere in the Bay Area on the two new freeways that passed nearby, and companies such as Hexcel, Triad, and Intel were locating to Livermore's new industrial park. As one observer put it:

> Livermore is not the same city it was ten years ago. . . . Housing developments have replaced cows on the dry hills surrounding old Livermore. Young and upscale, the new residents—who likely as not commute to San Francisco each day—have no ties to Livermore's past. In 1987 the city council voted to consider cutting the whirling electrons symbolizing atomic energy from the city's insignia. . . . Nothing was done, but the debate itself was significant.[22]

Close scrutiny of donations to candidates in Livermore's 1989 municipal election shows that city politics was by now organized around two evenly matched patronage communities, a lab-centered community and a development-centered community.[23] Many of the newer residents looked to the developers and new business interests more than to the laboratory for Livermore's future, whereas lab employees were more likely to yearn for the smaller, quieter community Livermore had been before the recent burst of development. Livermore politics in the late 1980s centered on a series of struggles between the laboratory community and the newer interests, especially over development issues. The city council, dominated in these years by development interests and led by a mayor who was a banker with strong ties to local developers, wanted to increase the pace of development in Livermore; the slow-growth movement, on the other hand, with lab employees at its core, sponsored a local ballot initiative in an attempt to block some of the new development. Meanwhile, the development-oriented mayor and council engaged in an unprecedented series of skirmishes with the lab, complaining about leaks of toxic chemicals into the city sewer system, insisting that the laboratory—a tax-exempt institution—contribute to the cost of road improvements nearby, blocking the lab's attempt to close a nearby road for security reasons, and, in an extraordinary move, hiring a lobbyist to maneuver against the laboratory in Washington, D.C., on these last two issues.[24]

By the late 1980s, then, Livermore was increasingly polarized over development issues. A situation had emerged in which powerful new interests in Livermore stood opposed to the lab community because its members threatened to obstruct continued development, not because they made nuclear weapons. Adjusting to this new situation in which the laboratory no longer dominated local politics, the local newspapers—already emboldened by national media investigations of the nuclear weapons facilities at Fernald, Hanford, and Rocky Flats—began to give noticeably more generous coverage to critics of and scandals at the lab.[25] This created just the opening Tri-Valley CAREs needed in their campaign against the Livermore laboratory.

Hearings

Much of the struggle between Tri-Valley CAREs and the laboratory took place in community hearings, mandated by the National Environmental Policy Act, for an environmental impact statement on both the proposed incinerator and the existing one operating under an interim permit. The laboratory approached these hearings as what I call "rituals of assent"— events in which lab scientists paternalistically displayed their superior knowledge in the expectation that the local population would then assent to their plans. At these hearings, interested members of the public assembled at a local high school where they were confronted with a series of highly polished, scripted presentations made by lab officials and scientists armed with glossy brochures, flip charts, and view graphs. The presentations were often very technical, seemingly designed as much to intimidate as to inform the layperson with their profusion of acronyms and preference for chemical abbreviations. (Plutonium, for example, was almost invariably represented in illustrations as Pu.) When it came to assessing the risk potentially posed to the community by the proposed incinerator, Livermore scientists used classic risk language, which mixes abstract statistical formulations with folksy comparisons from everyday life; for example, the scientists expected 3.1 diagnoses of cancer over seventy years for every one million MEIs (mean exposed individuals), which they compared to the increased risk of cancer from eating one banana, smoking four cigarettes, or taking one cross-country plane trip. Sometimes the moderator of the hearings tried to enforce a rule of one question per member of the public and a strict 9 p.m. deadline for the end of the hearing "so that people can get home to their families." Both of these rules in effect cut off debate, while the one question per audience member restricted the speech of Tri-Valley CAREs members who came to the hearings with a number of prepared questions based on their prior research.

In their battle for position, Tri-Valley CAREs activists sought to put the laboratory on the defensive and disrupt its script for the hearings by adopting three different and to some degree contradictory strategies: explicitly attacking the hearings as rituals of assent, fielding their own experts to undermine the expert authority of lab scientists, and challenging the very validity of the expert discourse on risk itself.

Attacking the Hearings as Rituals of Assent

A number of Tri-Valley CAREs members attempted to delegitimate the hearing process itself by explicitly questioning the openness of the hearings and the impartiality of the state officials in charge of them. At one hearing on the existing incinerator, Tri-Valley CAREs member Joann Frisch said, "You're only complying with some rule of the law that you have to have so many hearings before you can pass a foregone conclusion that the lab will continue to do whatever it wants to, and we are all the guinea pig."[26] At the same hearing, Tri-Valley CAREs member Roman Morkowski, complaining that the state official running the meeting seemed biased toward the laboratory and invoking the symbolic power of the U.S. Constitution to legitimate his complaint, said: "As a government agency, remember that . . . in the preamble of the Constitution it says, 'We the people, in order to form a more perfect government [sic] . . . must promote the general welfare,' and you people there are promoting General Motors, General Dynamics, General Foods, and you must, according to the Constitution, only protect the welfare of the Livermore community, not the rad lab." He went on: "You guys [from state government regulatory agencies] remind me of the people from the rad lab. They never send anybody that has the answers. Or if they do have the answers they don't have the authority to give them. Is it possible that the next time that this group comes that somebody from the State comes here that has some authority to say something?"[27]

Tri-Valley CAREs' great breakthrough in challenging the legitimacy of the hearing process and the sincerity of the agencies managing it came after the very first community hearing on the proposed new incinerator on August 23, 1988. The U.S. Department of Energy (DOE), which called the hearing, had advertised it as a hearing on a "decontamination and waste treatment facility," studiously avoiding the word *incinerator*, and had, according to Tri-Valley CAREs, not publicized the meeting widely enough.[28] Many local residents, when they read about the hearing in the local newspapers after the fact, were annoyed not to have known that the meeting was about an incinerator. Tri-Valley CAREs, accusing the DOE of deviousness in its public notice strategy, promptly started a campaign for a second hearing. In calling for a second hearing it won the support of the council and the mayor, Dale Turner, who complained that the DOE's notice for the initial hearing made it sound as if it were a hearing for the sewer upgrade under way at LLNL at the same time.[29]

In a move that with the benefit of hindsight can only be called disastrous, Jo Ann Elferink, regional manager of the DOE, summarily refused a second hearing. In one stroke, she thus inflamed usually moderate local opinion in Livermore, transformed Tri-Valley CAREs from a marginal group of malcontents into the local guardians of democracy, and gave the impression that the government and the lab sought to avoid a genuine hearing. The city council sent the mayor to Washington, D.C., to lobby for a second hearing over Elferink's head, and the nearby city of Pleasanton passed a resolution supporting Livermore's call for a second hearing. Meanwhile, Representative Pete Stark threatened to hold a congressional hearing on the incinerator if the DOE did not relent, and editorials in the local newspapers backed him and condemned the high-handedness of the DOE. The *Tri-Valley Herald,* the local newspaper with the largest circulation, editorialized: "We encourage Stark to proceed with the hearing, regardless of whether the Energy Department reconsiders its stupid decision on public hearings. . . . The congressman can subpoena experts to testify so residents can thoroughly understand the issue instead of getting the laundered version from the Energy Department."[30] After letting the dispute drag on for three months, the DOE relented and agreed to a second hearing, but by now the damage was done: the good faith of the DOE and the authority of the hearing process itself had been compromised.[31]

A Counterexpert

Harvey Sapolsky has argued in "The Politics of Risk" that when expert opinion is openly divided about the safety of a proposed new technology, the public loses trust in the technology in question. Tri-Valley CAREs recruited academic experts from outside Livermore to talk about alternatives to waste incineration and about the public health dangers represented by even small quantities of plutonium in the air. But their most effective expert advocate by far was Marion Fulk. Fulk was a retired chemist who had spent much of his career analyzing fallout from nuclear tests for the Livermore laboratory. A longtime cold warrior, he was clearly no antinuclear ideologue, and was thus an improbable ally for a group of citizens seeking ultimately to end nuclear weapons work at the lab. Fulk was concerned about the incinerator, however, and he and Tri-Valley CAREs were able to forge a comfortable working relationship. At the hearings, Fulk expressed his doubts that the HEPA filters on the proposed incinerator would stop plutonium particles from escaping into the atmosphere. He also reviewed the calculations in the lab's draft environmental impact statement and concluded that the statement only calculated emissions of plutonium for normal daily activities, omitting the four accidental releases a year that were expected according to a separate report. The laboratory was forced to concede Fulk's calculation that the draft environmental impact statement thus underestimated the incinerator's emission rate for plutonium by a factor of 3,000.[32] This did not sit well with public opinion.

Challenging Expert Discourse

Finally, even as Tri-Valley CAREs worked with Marion Fulk within the framework of expert discourse to delegitimate the accuracy of the draft environmental impact statement on the incinerator, it also, working simultaneously on an opposed rhetorical plane, questioned the legitimacy of scientists' risk language itself. This strategy was particularly used by female members of Tri-Valley CAREs who tried to disrupt the formal risk discourse of lab scientists by attacking the abstraction central to the discourse and valorizing more emotional responses to the incinerator. "None of us breathes average annual air," said Tri-Valley CAREs' founder, Marylia Kelley, at one hearing. "Have you ever seen anyone die of cancer?" asked Karen Hogan, angrily interrupting a scientist's presentation from her front row seat. "This is what makes people angry, the way you use numbers like this to say nothing. How does one-tenth of a person get cancer?" Dot Mathers, another Tri-Valley CAREs member, spoke emotionally of her son's hyperthyroid condition and, aiming her comment at young families at the hearing, concluded, "I'm concerned for the young mothers raising children in the valley."[33]

In all these ways, Tri-Valley CAREs members and ordinary citizens in Livermore were able to unravel the public hearing process and turn what were supposed to be rituals of assent into forums for dissension. The critique of expert discourse worked synergistically with Tri-Valley CAREs' other rhetorical strategies in casting doubt on the impartiality of the hearings, the competence and good faith of lab scientists, and the appropriateness of their frame of reference for thinking about the incinerator. As the debate over the incinerator went on, the laboratory increasingly lost control of public hearings, local media coverage grew progressively more negative, and, in the battle for position between Tri-Valley CAREs and the lab, the formerly uncommitted middle became more skeptical about the incinerator. To fully understand this, we need to situate the public debate on the incinerator in the context of other environmental developments in Livermore.

The Remainder of Livermore's Environmental Drama

In parallel with the public debate on the proposed incinerator, there were embarrassing revelations about prior contamination at the lab and about the older existing incinerator. The newly aggressive local press covered these revelations extensively, which, in the context of the national media coverage of the environmental costs of the cold war during this time, helped establish Tri-Valley CAREs' legitimacy as a watchdog organization while amplifying local concern about the environmental safety of the facility.

The lab's environmental problems began in earnest in late 1987 when the EPA put the site on its Superfund list because the groundwater beneath the facility had been contaminated, largely by the naval air base that preceded the weapons lab at this site, with carcinogenic solvents up to 120 times and benzene up to 9,000 times the federal limit. The contaminated groundwater was slowly seeping toward a local housing development and had already forced the sealing of private wells owned by nearby residents.[34] This development was important not only in embarrassing the lab but also in enabling Tri-Valley CAREs to apply, as provided for in the Superfund legislation, for a $50,000 grant to hire consultants and monitor the cleanup. Winning this grant gave Tri-Valley CAREs increased legitimacy in the community and enabled it to expand its profile and organizational capability.[35]

The lab's image suffered further when the local media began to report on a series of environmental infractions from the past. This local reporting took place against a backdrop of unprecedented national media revelations at the end of the cold war of health and environmental scandals at other facilities in the nuclear weapons complex. For example, the national media, television as well as print, were reporting that the managers of the Fernald uranium facility in Ohio had for twenty years knowingly allowed uranium to contaminate local air, water, and soil;[36] that enough plutonium to cause a spontaneous critical reaction had accumulated in ventilation ducts at the Rocky Flats facility in Denver, a facility the secretary of energy ordered closed in 1989 for its record of chronic safety violations and illegal waste disposal activities;[37] and that the Hanford facility in Washington had tanks containing volatile mixtures of wastes it could not dispose of, had deliberately released a huge dose of radioactive iodine into the air in 1949 as part of an experiment that later caused a local epidemic of thyroid problems, and had exposed neighbors to radioactivity at more than 1,000 times what was considered the safe dose in the late 1980s.[38]

Against the background of these stories, local media revelations took on added significance. These included the unannounced release of 700,000 to 800,000 curies of tritium into the air over fifteen years; the release of plutonium, americium, chromium, and sulfuric acid into the city sewer system; leakage of polychlorinated biphenyls (PCBs); the accidental transportation of americium to the county dump site; and an explosion at the lab's waste yard.[39] The juxtaposition in the local media of officials' insistence that their proposed incinerator would be safe with revelations of untold past accidents did not work to the laboratory's advantage, and at the hearings local citizens would often refer to the full range of the lab's environmental problems despite frequent reminders from the moderators that the hearings were supposed to focus on the proposed incinerator only rather than growing into inquisitions with regard to the facility's entire environmental record.

Finally, the coup de grâce, just as the laboratory was arguing that its new incinerator would be safe, its old incinerator failed two trial burns of liquid hazardous waste administered by the EPA in late 1988 and early 1989 as part of its licensing process. Laboratory managers had professed confidence that the old incinerator would pass the trial burns. After the lab's Environmental Protection Department failed to meet the EPA's deadline in November 1989 for submission of documents on behalf of the incinerator, the EPA ordered the old incinerator closed.[40]

With the gathering environmental scandal, Tri-Valley CAREs mounted a petition campaign against the proposed new incinerator, gathering signatures at local supermarkets. By 1990, LLNL found itself in a situation where 10,000 local residents (in a city of fewer than 60,000) had signed the petition against the incinerator;[41] the nearby town of Pleasanton's environmental monitoring committee had appealed to the lab to redo its environmental study of the incinerator;[42] the local *Tri-Valley Herald* had run a front-page story about people in Livermore who were considering selling their homes if the new incinerator was built;[43] and Representative Stark had threatened to sue if the incinerator was built without further study.[44]

Death of an Incinerator

In late 1988, while Tri-Valley CAREs and the city council were in the midst of their campaign for a second public hearing, lab director John Nuckolls had commissioned an internal committee to report to him on the safety and advisability of the proposed new incinerator. The committee was chaired by Mort Mendelsohn, director for biomedical and environmental research. Mendelsohn's committee issued an interim report on March 9, 1989 (after the second hearing had been granted but before it had taken place and before the existing incinerator had been ordered closed by EPA). The interim report stated that "there is no reasonable alternative to incineration for some fraction of the Laboratory's waste," that "incineration of hazardous waste is a safe, practical, prevalent technology," and that "incineration is best done here on the Livermore site. Ground transportation of untreated land ban mixed waste carries a high risk, increasing with distance."

Almost one year later, on February 21, 1990, at a point when the crisis over the incinerator had deepened, Mendelsohn's committee issued its final report. It concluded:

> We view incineration as a violation of the cardinal principle of radioactive waste treatment; namely, containing radioactivity rather than spreading it. . . . It seems prudent to avoid placing a mixed waste incinerator in the midst of a rapidly growing, increasingly residential environment. . . . Whether fears about incinerators are real or imaginary and regardless of how well an incinerator might be designed and run, incineration is regarded negatively by most California communities, including those near the Laboratory's sites. This psychological consideration may prove to be as important in our search for a suitable waste treatment system as any technical or economic factor.

The committee recommended transporting lab waste off-site for treatment— the option it had identified in its interim report a year earlier as the riskiest.

In February 1990, lab director Nuckolls ended the crisis by accepting his committee's recommendations and canceling the proposed incinerator.

Conclusion

Why did the Livermore lab's attempt to build an incinerator fail? It would be all too easy to attribute the outcome of this conflict, as does the Mendelsohn Report itself, to a generalized popular hostility toward incinerators. At the time lab managers proposed this incinerator, two hundred broadly comparable models were already in operation across the country. Somehow communities were persuaded to accept them. I believe, based on my experience as a close observer of Livermore politics and society, that had officials proposed Livermore's incinerator five years earlier, it would be up and running today; then, we might be discussing why it is so difficult to mobilize successful campaigns against incinerators, not why Tri-Valley CAREs' campaign succeeded.

Tri-Valley CAREs' campaign succeeded because of a particular conjunctural configuration of circumstances and because of a combination of strategic blunders by the incinerator's backers and savvy tactics on the part of its opponents. The enabling background circumstances include the lessening of cold war tensions thanks to Gorbachev's reforms; a national media campaign, mysterious in origin but powerful in its execution, to publicize decades of health and environmental problems at nuclear weapons facilities around the country; and federal environmental legislation that enabled Tri-Valley CAREs to apply for a federal grant, which forced LLNL to hold public hearings and, quite fortuitously, mandated embarrassing trial burns of the old incinerator right in the middle of the hearing process for the new incinerator. Meanwhile, shifts in the political economy of Livermore itself had produced a population of young professional and working families who were not beholden to the lab for their livelihood and had brought to office (for a very limited time, it turned out) a mayor and a council more oriented to the local development community than to the laboratory and, therefore, willing to confront the lab as their predecessors had not.

Within this context, the backers of the incinerator made things worse by means of some blunders. Foremost among these was Elferink's decision to deny a second hearing on the incinerator in Livermore, a decision that helped cement a coalition between Tri-Valley CAREs, the mayor, the council, and Representative Pete Stark. Whatever their differences of opinion on the incinerator itself, they could all agree on the need for a more extended and open process of discussion about it, and because of Elferink, the opponents of the incinerator shifted the debate for several months from the more divisive question of the desirability of the incinerator itself to the more unifying question of whether the residents of Livermore deserved another hearing on the issue.

Finally, Tri-Valley CAREs members played their roles skillfully. Maneuvering adeptly to capture the allegiance of the uncommitted middle in Livermore politics, they carefully separated their opposition to the incinerator from their opposition to the laboratory's overall mission of nuclear weapons design; they connected the incinerator debate to revelations of deeper environmental problems at the lab, preventing its managers from framing the incinerator as a self-contained issue; they forged alliances on the incinerator issue with local politicians whose progrowth priorities they, for the most part, did not share; they worked with a respected lab scientist whose criticisms of the incinerator carried weight with his former colleagues and in the wider community; and they found the correct rhetorical pressure points in the public hearing process to put lab spokespersons on the defensive. Just as students at military academies study old battles to prepare for new ones, so students of environmental politics would do well to study carefully the battle for position in local struggles such as this to understand how, sometimes, small groups can win big victories against powerful institutions.

(2000)

Postscript

Tall Tales and Deceptive Discourses: Nuclear Weapons in George W. Bush's America

Weapons systems, treaties, and strategies come to seem right (or wrong) in the context of the stories we tell ourselves about them. Social scientists and historians call these stories discourses. Sometimes new discourses (like our discourse on civil rights) originate from below and eventually gain enough credibility that they are co-opted by the government. Other discourses (like the discourse on deterrence during the cold war) originate within the government, and within the tight circle of think tanks that speak to the government, and are then propagated outward through society by waves of speech making and media dissemination. From time to time there are sharp historical breaks as new stories and propositions become accepted with startling suddenness. Senior officials in the Bush administration are now trying to create this kind of radical shift in our discourse about nuclear weapons.

The cold war saw the rise of an official discourse on nuclear weapons that is now looking more than a little tattered. Its chief assumptions were as follows: that the genie having escaped the bottle in a dangerous world, nuclear weapons could not be abolished, and anyone who thought otherwise was naive or worse; that even though the two superpowers were inevitable rivals racing to improve their arsenals, they were rational enough to manage their competition in ways that would not cause a nuclear war; that the arms race could be channeled and disciplined, though not prevented, by arms control treaties; and that certain avenues of competition were destabilizing and should therefore be foreclosed by mutual agreement. These included a race to build defensive antimissile systems and to put nuclear, antisatellite, or antiballistic weapons in space.

After the cold war, this way of looking at the world began to seem increasingly outmoded. The Clinton administration attempted to strike up some new discursive themes, but its efforts were undercut by its own half-heartedness. For example, the administration made vague remarks about moving toward a world without nuclear weapons, but it failed to negotiate any new arms reductions and it proclaimed through its *Nuclear Posture Review* that the United States would rely on nuclear weapons for its security for the indefinite future. Similarly, Clinton administration officials said that they supported the Anti-Ballistic Missile (ABM) Treaty only to sponsor research and development programs that pointed in the direction of its erosion or demise. And President Clinton spoke of a new global order founded on strong international treaties and institutions only to wage war in Kosovo without UN approval and to walk away from an international convention on land mines.

The administration of George W. Bush, on the other hand, has attempted to use the debate about ballistic missile defense to transform the official discourse on nuclear weapons and arms control. It has sought to dramatically redefine the U.S.-Russian relationship, the morality and effectiveness of deterrence, and the significance of arms control. If some of the statements made by administration officials had been uttered by President Clinton, they would have met with Republican derision. The Bush administration has also appropriated some of the antinuclear movement's rhetoric, only to use it in support of a further round of militarization.

The new discourse, like its predecessor, starts with the assumption that the world is a very dangerous place, although the source of danger is no longer Soviet-style militant communism but rather the proliferation of weapons of mass destruction to "rogue states." As Deputy Secretary of Defense Paul Wolfowitz recently testified to Congress: "The short-range missile threat to our friends, allies, and deployed forces arrived a decade ago; the intermediate missile threat is now here; and the long-range threat to American cities is just over the horizon—a matter of years, not decades, away—and our people and territory are defenseless."[1]

Within the old discourse, missile threats from abroad were used to justify nuclear deterrence. No longer. Remarkably, it is now becoming axiomatic that leaders of "rogue states," unlike the old Soviet leaders, cannot be deterred by nuclear weapons. This axiom is being used to justify not only the development of missile defenses but also a new earth-penetrating "mininuke" that would supposedly hold the leaders of "rogue states" per-sonally at risk in their underground bunkers. Although there is no evidence to support it, and the argument only seems plausible within the context of racist assumptions about Third World leaders' lack of rationality, the proposition that nuclear deterrence does not work on "rogue states" is now treated as self-evident by government officials.

Just as an earlier generation of government officials would have said "nuclear weapons keep the peace," as if merely articulating the obvious, so our current officials simply state as fact the claim that leaders of countries like Iraq, Iran, and North Korea cannot be deterred by nuclear weapons. Thus, Richard Perle said of Saddam Hussein, "I really don't want to count on the rational judgment of a man who used poison gas against his own people."[2] And Wolfowitz asked rhetorically, "If Saddam Hussein had the ability to strike a Western capital with a nuclear weapon, would he really be deterred by the prospect of a U.S. nuclear strike that would kill millions of Iraqis?"[3]

Those who thought the answer to Wolfowitz's question would be, "Yes, of course he would be deterred," would find themselves in disagreement with the editors of the New York Times, whose reaction has typified the extraor-dinary credulousness with which the media have received such claims. A May 2 New York Times editorial, repeating the new common sense, said, "By their nature, rogue nations, sometimes ruled by irrational dictators, can-not be assumed to respond to the Cold War deterrence of 'mutually assured destruction.'" The next day, Times columnist William Safire drove the point home, asking, "Why should we make it possible for some tinpot dictator, unconcerned about retaliation, to hold an American city hostage?"[4] What we see happening here—aided and abetted by a striking lack of skepticism in the media—is the creation of a new axiom for what Jonathan Schell has called the "second nuclear age."

The flip side of the emphasis on new threats from rogue states is an insistence that the old threat, Russia, is no longer an enemy. For example, Wolfowitz told the Senate that "we are engaged in discussions with Russia on a new security framework that reflects the fact that the Cold War is over and that the U.S. and Russia are not enemies."[5] And George Bush, taking aim at the ABM Treaty, said that "Russia is not an enemy of the United States and yet we still go to a treaty that assumes Russia is the enemy, a treaty that says the whole concept of peace is based on us blowing each other up. I don't think that makes sense any more."[6]

The truth is, of course, that Russia may no longer be the enemy it once was, but it is not exactly a friend either. Friends do not keep thousands of nuclear weapons on hair-trigger alert targeted against one another. Nor do they expel one another's diplomats forty at a time. The new discourse overstates the transformation of U.S.-Russian relations so as to delegitimate the ABM Treaty the two countries signed in 1972 as a relic of the past, opening the way for construction of George W. Bush's cherished missile defense system. Bush administration officials have even suggested that treaties in general have become useless fetishes, revered out of habit, and that the fast-moving world of today requires a more flexible approach than treaties allow. Condoleezza Rice, Bush's national security adviser, has said, for example, "There's a good reason not to get into 15-year negotiations, which is what it has taken to create arms-control treaties."[7] She also made the following remarkable statement in a July 12, 2001, press conference:

> I was one of the high priestesses of arms control—a true believer. Like so many others, I eagerly anticipated those breathtaking moments of summitry where the centerpiece was always the signing of the latest arms control treaty; the toast; the handshake; and with Brezhnev, the bear hug. For those precious few moments the world found comfort in seeing the superpowers affirm their peaceful intent. And the scientists would set the clock back a few minutes further away from midnight. Deep down we knew that arms control was a poor substitute for a real agenda based on common aspirations. . . . But along the way to the next summit something happened. History happened. 1989. So, while many of us were debating the implications of MIRVs [multiple independent reentry vehicles] on SS-18s and Peacekeepers like so many angels dancing on a warhead, the forces of history were making the old paradigm obsolete. . . . We cannot cling to the old order—like medieval scholars clinging to a Ptolemaic system even after the Copernican revolution. We must recognize that the strategic world we grew up in has been turned upside down.

This futuristic rhetoric is one of the most striking features of the new nuclear discourse, and it signifies a bold theft of the disarmament movement's rhetorical fire by the ideologues of the Pentagon. Cold war nuclear discourse was full of appeals for "caution," "realism," and "stability," making a virtue of its distrust for radical measures, where the new nuclear discourse is all about futuristic weapons and bold measures. One might have expected to hear of the need for visionary thinking, the hopeful possibilities if only we could break with the assumptions of yesterday, from partisans of disarmament. Instead, we hear it from Dick Cheney, Donald Rumsfeld, Richard Perle, and Paul Wolfowitz—veteran cold warriors all— who use it as a battering ram against the ABM Treaty.

"The ABM Treaty is a relic of the past," said George W. Bush recently.

"The days of the Cold War have ended, and so must the Cold War mentality as far as I'm concerned."[8]

Wolfowitz used similar language: "A 30-year-old treaty designed to preserve the balance of terror during the Cold War must not be allowed to prevent us from taking steps to protect our people, our forces, and our allies."[9]

Virginia's John Warner, the ranking Republican on the Senate Armed Services Committee, concurred: "The ABM Treaty has outlived its justification and foundations."[10] Likewise, his colleague, North Carolina's Jesse Helms, said, "Russia must come to grips with the fact that the Cold War is over. It is time to scrap the ABM Treaty."[11]

The new rhetoric is more indebted to the logic of advertising than that of strategic thinking. Advertisers use rhetoric glibly to create perceptions rather than to argue for truths, and they have learned that one of the easiest ways to discredit rival products, whatever their manifest virtues, is to make them seem old and outdated compared to one's own. While it is arguably the thinking of Rumsfeld, Cheney, and Wolfowitz that is old and outdated, these creators of the new nuclear discourse have learned that by simply likening the ABM Treaty to Mom and Dad's Oldsmobile they do not need to get their hands dirty with arguments about the precise relationship between the ABM Treaty and strategic stability.

Perhaps the most extraordinary achievement of these purveyors of the new nuclear discourse is to have appropriated antinuclear critiques of nuclear deterrence in the service of a new generation of weaponry. Officials who only a decade ago would have derided the naïveté of disarmament advocates who criticized nuclear deterrence now sound like their erstwhile opponents. Wolfowitz, for example, striking a sentimental note, began his recent testimony to the Senate Armed Services Committee by saying that, in Israel during the Gulf War, "We saw children walking to school carrying gas masks in gaily decorated boxes—no doubt to try to distract them from the possibility of facing mass destruction. They were awfully young to have to think about the unthinkable."[12]

Jesse Helms, a staunch defender of deterrence throughout the cold war, told the Senate two months earlier that it was time to "dispense with the illogical and immoral concept of mutually assured destruction."[13] And Rice, recycling an argument often made by the antinuclear movement in the 1980s, stated in her July 12 press conference that "we need to recognize that just as peace is not the absence of war, stability is not a balance of terror."

The new nuclear discourse holds out the hope that the United States and Russia can be friends and that, although rising military powers in the Third World may not be rational, we can be safe from their weapons of mass destruction, and indeed from the entire depressing logic of mutually assured destruction, if only we can let go of the ABM Treaty and build a new generation of defensive weapons that are almost within our technical grasp. Such weapons, being purely defensive, "threaten no one," in the words of Donald Rumsfeld. "They bother no one, except a country . . . that thinks they want [to] have ballistic missiles to impose their will on their neighbors."[14]

"Once people begin to realize that this is not something that is a matter of gaining advantage over anyone but is a matter of reducing vulnerability for everybody, then I think they begin to look at it differently," Wolfowitz told a press conference in Paris on May 9, 2001.

All discourses, especially government discourses, have something to hide, and this one is no exception. Although the Bush administration speaks of missile defense as a purely defensive technology designed to protect the United States from "rogue states" and not to change the balance of power with established nuclear powers, I have it on good authority from sources in the Clinton White House that, in their conversations out of public view, Pentagon planners are very interested in ways in which missile defense might be able to neutralize the twenty single-warhead missiles in China capable of hitting the United States, thus effectively disarming China.

Although Bush administration officials like to tell the public that missile defense is not "a matter of gaining advantage over anyone," they tell the Senate something different. Thus Wolfowitz recently testified that "the countries pursuing these [ballistic missile] capabilities are doing so because . . . they believe that if they can hold the American people at risk, they can . . . deter us from defending our interests around the world. . . . They may secure, in their estimation, the capability to prevent us from forming international coalitions to challenge their acts of aggression and force us into a truly isolationist posture. And they would not even have to use the weapons in their possession to affect our behavior and achieve their ends."[15] In other words, ballistic missile defense is a new means to the old dream of the cold warriors: achieving nuclear superiority. Insofar as it is about doing away with deterrence, it is only about abolishing the ability of other countries to deter the United States. As British antinuclear activist Helen Johns put it: "Ballistic missile defense is the armed wing of globalization. It is a euphemism for plans to ensure U.S. military and economic domination of the planet."[16]

The new nuclear discourse puts the disarmament movement in an awkward position. Its traditional rhetoric about the possibility of reconciliation with Russia and the existential darkness of deterrence has been hijacked by today's superannuated cold warriors as a way of justifying the abrogation of old arms control treaties, the construction of new weapons, and the militarization of space. Thus the movement is left either defending nuclear deterrence or arguing for nuclear abolition—a goal that strikes much of the public as no less idealistic than the Pentagon's Buck Rogers schemes for missile defense. But unless the disarmament movement learns to tell a compelling new story soon, very soon, the tall stories being told by the Bush administration will become the stories for our age.

(2001)

Notes

Introduction

1. The best source on this moment in nuclear history is still Scheer, *With Enough Shovels*.

2. On this movement, see Epstein, *Political Protest and Cultural Revolution*; Glass, *Citizens against the MX*; Loeb, *Hope in Hard Times*; McCrea and Markle, *Minutes to Midnight*; Meyer, *A Winter of Discontent*; Miller, *Geography and Social Movements*; and Solo, *From Protest to Policy*.

3. The protest is documented in Peter Adair's 1983 film, *Stopping History*, and by Cabasso and Moon, *Risking Peace*.

4. I usually devise pseudonyms for nuclear weapons scientists in my writing. In this case I have not since Tom has published his own account of this episode (Gusterson, *Nuclear Rites*, 245–47). In an interesting twist, Tom would attend my wedding, in Livermore, sixteen years later.

5. See Gusterson, "Exploding Anthropology's Canon in the World of the Bomb."

6. Interestingly, the abolitionists won support for their campaign from some unlikely establishment figures—for example, General Lee Butler, a former commander of American nuclear forces, and Richard Butler, a former head of the UN inspection team sent to disarm Iraq after the first Gulf War. Richard Butler lays out his case in *Fatal Choice*. The best source on the abolitionist movement overall is Schell, *The Abolition* and *The Gift of Time*.

7. See Barnett, "Peacekeeping, Indifference, and Genocide in Rwanda," and Powers, *A Problem from Hell*.

8. On India's program, see Perkovich, *India's Nuclear Bomb*, and Abraham, *The Making of the Indian Atomic Bomb*. On the North Korean program, see Albright, "How Much Plutonium Does North Korea Have?"; Norris, Kristensen, and Handler, "North Korea's Nuclear Program, 2003"; and Sigal, *Disarming Strangers*.

9. This appeared as the quote of the month in the *Bulletin of the Atomic Scientists* 52 (1996): 5.

10. Jonathan Schell, speech at Scripps College, October 17, 2002.

11. Appadurai, *Modernity at Large*.

12. Friedman, *The Lexus and the Olive Tree*, and Kaplan, *The Coming Anarchy*. For anthropological work on Guatemala, Mozambique, and Sri Lanka, see Nelson, *A Finger in the Wound*; Schirmer, *The Guatemalan Military Project*; Nordstrom, *A Different Kind of War Story*; and Tambiah, *Leveling Crowds*.

13. Nordstrom (forthcoming) provides an important corrective to this point of view.

14. Gusterson, "Studying Up Revisited."

15. The critical security studies literature is huge, but useful introductory readings include Campbell, *Writing Security*; Krause and Williams, *Critical Security Studies*; and Weldes et al., *Cultures of Insecurity*.

16. Cohn, "Sex and Death in the Rational World of Defense Intellectuals."

17. Gusterson, "Feminist Militarism."

18. Key texts in this tradition include Collins, *Changing Order*; Collins and Pinch, *The Golem*; Knorr-Cetina, *The Manufacture of Knowledge* and *Epistemic Cultures*; Latour, *Science in Action* and *The Pasteurization of France*; and Pickering, *Constructing Quarks*.

19. Krugman, "Behind the Great Divide."

20. Jackson, "What about the Death Toll?"

1. Becoming a Weapons Scientist

This chapter has benefited from the comments of a number of colleagues. I am particularly grateful to Leslie Eliason, Michael Fischer, Jean Jackson, Evelyn Fox Keller, Kim Fortun, George Marcus, Sherry Turkle, and Sylvia Yanagisako for their comments. I would also like to thank the NYU anthropology department, the Williams College anthropology department, the cultural studies group at the University of Washington, and the Program in Science, Technology, and Society at MIT for inviting me to present earlier versions of this piece, and for the helpful advice I was given at those presentations. Finally, my thanks to everyone at the Late Editions editorial workshop at Rice University.

1. As with all the names in this chapter, "Sylvia" is a pseudonym.

2. For ethnographic commentaries on these women-only peace camps, see Krasniewicz, *Nuclear Summer*, and Wilson, "Power and Epistemology." For accounts of the San Francisco Bay Area antinuclear movement that emphasize the importance of women's leadership and feminist consciousness in that movement, see Epstein, "The Culture of Direct Action" and "The Politics of Prefigurative Community," and Starhawk, *Dreaming the Dark*.

3. Cohn, "Sex and Death"; Enloe, *Bananas, Beaches, and Bases* and *Does Khaki Become You?*; and Ruddick, *Maternal Thinking*.

4. Krasniewicz, *Nuclear Summer*, 48.

5. Rogers, "Lab to Improve Minority Hiring Policies," and LLNL, *LLLWA Salary Study Committee Report*.

6. Caldicott, *Missile Envy*, and Ruddick, *Maternal Thinking*, offer two influential examples of essentialist texts that argue for a triangular correlation between womanhood, motherhood, and peace consciousness. See also Chodorow, *The Reproduction of Mothering*.

7. Lifton, "Imagining the Real"; Lifton and Markusen, *The Genocidal Mentality*; and Mack, "Toward a Collective Psychopathology of the Nuclear Arms Competition."

8. Gusterson, "Coming of Age in a Weapons Lab" and *Nuclear Rites*.

9. Traweek, *Beamtimes and Lifetimes*, x–xi.

10. DeWitt, "The Nuclear Arms Race as Seen by a Nuclear Weapons Lab Staff Member," 3.

11. My thanks to Rich Doyle for this insight.

12. Gusterson, "Coming of Age in a Weapons Lab" and *Nuclear Rites,* as well as chapter 8, this volume.

13. Malinowski, *Magic, Science, and Religion and Other Essays.*

2. Nuclear Weapons and the Other in the Western Imagination

The research for and writing of this chapter were helped by a Mellon New Directions Fellowship at Stanford University, an SSRC-MacArthur Fellowship in International Peace and Security, and an Arms Control Fellowship at Stanford University's Center for International Security and Arms Control (CISAC). Drafts were presented at the Conference on Discourse, Peace, Security, and International Security in Ballyvaughn, Ireland, August 6–12, 1988; the International Studies Association Meetings in London, April 1989; the University of Chicago colloquium titled Boundaries of Power, Boundaries of Communication, April 28, 1990; and the Social Science Seminar at Stanford University's Center for International Security and Arms Control on June 11, 1998. An earlier version was printed as working paper number 47 by the Center for Psychosocial Studies, Chicago.

I am indebted to the following people for their comments as I was rewriting this chapter: Adekeye Adebajo, Bart Bernstein, Larry Brown, George Bunn, Gary Downey, Lynn Eden, Leslie Eliason, Mike Fischer, Brad Klein, Mark Laffey, Gail Lapidus, Robert Manoff, Hugh Mehan, Jennifer Mnookin, Don Moore, Merwin Pond, Mary Pratt, George Rathjens, Renato Rosaldo, Scott Sagan, Michael Salmon, Dan Segal, Greg Urban, and Celeste Wallander. Thanks also to all the participants at the Ballyvaughn conference in 1988, the University of Chicago colloquium in 1990, and CISAC's Social Science Seminar for their comments. Also, this chapter would have been impossible to prepare without assistance from New York University's Center for War, Peace, and the News Media and from Ike Jeans in locating relevant news coverage.

1. See Gusterson, *Nuclear Rites.*

2. *Nuclear Weapons Work at LLNL,* 1.

3. Geertz, "Common Sense as a Cultural System."

4. The presumption that nuclear weapons are most dangerous in the hands of ethnic others has also found its way into video game culture. Electronic Arts markets a video game called Nuclear Strike™ that "drops players into the jungles of Southeast Asia in a fight to stop a tyrant [Colonel LeMonde] who is holding the world hostage with a nuclear threat" (*Business Wire,* "Electronic Arts Ships Nuclear Strike for the PC").

5. Adelman addressed his comments to the San Francisco Commonwealth Club on June 9, 1988; the speech was broadcast on National Public Radio. For Bethe, see Bernard, "Atomic Bomb Saved Lives in WWII, Bethe Says"; also quoted in Shroyer, *Secret Mesa,* 24.

6. Abrams, "US: Nuclear Situation Serious."

7. Moore and Khan, "Kashmir: A South Asian Flash Point."

8. Albright and Hibbs, "Hyping the Iraqi Bomb," and Gordon, "U.S. Aides Press Iraqi Nuclear Threat."

9. Perle, "Keeping the Bomb from Iraq"; Safire, "The Saddam Bomb"; Rosenthal, "A Story of Two Stories," and "Iraq and Atom Bombs"; and Kranish, "Senator Hints at Force over Reported Iraqi Threat."

10. See Douglas and Wildavsky, *Risk and Culture,* and Lindenbaum, *Kuru Sorcery.*

11. In this chapter I treat the Western discourse about the established nuclear powers as a single unit for heuristic purposes, although the five official nuclear nations are not all treated alike within the discourse. Since the disintegration of the Soviet Union, in Hollywood films such as *The Peacemaker,* for example, Russia has increasingly been portrayed in the Western media in the alarmist terms formerly reserved for Third World nations (Cockburn and Cockburn, *One Point Safe*). China was perceived as what we would now call a "rogue state" when it first acquired nuclear weapons. These days its nuclear status is mostly ignored in the discourse on nuclear proliferation—as is Israel's. Israel occupies an interesting and structurally anomalous position. As an outpost in the Middle East of the Judeo-Christian tradition, it tends to be exempted from criticism even though, in formal terms, it has more in common with such threshold states as Pakistan and Iraq than with the official nuclear powers: it has adversaries at its border; it has ancient and passionate—at root, religious—enmities with its neighbors; its command and control procedures over nuclear weapons are uncertain; and the power of the military within the nation is high by Western democratic standards.

12. Blacker and Duffy, *International Arms Control,* 395.

13. My thanks to George Bunn and Gail Lapidus for pointing this out to me.

14. Klare, *Rogue States and Nuclear Outlaws.*

15. The START II Treaty cuts the strategic arsenals to 3,500 deployed weapons on each side—though many thousands more weapons will be retained in strategic reserves. The Moscow Treaty of 2002 mandates further cuts to 2,200 deployed weapons for each country by 2012.

16. Panofsky, "Dismantling the Concept of 'Weapons of Mass Destruction,'" and Sloyan, "U.S. Has Policy Allowing Nuclear Attack on Iraq."

17. On the notion of dominant discourses, see especially Foucault, *Power/ Knowledge* and *The History of Sexuality.* See also Scott, *Domination and the Arts of Resistance,* Terdiman, *Discourse/Counter-discourse,* and Williams, *Marxism and Literature.*

18. Gupta, *Postcolonial Developments,* and Lutz and Collins, *Reading National Geographic.*

19. Classic sources on the theory and practice of deterrence include Brodie, *Strategy in the Missile Age*; Jervis, *The Illogic of American Nuclear Strategy*; Kahn, *On Thermonuclear War*; Schelling, *The Strategy of Conflict* and *Arms and Influence*; and Wohlstetter, "The Delicate Balance of Terror." See Freedman, *The Evo-*

lution of Nuclear Strategy, and Morgan, *Deterrence,* for overviews of this body of thought.

20. Waltz, "More May Be Better."

21. *New York Times,* "India, Uninvited, Joins the Nuclear Club."

22. McGrory, "Doomsday and Dalliance"; Cornwell, "Listen Here India."

23. Gokhale, "Columnist Erred on India's Military Spending."

24. The first figure was supplied by the National Law Center on Homelessness and Poverty in Washington, D.C.; www.nlchp.org. On Americans living below the poverty line, see Mattern, "The Poverty amid Riches."

25. Edelman, "Kids First."

26. Rathjens, "Preventing Proliferation," 267.

27. Potter, *Nuclear Power and Non-Proliferation,* 157.

28. The leading proponents of the view that the cold war was, in Gaddis's words, a "long peace" stabilized by nuclear deterrence are Gaddis, *Strategies of Containment,* and Mearsheimer, "Why We Will Soon Miss the Cold War."

29. Quoted in News Network International, "All the Tests Successful."

30. Here I focus on the argument that a common border is dangerous because it leads to very short missile flight times. One sometimes also sees the argument that deterrence between India and Pakistan will be unstable because, sharing a border, they are more likely to fight directly—for example, over Kashmir. China and the Soviet Union, however, practiced stable deterrence across a shared border. Also, one could as easily argue that a common border enhances deterrence because there is less chance of escaping radioactive fallout if one uses nuclear weapons against a nearby enemy.

31. Lev, "India, Pakistan."

32. On "incitement to discourse," see Foucault, *History of Sexuality,* chapter 1.

33. Power, "India and Pakistan Face the Prospect of a Nuclear War."

34. See Waltz, "Toward Nuclear Peace," "More May Be Better," and "Waltz Responds to Sagan."

35. Waltz, "Toward Nuclear Peace" and "More May Be Better."

36. Aldridge, *First Strike!;* Gray and Payne, "Victory Is Possible," and Scheer, *With Enough Shovels.*

37. Blair, *The Logic of Accidental Nuclear War,* and Sagan, *The Limits of Safety.*

38. Blair, Feiveson, and von Hippel, "Taking Nuclear Weapons off Hair-Trigger Alert," and Turner, *Caging the Nuclear Genie.*

39. Unfortunately, Pakistan has declared its intention to put warheads on the Ghauri missile, so this contrast between South Asia and the behavior of the principal nuclear powers may be disintegrating.

40. Sagan, "More Will Be Worse," 90–91. For a variant on this argument, see Perkovich, "A Nuclear Third Way in South Asia."

41. Brito and Intriligator, "Proliferation and the Probability of War," 137.

42. Anderson, "Confusion Dominates Arms Race."

43. One reason given by defense intellectuals for not sharing such safety technologies with India and Pakistan is that it would signal U.S. acceptance of their nuclear weapons capability.

44. Drell, Foster, and Townes, "How Safe Is Safe?" and Smith, "Lab Spreads Radiation in Air."

45. Sagan, *The Limits of Safety*, 228–29.

46. Ibid., 230.

47. Ibid., 130–31.

48. Ibid., 1, 99.

49. Sagan, *The Limits of Safety*, 185, and Williams and Cantelon, *The American Atom*, 239–45.

50. Barasch, *The Little Black Book of Atomic War*, 41.

51. Ibid.

52. Sagan, *The Limits of Safety*, 156–203.

53. Sagan, *The Limits of Safety*, 184, and Smith, "America's Arsenal of Nuclear Time Bombs."

54. Potter, *Nuclear Power and Non-Proliferation*, 143. By contrast, George Perkovich has suggested that authoritarian regimes may actually find it easier to denuclearize than democracies. He points out that the governments of South Africa, Brazil, and Argentina actually decided to abandon their nuclear weapons programs before their transition to democracy (Perkovich, "Exploding Myths about the Bomb").

55. McCrea and Markle, *Minutes to Midnight*, 111.

56. I am indebted to Avner Cohen and George Rathjens for pointing this out to me.

57. Dahl, *Controlling Nuclear Weapons*, Falk, "Nuclear Weapons and the End of Democracy," and Scarry, *The Body in Pain*, all argue that nuclear weapons have a corrosive effect on democracy, subverting it from within. Dahl contends that the secrecy and arcane expertise surrounding nuclear weapons decisions as they are currently made exclude the public from those decisions. Falk and Scarry argue that, because the use of nuclear weapons could be initiated by a small elite within U.S. society, the citizenry has lost its prerogative, central to liberal society, to consent to war.

58. Abrams, "US: Nuclear Situation Serious."

59. Perle, "Keeping the Bomb from Iraq." It bears noting here that, despite the popular U.S. conception of Saddam Hussein as a madman, his conduct of the Gulf Crisis and eventual Gulf War was, by the standards of realpolitik, shrewd and rational, even if it was also ruthless and, ultimately, unsuccessful. In his conversation with U.S. Ambassador April Glaspie a few days before invading Kuwait, Hussein attempted to make sure he would not be trespassing on U.S. vital interests. In subsequent months Hussein attempted to buy time and split the coalition before the war. When that failed, his attacks on Israel were an intelligent (albeit amoral) strategy to split the Arab coalition. He was wise to keep his air force well away from the U.S. Air Force during the war. Finally, in surrendering and surviving as

leader of his country, Hussein showed that he was not quite like Hitler after all (see Waltz, "More May Be Better" and "Waltz Responds to Sagan").

60. Kennedy, "Prologue," ix.

61. *Congressional Quarterly Weekly,* "As the Dust Settles in India, U.S. Rethinks Nuclear Policy," 1367–68.

62. Mayer, "Subcontinent Nuclear Tests Bother Teller," B1.

63. Said, *Orientalism,* 287; Kennedy, "Prologue," ix; Associated Press, "Senator Daniel Patrick Moynihan Says Nuclear Threat Is Not India"; McGrory, "Nuclear Boys Behaving Badly"; Kempster, "Iraq Sacrificed Billions for Its Arms."

64. Kondracke, "Watch Out for Those 'Little' Nuclear Wars."

65. Wouters, "Nuclear Powder Keg."

66. See, for example, Marquand, "India Bomb Hits Chord for Hindus."

67. Ghosh, "Letter to the Editor."

68. Brito and Intiligator, "Proliferation and the Probability of War," 140.

69. Said, *Orientalism,* 287.

70. Aeppel, "A-Bomb Technology Spreads"; Spector, *Nuclear Ambitions,* 18.

71. Sagan, *The Limits of Safety,* 81–91; "More Will Be Worse," 78–79.

72. Sagan, *The Limits of Safety,* 189.

73. Sagan, "More Will Be Worse," 62.

74. Rhodes, *Dark Sun,* 564.

75. U.S. Air Force, *Oral History of General Horace M. Wade,* 307–9; quoted in Sagan, *The Limits of Safety,* 150.

76. Stevens, "General Removed over War Speech"; quoted in Sagan, "More Will Be Worse," n. 25.

77. Gusterson, *Nuclear Rites* and "Remembering Hiroshima at a Nuclear Weapons Laboratory"; see also Mojtabai, *Blessed Assurance.*

78. Sagan, *The Limits of Safety,* 54.

79. Bundy, *Danger and Survival,* 238–39, 266–70, 277–83, 384; Cheng, "To the Nuclear Brink"; Ellsberg, "Call to Mutiny," v–vi.

80. Said, *Orientalism,* 1–2.

81. Reid, "Pakistan, India Loans Blocked."

82. Perlmutter, "A Bomb for the Butcher?" emphasis added.

83. Weiner, "U.S. and China Helped Pakistan Build Its Bomb."

84. *New York Times,* "Punish Pakistan's Perfidy on the Bomb" and "Stop Pakistan's Nuclear Bomb."

85. Smith, "A-Bomb Ticks in Pakistan," 38.

86. Hence William Safire's comment in the debate as to whether or not the United States should undertake air strikes on Iraq that President Clinton "cannot, as head of the only willing world police power, do less" ("Support Your President").

87. News Network International, June 1, 1998.

88. Haraway, *Primate Visions*; Merchant, *The Death of Nature*; and Rosaldo, "Woman, Culture, and Society."

89. *New York Times,* "Punish Pakistan's Perfidy on the Bomb"; Rosenfeld, "Nuclear Nightmare"; Markey, "Hold Pakistan to Non-Proliferation Law."

90. *Washington Post,* "Second Best."

91. Smith, "A-Bomb Ticks in Pakistan," 104.

92. Molander, "Must They All Go Nuclear?"

93. Marshall, "India, Pakistan"; Sanders, "Avoiding the Worst of All Possible Worlds," 25; Chapman, "Hiding from Reality"; *New York Times,* "Punish Pakistan's Perfidy"; Smith, "A-Bomb Ticks in Pakistan," 106; *New York Times,* "Punish Pakistan's Perfidy."

94. Smith, "Indian Tests Shatter West's Containment Policy."

95. Marshall, "South Asia Testing."

96. McFarlane, "Pakistan's Catch-22."

97. McGrory, "Doomsday and Dalliance."

98. Chomsky, "Strategic Arms, the Cold War, and the Third World."

99. Thus, for example, Eric Ehrmann, worried by evidence that Iraq, Brazil, and Argentina were working together on the bomb, fears that "with Latin-developed mass-destruction technologies in hand, Saddam's nonaligned populism could transcend the politics of Islam and shift the global balance of power" ("Iraq's Nuclear Wildcards"). He fears a global alliance, protected by its own nuclear umbrella, between "Saddam Hussein's challenge to the oil sheikhdoms and the struggle of Latin populists against their traditional oligarchies."

Richard Perle wonders: "Would the U.S. have sent 100,000 troops within range of Iraqi nuclear missiles? With nuclear weapons Saddam would rule the gulf and control the world's supply of oil" ("Keeping the Bomb from Iraq"). William Safire agrees: "Once he gets his Saddam bomb, no land force, no matter how powerful, would dare invade; and, as his Tammuz missile is perfected, he can impose nuclear blackmail on the superpowers" ("Giving Iraq Time").

Gary Milhollin ("Attention, Nuke-Mart Shoppers!") argues that, now that the cold war is over, the main threat to "our" security comes from the Third World. He argues that CoCom (Coordinating Committee for Multilateral Export Controls), the institution established to prevent Eastern bloc countries from acquiring advanced Western technology during the cold war, should be reformed to admit former Eastern bloc countries and prevent Third World countries from acquiring advanced, especially nuclear, technology.

100. Burns, "On Kashmir's Dividing Line."

101. Green, "The Iraqi Bomb," 18.

102. Lewis, "Are States All Equal?"

103. Rushdie, *Shame,* 219.

104. Ground Zero, *Nuclear War,* 221.

105. Kennan, "Two Views of the Soviet Problem," 62.

3. Short Circuit

I am grateful to Jane Caputi, Michael Fischer, Chris Gray, and anonymous reviewers for the *Journal of Popular Film and Television* for comments that helped me revise this chapter. As always, responsibility for remaining idiocies is mine alone. The research upon which this chapter is based would not have been possible without the financial support of a Mellon New Directions Fellowship at Stanford University and an SSRC-MacArthur Fellowship in International Peace and Security.

1. "Ray" is a pseudonym. I have also taken the liberty of disguising some of the circumstantial details I give about Ray's life in order to make it harder to identify him. In accordance with the prevailing, but unfortunate, convention in anthropology, and for want of a better word, I call Ray an informant, though I dislike this word's connotations of surveillance and betrayal.

2. Fish, *Is There a Text in This Class?*

3. Hobson, *Crossroads,* 17; quoted in Radway, *Reading the Romance,* 9.

4. Besides Radway, my approach here is also influenced by a classic anthropological article by Laura Bohannon ("Shakespeare in the Bush"), which explores the different ways Bohannon and her African Tiv hosts understood Shakespeare's *Hamlet.* The present chapter can be read as an updating of Bohannon's argument for the age of film and video.

5. The founding and early history of the laboratory are best described in the writings of Herb York, its first director (York, "The Origins of the Lawrence Livermore Laboratory" and *Making Weapons, Talking Peace*).

6. For overviews of the laboratory's programs, see Cochran et al., *Nuclear Weapons Databook,* vol. 2, and a special issue of the laboratory's *Energy and Technology Review* ("The State of the Laboratory"). An excellent but unpublished overview appears in Senate Policy Committee, "The University of California, The Lawrence Livermore National Laboratory, and the Los Alamos National Laboratory."

7. On the rise and fall of the Nuclear Freeze Campaign, see Solo, *From Protest to Policy,* and Waller, *Congress and the Nuclear Freeze.* For a more general portrait of the antinuclear movement in the 1980s, see Loeb, *Hope in Hard Times.* Barbara Epstein, in "The Culture of Direct Action" and "The Politics of Prefigurative Community," gives an excellent description and analysis of the Livermore Action Group, which organized the mass blockades of the laboratory, one of which attracted about five thousand participants. Thirteen hundred people were arrested for civil disobedience at this protest in 1982, making it one of the biggest civil disobedience actions in American history. For an account of one of the mass blockades, see Cabasso and Moon, *Risking Peace.*

8. For an exploration of the growing opposition to the arms race within America's mainstream churches, see the interviews in Wallis, *Peacemakers.* The bishop who was arrested at the gates of the laboratory was Leontine Kelley, a Methodist.

9. For a more detailed exploration of Livermore scientists' thinking about nuclear ethics, see Gusterson, *Nuclear Rites,* chapter 3.

10. In my writing I usually treat nuclear weapons scientists' political statements as material for cultural analysis, bracketing the contentious question of whether these statements should be seen as "true" or "false." In this case, however, I feel compelled as commentator to make an exception to my own policy in order to refute what must in all candor be described as disinformation about the antinuclear movement promulgated by the Reagan administration. Based on my experience,

first as a participant in and later as a researcher on the northern California anti-nuclear movement of the 1980s, I am quite sure that this movement was not funded by the KGB. I spent a year of my life deeply involved in fund-raising for the San Francisco Nuclear Freeze and got to see firsthand, when the mail was opened, where the money came from (mostly from lots of small donors). I also spent years watching antinuclear organizations sink into debt, fall behind in paying their employees' minimal salaries, and keep having to neglect their political goals in order to organize fund-raising events to keep themselves afloat. This was a movement that was starved of resources (see Gusterson, "Exploding Anthropology's Canon in the World of the Bomb").

11. Ironically, the jewel in the Livermore Laboratory's technological crown in the 1980s was its Nova laser—the most powerful laser in the world—used for both military and alternative-energy experiments.

4. Hiroshima, the Gulf War, and the Disappearing Body

This essay has been created for this volume by combining and rewriting "Nuclear War, the Gulf War, and the Disappearing Body" and "Remembering Hiroshima at an American Nuclear Weapons Laboratory." Part of the argument was first presented at the American Anthropological Association Meetings in 1988 and to a lively meeting of the anthropology dissertation writers seminar at Harvard University in 1990. My thanks to Carol Cohn, Paul Gelles, Art Hudgins, John Mack, and Cynthia Nitta for their comments, as well as to the Livermore scientist for whom I invented the pseudonym "Tom."

1. Scarry, *The Body in Pain*; Foucault, *Discipline and Punish* and *The History of Sexuality*.

2. Foucault, *Discipline and Punish*; Asad, "Notes on Body Pain and Truth in Medieval Christian Ritual."

3. On the Iroquois, see Wallace, *The Death and Rebirth of the Seneca*; see also Chagnon, *Yanomamo*; Heider, *Grand Valley Dani*; and Rosaldo, *Ilongot Head-hunting, 1883–1974*.

4. This estimate comes from Keegan, *War and Our World*, 2.

5. Examples of the revisionist perspective include Alperovitz, *Atomic Diplomacy* and *The Decision to Use the Atomic Bomb*; Bernstein, *The Atomic Bomb*; Boyer, *Fallout*; Goldberg, "What Did Truman Know and When Did He Know It?"; Kolko, *The Politics of War*; and Norris, *Racing for the Bomb*.

6. For more on the dispute over the Smithsonian exhibition, see Goldberg, "Smithsonian Suffers Legionnaire's Disease"; Lifton and Mitchell, *Hiroshima in America*; and Nobile, *Judgment at the Smithsonian*.

7. Krauthammer, "Exhibit Distorts Historical Context of the A-Bombing of Japan."

8. York, *Making Weapons, Talking Peace*, 23.

9. Myslinski, "Memory Haunts Nagasaki Survivor."

10. On Western science's historical antipathy to emotional, personal, situated

accounts of the natural world, see Keller, *Reflections on Gender and Science*. In a fascinating autobiographical account of his socialization as an engineer, Pepper White recalls hearing as a graduate student that one of his friends had gassed herself to death in her car. His first reaction was to calculate in his mind the flow of carbon monoxide and the time it would have taken to kill her. It was at this moment that he realized he'd been resocialized by his training at MIT, saying to himself, "[T]hey've got me" (White, *The Idea Factory*, 255). Mark Selden (personal communication), foregrounding the roots of this objectifying impulse in the culture of science itself, points out that Japanese scientists represented the suffering bodies of A-bomb victims in strikingly similar terms—though they also criticized their American counterparts for treating the A-bomb victims like guinea pigs and for studying their symptoms without offering treatment.

11. On U.S. censorship of news about the bombing, see Hook, "Censorship and Reportage of Atomic Damage in Hiroshima and Nagasaki," and Mitchell, "Hiroshima Day."

12. Rhodes, *The Making of the Atomic Bomb*, 734.

13. See Caulfield, *Multiple Exposures*; Committee for the Compilation of Materials on the Damage Caused by the Atomic Bombs in Hiroshima and Nagasaki, *Hiroshima and Nagasaki*; Glasstone and Dolan, *The Effects of Nuclear Weapons*; Neel, Beebe, and Miller, "Delayed Biomedical Effects of the Bomb"; and Postol, "Nuclear War."

14. See Gallagher, *American Ground Zero*; Rosenberg, *Atomic Soldiers*; and Welsome, *The Plutonium Files*.

15. Some footage of this gruesome experiment can be seen in the 1982 documentary film *Dark Circle*. The documentary footage is also incorporated into a fictionalized re-creation of the events in the 1989 Hollywood film *Nightbreaker*.

16. McClatchy News Service, "History Has Glow in Desert"; Norris and Arkin, "Hot Dogs."

17. Foucault, *Discipline and Punish*; Scarry, *The Body in Pain*.

18. My thanks to Laura Hein and Mark Selden for this point.

19. Glasstone and Dolan, *The Effects of Nuclear Weapons*, 548.

20. On the human cost of Hiroshima and Nagasaki, see the varying casualty estimates of Bernstein, *The Atomic Bomb*, vii; Bundy, *Danger and Survival*, 80; Postol, "Nuclear War," 519; and Rhodes, *The Making of the Atomic Bomb*, 734, 740. The Gulf War casualty estimate is discussed in Jackson, "What about the Death Toll?"

21. Schmitt, "Racing through the Dark in Pursuit of Scuds."

22. Thomas and Barry, "War's New Science."

23. Farrell and Kornblut, "War in Iraq Selective Strikes/Strategy."

24. *World News Tonight with Peter Jennings*, February 28, 1991.

25. Schmitt, "Racing through the Dark in Pursuit of Scuds."

26. Farrell, "Where We Shroud Our Heroes." The White House reinstated this ban during the second Gulf War in 2003.

27. Jackson, "What about the Death Toll?"

28. Some of these examples come from an insightful article on the language of the Gulf War by Diane White: "Everyday Uses for Gulfspeak."

29. Mathews, "Saddam's Last Stand."

30. *This Week with David Brinkley,* March 3, 1991.

31. Boustany, "'Show No Mercy,' Saddam Tells His Troops"; Cowell, "Hussein Orders 'No Mercy' for Foe."

32. Kelly, "In Morgues, Terror's Grisly Remains."

33. For a highly readable critique of these hyperrational nuclear war plans, see Scheer, *With Enough Shovels.*

34. See Lifton, *The Broken Connection*; Lifton and Falk, *Indefensible Weapons*; and Lifton and Markusen, *The Genocidal Mentality.* For classic articulations of the feminist perspective, see Caldicott, *Missile Envy,* as well as Cohn, "Sex and Death in the Rational World of Defense Intellectuals."

35. "Tom" is a pseudonym.

36. Specialists in nuclear ethics refer to this position as "consequentialist" because, instead of focusing on the morality of the means employed, it stresses the morality of the consequences achieved by actions that, although ethically problematic in themselves, may become ethical in the context of their consequences. For more on this see Nye, *Nuclear Ethics.*

37. Hersey, *Hiroshima,* p.29

38. See Gusterson, "Tales of the City."

5. Presenting the Creation

This chapter has benefited from comments by Barton Bernstein and Paul Chilton as well as the participants at the conference "NATO's First Decade" at Oxford University, April 9–12, 1990, where it was first presented. The research for this chapter was conducted while the author was the recipient of an SSRC-MacArthur Fellowship in International Peace and Security; the chapter was revised for publication under the auspices of an Arms Control Fellowship at Stanford University's Center for International Security and Arms Control.

1. See Kaplan, *NATO and the United States,* 8. In his first inaugural address of 1801, Thomas Jefferson seconded Washington's sentiments, saying famously, "Peace, commerce and honest friendship with all nations; entangling alliances with none."

2. Calleo, *The Atlantic Fantasy,* 3.

3. Kaplan, *NATO and the United States,* 1.

4. Wallace, a former presidential candidate for the Progressive Party, opposed the treaty on the grounds that it abridged the constitutional right of Congress to, alone, commit the United States to war; that "it would replace the United Nations concept of one world with two irreconcilable blocs of nations" (*New York Times,* "Wallace Urges Protest"); and that it would tighten the noose of military encirclement too tightly around Russia's neck. On March 28, 1949, he shared these views with the American people in a half-hour radio broadcast on CBS.

Senator Taft saw the North Atlantic Treaty, accurately as it turned out, as the first act in a long drama of U.S. military commitments to Europe that he opposed on fiscal as well as diplomatic grounds.

George Kennan felt that the Soviet threat toward Western Europe was political rather than military, and that an expensive alliance would just waste money that might be better spent inoculating the war-ravaged economies and societies of Europe against their domestic communist movements. For more on Kennan's views, see Gaddis, *Strategies of Containment* and "The United States and the Question of a Sphere of Influence in Europe."

5. Secretary of State Dean Acheson, for example, gave a "clear and absolute no" when Republican Senator Bourke Hickenlooper of Iowa asked him during the Senate ratification hearings whether U.S. troops would, as a consequence of the North Atlantic Treaty, be stationed permanently or semipermanently in Europe. In his memoirs he claims that his answer was "deplorably wrong" and "stupid," but "not intended to deceive." See Acheson, *Present at the Creation*, 285.

6. Calleo, *The Atlantic Fantasy*, 25.

7. See Edwards, *The Closed World*; Herman and Chomsky, *Manufacturing Consent*; and Chomsky, *Necessary Illusions*.

8. Acheson, *Present at the Creation*, 282. Acheson's own typed copy of the speech, with his handwritten emendations, can be found at www.trumanlibrary.org/nato/doc5.htm.

9. For a good introduction to critical security studies, see Krause and Williams, *Critical Security Studies*. Other useful texts include Booth and Smith, *International Relations Theory Today*; Campbell, *Writing Security*; Chilton, *Security Metaphors*; Der Derian and Shapiro, *International/Intertextual Relations*; Gusterson, *Nuclear Rites*; Shapiro, *Violent Cartographies*; Walker, *Inside/Outside*; and Weldes et al., *Cultures of Insecurity*.

10. On the importance of these factors in the creation of the NATO alliance, see Lafeber, *America, Russia, and the Cold War*, 50–85.

11. On the naturalizing power of ideology, see Althusser, "Ideology and Ideological State Apparatuses," 121–73; Berger and Luckmann, *The Social Construction of Reality*; Eagleton, *Ideology*; Foucault, *Discipline and Punish*, *Power/Knowledge*, and *The History of Sexuality*; Geertz, "Common Sense as a Cultural System"; Giddens, "Four Theses on Ideology"; and Nader, *Harmony Ideology*.

12. See Benjamin, "Theses on the Philosophy of History."

13. See Kennan, "A Fateful Error."

14. See Calleo, *The Atlantic Fantasy*, 28; and Gaddis, "The United States and the Question of a Sphere of Influence in Europe."

15. Gaddis, "The United States and the Question of a Sphere of Influence in Europe," 66.

16. Quoted in ibid., 22.

17. Gaddis, ibid., 25–88; Calleo, *Beyond American Hegemony*, 29–30; Kaplan, *NATO and the United States*, 14; and Lafeber, *America, Russia, and the Cold War*, 59–68.

18. Gaddis, "The United States and the Question of a Sphere of Influence in Europe," 83.

19. Calleo, *Beyond American Hegemony*, 34.

20. Ibid., 34–35.

21. Kaplan, *NATO and the United States*, 34.

22. Ibid., chapter 1.

23. Ibid., 37.

24. Acheson, *Present at the Creation*, 280.

25. Callender, "U.S. Aid Guarantee Hailed by France."

26. *New York Times* (1949).

27. Calleo, *Beyond American Hegemony*, 38–39.

28. Gaddis, "The United States and the Question of the Sphere of Influence in Europe," 64.

29. Kaplan, *NATO and the United States*, 36–37.

30. Ibid., 36.

31. Quoted in Reston, "New Pact Marks Historic Change in Our Policy."

32. For a discussion of such persuasive techniques in advertising and other contexts, see Cialdini, *Influence: Science and Practice*.

33. Kaplan, *NATO and the United States*, 36.

34. See article 3 of the North Atlantic Treaty (www.nato.int/docu/basictxt/treaty.htm).

35. *New York Times,* "Wallace Urges Protest."

36. Calleo, *The Atlantic Fantasy*, 43.

37. On this point, see Giddens, *Central Problems in Social Theory*.

38. Acheson, *Present at the Creation*, 279.

39. Ibid.

40. For more discussion of the use of "the Other" to construct community, see Connolly, *Identity/Differences,* and Said, *Orientalism*.

41. Truman used the same device in a speech at the signing of the North Atlantic Treaty, April 4, 1949, saying that efforts to make the United Nations work "have been blocked by one of the major powers." He never names the power explicitly.

42. Calleo, *The Atlantic Fantasy*, 24.

43. Halen, "Senator Hails Tie," and Lawrence, "Pact Itself Hailed."

44. Kaplan, *NATO and the United States*, 37.

45. Acheson, *Present at the Creation*, 280.

6. Missing the End of the Cold War in Security Studies

My thanks to Stanford University's Center for International Security and Arms Control for inviting me to present an early version of the chapter, and to Noam Chomsky, Lynn Eden, Peter Katzenstein, Steve Miller, Robert Latham, Stephanie Platz, Scott Sagan, and Steve Van Evera for their thoughtful responses to earlier drafts. Thanks also go to Roberta Brawer for showing me the relevance of the "trading zone" literature. Above all, I thank all the participants in the "Cultures of

Insecurity" project for their comments in successive workshops in which this essay was presented.

1. The field discussed in this chapter goes by a number of names, each with its own nuance. These names include security studies, strategic studies, international relations, and peace and conflict studies. I call the field international security studies following the usage of Nye and Lynn-Jones, "International Security Studies."

2. One could make the case (as Cynthia Enloe has pointed out) for many endings of the cold war (see Booth, "Security and Self," 85). In putting the end of the cold war in the fall of 1989, I am following the dominant convention, which ties the end of the cold war to the fall of the Berlin Wall in November 1989.

3. Lebow and Risse-Kappen, *International Relations Theory and the End of the Cold War*, 2.

4. See Cohn, "Sex and Death in the Rational World of Defense Intellectuals"; Herken, *Counsels of War*; and Kaplan, *Wizards of Armageddon*.

5. Galison, *Image and Logic*.

6. It is a hallmark of the kind of knowledge developed in trading zones that it is as likely to be elaborated in adjunct centers at universities or freestanding institutes (the Santa Fe Institute being the classic example) as institutionalized in university departments.

7. Nye and Lynn-Jones, "International Security Studies."

8. Forsberg, "A Bilateral Nuclear Weapons Freeze" and "The Freeze and Beyond"; McCrea and Markle, *Minutes to Midnight*; Solo, *From Protest to Policy*; Waller, *Congress and the Nuclear Freeze*.

9. New Left Review, *Exterminism and Cold War*; Thompson, *Beyond the Cold War* and *Heavy Dancers*; Thompson and Smith, *Protest and Survive* and *Prospectus for a Habitable Planet*.

10. Many mainstream security studies specialists, defending their failure to foresee the end of the cold war, have told me that the end of the cold war was an extraordinary event that no one predicted. This depends on what one means by "predict." By the mid-1980s, many in the peace movement, without putting their money on a specific date, argued that the end of the cold war was a possibility to work toward (New Left Review, *Exterminism and Cold War*; Thompson, *Beyond the Cold War*).

11. Cohn, "Sex and Death in the Rational World of Defense Intellectuals."

12. See Cohn, "Sex and Death in the Rational World of Defense Intellectuals," and Gusterson, "Realism and the International Order after the Cold War" for an elaboration of these criticisms. On a more philosophical note, security studies was also almost entirely untouched by the critiques of positivism and eruptions of critical theory that were turning neighboring fields of knowledge upside down in the 1980s, producing the reflexive and feminist turns in anthropology, deconstruction in literary studies, social constructivism in science studies, and the view from below in history. Since the late 1980s, however, security studies has changed, opening itself to new voices (anthropologists, for example) and to new issues (ethnic conflict, environmental security, etc.).

13. For a systematic critique of security studies in the 1980s as an "ancien régime" worldview, written by a self-described "fallen realist," see Booth, "Security and Self."

14. Carnesale and Haass, *Superpower Arms Control,* 355.

15. Hoffman, "On the Political Psychology of Peace and War," 5.

16. Marcus, "Foreword."

17. Weldes, *Constructing National Interests*; Milliken, "Intervention and Identity."

18. The argument here is, of course, broadly Kuhnian: that successful theoretical paradigms work to render certain kinds of anomalous patterns invisible (Kuhn, *The Structure of Scientific Revolutions*). Seen in this light, international security specialists in the 1980s were like those gifted medieval astronomers who were more interested in elaborating the considerable successes of the Ptolemaic paradigm than in attending to a few observations that did not fit comfortably within it.

19. Booth, "Dare Not to Know," 333–34.

20. My argument here is strongly indebted to Starn, "Missing the Revolution." Starn asks how it was that Andeanists in anthropology were so taken by surprise by the eruption of the Maoist Sendero Luminoso and of civil war in Peru in the 1980s. He finds the answer primarily in a common trope in anthropological writing of peasants as isolated bearers of unchanging traditions, arguing that this intellectual predisposition obstructed anthropologists from seeing the degree to which, despite colorful folkloric costumes, these peasants had been absorbed into global capitalist society. I would argue that there is an isomorphism between one kind of anthropology's nostalgic emphasis on the unchanging traditionalism of peasant life and one kind of security studies' focus on enduring anarchy and military rivalry as defining features of the international system.

21. Contributors have included theorists such as Hedley Bull, Kenneth Waltz, John Mearsheimer, Stephen Walt, and Robert Keohane and practitioners such as Robert McNamara and McGeorge Bundy.

22. Examples of analyses of discourse communities include Foucault, *The Order of Things, Discipline and Punish,* and *The History of Sexuality*; Lutz and Collins, *Reading National Geographic*; and Said, *Orientalism.* Analyses of the discourse of Western defense communities include Chilton, *Language and the Nuclear Arms Debate*; Cohn, "Sex and Death"; Der Derian and Shapiro, *International/Intertextual Relations*; Gusterson, "Endless Escalation"; Manoff, "Modes of War and Modes of Address"; and Taylor, "Reminiscences of Los Alamos."

23. Haraway, *Primate Visions* and *Simians, Cyborgs, and Women.*

24. Gusterson, "Endless Escalation."

25. Blechman and Utgoff, "The Macroeconomics of Strategic Defenses," 63.

26. Perle's claim that the Soviets led in strategic bombers would not have been accepted by most defense analysts. In the same issue of the journal, for example, Sloss ("A World without Ballistic Missiles," 184–85) says that the Soviets were behind the United States in strategic bombers.

27. Schelling, "Abolition of Ballistic Missiles"; Sloss "A World without Ballistic Missiles," 187.

28. In a situation of extended deterrence, the U.S. nuclear umbrella is extended over allies. In a situation of existential deterrence, nuclear weapons exist only to deter the use of nuclear weapons against one's own country.

29. May, Bing, and Steinbruner, "Strategic Arsenals after START," 132–33.

30. Mustin, "The Sea-Launched Cruise Missile"; Brooks, "Nuclear SLCMs Add to Deterrence and Security"; Gottemoeller, "Finding Solutions to SLCM Arms Control Problems"; Postol, "Banning Nuclear SLCMs."

31. The other two articles are Lepingwell, "Soviet Strategic Air Defense and the Stealth Challenge," and Welch, "Assessing the Value of Stealthy Aircraft and Cruise Missiles."

32. MIRV stands for "multiple independently targetable reentry vehicles." A MIRVed missile bears several warheads, each capable of hitting a separate preprogrammed target. Thus, one MX missile could, in theory at least, knock out ten different targets.

33. Glass, *Citizens against the MX.*

34. The other articles are Chayes, "Managing the Politics of Mobility"; Dougherty, "The Value of ICBM Modernization"; Fridling and Harvey, "On the Wrong Track?"; Hicks, "ICBM Modernization"; Lodal, "SICBM Yes, HML No"; and Toomay, "Strategic Forces Rationale."

35. These articles also slight the importance of U.S. domestic politics. The Carter administration's plans for deployment of the MX had collapsed in the face of grassroots and congressional political opposition, and the eruption of a massive antinuclear movement in the United States in the early 1980s was complicating the Reagan administration's search for an alternative deployment plan (Glass, *Citizens against the MX*). The authors refer only obliquely to such phenomena, however. Toomay ("Strategic Forces Rationale," 193), for example, refers to "political, economic, and social issues which create cross-currents in the decision-making process."

36. Hicks, "ICBM Modernization," 174.

37. As Steven Miller (personal communication) points out, there was, on the other hand, a coup attempt in the Soviet Union when it became clear that the Soviet empire was collapsing.

38. Lebow, "The Long Peace," 35.

39. For a broader discussion of the implications of the end of the cold war for security studies, especially for international relations theory, see also Halliday, "The End of the Cold War and International Relations"; Hogan, *The End of the Cold War*; and Lebow and Risse-Kappen, *International Relations Theory and the End of the Cold War.*

40. Besides the articles discussed here, *International Security* also published a cluster of articles attacking neoliberal institutionalism and democratic peace theory and arguing for the continuing importance of anarchy as the defining feature of the international system. See Layne, "Kant or Cant"; Mearsheimer, "The

False Promise of International Institutions"; and Spiro, "The Insignificance of the Liberal Peace," for example.

41. We might note here that, in Ken Booth's words, "we talk about peace (as in 'We've had peace since 1945') in such a way that peace can only mean the 'absence of world war.' This is a bizarre conception . . . when it cloaks well over twenty million violent deaths" ("Dare Not to Know," 334).

42. Mearsheimer's argument is, throughout, played out with a deck stacked in favor of neorealism. He claims to demonstrate that the underlying features of the international system have not changed by testing two rival theories, one of which (neoliberalism) assumes evolution in the international system while the other (neorealism) assumes constancy. He then tests the rival theories in terms of their ability to predict past behavior in the system. Thus, the conclusion (that the anarchy of the state system persists) is smuggled into the method.

43. In a prediction that may come back to haunt him, Waltz also—pointing out that "balance-of-power theory leads one to expect that states, if they are free to do so, will flock to the weaker side"—predicts the decay of NATO and the Western alliance as European states move to balance American power ("The Emerging Structure of International Politics," 74–75).

44. Lebow and Risse-Kappen, *International Relations Theory and the End of the Cold War,* 1.

45. Lebow, "The Long Peace," 36.

46. See Evans-Pritchard, *Witchcraft, Oracles and Magic among the Azande.*

7. Cultures as Strategic Hamlets

I have presented the ideas in this chapter in various venues, including the annual meeting of the American Anthropological Association in 1999 and 2000 and a special workshop at the York University in Toronto in 1999. I am grateful to everyone in both contexts for their thoughts. Special thanks go to Marshall Beier for his support, and to Ulf Hannerz for his comments.

1. See Gusterson, "Endless Escalation," "Realism and the International Order after the Cold War," and *Nuclear Rites*; as well as Weldes et al., *Cultures of Insecurity.*

2. Hannerz, "Reflections on Varieties of Culturespeak," 403.

3. Jervis, "The Clash of Civilizations," 308.

4. Bozeman, "Civilizations Under Stress," 1, quoted in Huntington, *The Clash of Civilizations,* 41. The latter author's own definition of civilization goes as follows: "a civilization is . . . the highest cultural grouping and the broadest level of cultural identity people have short of that which distinguishes humans from other species. It is defined both by common objective elements, such as language, history, religion, customs, institutions, and by the subjective self-identification of people" (43).

5. Huntington gives his list of civilizations on pp. 46–47 of *The Clash of Civilizations.* If Africa is not a separate civilization, it is unclear, according to Hunting-

ton what exactly it is, since, unlike the Latin American case, it seems doubtful an argument could be made that it belongs to one of the other civilizations. Implicitly, in Huntington's schema, Africans are a people without civilization.

6. Walt, "Building Up New Bogeymen," 189.

7. Kaldor, *New and Old Wars,* 143.

8. *The Clash of Civilizations* was also much discussed outside the West, where it found what might at first blush seem like strange admirers: some Hindu nationalists in India praised its portrayal of Muslims as bellicose expansionists, for example, while some Asian leaders (including senior officers in the Chinese military) embraced Huntington's depiction of Asian cultures as hierarchical and disciplined, but ill-suited to democracy (Ong, *Flexible Citizenship,* 187).

9. Ahrari, "The Clash of Civilizations," 57.

10. A similar argument is made by Chan, "Too Neat and Under-Thought a World Order." On Kennan's birthing of the containment vision for the cold war era, see Gaddis, *Strategies of Containment.*

11. See Fukuyama, "The End of History," and *The End of History and the Last Man.* See Huntington, "No Exit," 3–11 for his rebuttal of Fukuyama's argument. On the "democratic peace," see Doyle, "Kant, Liberal Legacies and Foreign Affairs," parts 1 and 2, and "Liberalism and World Politics." See also Ember, Ember, and Russett, "Peace between Participatory Polities."

12. Alluding to Huntington's earlier role as an adviser to the Johnson administration on Vietnam, Michael Ignatieff remarks that "it is a significant change of heart for a former architect of American policy in Vietnam to assert that 'Western intervention in the affairs of other civilizations is probably the single most dangerous source of instability and potential global conflict in a multi-civilizational world.'" ("The Clash of Civilizations," 13).

13. This last point is made by Chan, "Too Neat and Under-Thought a World Order," 138.

14. Rosencrance, "The Clash of Civilizations," 979.

15. Ignatieff, "The Clash of Civilizations," 13. Ahrari, "The Clash of Civilizations," makes the same point.

16. A symptom of Huntington's difficulty here is encountered in his discussion of Ukraine, which he characterizes as a "cleft state" divided between Western- and Orthodox-oriented peoples. Yet he acknowledges that the country seems likely to remain stable and unified because "these are two Slavic, primarily Orthodox peoples who have had close relationships for centuries and between whom intermarriage is common" (167). In other words, he explains why, in apparent violation of his model, two peoples can happily share a state across a civilizational fault line by making use of an analytical "patch"—the invocation of intermarriage and shared historical closeness (an argument, by the way, that would have seemed predictive of calm in Rwanda and in many parts of Yugoslavia twenty years ago). He is arguing, then, that civilizational fissures within a state generate conflict except when there is a close and friendly relationship between members of the different

civilizations—an argument we would have to characterize as more tautological than predictive.

17. This point is also made by Walt, "Building Up New Bogeymen," and by Glynn, "The Clash of Civilizations," 10. Huntington himself briefly "explains" U.S. support for Bosnia as follows: "The absence of an Islamic core state which could legitimately and authoritatively relate to the Bosnians, as Russia did to the Serbs and Germany to the Croats, impelled the United States to attempt that role" (156). This is a curious statement since nothing in the book explains why the U.S. should feel "impelled" to do any such thing.

18. Cheng, "To the Nuclear Brink."

19. Katzenstein, *The Culture of National Security*; Price, *The Chemical Weapons Taboo*; Kier, *Imagining War*.

20. In anthropology these arguments have been most forcefully made in Appadurai, *Modernity at Large*.

21. The allusion is to the annual meetings in the Swiss town of Davos of the political, economic, and intellectual movers and shakers of globalization.

22. For a study by an international relations theorist of the role of culture in foreign policy that uses a concept of culture less flat, deterministic, and reified than Huntington's, see Payne, *The Clash of Distant Cultures*.

23. This way of thinking was beautifully expressed in Ruth Benedict's *Patterns of Culture* and in her later national character study of Japanese culture, *The Chrysanthemum and the Sword*. The argument that cultures have rules that, like linguistic grammars, can be codified is most strongly stated in Goodenough, *Culture, Language, and Society*. For influential critiques of this model in anthropology in recent years, see Clifford, *The Predicament of Culture*; Clifford and Marcus, *Writing Culture*; Marcus and Fischer, *Anthropology as Cultural Critique*; and Rosaldo, *Culture and Truth*. A useful short survey of the status of the concept of culture in anthropology is given, together with a critique of Huntington's view of culture, in Hannerz, "Reflections on Varieties of Culturespeak."

24. In one of the most cited articles in the history of anthropology, the culture-as-text model was suggested by Clifford Geertz in chapter 1 of his *The Interpretation of Cultures*.

25. Rosaldo, *Culture and Truth*.

26. Hannerz, "Reflections on Varieties of Culturespeak," 395.

27. Durkheim, *The Division of Labor in Society*, one of the founding fathers of contemporary sociology and anthropology, saw culture as a unifying set of norms shared by members of a social group. For critiques of this perspective, see, inter alia, Rosaldo, *Culture and Truth*, chapter 4; and Giddens, *Central Problems in Social Theory*.

28. In his book *Islam Observed*, Geertz, who has done fieldwork at the two geographical poles of the Islamic world in Morocco and Indonesia, carefully traces the interwoven threads of similarity and difference through the Islamic world. Ironically, Huntington himself (154) speaks of the "strength, resilience, and viscosi-

ty of indigenous cultures, and their ability to resist, contain and adapt" foreign cultures when analyzing the difficulties in the contemporary world of Westernizing other cultures; it seems not to have occurred to him that this generalization applies backward in time and that all the civilizations he describes—but especially Islamic civilization—are agglomerations of myriad local resistances and adaptations.

29. Ong, *Flexible Citizenship*, 188. Making essentially the same point but hitting closer to home, Stephen Chan asks, "In a polyglot world in which plural societies predominate, what exactly is 'the West' Huntington seeks to defend? Is it a London with mosques and ashrams?" ("Too Neat and Under-Thought a World Order," 138).

30. Rosaldo, *Culture and Truth*, 208; Anzaldúa, *Borderlands?*; Hannerz, "Borders," 537–48.

31. In his discussion of Islamic immigration to Europe (199–203), Huntington suggests that these migrants will not assimilate and may therefore become a transnational thirteenth nation, a nation of Islam in Europe.

32. In what strikes this reader as a throwback to fascist ideologies of the mid-twentieth century (especially given its association with metaphors of infection), Huntington repeatedly indexes civilizational strength to rates of demographic expansion. Given that, in his model, people retain the civilizational culture into which they are born, those cultures with the highest birthrates may overwhelm others. The United States has, historically, always supplemented its birthrate by importing immigrants, but, in Huntington's model, this way of achieving demographic expansion can only be self-destructive.

33. The last sentence, spoken on behalf of a putatively homogeneous category of "Americans," is extraordinary given that, for recent waves of immigrants from Central America, Vietnam, Cambodia, Laos, the Philippines, Korea, and so on, Europe is hardly where they look for their roots.

34. One of the most influential formulations of this perspective is Robert Kaplan's *Balkan Ghosts*, reading of which is said to have persuaded Bill Clinton to keep out of the Bosnian conflict until late in the day.

35. On Rwanda, see Gourevitch, *We Wish to Inform You That Tomorrow We Will Be Killed with Our Families*. On Bosnia, see Bringa, *Being Muslim the Bosnian Way*; Christie, *Bosnia*; Ignatieff, *Blood and Belonging*; and Crawford and Lipschutz, "Discourses of War." For a more general discussion, see Naimark, *Fires of Hatred*. To be fair to Huntington, there is a processual edge to his theory of civil war in his discussion of the "hate dynamic" (266) that precedes civil wars as each side gets caught in an escalating cycle of mistrust and hostile misreadings of signals while moderates are increasingly marginalized. His discussion here (266–67) is perceptive and interesting, but it lacks any sense of human agency and it presumes a sort of conservation of identities and suspicions that—like tinder in a forest—are just awaiting the next cycle of combustion. Hence his formula: "fault line wars are intermittent; fault line conflicts are interminable" (291), and his observation that such conflicts have an "off-again-on-again quality" (ibid.).

36. This, again, replicates a weakness in older anthropological theorizing. As Rosaldo, *Culture and Truth,* 209, observes in his own critique of this theorizing, it was presumed that "if it's moving it isn't cultural."

37. Senghaas, "A Clash of Civilizations," 129.

38. It bears mentioning here that Huntington was one of those personally responsible for this policy in Vietnam, a policy whose consequences he denies by misreading them as symptoms of a timeless Asian culture.

39. For work in this direction, see Haas, "Knowledge, Power, and International Policy Coordination." For a study of the culture of defense intellectuals that has not received the attention it deserves in the field of security studies, see Cohn, "Sex and Death in the Rational World of Defense Intellectuals."

40. See Abraham, *The Making of the Indian Atomic Bomb.*

41. For a magisterial answer to this question, see Dower, *Embracing Defeat.*

42. See chapter 5.

43. Pedelty, *War Stories.*

44. For example, here is Huntington on different cultural groups within "cleft" states: "The forces of repulsion drive them apart and they gravitate toward civilization magnets in other countries" (138).

45. For this metaphor for culture I am partly indebted to Susan Harding's address to the American Ethnological Association at its May 2001 meeting in Montreal.

8. Nuclear Weapons Testing as Scientific Ritual

This chapter is based on fieldwork funded by a Mellon New Directions Fellowship at Stanford and a Social Sciences Research Council MacArthur Fellowship in International Peace and Security. Writing was facilitated by a Weatherhead Fellowship at the School of American Research and a John D. and Catherine T. MacArthur Foundation Grant in Research and Writing in the Program on Peace and International Security. My thanks to David Dearborn, Steve Flank, Bill Zagotta, and Routledge's anonymous reviewer for detailed comments on drafts of this material, and to colloquium audiences at the Massachusetts Institute of Technology and Arizona State University West for their comments. This chapter is adapted from my book *Nuclear Rites: A Nuclear Weapons Laboratory at the End of the Cold War.*

1. The Livermore Laboratory, located about forty miles east of San Francisco, is the younger of two nuclear weapons laboratories in the United States, the other being Los Alamos, where the bombs dropped on Japan were designed. The Sandia Laboratory provides engineering support. Livermore was established in 1952. Its scientists designed the neutron bomb and the warheads for the MX, Polaris, Minuteman II, and ground-launched cruise missiles. For more information on the laboratory, see Broad, *Star Warriors* and *Teller's War;* Cochran et al., *Nuclear Weapons Databook,* volume 2, 44–52; and Gusterson, *Nuclear Rites.*

2. Divine, *Blowing on the Wind.*

3. Blum, "Nuclear Labs."

4. DeWitt, "Labs Drive the Arms Race," 104.

5. See the 1981 interview with Harold Agnew in *Los Alamos Science*; also, York, *Making Weapons, Talking Peace*.

6. This letter is reproduced in appendix K of Kidder, *Maintaining the U.S. Stockpile of Nuclear Weapons during a Low-Threshold or Comprehensive Test Ban*.

7. Miller, Brown, and Alonso, *Report to Congress on Stockpile Reliability*.

8. Wilson, *The Disarmer's Handbook*, 199.

9. Cochran et al., *Nuclear Weapons Databook*, 44. For a more detailed exploration of the issues at stake in this debate, see Fetter, "Stockpile Confidence under a Nuclear Test Ban" and *Toward a Comprehensive Test Ban*; and Immele and Brown, "Correspondence."

10. Reliability is officially defined in such a way that, if a weapon certified at 100 kilotons only produced an 80-kiloton yield, it would be deemed unreliable—even though the explosion would still be many times more powerful than that at Hiroshima.

11. On incitement to discourse, see Foucault, *The History of Sexuality*, chapter 1.

12. The names, and sometimes genders, of all scientists in this chapter have been changed to protect their privacy.

13. Broad, *Teller's War*, 196.

14. For other attempts to apply ritual theory to science, see Abir-Am, "A Historical Ethnography of a Scientific Anniversary in Molecular Biology"; Davis-Floyd, *Birth as an American Rite of Passage*; and Reynolds, *Stealing Fire*.

15. Durkheim, *The Elementary Forms of the Religious Life*; Gluckman, *Rituals of Rebellion in South-East Africa*; Turner, *The Ritual Process*.

16. Evans-Pritchard, *Witchcraft, Oracles, and Magic among the Azande*; Homans, "Anxiety and Ritual"; Malinowski, *Magic, Science, and Religion and Other Essays*.

17. Turner, *The Forest of Symbols*; Van Gennep, *The Rites of Passage*.

18. Benedict, *Patterns of Culture*; Geertz, *The Interpretation of Cultures*.

19. Quoted in Stober, "Lawrence Livermore Braces for Change."

20. Pinch, "Testing—One, Two Three."

21. Bourdieu, *Outline of a Theory of Practice*.

22. Drell, Foster, and Townes, "How Safe Is Safe?"; Smith, "America's Arsenal of Nuclear Time Bombs."

23. Easlea, *Fathering the Unthinkable*, 103, 130. By contrast, when India's scientists succeeded in exploding a nuclear device, they cabled their government with the message, "The Buddha is smiling" (Markey, *Nuclear Peril*, xiii).

24. See Foucault, *Power/Knowledge*.

25. Evans-Pritchard, *Witchcraft, Oracles, and Magic among the Azande*; Horton, "African Traditional Thought and Western Science"; Lévi-Strauss, *The Savage Mind*.

9. The Virtual Nuclear Weapons Laboratory in the New World Order

This chapter draws on research funded by a John D. and Catherine T. MacArthur Foundation Grant in Research and Writing in the Program on Peace and International Security, and by an Old Dominion Fellowship at MIT. Interview transcription was funded by an NSF grant on the Societal Dimensions of Engineering, Science, and Technology (grant number SBR-9712223). The chapter was written under the auspices of a fellowship at Stanford University's Center for International Security and Arms Control, and is based on talks given at Harvard's History of Science Department, the 1997 CASTAC conference at Rensselaer Polytechnic Institute, the 1997 Social Studies of Science Conference in Tucson, the Energy and Resources Group colloquium at UC Berkeley, and at the Anthropology Department, the History and Philosophy of Science Program, and the Center for International Security and Arms Control at Stanford University. My thanks to the many people at these presentations, too numerous to name individually, who suggested new perspectives on this material. I am particularly grateful for suggestions from Joe Dumit, Lynn Eden, Roger Hart, Stefan Helmreich, Tim Lenoir, Allison Macfarlane, Don Moore, Pief Panofsky, Trevor Pinch, Heinrich Schwarz, and Sylvia Yanagisako.

1. Exceptions to this generalization include Cohn, "Sex and Death in the Rational World of Defense Intellectuals"; Freer, "Atomic Pioneers and Environmental Legacy at the Hanford Site" on the Hanford plutonium facility; Garb, "Complex Problems and No Clear Solutions" (as well as her contribution to Dalton et al., *Critical Masses*), on the Chelyabinsk nuclear complex in Russia; Krasniewicz, *Nuclear Summer* (an ethnography of the women's peace camp at Seneca Falls); Masco, "The Nuclear Borderlands" and "States of Insecurity" (studies of the Los Alamos National Laboratory and the surrounding region); McNamara, "Ways of Knowing about Nuclear Weapons" (a Ph.D. dissertation on the internal culture of the Los Alamos National Laboratory); Schoch-Spana, "Reactor Control and Environmental Management" (a Ph.D. dissertation on the Savannah River facility); Wilson, "Power and Epistemology" (on the women's peace camp at Greenham Common); Yoneyama, *Hiroshima Traces* (on collective memories of Hiroshima); the essays collected by Rubinstein and Foster, *The Social Dynamics of Conflict* and *Peace and War*; Turner and Pitt, *The Anthropology of War and Peace*; and my own ethnography (Gusterson, *Nuclear Rites*) of the Lawrence Livermore National Laboratory.

2. See, for example, Krause and Williams, *Critical Security Studies*.

3. Clifford, "Spatial Practices"; des Chene, "Locating the Past"; Gupta and Ferguson, *Culture, Power, Place*; Gusterson, "Studying Up Revisited"; Marcus, "Ethnography in/of the World System"; Martin, *Flexible Bodies*.

4. On the Los Alamos National Laboratory, see Masco, "The Nuclear Borderlands" and "States of Insecurity"; Rhodes, *The Making of the Atomic Bomb*; Rosenthal, *At the Heart of the Bomb*; Shroyer, *Secret Mesa*; and Taylor, "Reminiscences of Los Alamos," "Remembering Los Alamos," and "The Politics of the Nu-

clear Test." On the Lawrence Livermore National Laboratory, see Broad, *Star Warriors* and *Teller's War*; Francis, "Warhead Politics"; and Gusterson, *Nuclear Rites*.

5. Appadurai, *Modernity at Large*; Featherstone, *Global Culture*; Gupta and Ferguson, "Discipline and Practice"; Hannerz, "Notes on the Global Ecumene" and *Transnational Connections*; Harvey, *The Condition of Postmodernity*; King, *Culture, Globalization, and the World-System*; Mintz, *Sweetness and Power*; Robertson, *Globalization*; and Wedel, *Collision and Collusion*.

6. Appadurai, *Modernity at Large*, 158–77; Hannerz, *Transnational Connections*, 81–90.

7. On globally networked defense intellectuals, see Cohn, "Sex and Death in the Rational World of Defense Intellectuals"; on spectacles of war, see Baudrillard, *The Gulf War Did Not Take Place*; Gibson, *Warrior Dreams*; Gray, *Postmodern War*; Gusterson, "Nuclear War, the Gulf War, and the Disappearing Body"; and Pedelty, *War Stories*.

8. My thanks to Sylvia Yanagisako for this insight.

9. Literature on the recent virtual turn in science includes Casti, *Would-be Worlds*; Helmreich, *Silicon Second Nature*; Starr "Seductions of Sim"; Turkle, *Life on Screen*; and Woolley, *Virtual Worlds*.

10. In constant 1997 dollars, the United States spent $3.7 billion per year on nuclear weapons design, testing, and production between 1948 and 1990. In 1997, the annual budget for science-based stockpile stewardship was $4.5 billion (Paine, "The Comprehensive Test Ban Treaty in the Current Nuclear Context," 54–55).

11. See Allison et al., *Avoiding Nuclear Anarchy*, and Cockburn and Cockburn, *One Point Safe* for "loose nukes" scenarios. See Klare, *Rogue States and Nuclear Outlaws* for an argument that the Pentagon fabricated the threat of "rogue states" at the end of the cold war in order to legitimate cold war defense budgets in the post–cold war era.

12. The phrase is indebted to Klare (*Rogue States and Nuclear Outlaws*, 23), who in turn adapted it from a statement by Admiral Carlisle Trost.

13. U.S. weapons designers worried that, where the Russian leadership had been deterred by U.S. threats to destroy major Russian population centers, leaders of rogue states were so ruthless and cared so little about their people that they would be deterred only by a threat against their own survival (Arkin, "Those Lovable Little Bombs"; Younger, *Nuclear Weapons in the Twenty-first Century*). Hence the suggestion of some at the weapons labs that the United States deploy an earth-penetrating mininuke that would burrow and destroy such leaders in their underground shelters.

14. By the time the Clinton administration took office, it was widely known that India, Pakistan, and Israel had nuclear weapons, and that North Korea was on the threshold of obtaining them, but these weapons were not publicly announced or acknowledged (at least until the Indian and Pakistani nuclear tests of May 1998), and the text of the Non-Proliferation Treaty formally enshrined the United States, the Soviet Union, Britain, France, and China as, in perpetuity (unless the treaty was amended), the only official nuclear powers.

15. Quoted in Blacker and Duffy, *International Arms Control*, 395.

16. Epstein, "Indefinite Extension—With Accountability"; Zamora Collina, "South Africa Bridges the Gap."

17. For comparison, the Hiroshima bomb was about twelve kilotons.

18. See Nuclear Weapons Stockpile Stewardship.

19. U.S. nuclear testing was suspended in September 1992. The Clinton administration discussed resuming a limited program of nuclear testing while negotiating the Comprehensive Test Ban Treaty (CTBT), but decided not to. The CTBT was eventually signed in September 1996. Although the U.S. Senate voted against ratification in 1999, the treaty remains in effect. So far, 155 countries have signed the CTBT and 55 have ratified it.

20. There is little published about the stockpile stewardship program except newspaper articles, official brochures, and the gray literature produced by nongovernmental organizations (NGOs) and review committees. Overviews of the program are given by Congressional Budget Office, *Preserving the Nuclear Weapons Stockpile Under a Comprehensive Test Ban*; Department of Energy, *The Stockpile Stewardship and Management Program*; Drell et al., *Science Based Stockpile Stewardship*; Easthouse, "Virtual Testing, Real Doubts"; Kidder, "Problems with Stockpile Stewardship"; Lichterman and Cabasso, *A Faustian Bargain*; Zerriffi and Makhijani, "The Stewardship Smokescreen" and *The Nuclear Safety Smokescreen*; Pasztor, "Building a Better Bomb"; and Veiluva et al., "Laboratory Testing in a Test Ban/Non-Proliferation Regime."

21. Gusterson, "NIF-ty Exercise Machine."

22. See Shankland, "Lab's Rebound Test Detonated as Planned"; and Wald, "Lab's Task."

23. Gibbs, "Computer Bombs."

24. Arkin, "Those Lovable Little Bombs"; Paine and McKinzie, *End Run*.

25. The text of the treaty can be accessed at www.state.gov/www/global/arms/treaties/ctb.html.

26. Holum's statement can be accessed at dosfan.lib.uic.edu/acda/ctbtpage/cd1.htm.

27. Veiluva et al., "Laboratory Testing in a Test Ban/Non-Proliferation Regime," 9.

28. Perry, *Annual Report to the President and the Congress*, 83–92.

29. If subjects are identified by their first name only, the name is a pseudonym.

30. Kidder, "Problems with Stockpile Stewardship," 646.

31. Barker's comments can be read at www.senate.gov/~armed_services/statement/1999/991007rb.pdf. A press release summarizing the Spence report is at http://armedservices.house.gov/openingstatementsandpressreleases/104thCongress/spdocpap.pdf.

32. Sokal makes this claim in "A Physicist Experiments with Cultural Studies." For another influential attack on the constructivist tradition in science studies, see Gross and Leavitt, *Higher Superstition*. See Ross, *Science Wars*, for a rebuttal of these critiques.

33. Classic texts in this tradition in science studies include Bloor, *Knowledge*

and Social Imagery; Kuhn, *The Structure of Scientific Revolutions*; Latour, *Science in Action* and *The Pasteurization of France*; Pickering, *Constructing Quarks*; Pinch and Collins, *The Golem*; and Shapin and Schaffer, *Leviathan and the Air-Pump*. A useful overview of this work is given in Hess, *Science Studies,* chapter 4.

34. Galison, *The Disunity of Science,* 3.

35. The phrase is from Latour, *Science in Action.*

36. See Katz, *Ban the Bomb.*

37. On this concept, see Fujimura, *Crafting Science.*

38. Galison, *Image and Logic*; Helmreich, *Silicon Second Nature.*

39. Galison, *The Disunity of Science* and *Image and Logic.*

40. Galison, *Image and Logic,* 691.

41. Zerriffi and Makhijani, *The Nuclear Safety Smokescreen.*

42. Derrida, "No Apocalypse, Not Now."

43. Luke, "What's Wrong with Deterrence?," 219, 223.

44. As Roger Hart (personal communication, March 14, 1998) points out, Luke's use of the term *postwarring* is problematic, since—in a recapitulation of the move for which I criticize Baudrillard—it implies through its use of the prefix *post* that war is a thing of the past, thus conceding to deterrence theory precisely the claim that the antinuclear movement has sought most strenuously to contest.

45. Der Derian, "Lenin's War, Baudrillard's Games"; Kroker, *Data Trash*; Stewart, *A Space on the Side of the Road.*

46. MacKenzie and Spinardi, "Tacit Knowledge, Weapons Design, and the Uninvention of Nuclear Weapons."

10. The Death of the Authors of Death

This chapter was first presented at the "What Is a Scientific Author?" conference at Harvard University in March 1997. My thanks to Mario Biagioli and Peter Galison for organizing the conference, for guiding me to unknown sources in the literature, and for giving me perceptive comments on the first draft of this chapter. I am also indebted to Babak Ashrafi, Roberta Brawer, James Howe, Allison Macfarlane, Abigail O'Sullivan, and Charles Thorpe for clarifying in discussion some of the ideas in this chapter, and to the four weapons scientists who answered my e-mail appeals for information on secrecy and authorship at the Livermore Laboratory.

1. Djerassi, the inventor of the birth control pill, has now completed a trilogy of what he calls "science in fiction" novels: novels that take scientists as their principal characters and explain the workings of science to the reader. In addition to *The Bourbaki Gambit,* the other novels are *Cantor's Dilemma* and *Menachem's Seed.*

2. On Big Science, see Galison, *Image and Logic,* and the essays in Galison and Hevly, *Big Science.* Panofsky's essay in the latter volume is particularly apposite to some of the issues discussed here. Sutton, "Organizational Autonomy and Professional Norms in Science," discusses the conjunction of military secrecy and Big Science at the Livermore Laboratory.

3. See Hoddeson, "Mission Change in the Large Laboratory"; Hoddeson et al., *Critical Assembly*; and Rhodes, *The Making of the Atomic Bomb.*

4. York, "The Origins of the Lawrence Livermore Laboratory," 13.

5. Ulam thought of making the hydrogen bomb a two-stage device in which the first stage (a fission bomb) would be used to compress, not just ignite, fuel in the secondary. Teller later thought of using radiation rather than neutrons from the atomic bomb to achieve compression (Rhodes, *Dark Sun*, chapter 23). Some weapons scientists have joked that Ulam "inseminated" Teller with the idea and that Teller is in fact the "mother of the H-bomb" (Easlea, *Fathering the Unthinkable*).

6. This approach also characterizes the biographies of two of the great Manhattan Project scientists: Lanouette's *Genius in the Shadows* biography of Leo Szilard and Gleick's *Genius* biography of Richard Feynman which, even in their titles, focus on the creativity and uniqueness of their subjects. As the literary theorist David Lodge has observed, commenting on the imperviousness of biography to new literary theories that decenter the subject, "Literary biography thus constitutes the most conservative branch of academic literary scholarship today. By the same token, it is the one that remains most accessible to the 'general reader'" (*The Practice of Writing*, 99).

7. Rhodes subsequently revealed the extraordinary labor that went into the research and writing of this paragraph. He had to visit London to see the intersection for himself, and he researched London weather records so that he could evoke the physical setting for Szilard's inspiration as precisely as possible.

8. The "Super" was the hydrogen bomb. If Rhodes's books use, wherever possible, the trope of sudden inspiration to narrate the origins of America's first- and second-generation nuclear weapons, it is interesting that William Broad's *Star Warriors* account of the stillborn genesis of third-generation nuclear weapons at the Livermore Laboratory in the 1980s contains exactly the same literary device in its description of Peter Hagelstein's sudden envisioning of a design for the X-ray laser at a review meeting where he was in a mystical state induced by sleep deprivation. For a playwright's use of exactly the same literary device, this time to evoke Alan Turing's breakthrough in cracking the Nazi Enigma code during World War II, see Whitemore, *Breaking the Code*. The Hollywood film *Fat Man and Little Boy*, in an appalling example of overwrought dramatization, uses the same device in portraying the inception of implosion—attributed in the film to Seth Neddermeyer—during the Manhattan Project.

9. See, for example, Hoddeson, "Mission Change in the Large Laboratory"; and Hoddeson et al., *Critical Assembly*.

10. Rhodes, *The Making of the Atomic Bomb*, 447.

11. Ibid., 570.

12. Holloway, *Stalin and the Bomb*, 202.

13. This is to speak as if Holloway wrote only about the Soviet scientists and Rhodes only about the Americans. In fact, portions of Rhodes's *Dark Sun* narrate the Soviet bomb project as well, though this part of his work has received less attention, and less acclaim, than his narration of the American hydrogen bomb project.

14. In the early 1990s this became a matter of some controversy in Russia as the intelligence services and veteran scientists of the original Soviet atomic bomb proj-

ect feuded over who should get most credit for the first Soviet nuclear test: the spies who obtained the design for America's first plutonium bomb or the scientists who figured out how to build it (Holloway, "Soviet Scientists Speak Out"; Khariton and Smirnov, "The Khariton Version"; Leskov, "Dividing the Glory of the Fathers"; Sagdeev, "Russian Scientists Save American Secrets").

15. See Holloway, *Stalin and the Bomb*, chapter 14.

16. Quoted in ibid., 198. Hawking meant by this that Zel'dovich seemed to have accomplished too much for one man. The admiration for Zel'dovich, and the sense of him as a great scientist, is also conveyed in a story told to me by a scientist at the Livermore Laboratory: when the Princeton physicist John Wheeler, who had worked on the American hydrogen bomb, finally met Zel'dovich, he presented him with a salt and pepper shaker, one male and one female in shape. Alluding to the greater elegance of the first Soviet H-bomb design compared to its American counterpart, he said that the male represented Zel'dovich and the female, Teller.

17. My thanks to Peter Galison for this point.

18. Woodmansee and Jaszi, *The Construction of Authorship*, 3. See also Woodmansee, *The Author and the Market*.

19. See Gusterson, *Nuclear Rites*, chapter 4.

20. At the end of the cold war there were fears that military budget cuts would finally destroy the job security of scientists at the weapons laboratories. Although roughly one thousand employees (mostly support staff rather than scientists) were laid off by Los Alamos in 1995, Livermore has had no forced layoffs (as opposed to voluntary early retirement programs) since 1973.

21. The organization of the laboratory and the social production of nuclear testing is described in greater detail in Gusterson, *Nuclear Rites*.

22. To date only one director of the laboratory, Roger Batzel, has not been a physicist. Batzel was a chemist. Similarly, at Los Alamos only one of the laboratory's directors (Sig Hecker, a metallurgist) has not been a physicist.

23. "Peter" is a pseudonym. Ironically, anthropology's conventional practice of shielding interviewees by giving them pseudonyms in this case becomes another way of killing the authors behind the barbed wire fence.

24. See Iglesias and Rogers, "Updated OPAL Opacities"; and Rogers, Swenson, and Iglesias, "OPAL Equation-of-State Tables for Astrophysical Applications."

25. The picture is, in fact, more complicated than this thumbnail sketch allows. Some weapons scientists lead a double life, finding ways to publish in the open literature at the same time as they do their weapons work. This enables them to build intellectual capital and authorial profiles outside the laboratory perimeter in a way that makes them potentially mobile in the scientific job and knowledge markets.

26. A hohlraum (German for "empty room") is a gold chamber inside which sits a pellet of deuterium and tritium in an inertial confinement experiment. When the laser beams strike and enter the hohlraum, it gives off an intense burst of X rays, which crush and heat the fuel in the pellet, initiating fusion.

The Soviets did not classify inertial confinement fusion research to the same degree as the Americans. This led to curious situations, such as one at a conference in the 1980s where Livermore fusion researchers were embarrassed that Russian scientists were openly presenting the results of their fusion experiments to an audience that included many Americans without security clearances—even though the rationale for hiding such knowledge from the uncleared was that they might share it with the Russians!

27. Sutton, "Organizational Autonomy and Professional Norms in Science," 208.

28. Bohannon, "The Impact of Money on an African Subsistence Economy."

29. For the story of the X-ray laser and allegations of misconduct in its promotion, see Blum, "Weird Science"; Broad, *Teller's War*; and Scheer, "The Man Who Blew the Whistle on Star Wars."

30. An interesting example here is Bruce Tartar, a recent director of the laboratory. One scientist told me that, curious to know more about his director's scientific career before he became director of the laboratory, he had tried to find what he had written, but was unable to find a single report or article by him listed anywhere.

31. Sutton, "Organizational Autonomy and Professional Norms in Science," 206.

32. This consideration has led MacKenzie and Spinardi to argue that, in the absence of nuclear testing, advanced nuclear weapons design knowledge might more or less fade away ("Tacit Knowledge, Weapons Design, and the Uninvention of Nuclear Weapons").

33. Merton, "The Normative Structure of Science."

34. Quoted in Gusterson, *Nuclear Rites*, 47–48.

35. See Benowitz, "Is Corporate Research Funding Leading to Secrecy in Science?"; Blumenstyk, "Berkley Pact with a Swiss Company Takes Technology Transfer to a New Level"; Blumenthal et al., "Withholding Research Results in Academic Life Science"; Cohen, "Share and Share Alike Isn't Always the Rule in Science"; and Marshall, "Secretiveness Found Widespread in Life Sciences."

11. How Not to Construct an Incinerator

The research on which this chapter is based was funded by a Mellon New Directions Fellowship at Stanford University and an SSRC-MacArthur Fellowship on Peace and International Security. The chapter was written under the auspices of a fellowship at Stanford University's Center for International Security and Arms Control. This chapter grew out of a paper originally presented at the Conference on Public Interest Science at the University of Oregon, April 13, 1996. My thanks to everyone at the conference who responded to the paper, especially to Laura Nader. Marion Fulk, Lee Gardizi, Marylia Kelley, and Allison Macfarlane commented on an earlier draft. Thanks also to Dave Elliott for helpful advice.

1. On the origins of the laboratory, see Francis, "Warhead Politics"; Lawrence Livermore National Laboratory, *Thirty Years of Technical Excellence*; York, "The Origins of the Lawrence Livermore National Laboratory"; and *Making Weapons, Talking Peace*, 65–67.

2. Studies of the lab in the 1980s include Broad, *Star Warriors* and *Teller's War*; and Gusterson, *Nuclear Rites*.

3. This figure comes from the Livermore Chamber of Commerce's economic profile for 1988–89 (5).

4. For description and analysis of these protests, see Cabasso and Moon, *Risking Peace*; Epstein, "The Politics of Prefigurative Community" and *Political Protest and Cultural Revolution*; and Gusterson, *Nuclear Rites*, chapters 7 and 8.

5. Gusterson, *Nuclear Rites*, 18.

6. For a brief history of Tri-Valley Citizens Against a Radioactive Environment, see Tompkins, "Whose Livermore Is It Anyway?"

7. On new social movements, see Beck, *The Risk Society*; McCrea and Markle, *Minutes to Midnight*; Parkin, *Middle Class Radicalism*; and Touraine, *The Voice and the Eye*. The term "battle for position" is from Gramsci's *Prison Notebooks*.

8. For an overview of these theories, see Krimsky and Golding, *Social Theories of Risk*; Margolis, *Risk*, chapter 2; and Sjoberg, *Risk and Society*.

9. See Raats and Shepherd, "Developing a Subject-Derived Terminology"; Roth et al., "What Do We Know about Making Risk Comparisons?"

10. See also Schwarz and Thompson, *Divided We Stand*. For a critique of Douglas and Wildavsky, see Downey, "Risk in Culture."

11. See Covello, *The Analysis of Actual versus Perceived Risks* and "Risk Comparisons and Risk Communication"; Flynn, Slovic, and Mertz, "Decidedly Different"; Gardener and Gould, "Public Perceptions of Risks and Benefits of Technology"; Margolis, *Risk*; and Weart, *Nuclear Fear*.

For attempts to bridge the divide between experts and the public and to theorize a democratic model of decision making about risk, see Fiorino, "Citizen Participation and Environmental Risk"; Frankenfeld, "Technological Citizenship"; and Perhac, "Comparative Risk Assessment."

12. The generalizing models I am critiquing here would have little to say, for example, about why the community around the Rocky Flats nuclear facility in Colorado mobilized to prevent construction of an incinerator, whereas the parallel community in Oak Ridge, Tennessee, did not.

13. This perspective is influenced by the work of social theorists such as Bourdieu, *Outline of a Theory of Practice*, and Giddens, *The Constitution of Society*, who have chided their colleagues for presenting individuals as mere carriers of social roles and for underestimating the importance of agency in producing conflicts and determining their outcomes.

14. For example, see Margolis, *Risk*, and Weart, *Nuclear Fear*.

15. For two other analyses that emphasize the importance of a lack of consensus among experts in unsettling public opinion, see Jasanoff, *The Fifth Branch*, and Sapolsky, "The Politics of Risk."

16. Radioactive waste was sent from Livermore to the Nevada Nuclear Test Site, hazardous waste to a company in Utah, and mixed waste to off-site incinerators, most of it going to Idaho (Stober, "Weapons Lab Incinerator Permit Iffy").

17. The legislation in question is the 1984 Hazardous and Solid Waste Amendments to the Resource Conservation and Recovery Act first implemented in 1980.

18. Rogers, "Incinerator Permit Denial Might Curtail Lab Research"; Stober, "Weapons Lab Incinerator Permit Iffy."

19. See Makhijani, Hu, and Yih, *Nuclear Wastelands,* for the definitive statement on these issues. On the consequences of nuclear testing in Nevada and, downwind, in Utah, see Fradkin, *Fallout;* Gallagher, *American Ground Zero;* Grant, *The Day We Bombed Utah;* and Rosenberg, *Atomic Soldiers.* On the consequences of Soviet nuclear testing in Kazakhstan, see McElroy, "Kazakhs Pay for Soviet Nuclear Tests." Dalton et al., *Critical Masses,* offers a fascinating and comprehensive overview of parallels in the contamination at Hanford and Chelyabinsk. For more details on the Soviet case, see also Cochran, Norris, and Bukharin, *Making the Russian Bomb.*

20. For example, see Barnet, *The Economy of Death;* Kotz, *Wild Blue Yonder;* Melman, *Pentagon Capitalism* and *The Permanent War Economy;* and Tirman, *The Militarization of High Technology.*

21. Kang, "Bumpkins and Eggheads."

22. Tompkins, "Whose Livermore Is It Anyway?"

23. See Dillon, "Developers, Lab Employees Boost Candidates"; and Jeffers, "Brown Tops in Fund-raising for City Races."

24. On toxic chemicals in the city sewers, see DeWolk, "Toxic Waste Dumps"; on the issue of LLNL contributing to road improvements and closing a road for security reasons, see Bodovitz, "DOE Relents, OKs Incinerator Hearing" and *Livermore Independent,* "Livermore to Fight East Avenue Closure"; see also *Livermore Independent,* "Lobbyist Hired to Deal with the Labs."

25. Two local journalists told me that by the late 1980s, the publishers of the *Tri-Valley Herald* were increasingly inclined to resent the lab as a bastion of local antigrowth sentiment and as an institution that took up a square mile of prime real estate without even paying taxes. Accordingly, they told their reporters to cover the lab's problems more aggressively.

26. Official transcript of the public hearing, May 24, 1989 (41).

27. Official transcript of the public hearing, May 24, 1989 (14, 21).

28. The U.S. Department of Energy had sent 330 letters giving advance notice of the meeting to residents and businesses within one mile of the proposed incinerator site and had sent out a press release publicizing the hearing (*Livermore Independent,* "Livermore Officials Castigate DOE").

29. Bodovitz, "DOE Refusal Angers Stark"; *Livermore Independent,* "Livermore Officials Castigate DOE."

30. *Tri-Valley Herald,* "Livermore Lab Hearings Needed."

31. Bodovitz, "Livermore Burns over Incinerator Plan."

32. *Livermore Independent,* "Data Missing from Incinerator Report."

33. These quotes are from my notes on the meeting, which took place May 9, 1989.

34. This development was not as alarming as it may sound, since the upper aquifer in the Livermore Valley was not of drinking quality anyway, having too high a concentration of metals (Lee Gardizi, personal communication, April 30, 1998).

35. Bodovitz, "Livermore Group Given EPA Grant."

36. *San Francisco Chronicle*, "U.S. Ignored A-Plant's Toxic Emissions"; *New York Times*, "New Uranium Pollution Is Found in Wells."

37. Schneider, "Decades of Plutonium Peril at an Arms Plant" and "U.S. Temporarily Shutting Down Nuclear Plant for Safety Problems"; Wald, "Plutonium Hazard Found at Nuclear Arms Plant"; Wartzman, "Rockwell Bomb Plant Is Repeatedly Accused of Poor Safety Record."

38. Hoversten, "N-Plant Radiation"; Schneider, "U.S. Tells of Peril in '40's Radiation to the Northwest" and "Report Warns of Impact of Hanford's Radiation"; Wald, "Secrecy Tied to Hanford Tanks' Trouble."

39. DeWolk, "Toxic Waste Dumps"; Rogers, "Toxic Water Escapes from LLL" and "Lab Downplays Effect on Plants"; Smith, "Lab Spreads Radiation in Air."

40. Rogers, "Lab Misses Incinerator Reporting Deadline" and "EPA Tells Lab Incinerator Days Are Over."

41. Smith, "Genius, Resources Grace Facility."

42. *Oakland Tribune*, "Pleasanton Panel Urges EIR on Lab Incinerator."

43. Bodovitz, "Questions Dog Lab's Neighbors."

44. Brewer, "Stark Threatens to Sue Lab."

Postscript

1. Wolfowitz, Testimony on Ballistic Missile Defense to Senate Armed Services Committee, July 12, 2001.

2. Quoted in Friedman, "MAD Isn't Crazy."

3. Wolfowitz, Testimony.

4. Safire, "Friendly Dissuasion."

5. Wolfowitz, Testimony.

6. Quoted in Reuters, "Bush."

7. Quoted in Kiefer, "Why Bush Team Is No Fan of Arms Control Treaties."

8. Quoted in Bruni, "In Spain, Bush Sells Missile Plan."

9. Wolfowitz, Testimony.

10. Diamond, "Congress Mulls Shield with an Eye on ABM Treaty."

11. Congressional Record, May 2, 2001.

12. Wolfowitz, Testimony.

13. Congressional Record, May 2, 2001.

14. Quoted by Kellerhals, "Rumsfeld Says U.S. Will Not Violate 1972 ABM Treaty."

15. Wolfowitz, Testimony.

16. Quoted in Bill Smirnow, "Peace Activist Hopes to Force Blair's Hand on NMD/Star Wars," May 9, 2001, e-mail message on Abolition 2000 listserv.

Bibliography

Abir-Am, Pnina. "A Historical Ethnography of a Scientific Anniversary in Molecular Biology: The First Protein X-Ray Photograph (1984, 1934)." *Social Epistemology* 6 (1992): 323–55.

Abraham, Itty. *The Making of the Indian Atomic Bomb: Science, Secrecy, and the Postcolonial State.* London: Zed Books, 1998.

Abrams, Jim. "US: Nuclear Situation Serious." Associated Press, May 31, 1998.

Acheson, Dean. *Present at the Creation: My Years in the State Department.* New York: W. W. Norton, 1969.

Adair, Peter. *Stopping History.* San Francisco: Adair and Armstrong Films, 1983.

Aeppel, T. "A-Bomb Technology Spreads." *Christian Science Monitor,* February 25, 1987.

Agnew, Harold. "The View from San Diego: Harold Agnew Speaks Out." *Los Alamos Science* (Summer/Fall 1981): 152–59.

Ahrari, M. E. "The Clash of Civilizations: An Old Story or New Truth?" *New Perspectives Quarterly,* Spring, 1997.

Albright, David. "How Much Plutonium Does North Korea Have?" *Bulletin of the Atomic Scientists* 50 (1994): 46–53.

Albright, David, and Mark Hibbs. "Hyping the Iraqi Bomb." *Bulletin of the Atomic Scientists* 47 (1991): 26–28.

Aldridge, Robert. *First Strike! The Pentagon's Strategy for Nuclear War.* Boston: South End Press, 1983.

Allison, Graham, Steven Miller, Owen Cote, and Richard Falkenrath. *Avoiding Nuclear Anarchy.* Cambridge, MA: MIT Press, 1996.

Alperovitz, Gar. *Atomic Diplomacy: Hiroshima and Potsdam: The Use of the Atomic Bomb and the American Confrontation with Soviet Power.* Boulder, CO: Pluto Press, 1994.

———. *The Decision to Use the Atomic Bomb and the Architecture of an American Myth.* New York: Knopf, 1995.

Althusser, Louis. "Ideology and Ideological State Apparatuses: Notes Towards an Investigation." In *Lenin and Philosophy and Other Essays,* 121–73. New York: Monthly Review Press, 1971.

Anderson, John Ward. "Confusion Dominates Arms Race." *Washington Post,* June 1, 1998.

Anzaldúa, Gloria. *Borderlands? La Frontera: The New Mestiza.* San Francisco: Spinsters/Aunt Lute, 1987.

Appadurai, Arjun. *Modernity at Large: Cultural Dimensions of Globalization.* Minneapolis: University of Minnesota Press, 1996.

Arkin, William. "Those Lovable Little Bombs." *Bulletin of the Atomic Scientists* 49 (1993): 22–27.

———. "What's 'New'?" *Bulletin of the Atomic Scientists* 53(1997): 22–27.

Asad, Talal. "Notes on Body Pain and Truth in Medieval Christian Ritual." *Economy and Society* 12 (1983): 287–327.

Associated Press. "Senator Daniel Patrick Moynihan Says Nuclear Threat Is Not India." May 25, 1998.

Barasch, Marc Ian. *The Little Black Book of Atomic War.* New York: Dell, 1983.

Barker, Robert. Prepared testimony of Dr. Robert B. Barker Before the Senate Governmental Affairs Committee Subcommittee on International Security, Proliferation and Federal Services, October 27, 1997.

Barnet, Richard. *The Economy of Death.* New York: Atheneum, 1969.

Barnett, Michael. "Peacekeeping, Indifference, and Genocide in Rwanda." In Jutta Weldes, Mark Laffey, Hugh Gusterson, and Raymond Duvall, eds., *Cultures of Insecurity: States, Communities, and the Production of Danger,* 173–202. Minneapolis: University of Minnesota Press, 1999.

Barthes, Roland. "The Death of the Author." Reprinted in K. M. Newton, ed., *Twentieth Century Literary Theory: A Reader,* 154–58. New York: St. Martin's Press, 1988.

———. *Mythologies.* New York: Hill and Wang, 1972.

Baudrillard, Jean. *The Gulf War Did Not Take Place.* Bloomington: Indiana University Press, 1991.

———. *Simulations.* New York: Semiotext(e), 1983.

Beck, Ulrich. *The Risk Society: Towards a New Modernity.* Newbury Park, CA: Sage, 1992.

Benedict, Ruth. *The Chrysanthemum and the Sword: Patterns of Japanese Culture.* Boston: Houghton Mifflin, 1946.

———. *Patterns of Culture.* Boston: Houghton Mifflin, 1934.

Benjamin, Walter. "Theses on the Philosophy of History." In *Illuminations,* edited by Hannah Arendt. New York: Schocken, 1969.

Benowitz, Steven. "Is Corporate Research Funding Leading to Secrecy in Science?" *Scientist* 10 (1996): 1, 6.

Berger, Peter, and Thomas Luckmann. *The Social Construction of Reality: A Treatise in the Sociology of Knowledge.* New York: Anchor Books, 1967.

Bernard, Larry. "Atomic Bomb Saved Lives in WWII, Bethe Says." *Cornell Chronicle,* April 14, 1994.

Bernstein, Barton. *The Atomic Bomb: The Critical Issues.* Boston: Little, Brown, 1976.

Blacker, Coit, and Gloria Duffy, eds. *International Arms Control: Issues and Agreements.* Stanford, CA: Stanford University Press, 1984.

Blair, Bruce. *The Logic of Accidental Nuclear War.* Washington, DC: Brookings Institution, 1993.

Blair, Bruce, Harold Feiveson, and Frank von Hippel. "Taking Nuclear Weapons off Hair-Trigger Alert." *Scientific American,* November 1997.

Blechman, Barry, and Victor Utgoff. "The Macroeconomics of Strategic Defenses." *International Security* 11(1986–87): 33–70.

Bloor, David. *Knowledge and Social Imagery.* Chicago: University of Chicago Press, 1991.

Blum, Deborah. "Nuclear Labs: Bulwark against Test Bans." *Sacramento Bee,* August 2, 1987.

———. "Weird Science: Livermore's X-ray Laser Flap." *Bulletin of the Atomic Scientists* 44 (1988): 7–13.

Blumenstyk, Goldie. "Berkeley Pact with a Swiss Company Takes Technology Transfer to a New Level." *Chronicle of Higher Education,* December 11, 1998.

Blumenthal, David, Eric G. Campbell, Melissa S. Anderson, Nancyanne Causino, and Karen Seashore Louis. "Withholding Research Results in Academic Life Science: Evidence from a National Survey of Faculty." *Journal of the American Medical Association* 227(1997): 1224–28.

Bodovitz, Sandra. "DOE Refusal Angers Stark." *Tri-Valley Herald,* October 26, 1988.

———. "DOE Relents, OKs Incinerator Hearing." *Tri-Valley Herald,* February 3, 1989.

———. "Livermore Burns over Incinerator Plan; Lab Says It's Safe." *Tri-Valley Herald,* May 21, 1989.

———. "Livermore Group Given EPA Grant." *Tri-Valley Herald,* February 4, 1989.

———. "Questions Dog Lab's Neighbors." *Tri-Valley Herald,* July 24, 1989.

Bohannon, Laura. "Shakespeare in the Bush." *Natural History,* August–September 1966.

Bohannon, Paul. "The Impact of Money on an African Subsistence Economy." In James P. Spradley, ed., *Conformity and Conflict: Readings in Cultural Anthropology,* 221–32. Boston: Little, Brown, 1984.

Booth, Ken. "Dare Not to Know: International Relations Theory versus the Future." In Ken Booth and Steve Smith, eds., *International Relations Theory Today,* 328–50. University Park: Pennsylvania State University Press, 1995.

———. "Security and Self: Reflections of a Fallen Realist." In Keith Krause and Michael C. Williams, eds., *Critical Security Studies: Concepts and Cases,* 83–120. Minneapolis: University of Minnesota Press, 1996.

Booth, Ken, and Steve Smith, eds. *International Relations Theory Today.* University Park: Pennsylvania State University Press, 1995.

Bourdieu, Pierre. *Outline of a Theory of Practice.* Cambridge: Cambridge University Press, 1977.

Bourgeois, Phillipe. "Just Another Night on Crack Street." *New York Times Magazine,* November 12, 1989.

Boustany, Nora. "'Show No Mercy,' Saddam Tells His Troops." *Washington Post,* February 25, 1991.

Boyer, Paul. *Fallout: A Historian Reflects on America's Half-Century Encounter with Nuclear Weapons.* Columbus: Ohio State University Press, 1998.

Bozeman, Adda B. "Civilizations Under Stress." *Virginia Quarterly Review* 51 (1975): 1–18.

Brasset, Donna. "U.S. Military Elites: Perceptions and Values." In Paul Turner and David Pitt, eds., *The Anthropology of War and Peace: Perspectives on the Nuclear Age,* 32–48. Westport, CT: Bergin & Garvey/Greenwood, 1989.

———. "Values and the Exercise of Power: Military Elites." In Robert Rubinstein and Mary LeCron Foster, eds., *The Social Dynamics of Peace and Conflict: Culture in International Security,* 81–90. Boulder, CO: Westview, 1988.

Brewer, Boni. "Stark Threatens to Sue Lab Over Toxics Incinerator." *Valley Times,* January 18, 1989.

Bringa, Tone. *Being Muslim the Bosnian Way: Identity and Community in a Central Bosnian Village.* Princeton, NJ: Princeton University Press, 1995.

Brito, Dagobert, and Michael Intriligator. "Proliferation and the Probability of War: Global and Regional Issues." In Dagobert Brito, Michael Intriligator, and Adele Wick, eds., *Strategies for Managing Nuclear Proliferation.* Lanham, MD: Lexington Books, 1982.

Broad, William. *Star Warriors: A Penetrating Look into the Lives of the Young Scientists behind Our Space Age Weapons.* New York: Simon and Schuster, 1985.

———. *Teller's War: The Top Secret Story behind the Star Wars Deception.* New York: Simon and Schuster, 1992.

Brodie, Bernard. *Strategy in the Missile Age.* Princeton, NJ: Princeton University Press, 1959.

Brooks, Linton. "Nuclear SLCMs Add to Deterrence and Security." *International Security* 13(1988–89): 169–74.

Brown, Michael. "The U.S. Manned Bomber and Strategic Deterrence in the 1990s." *International Security* 14(1989): 5–46.

Bruni, Frank. "In Spain, Bush Sells Missile Plan." *New York Times,* June 13, 2001.

Bundy, McGeorge. *Danger and Survival: Choices about the Bomb in the First Fifty Years.* New York: Vintage Books, 1988.

Burns, John F. "On Kashmir's Dividing Line, Nuclear Fears Enforce Calm." *New York Times,* June 14, 1998.

Business Wire, "Electronic Arts Ships Nuclear Strike for the PC," October 29, 1997.

Butler, Richard. *Fatal Choice: Nuclear Weapons and the Illusion of Missile Defense.* Boulder, CO: Westview, 2001.

Cabasso, Jackie, and Susan Moon. *Risking Peace: Why We Sat in the Road.* Berkeley: Open Books, 1985.

Calder, Nigel. *Nuclear Nightmares.* London: Penguin, 1979.

Caldicott, Helen. *Missile Envy: The Arms Race and Nuclear War.* New York: Bantam Books, 1986.

Callender, Harold. "U.S. Aid Guarantee Hailed by France." *New York Times,* March 19, 1949.

Calleo, David. *The Atlantic Fantasy: The U.S., NATO, and Europe.* Baltimore: The Johns Hopkins University Press, 1987.

———. *Beyond American Hegemony: The Future of the Western Alliance.* New York: Basic Books, 1987.

Campbell, David. *Writing Security: United States Foreign Policy and the Politics of Identity.* Minneapolis: University of Minnesota Press, 1992.

Carnesale, Albert, and Richard Haass. "Conclusions: Weighing the Evidence." In Albert Carnesale and Richard Haass, eds., *Superpower Arms Control: Setting the Record Straight,* 329–55. Cambridge, MA: Ballinger, 1987.

Casti, John L. *Would-be Worlds: How Simulation Is Changing the Frontiers of Science.* New York: John Wiley and Sons, 1997.

Caulfield, Catherine. *Multiple Exposures: Chronicles of the Radiation Age.* New York: Harper and Row, 1989.

Chagnon, Napoleon. *Yanomamo: The Fierce People.* New York: Holt, Rinehart and Winston, 1977.

Chan, Stephen. "Too Neat and Under-Thought a World Order: Huntington and Civilizations." *Millennium* 26 (1997): 137–40.

Chapman, Steve. 1998. "Hiding From Reality on Nuclear Proliferation." *Chicago Tribune,* May 31, 1998.

Chayes, Abram. "Legal Case for U.S. Action in Cuba. Address at Harvard Law School, November 3." *Department of State Bulletin,* November 19, 1962, 763–65.

Chayes, Antonia Handler. "Managing the Politics of Mobility." *International Security* 12(1987): 154–62.

Cheng, Gordon. "To the Nuclear Brink: Eisenhower, Dulles, and the Quemoy-Matsu Crisis." *International Security* 12 (1988): 96–122.

Chilton, Paul, ed. *Language and the Nuclear Arms Debate: Nukespeak Today.* London: Frances Pinter, 1985.

———. *Security Metaphors: Cold War Discourse from Containment to Common House.* New York: Lang, 1996.

Chodorow, Nancy. *The Reproduction of Mothering: Psychoanalysis and the Sociology of Gender.* Berkeley: University of California Press, 1978.

Chomsky, Noam. *Necessary Illusions: Thought Control in Democratic Societies.* Boston: South End Press, 1989.

———. "Strategic Arms, the Cold War, and the Third World." In New Left Review, ed., *Exterminism and Cold War,* 223–36. London: New Left Books, 1982.

Christian Science Monitor, "Saddam and the Bomb" (editorial). November 28, 1990.

Christie, Deborah. *Bosnia: We Are All Neighbors.* London: Granada TV Film, 1993.

Cialdini, Robert. *Influence: Science and Practice.* Glenview, IL: Scott Foresman, 1988.

Clausewitz, Carl von. *On War.* Princeton, NJ: Princeton University Press, 1976.

Clifford, James. "On Ethnographic Authority." *Representations* 1 (1983): 118–44.

———. *The Predicament of Culture: Twentieth-Century Ethnography, Literature and Art.* Cambridge, MA: Harvard University Press, 1987.

———. "Spatial Practices: Fieldwork, Travel, and the Disciplining of Anthropology." In Akhil Gupta and James Ferguson, eds., *Anthropological Locations:*

Boundaries and Grounds of a Field Science, 185–222. Berkeley: University of California Press, 1997.

Clifford, James, and George Marcus. *Writing Culture: The Poetics and Politics of Ethnography*. Berkeley: University of California Press, 1986.

Cochran, Thomas, William Arkin, Robert Norris, and Milton Hoenig. *Nuclear Weapons Databook*, volume 2. Cambridge, MA: Ballinger, 1987.

Cochran, Thomas, Stan Norris, and Oleg Bukharin. *Making the Russian Bomb: From Stalin to Yeltsin*. Boulder, CO: Westview Press, 1995.

Cockburn, Andrew, and Leslie Cockburn. *One Point Safe*. New York: Anchor Books, 1997.

Cohen, Jon. "Share and Share Alike Isn't Always the Rule in Science." *Science* 268 (1995): 1715–18.

Cohn, Carol. "Sex and Death in the Rational World of Defense Intellectuals." *Signs* 12 (1987): 687–718.

Collins, Harry. *Changing Order: Replication and Induction in Scientific Practice*. London: Sage, 1985.

Collins, Harry, and Trevor Pinch. *The Golem: What Everyone Should Know about Science*. Cambridge: Cambridge University Press, 1993.

Committee for the Compilation of Materials on the Damage Caused by the Atomic Bombs in Hiroshima and Nagasaki. *Hiroshima and Nagasaki: The Physical, Medical, and Social Effects of the Atomic Bombings*. New York: Basic Books, 1981.

Comprehensive Test-Ban Treaty. Electronic document: www.state.gov/www/global/arms/treaties/ctb.html (accessed December 1, 2000).

Congressional Budget Office. *Preserving the Nuclear Weapons Stockpile Under a Comprehensive Test Ban*. Washington, DC: Congressional Budget Office, 1997.

Congressional Quarterly Weekly. "As the Dust Settles in India, U.S. Rethinks Nuclear Policy," May 23, 1998, 1365–68.

Congressional Record. *Proceedings and Debates of the U.S. Congress*, 135 (197), August 2. Washington, DC: U.S. Government Printing Office, 1986.

Congressional Record. Office of International Information Programs, Department of State (usinfo.state.gov), May 2, 2001.

Connolly, William. *Identity/Difference: Democratic Negotiations of Political Paradox*. Ithaca, NY: Cornell University Press, 1991.

Cornwell, Rupert. "Listen Here India—Do as Nuclear Nations Say, Not as They Do." *Independent*, May 14, 1998.

Covello, V. *The Analysis of Actual versus Perceived Risks*. New York: Plenum, 1983.

———. "Risk Comparisons and Risk Communication." In Roger Kasperson and Pieter Jan M. Stallen, eds., *Communicating Risks to the Public*. Dordrecht: Kluwer, 1992.

Cowell, Alan. "Hussein Orders 'No Mercy' for Foe But Hints Iraq May Face 'Abyss.'" *New York Times*, February 25, 1991.

Crawford, Beverly, and Ronnie Lipschutz. "Discourses of War: Security and the Case of Yugoslavia." In Keith Krause and Michael C. Williams, eds., *Critical Security Studies*, 149–85. Minneapolis: University of Minnesota Press, 1997.

Dahl, Robert. *Controlling Nuclear Weapons: Democracy versus Guardianship.* Syracuse, NY: Syracuse University Press, 1985.

Dalton, Russell, Paula Garb, Nicolas P. Lovrich, John C. Pierce, and John M. Whiteley. *Critical Masses: Citizens, Nuclear Weapons Production, and Environmental Destruction in the United States and Russia.* Cambridge, MA: MIT Press, 1999.

Daner, Francine. *The American Children of Krsna: A Study of the Hare Krsna Movement.* New York: Holt, Rineholt, and Winston, 1976.

Davis-Floyd, Robbie. *Birth as an American Rite of Passage.* Berkeley: University of California Press, 1992.

Department of Energy. *The Stockpile Stewardship and Management Program: Maintaining Confidence in the Safety and Reliability of the Enduring U.S. Nuclear Weapon Stockpile.* Washington, DC: Office of Defense Programs, U.S. Department of Energy, 1995.

Der Derian, James. "Lenin's War, Baudrillard's Games." In Gretchen Bender and Timothy Druckrey, eds., *Culture on the Brink: Ideologies of Technology*, 267–76. Seattle: Bay Press, 1994.

Der Derian, James, and Michael Shapiro, eds. *International/Intertextual Relations: Postmodern Readings of World Politics.* Lexington, MA: D. C. Heath, 1989.

Derrida, Jacques. "No Apocalypse, Not Now (Full Speed Ahead, Seven Missiles, Seven Missives)." *Diacritics* 14 (1984): 20–31.

des Chene, Mary. "Locating the Past." In Akhil Gupta and James Ferguson, eds., *Anthropological Locations: Boundaries and Grounds of a Field Science*, 66–85. Berkeley: University of California Press, 1997.

DeWitt, Hugh. "Labs Drive the Arms Race." In Len Ackland and Steven McGuire, eds., *Assessing the Nuclear Age.* Chicago: Educational Foundation for Nuclear Science, 1986.

———. "The Nuclear Arms Race as Seen by a Nuclear Weapons Lab Staff Member." *SANA Update: Scientists Against Nuclear Arms Newsletter* 74 (1989): 2–4.

DeWolk, Roland. "Toxic Waste Dumps, Secrecy Sour Town's Relationship to the Facility." *Oakland Tribune*, August 13, 1989.

Diamond, John. "Congress Mulls Shield with Eye on ABM Treaty." *Chicago Tribune*, July 20, 2001.

Dillon, John. "Developers, Lab Employees Boost Candidates." *Valley Times*, September 28, 1989.

Divine, Robert. *Blowing on the Wind: The Nuclear Test Ban Debate 1954–1960.* New York: Oxford University Press, 1978.

Djerassi, Carl. *The Bourbaki Gambit.* New York: Penguin, 1994.

———. *Cantor's Dilemma.* New York: Penguin, 1991.

———. *Menachem's Seed.* Athens: University of Georgia Press, 1997.

Dougherty, Russell E. "The Value of ICBM Modernization." *International Security* 12(1987): 163–72.

Douglas, Mary, and Aaron Wildavsky. *Risk and Culture.* Berkeley: University of California Press, 1982.

Dower, John. *Embracing Defeat: Japan in the Wake of World War II.* New York: Free Press, 1999.

Downey, Gary. "Risk in Culture: The American Conflict over Nuclear Power." *Cultural Anthropology* 1 (1986): 388–412.

Doyle, Michael. "Kant, Liberal Legacies and Foreign Affairs. Part 1." *Philosophy and Public Affairs* 12 (1983): 205–35.

———. "Kant, Liberal Legacies and Foreign Affairs. Part 2." *Philosophy and Public Affairs* 12 (1983): 323–53.

———. "Liberalism and World Politics." *American Political Science Review* 89(1986): 1151–69.

Drell, Sidney, C. Callan, M. Cornwall, D. Eardley, J. Goodman, D. Hammer, W. Happer, J. Kimble, S. Koonin, R. LeLevier, C. Max, W. Panofsky, M. Rosenbluth, J. Sullivan, P. Weinburger, H. York, and F. Zachariasen. *Science Based Stockpile Stewardship.* JSR-94-345, JASON. McLean, VA: Mitre Corporation, 1994.

Drell, Sidney, John Foster, and Charles Townes. "How Safe Is Safe?" *Bulletin of the Atomic Scientists* 47 (1991): 35–40.

Durkheim, Émile. *The Division of Labor in Society.* Glencoe, IL: Free Press, 1964.

———. *The Elementary Forms of the Religious Life.* New York: Free Press, 1954.

Eagleton, Terry. *Ideology.* New York: Verso, 1991.

Easlea, Brian. *Fathering the Unthinkable: Masculinity, Scientists, and the Arms Race.* London: Pluto Press, 1983.

Easthouse, Keith. "Virtual Testing, Real Doubts." *New Mexican* series (1998): May 3: A1, A7–A8; May 4: A1, A11–A12; May 5: A1, A7–A9.

Edelman, Marian Wright. "Kids First." *Mother Jones* 16(1991): 31–77.

Eden, Lynn. "Oblivion Is Not Enough: How the U.S. Air Force Thinks about Nuclear War." Lecture presented to the Program in Science, Technology, and Society, MIT, October 16, 1989.

Edwards, Paul. *The Closed World: Computers and the Politics of Discourse in Cold War America.* Cambridge, MA: MIT Press, 1996.

Ehrmann, Eric. "Iraq's Nuclear Wildcards." *Christian Science Monitor,* September 4, 1990.

Ellsberg, Daniel. "Call to Mutiny." In Dan Smith and E. P. Thompson, eds., *Protest and Survive,* i–xxviii. New York: Monthly Review Press, 1981.

Else, J., director. *Day After Trinity.* San Jose, CA: KTEH Television, 1980.

Elshtain, Jean Bethke. *Women and War.* New York: Basic Books, 1987.

Ember, Carol, Melvin Ember, and Bruce Russett. "Peace between Participatory Polities: A Cross-Cultural Test of the 'Democracies Really Fight Each Other' Hypothesis." *World Politics* 44(1992): 573–99.

Enloe, Cynthia. *Bananas, Beaches, and Bases: Making Feminist Sense of International Politics.* Berkeley: University of California Press, 1990.

———. *Does Khaki Become You? The Militarization of Women's Lives.* Boston: South End Press, 1983.

Epstein, Barbara. "The Culture of Direct Action." *Socialist Review* 82–83 (1985): 31–61.

———. "The Politics of Prefigurative Community: The Non-Violent Direct Action Movement." In Mike David and Michael Spriker, eds., *Reshaping the U.S. Left: Popular Struggles in the 1980s,* 63–92. London: Verso Books, 1988.

———. *Political Protest and Cultural Revolution: Nonviolent Direct Action in the 1970s and 1980s.* Berkeley: University of California Press, 1991.

Epstein, William. "Indefinite Extension—With Accountability." *Bulletin of the Atomic Scientists* 51(1995): 27–30.

Evans-Pritchard, E. E. *Witchcraft, Oracles and Magic among the Azande.* Oxford: Oxford University Press, 1937.

Falk, Richard. "Nuclear Weapons and the End of Democracy." *Praxis International* 2 (1982): 1–11.

Farrell, John Aloysius. "Where We Shroud Our Heroes." *Boston Globe,* February 27, 1991.

Farrell, John, and Anne Kornblut. "War in Iraq Selective Strikes/Strategy; Technological Advances Define U.S. Approach." *Boston Globe,* March 23, 2003.

Featherstone, Michael. *Global Culture: Nationalism, Globalization and Identity.* Newbury Park, CA: Sage, 1990.

Fetter, Steve. "Stockpile Confidence under a Nuclear Test Ban." *International Security* 12 (1987–88): 132–67.

———. *Toward a Comprehensive Test Ban.* Cambridge, MA: Ballinger, 1988.

Fiorino, Daniel J. "Citizen Participation and Environmental Risk: A Survey of Institutional Mechanisms." *Science, Technology, and Human Values* 15(1990): 226–43.

Fish, Stanley. *Is There a Text in This Class? The Authority of Interpretive Communities.* Cambridge, MA: Harvard University Press, 1980.

Flynn, J., P. Slovic, and C. K. Mertz. "Decidedly Different: Expert and Public Views of Risks from a Radioactive Waste Repository." *Risk Analysis* 13(1993): 643–48.

Forsberg, Randall. "A Bilateral Nuclear Weapons Freeze." *Scientific American* 247(1982): 52–61.

———. "The Freeze and Beyond: Confining the Military to Defense as a Route to Disarmament." *World Policy Journal* 1(1984): 285–318.

Foucault, Michel. *Discipline and Punish: The Birth of the Prison.* New York: Vintage Books, 1979.

———. *The History of Sexuality. Volume 1: An Introduction.* New York: Vintage Books, 1980.

———. *The Order of Things: An Archaeology of the Human Sciences.* New York: Vintage Books, 1973.

————. *Power/Knowledge: Selected Interviews and Other Writings, 1972–1977.* New York: Pantheon Books, 1980.

————. "What Is an Author?" In Josue V. Harari, ed., *Textual Strategies: Perspectives in Post-Structuralist Criticism,* 141–60. Ithaca, NY: Cornell University Press, 1979.

Fradkin, Philip. *Fallout: An American Nuclear Tragedy.* Tucson: University of Arizona Press, 1989.

Francis, Sybil. "Warhead Politics: Livermore and the Competitive System of Nuclear Weapon Design." Ph.D. dissertation, Massachusetts Institute of Technology, 1996.

Frankenfeld, Philip J. "Technological Citizenship: A Normative Framework for Risk Studies." *Science, Technology, and Human Values* 17 (1992): 459–84.

Freedman, Lawrence. *The Evolution of Nuclear Strategy.* New York: St. Martin's Press, 1981.

Freer, Brian. "Atomic Pioneers and Environmental Legacy at the Hanford Site." *Canadian Review of Sociology and Anthropology* 31(1994): 305–24.

Fridling, Barry, and John Harvey. "On the Wrong Track? An Assessment of MX Rail Garrison Basing." *International Security* 13(1988–89): 113–41.

Friedman, Thomas. *The Lexus and the Olive Tree: Understanding Globalization.* New York: Farrar, Straus and Giroux, 1999.

————. "MAD Isn't Crazy." *New York Times,* July 24, 2001.

Fujimura, Joan. *Crafting Science: A Sociohistory of the Quest for the Genetics of Cancer.* Cambridge, MA: Harvard University Press, 1996.

Fukuyama, Francis. "The End of History." *National Interest,* no. 16 (Summer 1989): 1–18.

————. *The End of History and the Last Man.* New York: Avon Books, 1993.

Gaddis, John Lewis. "International Relations Theory and the End of the Cold War." *International Security* 17(1992–93): 5–58.

————. *Strategies of Containment: A Critical Appraisal of Postwar American National Security Policy.* New York: Oxford University Press, 1982.

————. "The United States and the Question of a Sphere of Influence in Europe, 1945–9." In Olav Riste, ed., *Western Security: The Formative Years.* Oslo: Norwegian University Press, 1985.

Galison, Peter. *The Disunity of Science: Boundaries, Context and Power.* Stanford, CA: Stanford University Press, 1996.

————. *Image and Logic: A Material Culture of Microphysics.* Chicago: University of Chicago Press, 1997.

Galison, Peter, and Bruce Hevly, eds. *Big Science: The Growth of Large-Scale Research.* Stanford, CA: Stanford University Press, 1992.

Gallagher, Carole. *American Ground Zero: The Secret Nuclear War.* Cambridge, MA: MIT Press, 1993.

Garb, Paula. "Complex Problems and No Clear Solutions: Difficulties of Defining and Assigning Culpability for Radiation Victimization in the Chelyabinsk Region of Russia." In Barbara Rose Johnston, ed., *Life and Death Matters:*

Human Rights at the End of the Millennium, 307–29. Walnut Creek, CA: Altamira Press, 1997.

Gardner, Gerald T., and Leroy C. Gould. "Public Perceptions of Risks and Benefits of Technology." *Risk Analysis* 9 (1989): 225–42.

Geertz, Clifford. "Common Sense as a Cultural System." In *Local Knowledge: Further Essays in Interpretive Anthropology,* 73–93. New York: Basic Books, 1983.

———. "From the Native's Point of View: On the Nature of Anthropological Understanding." In *Local Knowledge,* 55–70.

———. *The Interpretation of Cultures.* New York: Basic Books, 1973.

———. *Islam Observed.* New Haven, CT: Yale University Press, 1968.

Ghosh, Amitav. Letter to the editor. *New York Times,* June 1, 1998.

Gibbs, W. Wayt. "Computer Bombs." *Scientific American,* March 1997, 14–15.

Gibson, James William. *Warrior Dreams: Violence and Manhood in Post-Vietnam America.* New York: Hill and Wang, 1994.

Gibson, William. *Neuromancer.* New York: Ace Books, 1984.

Giddens, Anthony. *Central Problems in Social Theory: Action, Structure and Contradiction in Social Analysis.* Berkeley: University of California Press, 1979.

———. *The Constitution of Society: Outline of the Theory of Structuration.* Cambridge, MA: Polity Press, 1984.

———. "Four Theses on Ideology." *Canadian Journal of Political and Social Theory* 7 (1983): 18–21.

Ginsburg, Faye. *Contested Lives: The Abortion Debate in an American Community.* Berkeley: University of California Press, 1989.

Glass, Matthew. *Citizens against the MX: Public Languages in the Nuclear Age.* Urbana: University of Illinois Press, 1993.

Glasstone, Samuel, and Philip Dolan. *The Effects of Nuclear Weapons.* Washington, DC: U.S. Department of Defense and Energy Research and Development Administration, 1977.

Gleick, James. *Genius: The Life and Times of Richard Feynman.* New York: Pantheon, 1992.

Glendinning, Chellis. *Waking Up in the Nuclear Age.* Philadelphia: New Society Publishers, 1987.

Gluckman, Max. *Rituals of Rebellion in South-East Africa.* Manchester, UK: Manchester University Press, 1954.

Glynn, Patrick. "The Clash of Civilizations." *Times Literary Supplement,* April 1, 1997.

Gokhale, Sunil. "Columnist Erred on India's Military Spending." *Boston Globe,* May 9, 1996.

Goldberg, Stanley. "Smithsonian Suffers Legionnaire's Disease." *Bulletin of the Atomic Scientists* 51 (1995): 28–34.

———. "What Did Truman Know and When Did he Know It?" *Bulletin of the Atomic Scientists* 54 (1998): 18–20.

Goodenough, Ward. *Culture, Language, and Society.* Menlo Park, CA: Benjamin/Cummings, 1981.

Gordon, Michael. "U.S. Aides Press Iraqi Nuclear Threat." *New York Times,* November 26, 1990.

Gottemoeller, Rose. "Finding Solutions to SLCM Arms Control Problems." *International Security* 13(1988–89): 175–83.

Gourevitch, Philip. *We Wish to Inform You That Tomorrow We Will Be Killed with Our Families: Stories from Rwanda.* New York: Picador, 1999.

Gramsci, Antonio. *Prison Notebooks.* New York: Columbia University Press, 1992.

Grant, John. *The Day We Bombed Utah.* New York: New American Library, 1984.

Gray, Chris. *Postmodern War: The New Politics of Conflict.* New York: Guilford Press, 1997.

Gray, Colin, and Keith Payne. "Victory Is Possible." *Foreign Policy* 39 (1980): 14–27.

Green, Stephen. "The Iraqi Bomb: Only Ourselves to Blame." *Christian Science Monitor,* April 20, 1990.

Griffin, Susan. "Ideologies of Madness." In Diana Russell, ed., *Exposing Nuclear Phallacies.* New York: Pergamon, 1989.

Gross, Paul, and Norman Leavitt. *Higher Superstition: The Academic Left and Its Quarrels with Science.* Baltimore: The Johns Hopkins University Press, 1994.

Ground Zero. *Nuclear War: What's in It for You?* New York: Pocket Books, 1982.

Gupta, Akhil. *Postcolonial Developments.* Durham, NC: Duke University Press, 1998.

Gupta, Akhil, and James Ferguson. *Culture, Power, Place: Explorations in Critical Anthropology.* Durham, NC: Duke University Press, 1997.

———. "Discipline and Practice: The 'Field' as Site, Method, and Location in Anthropology." In Akhil Gupta and James Ferguson, eds., *Anthropological Locations: Boundaries and Grounds of a Field Science,* 1–46. Berkeley: University of California Press, 1997.

Gusterson, Hugh. "Coming of Age in a Weapons Lab: Culture, Tradition and Change in the House of the Bomb." *The Sciences,* May–June 1992, 16–22.

———. "Endless Escalation: The Cold War as Postmodern Narrative." *Tikkun* 6 (1991): 45–92.

———. "Exploding Anthropology's Canon in the World of the Bomb: Ethnographic Writing on Militarism." *Journal of Contemporary Ethnography* 22 (1993): 59–79.

———. "Feminist Militarism." *Political and Legal Anthropology Review* 22(1999): 17–26.

———. "NIF-ty Exercise Machine." *Bulletin of the Atomic Scientists* 51 (1995): 22–26.

———. *Nuclear Rites: A Nuclear Weapons Laboratory at the End of the Cold War.* Berkeley: University of California Press, 1996.

———. "Nuclear War, the Gulf War, and the Disappearing Body." *Journal of Urban and Cultural Studies* 2(1991): 45–55.

———. "Nuclear Weapons and the Other in the Western Imagination." *Cultural Anthropology* 14(1999): 111–43.

———. "Presenting the Creation: Dean Acheson and the Rhetorical Legitimation of NATO." *Alternatives* 24(1999): 39–57.

———. "Realism and the International Order after the Cold War." *Social Research* 60(1993): 279–300.

———. "Remembering Hiroshima at a Nuclear Weapons Laboratory." In Laura Hein and Mark Selden, eds., *Living with the Bomb: American and Japanese Cultural Conflicts in the Nuclear Age*. Armonk, NY: M. E. Sharpe, 1997.

———. "Studying Up Revisited." *Political and Legal Anthropology Review* 20 (1997): 114–19.

———. "Tales of the City." *Technology Review* 98 (1995): 56–57.

Haas, Peter, ed. "Knowledge, Power, and International Policy Coordination." Special issue, *International Organization* 46(1992).

Halen, Bertram. "Senator Hails Tie." *New York Times,* March 20, 1949.

Halliday, Fred. "The End of the Cold War and International Relations: Some Analytic and Theoretical Conclusions." In Ken Booth and Steve Smith, eds., *International Relations Theory Today*, 38–61. University Park: Pennsylvania State University Press, 1995.

Hannerz, Ulf. "Borders." *International Social Science Journal* 154 (1997): 537–48.

———. "Notes on the Global Ecumene." *Public Culture* 1(1989): 66–75.

———. *Transnational Connections: Culture, People, Places*. New York: Routledge, 1996.

———. "Reflections on Varieties of Culturespeak." *European Journal of Cultural Studies* 2(1999): 393–407.

Haraway, Donna. "A Manifesto for Cyborgs: Science, Technology, and Socialist Feminism in the 1980s." In Linda Nicholson, ed., *Feminism/Postmodernism*, 190–233. New York: Routledge, 1990.

———. *Primate Visions: Gender, Race, and Nature in the World of Modern Science*. New York: Routledge, 1990.

———. *Simians, Cyborgs, and Women: The Reinvention of Nature*. New York: Routledge, 1991.

———. "Situated Knowledges: The Science Question in Feminism and the Privilege of Partial Perspective." *Feminist Studies* 14 (1988): 575–99.

Harding, Susan. "Representing Fundamentalism: The Problem of the Repugnant Cultural Other." *Social Research* 58 (1991): 373–93.

Harvey, David. *The Condition of Postmodernity: An Enquiry into the Origins of Cultural Change*. Cambridge, MA.: Basil Blackwell, 1989.

Heider, Karl. *Grand Valley Dani: Peaceful Warriors*. New York: Holt, Rinehart, and Winston, 1979.

Helmreich, Stefan. *Silicon Second Nature: Culturing Artificial Life in a Digital World*. Berkeley: University of California Press, 1998.

Herken, Gregg. *Counsels of War.* New York: Alfred A. Knopf, 1985.

Herman, Edward, and Noam Chomsky. *Manufacturing Consent: The Political Economy of the Mass Media*. New York: Pantheon, 1988.

Hersey, John. *Hiroshima*. 1946. Reprint, New York: Vintage, 1985.

Hess, David. *Science Studies: An Advanced Introduction*. New York: New York University Press, 1997.

Hicks, Donald. "ICBM Modernization: Consider the Alternatives." *International Security* 12(1987): 173–81.

Hirsh, Daniel, and William Mathews. "The H-Bomb: Who Really Gave Away the Secret?" *Bulletin of the Atomic Scientists* 46 (1990): 24–26.

Hobson, Dorothy. *Crossroads: The Drama of a Soap Opera*. London: Methuen, 1982.

Hoddeson, Lillian. "Mission Change in the Large Laboratory: The Los Alamos Implosion Program, 1943–1945." In Peter Galison and Bruce Hevly, eds., *Big Science: The Growth of Large-Scale Research*, 265–89. Stanford, CA: Stanford University Press, 1992.

Hoddeson, Lillian, Paul W. Henrikson, Roger A. Meade, and Catherine Westfall. *Critical Assembly: A Technical History of Los Alamos during the Oppenheimer Years, 1943–1945*. Cambridge: Cambridge University Press, 1993.

Hoffman, Stanley. "On the Political Psychology of Peace and War: A Critique and an Agenda." *Political Psychology* 7(1986): 1–21.

Hogan, Michael J., ed. *The End of the Cold War: Its Meaning and Implications*. Cambridge: Cambridge University Press, 1992.

Holloway, David. "Soviet Scientists Speak Out." *Bulletin of the Atomic Scientists* 49(1993): 18–19.

———. *Stalin and the Bomb*. New Haven, CT: Yale University Press, 1994.

Holt, Robert R. "Can Psychology Meet Einstein's Challenge?" *Political Psychology* 7(1984): 199–225.

Holum, John. Statement to the United States Delegation to the Conference on Disarmament, Geneva, Switzerland. dosfan.lib.uic.edu/acda/ctbtpage/cd1.htm (accessed January 23, 1996.)

Homans, George. "Anxiety and Ritual: The Theories of Malinowski and Radcliffe-Brown." *American Anthropologist* 43 (1941): 164–72.

Hook, Glen. "Censorship and Reportage of Atomic Damage in Hiroshima and Nagasaki." *Multilingua* 7 (1988): 133–58.

Horton, Robin. "African Traditional Thought and Western Science." *Africa* 37 (1967): 50–71, 155–87.

Hoversten, Paul. "N-Plant Radiation: 13,500 Exposed." *USA Today,* July 13, 1990.

Huntington, Samuel P. *The Clash of Civilizations and the Remaking of World Order*. New York: Touchstone Books, 1996.

———. "No Exit: The Errors of Endism." *National Interest* 17 (1989): 3–11.

Iglesias, C. A., and F. J. Rogers. "Updated OPAL Opacities." *Astrophysical Journal* 464 (1996): 943–53.

Ignatieff, Michael. *Blood and Belonging: Journeys into the New Nationalism*. New York: Farrar, Straus and Giroux, 1993.

———. "The Clash of Civilizations." *New York Times Book Review,* December 1, 1996.

Immele, John, and Paul Brown. "Correspondence." *International Security* 13 (1988): 196–210.

Irving, J., director. *Dark Circle*. New York: New Yorker Films, 1982.

Jackson, Derrick. "What about the Death Toll?" *Boston Globe,* February 14, 2003.

Jasanoff, Sheila. *The Fifth Branch: Science Advisers as Policymakers*. Cambridge, MA: Harvard University Press, 1990.

Jeffers, Michelle. "Brown Tops in Fund-raising for City Races." *Tri-Valley Herald,* October 1, 1989.

Jenkins, Henry. *The Textual Poachers*. New York: Routledge, 1992.

Jervis, Robert. "The Clash of Civilizations." *Political Science Quarterly* 112(1997): 308.

———. *The Illogic of American Nuclear Strategy*. Ithaca, NY: Cornell University Press, 1984.

Joffe, Roland. *Fat Man and Little Boy*. Paramount Pictures, 1989.

Kahn, Herman. *On Thermonuclear War*. Princeton, NJ: Princeton University Press, 1960.

Kaldor, Mary. *New and Old Wars: Organized Violence in a Global Era*. Cambridge, UK: Polity Press, 1999.

Kang, David. "Bumpkins and Eggheads: A Cultural Look at Livermore in the 1950s." Honors Thesis, Anthropology Department, Stanford University, 1987.

Kaplan, Fred. *Wizards of Armageddon*. New York: Simon and Schuster, 1983.

Kaplan, Lawrence. *NATO and the United States: The Enduring Alliance*. Boston: Twayne, 1988.

Kaplan, Robert. *Balkan Ghosts*. New York: St. Martin's Press, 1993.

———. *The Coming Anarchy: Shattering the Dreams of the Post Cold War*. New York: Random House, 2000.

Katz, Milton. *Ban the Bomb: A History of SANE, the Committee for a Sane Nuclear Policy, 1957–1985*. Westport, CT: Greenwood Press, 1980.

Katzenstein, Peter, ed. *The Culture of National Security: Norms and Identity in World Politics*. New York: Columbia University Press, 1996.

Keegan, John. *War and Our World*. New York: Vintage, 1998.

Keiser, Lincoln. *The Vicelords: Warriors of the Streets*. New York: Holt, Rinehart and Winston, 1969.

Keller, Evelyn Fox. *Reflections on Gender and Science*. New Haven, CT: Yale University Press, 1985.

Kellerhals, Merle D., Jr. "Rumsfeld Says U.S. Will Not Violate 1972 ABM Treaty." Washington file, July 13, 2001. Office of International Information Programs, Department of State (usinfo.state.gov).

Kelly, Michael. "In Morgues, Terror's Grisly Remains." *Boston Globe* March 2, 1991.

Kempster, Norman. "Iraq Sacrificed Billions for Its Arms." *San Francisco Examiner,* February 8, 1998.

Kennan, George. "A Fateful Error." *New York Times,* February 5, 1997.

———. "Two Views of the Soviet Problem." *New Yorker,* November 2, 1981.

Kennedy, Edward. "Prologue." In Edward Markey, *Nuclear Peril: The Politics of Proliferation.* Cambridge, MA: Ballinger, 1982.

Khariton, Yuli, and Yuri Smirnov. "The Khariton Version." *Bulletin of the Atomic Scientists* 49(1993): 20–31.

Kidder, Ray. *Maintaining the U.S. Stockpile of Nuclear Weapons during a Low-Threshold or Comprehensive Test Ban.* Document UCRL-53820, Lawrence Livermore National Laboratory, 1987.

———. "Problems with Stockpile Stewardship." *Nature,* April 17, 1997.

Kiefer, Francine. "Why Bush Team Is No Fan of Arms Control Treaties." *Christian Science Monitor,* July 20, 2001.

Kier, Elizabeth. *Imagining War: French and British Military Doctrines between the Wars.* Princeton, NJ: Princeton University Press, 1988.

King, Anthony, ed. *Culture, Globalization, and the World-System: Contemporary Conditions for the Representation of Identity.* 1991. Reprint, Minneapolis: University of Minnesota Press, 1997.

Klare, Michael. *Rogue States and Nuclear Outlaws: America's Search for a New Foreign Policy.* New York: Hill and Wang, 1995.

Knorr-Cetina, Karin. *Epistemic Cultures: How the Sciences Make Knowledge.* Cambridge, MA: Harvard University Press, 1999.

———. *The Manufacture of Knowledge: An Essay on the Constructivist and Contextual Nature of Knowledge.* New York: Pergamon, 1981.

Kolko, Gabriel. *The Politics of War: The World and United States Foreign Policy, 1943–1945.* New York: Random House, 1968.

Kondracke, Morton. "Watch Out for Those 'Little' Nuclear Wars." *Los Angeles Times,* July 22, 1983.

Kopit, Arthur. *End of the World with Symposium to Follow.* New York: Samuel French, 1984.

Kotz, Nick. *Wild Blue Yonder: Money, Politics, and the B-1 Bomber.* Princeton, NJ: Princeton University Press, 1988.

Kramer, Mark. "Beyond the Brezhnev Doctrine: A New Era in Soviet-East European Relations?" *International Relations* 14(1989–90): 25–67.

Kranish, Michael. "Senator Hints at Force over Reported Iraqi Threat." *Boston Globe,* April 2, 1990.

Krasniewicz, Louise. *Nuclear Summer: The Clash of Communities at the Seneca Women's Peace Encampment.* Ithaca, NY: Cornell University Press, 1992.

Krause, Keith, and Michael C. Williams. *Critical Security Studies.* Minneapolis: University of Minnesota Press, 1997.

Krauthammer, Charles. "Exhibit Distorts Historical Context of the A-Bombing of Japan." *Albuquerque Journal,* August 21, 1994.

Krimsky, Sheldon, and Dominic Golding, eds. *Social Theories of Risk.* New York: Praeger, 1992.

Kroker, Arthur. *Data Trash: The Theory of the Virtual Class.* New York: St. Martin's, 1994.

Krugman, Paul. "Behind the Great Divide." *New York Times,* February 18, 2003.

Kuhn, Thomas. *The Structure of Scientific Revolutions.* Chicago: University of Chicago Press, 1962.

Kull, Steven. *Minds at War: Nuclear Reality and the Inner Conflicts of Defense Policymakers.* New York: Basic Books, 1988.

———. "Nuclear Nonsense." *Foreign Policy* 58 (1985): 28–52.

Laclau, Ernesto, and Chantal Mouffe. *Hegemony and Socialist Strategy: Towards a Radical Democratic Politics.* London: Verso Books, 1985.

Lafeber, Walter. *America, Russia, and the Cold War, 1945–1975.* New York: John Wiley, 1985.

Lanouette, William. *Genius in the Shadows: A Biography of Leo Szilard, the Man behind the Bomb.* Chicago: University of Chicago Press, 1992.

Latour, Bruno. 1988. *The Pasteurization of France.* Cambridge, MA: Harvard University Press, 1988.

———. *Science in Action: How to Follow Scientists and Engineers through Society.* Cambridge, MA: Harvard University Press, 1987.

Latour, Bruno, and Steve Woolgar. *Laboratory Life: The Construction of Scientific Facts.* Beverly Hills, CA: Sage, 1979.

Lawrence, W. H. "Pact Itself Hailed." *New York Times,* March 19, 1949.

Lawrence Livermore National Laboratory. *Nuclear Weapons Work at LLNL.* Visitors Center leaflet, May 4, 1990.

———. "The State of the Laboratory." *Energy and Technology Review,* July–August 1990.

———. *Thirty Years of Technical Excellence.* Livermore, CA: Lawrence Livermore National Laboratory Communications Resources Office, 1982.

Layne, Christopher. "Kant or Cant: The Myth of the Democratic Peace." *International Security* 19(1994): 5–49.

Lebow, Richard Ned. "The Long Peace, the End of the Cold War, and the Failure of Realism." In Richard Ned Lebow and Thomas Risse-Kappen, eds., *International Relations Theory and the End of the Cold War.* New York: Columbia University Press, 1995.

Lebow, Richard Ned, and Thomas Risse-Kappen, eds. *International Relations Theory and the End of the Cold War.* New York: Columbia University Press, 1995.

Lepingwell, John. "Soviet Strategic Air Defense and the Stealth Challenge." *International Security* 14(1998): 64–100.

Leskov, Sergei. "Dividing the Glory of the Fathers." *Bulletin of the Atomic Scientists* 49(1993): 37–39.

Lev, Michael A. "India, Pakistan: Hard Road to Nuclear Intelligence." *San Francisco Examiner,* June 7, 1998.

Lévi-Strauss, Claude. *The Savage Mind.* Chicago: University of Chicago Press, 1966.

Lewis, Flora. "Are States All Equal?" *New York Times,* November 10, 1990.

Lichterman, Andrew, and Jacqueline Cabasso. *A Faustian Bargain: Why "Stockpile Stewardship" is Fundamentally Incompatible with the Process of Nuclear Disarmament.* Oakland, CA: Western States Legal Foundation, 2000.

Lifton, Robert Jay. *The Broken Connection: On Death and the Continuity of Life.* New York: Basic Books, 1983.

———. "Imagining the Real." In Robert Jay Lifton and Richard Falk, *Indefensible Weapons: The Political and Psychological Case against Nuclearism.* New York: Basic Books, 1982.

Lifton, Robert Jay, and Richard Falk. *Indefensible Weapons: The Political and Psychological Case against Nuclearism.* New York: Basic Books, 1982.

Lifton, Robert Jay, and Eric Markusen. *The Genocidal Mentality: Nazi Holocaust and Nuclear Threat.* New York: Basic Books, 1990.

Lifton, Robert Jay, and Greg Mitchell. *Hiroshima in America: Fifty Years of Denial.* New York: Putnam, 1995.

Lindenbaum, Shirley. *Kuru Sorcery: Disease and Danger in the New Guinea Highlands.* Palo Alto, CA: Mayfield, 1974.

Livermore Independent, "Data Missing from Incinerator Report," March 8, 1989.

———. "Lobbyist Hired to Deal with the Labs," June 15, 1988.

———. "Livermore Officials Castigate DOE for Denying Request for Hearing," October 26, 1988.

———. "Livermore to Fight East Avenue Closure," May 11, 1988.

LLNL Women's Association. *LLLWA Salary Study Committee Report.* Livermore, CA: LLNL Women's Association, 1988.

Lodal, Jan. "SICBM Yes, HML No." *International Security* 12(1987–88): 182–86.

Lodge, David. *The Practice of Writing.* New York: Penguin, 1996.

Loeb, Paul. *Hope in Hard Times: America's Peace Movement and the Reagan Era.* Lanham, MD: Lexington Books, 1987.

Luke, Timothy. "What's Wrong with Deterrence? A Semiotic Interpretation of National Security Policy." In James Der Derian and Michael Shapiro, eds., *International/Intertextual Relations: Postmodern Readings of World Politics,* 207–30. Lanham, MD: Lexington Books, 1989.

Lutz, Catherine, and Jane Collins. *Reading National Geographic.* Chicago: University of Chicago Press, 1993.

Mack, John. "Nuclear Weapons and the Dark Side of Humankind." *Political Psychology* 7 (1986): 223–33.

———. "Toward a Collective Psychopathology of the Nuclear Arms Competition." *Political Psychology* 6 (1985): 291–321.

MacKenzie, Donald, and Graham Spinardi. "Tacit Knowledge, Weapons Design, and the Uninvention of Nuclear Weapons." In Donald MacKenzie, *Knowing Machines: Essays on Technical Change,* 215–60. Cambridge, MA: MIT Press, 1996.

Makhijani, Arjun, Howard Hu, and Katherine Yih, eds. *Nuclear Wastelands: A Global Guidebook to Nuclear Weapons Production and Its Health and Environmental Effects.* Cambridge, MA: MIT Press, 1995.

Malinowski, Bronislaw. *Magic, Science, and Religion and Other Essays.* 1925. Reprint, Garden City, NY: Doubleday Anchor, 1948.

Manoff, Robert. "Modes of War and Modes of Address: The Text of SDI." *Journal of Communication* 39(1989): 59–83.

Marcus, George. "Ethnography in/of the World System: The Emergence of Multi-sited Ethnography." *Annual Review of Anthropology* 24 (1995): 95–117.

———. "Foreword." In Jutta Weldes, Mark Laffey, Hugh Gusterson, and Raymond Duvall, eds., *Cultures of Insecurity: States, Communities and the Production of Danger*, vii–xv. Minneapolis: University of Minnesota Press, 1999.

Marcus, George, and Michael Fischer. *Anthropology as Cultural Critique: An Experimental Moment in the Human Sciences*. Chicago: University of Chicago Press, 1986.

Margolis, Howard. *Risk: Why the Public and the Experts Disagree on Environmental Issues*. Chicago: University of Chicago Press, 1992.

Markey, Edward. "Hold Pakistan to Non-Proliferation Law." *Washington Post*, November 3, 1987.

———. *Nuclear Peril: The Politics of Proliferation*. Cambridge, MA: Ballinger, 1982.

Markle, Peter, director. *Nightbreaker.* Turner Home Entertainment. 1989.

Marquand, Robert. "India Bomb Hits Chord for Hindus." *Christian Science Monitor,* June 4, 1998.

Marshall, Eliot. "Secretiveness Found Widespread in Life Sciences." *Science* 276 (1997): 525.

Marshall, Tyler. "India, Pakistan Told to Put Weapons Away." *San Francisco Chronicle,* May 28, 1998.

———. "South Asia Testing May Blast a Hole in 3-Decade Old Double Standard." *Los Angeles Times,* June 5, 1998.

Martin, Emily. *Flexible Bodies: Tracking Immunity in America from the Days of Polio to the Age of AIDS*. Boston: Beacon Press, 1994.

Marx, Karl. *Capital,* Book 1. 1867. Reprint, London: Everyman Library, 1972.

Masco, Joseph. "The Nuclear Borderlands: The Legacy of the Manhattan Project in Post-Cold War New Mexico." Ph.D. dissertation, University of California at San Diego, 1999.

———. "States of Insecurity: Plutonium and Post-Cold War Anxiety in New Mexico, 1992–1996." In Jutta Weldes, Mark Laffey, Hugh Gusterson, and Raymond Duvall, eds., *Cultures of Insecurity: States, Communities, and the Production of Danger*, 203–31. Minneapolis: University of Minnesota Press, 1999.

Mathews, Tom. "Saddam's Last Stand." *Newsweek,* March 4, 1991.

Mattern, Douglas. "The Poverty amid Riches." *San Francisco Chronicle,* January 5, 1998.

May, Michael, George Bing, and John Steinbruner. "Strategic Arsenals after START." *International Security* 13(1988): 90–133.

Mayer, Nancy. "Subcontinent Nuclear Tests Bother Teller." *Livermore Tri-Valley Herald,* June 5, 1998.

McClatchy News Service, "History Has Glow in Desert," *Tri-Valley Herald,* November 13, 1994.

McCrea, Frances, and Gerald Markle. *Minutes to Midnight: Nuclear Weapons Protest in America.* Newbury Park, CA: Sage, 1989.

McElroy, Claudia. "Kazakhs Pay for Soviet Nuclear Tests." *Manchester Guardian Weekly,* March 29, 1998.

McFarlane, Robert. "Pakistan's Catch-22." *New York Times,* May 30, 1998.

McGrory, Mary. "Doomsday and Dalliance." *Washington Post,* June 4, 1998.

———. "Nuclear Boys Behaving Badly." *Washington Post,* May 31, 1998.

McNamara, Laura. "Ways of Knowing about Nuclear Weapons." Ph.D. dissertation, University of New Mexico, 2001.

McNamara, Robert. *Blundering into Disaster: Surviving the First Century of the Nuclear Age.* New York: Pantheon, 1986.

Mearsheimer, John. "Back to the Future: Instability in Europe after the Cold War." *International Security* 15(1990): 5–56.

———. "The False Promise of International Institutions." *International Security* 19(1994–95): 5–49.

———. "Why We Will Soon Miss the Cold War." *Atlantic Monthly,* August 1990, 35–50.

Mehan, Hugh, James Skelly, and Charles Nathanson. "Nuclear Discourse in the 1980s: The Unraveling Conventions of the Cold War." *Discourse and Society* 1(1990): 133–65.

Mehan, Hugh, and John Wells. "MEND: A Nurturing Voice in the Nuclear Arms Debate." *Social Problems* 35(1988): 363–83.

Melman, Seymour. *Pentagon Capitalism: The Political Economy of War.* New York: McGraw-Hill, 1970.

———. *The Permanent War Economy.* New York: Touchstone Books, 1974.

Merchant, Carolyn. *The Death of Nature.* San Francisco: Harper, 1980.

Merton, Robert. "The Normative Structure of Science." In *The Sociology of Science: Theoretical and Empirical Investigations,* 267–78. Chicago: University of Chicago Press, 1942.

Meyer, David S. *A Winter of Discontent: The Nuclear Freeze and American Politics.* New York: Praeger, 1990.

Meyer, Steven. "The Sources and Prospects of Gorbachev's New Political Thinking on Security." *International Security* 13(1998): 124–63.

Milhollin, Gary. "Attention, Nuke-Mart Shoppers!" *Washington Post,* July 22, 1990.

Miller, Byron A. *Geography and Social Movements: Comparing Antinuclear Activism in the Boston Area.* Minneapolis: University of Minnesota Press, 2000.

Miller, George, Paul Brown, and Carol Alonso. *Report to Congress on Stockpile Reliability, Weapon Manufacture, and the Role of Nuclear Testing.* Document UCRL-53822. Livermore, CA: Lawrence Livermore National Laboratory, 1987.

Milliken, Jennifer. "Intervention and Identity: Reconstructing the West in Korea." In Jutta Weldes, Mark Laffey, Hugh Gusterson, and Raymond Duvall, eds.,

Cultures of Insecurity: States, Communities, and the Production of Danger, 91–117. Minneapolis: University of Minnesota Press, 1999.

Mintz, Sidney. *Sweetness and Power.* New York: Penguin, 1985.

Mitchell, Greg. "Hiroshima Day." *Progressive,* August 1994.

Mojtabai, A. G. *Blessed Assurance: At Home with the Bomb in Amarillo, Texas.* Boston: Houghton Mifflin, 1986.

Molander, Roger. "Must They All Go Nuclear?" *Los Angeles Times,* August 6, 1986.

Moore, Molly, and Kamran Khan. "Kashmir: A South Asian Flash Point." *Washington Post,* June 3, 1998.

Moore, Sally F., and Barbara Myerhoff, eds. *Secular Rituals.* Amsterdam: Van Gorcum, 1997.

Morgan, Henry Louis. *League of the Ho-de-no-sau-nee or Iroquois.* 1851. Reprint, New York: Corinth, 1962.

Morgan, Patrick. *Deterrence: A Conceptual Analysis.* Beverly Hills, CA: Sage, 1977.

Mustin, Henry. "The Sea-Launched Cruise Missile: More Than a Bargaining Chip." *International Security* 13(1988–89): 184–90.

Myslinski, M. "Memory Haunts Nagasaki Survivor." *Valley Herald,* August 6, 1982.

Nader, Laura. *Harmony Ideology.* Stanford, CA: Stanford University Press, 1990.

———. "Up the Anthropologist: Perspectives Gained from Studying Up." In Dell Hymes, ed., *Reinventing Anthropology,* 284–311. New York: Vintage, 1974.

Naimark, Norman. *Fires of Hatred: Ethnic Cleansing in Twentieth Century Europe.* Cambridge, MA: Harvard University Press, 2001.

Nash, Henry. "The Bureaucratization of Homicide." In E. P. Thompson and Dan Smith, eds., *Protest and Survive,* 284–311. New York: Monthly Review Press, 1981.

National Conference of Catholic Bishops. *The Challenge of Peace: God's Promise and Our Response.* Washington, DC: U.S. Catholic Conference, 1983.

Neale, Mary. "Balancing Passion and Reason: The Physicians Movement against Nuclear Weapons." Ph.D. dissertation, University of California at San Francisco, 1988.

Neel, James V., Gilbert Beebe, and Robert W. Miller. "Delayed Biomedical Effects of the Bomb." *Bulletin of the Atomic Scientists* 41 (1985): 72–75.

Nelson, Diane. *A Finger in the Wound: Body Politics in Quincentennial Guatemala.* Berkeley: University of California Press, 1999.

New Left Review, ed. *Exterminism and Cold War.* London: Verso, 1982.

New York Times. "India, Uninvited, Joins the Nuclear Club," May 19, 1974.

———. "New Uranium Pollution Is Found in Wells at U.S. A-plant in Ohio," January 4, 1990.

———. "Nuclear Risks in South Asia," May 25, 1998.

———. "On to Armageddon," May 20, 1974.

———. "Punish Pakistan's Perfidy on the Bomb," July 17, 1987.

————. "Stop Pakistan's Nuclear Bomb," March 13, 1987.

————. "Wallace Urges Protest," March 19, 1949.

News Network International. "All the Tests Successful: Dr. Qadeer." *NNI-News of Pakistan*, June 1, 1998.

Nobile, Philip, ed. *Judgment at the Smithsonian*. New York: Marlowe, 1995.

Nordstrom, Carolyn. *A Different Kind of War Story (Ethnography of Political Violence)*. Philadelphia: University of Pennsylvania Press, 1997.

————. "Illuminating the Shadows: Globalization of the Illicit." In Catherine Besteman and Hugh Gusterson, eds., *Why America's Top Pundits Are Wrong*. Berkeley: University of California Press, forthcoming.

Norris, Robert, and William Arkin. "Hot Dogs." *Bulletin of the Atomic Scientists* 46 (1990): 56.

Norris, Stanley. *Racing for the Bomb: General Leslie R. Groves, the Manhattan Project's Indispensible Man*. South Royalton, VT: Steerforth Press, 2002.

Norris, Stanley, Hans Kristensen, and Joshua Handler. "North Korea's Nuclear Program, 2003." *Bulletin of the Atomic Scientists* 59 (2003): 74–77.

Nuclear Weapons Stockpile Stewardship. *Nuclear Weapons Stockpile Stewardship*. mit.edu/sts/SSBS (accessed November 28, 2000).

Nye, Joseph. *Nuclear Ethics*. New York: Free Press, 1986.

Nye, Joseph S., Jr., and Sean M. Lynn-Jones. "International Security Studies: A Report on a Conference on the State of the Field." *International Security* 12(1988): 5–27.

Oakland Tribune, "Pleasanton Panel Urges EIR on Lab Incinerator," May 3, 1989.

Ong, Aihwa. *Flexible Citizenship: The Cultural Logics of Transnationality*. Durham, NC: Duke University Press, 1999.

Paine, Christopher. "The Comprehensive Test Ban Treaty in the Current Nuclear Context." In Matthew McKinzie, ed., *The Comprehensive Test Ban Treaty: Issues and Answers*. Occasional Paper 21. Ithaca, NY: Cornell University Peace Studies Program, 1997.

Paine, Christopher, and Matthew McKinzie. *End Run: Simulating Nuclear Explosions under the Comprehensive Test Ban Treaty*. Washington, DC: Natural Resources Defense Council, 1997.

Panofsky, Wolfgang. "Dismantling the Concept of 'Weapons of Mass Destruction.'" *Arms Control Today*, April 1992, 3–8.

————. "SLAC and Big Science: Stanford University." In Peter Galison and Bruce Hevly, eds., *Big Science: The Growth of Large-Scale Research*, 129–46. Stanford: Stanford University Press, 1992.

Parkin, David. *Middle Class Radicalism*. Manchester, UK: Manchester University Press, 1968.

Pasztor, David. "Building a Better Bomb." *San Francisco Weekly*, May 27, 1998.

Payne, Keith, and Colin Gray. "Victory Is Possible." *Foreign Affairs* 39 (1980): 14–27.

Payne, Richard. *The Clash of Distant Cultures: Values, Interests, and Force in American Foreign Policy*. Albany: SUNY Press, 1995.

Peattie, Lisa. "The Defense of Daily Life." *IUAES Commission on the Study of Peace Newsletter* 4(1986): 3–12.

———. "Economic Conversion as a Set of Organizing Ideas." *Bulletin of Peace Proposals* 19(1988): 11–20.

Pedelty, Mark. *War Stories: The Culture of Foreign Correspondents.* New York: Routledge, 1995.

Perhac, Ralph M. "Comparative Risk Assessment: Where Does the Public Fit In?" *Science, Technology, and Human Values* 23 (1998): 221–41.

Perkovich, George. "Exploding Myths about the Bomb: The Theoretical and Policy Implications of India's Nuclear Weapon Program." Lecture at Center for International Security and Arms Control, Stanford University, 1998.

———. *India's Nuclear Bomb: The Impact on Global Proliferation.* Berkeley: University of California Press, 1999.

———. "A Nuclear Third Way in South Asia." *Foreign Policy* 91 (1993): 85–105.

Perle, Richard. "Keeping the Bomb from Iraq." *Wall Street Journal,* August 22, 1990.

———. "Reykjavik as a Watershed in U.S.-Soviet Arms Control." *International Security* 12(1987): 175–78.

Perlmutter, Amos. "A Bomb for the Butcher?" *Washington Times,* April 10, 1990.

Perry, William. *Annual Report to the President and the Congress.* Washington, DC: Government Printing Office, 1995.

Pickering, Andrew. *Constructing Quarks: A Sociological History of Particle Physics.* Chicago: University of Chicago Press, 1984.

Pinch, Trevor. "Testing—One, Two, Three . . . Testing: Towards a Sociology of Testing." *Science, Technology, and Human Values* 18 (1993): 25–41.

Pinch, Trevor, and Harry Collins. *The Golem: What Everyone Should Know about Science.* Cambridge: Cambridge University Press, 1993.

Postol, Theodore. "Banning Nuclear SLCMs: It Would Be Nice if We Could." *International Security* 13(1988–89): 191–202.

———. "Nuclear War." *Encyclopaedia Americana,* 519–32. Danbury, CT: Grolier, 1987.

Potter, William. *Nuclear Power and Non-Proliferation: An Inter-Disciplinary Perspective.* Cambridge, MA: Oelgeschlager, Gunn, and Hain, 1982.

Power, Jonathan. "India and Pakistan Face the Prospect of a Nuclear War." *Minneapolis Star Tribune,* November 2, 1997.

Powers, Samantha. *A Problem from Hell: America and the Age of Genocide.* New York: Basic Books, 2002.

Powers, Thomas. *Thinking about the Next War.* New York: Mentor Books, 1982.

Price, Richard. *The Chemical Weapons Taboo.* Ithaca, NY: Cornell University Press, 1997.

Raats, M. M., and R. Shepherd. "Developing a Subject-Derived Terminology to Describe Perceptions of Chemicals in Food." *Risk Analysis* 16 (1996): 133–47.

Rabinow, Paul. *Making PCR: A Story of Biotechnology.* Chicago: University of Chicago Press, 1996.

Radway, Janice. *Reading the Romance: Women, Patriarchy, and Popular Literature*. Chapel Hill: University of North Carolina Press, 1991.

Rathjens, George. "Preventing Proliferation." In Dagobert Brito and Michael Intriligator, eds., *Strategies for Managing Nuclear Proliferation*, 265–72. Lanham, MD: Lexington Books, 1982.

Reid, T. R. "Pakistan, India Loans Blocked: G-8 Nations Move to Punish Nuclear Outlaws." *San Francisco Chronicle*, June 13, 1998.

———. "U.S. A-Bomb Stamp Called 'Heartless.'" *Washington Post*, December 3, 1994.

Reston, James. "New Pact Marks Historic Change in Our Policy." *New York Times*, March 13, 1949.

Reuters. "Bush: Allies Have Say on Missile Shield Development," June 11, 2001.

Reynolds, Peter. *Stealing Fire: The Atomic Bomb as Symbolic Body*. Palo Alto, CA: Iconic Anthropology Books, 1991.

Rhodes, Richard. *Dark Sun: The Making of the Hydrogen Bomb*. New York: Simon and Schuster, 1995.

———. *The Making of the Atomic Bomb*. New York: Simon and Schuster, 1988.

Robertson, Roland. *Globalization: Social Theory and Global Culture*. Newbury Park, CA: Sage, 1992.

Rogers, F. J., F. J. Swenson, and C. A. Iglesias. "OPAL Equation-of-State Tables for Astrophysical Applications." *Astrophysical Journal*, January 10, 1996, 902–8.

Rogers, Keith. "EPA Tells Lab Incinerator Days Are Over." *Valley Times*, September 12, 1990.

———. "Incinerator Permit Denial Might Curtail Lab Research." *Valley Times*, November 9, 1989.

———. "Lab Downplays Effect on Plants in Spiked Garden." *Valley Times*, September 10, 1989.

———. "Lab Misses Incinerator Reporting Deadline." *Valley Times*, November 7, 1989.

———. "Lab to Improve Minority Hiring Policies." *Livermore Valley Times*, May 25, 1989.

———. "Toxic Water Escapes from LLL." *Valley Times*, May 22, 1987.

Rosaldo, Michelle. "Woman, Culture, and Society: A Theoretical Overview." In Michelle Rosaldo and Louise Lamphere, eds., *Woman, Culture, and Society*, 17–42. Stanford, CA: Stanford University Press, 1974.

Rosaldo, Renato. *Culture and Truth: The Remaking of Social Analysis*. Boston: Beacon Press, 1989.

———. *Ilongot Headhunting, 1883–1974: A Study in Society and History*. Stanford, CA: Stanford University Press, 1980.

Rosenberg, Howard L. *Atomic Soldiers: American Victims of Nuclear Experiments*. Boston: Beacon Press, 1980.

Rosencrance, Richard. "The Clash of Civilizations." *American Political Science Review* 92(1998): 978–80.

Rosenfeld, Peter. "Nuclear Nightmare." *Washington Post*, March 13, 1987.

Rosenthal, A. M. "Iraq and Atom Bombs." *New York Times,* August 16, 1990.

———. "A Story of Two Stories." *New York Times,* February 3, 1998.

Rosenthal, Debra. *At the Heart of the Bomb: The Deadly Allure of Weapons Work.* Reading, MA: Addison-Wesley, 1990.

Ross, Andrew, ed. *Science Wars.* Durham, NC: Duke University Press, 1996.

Roth, Emilie, M. Granmger Morgan, Baruch Fischhoff, Lester Lave, and Ann Bostrom. "What Do We Know about Making Risk Comparisons?" *Risk Analysis* 10 (1990): 375–87.

Rubinstein, Robert, and Mary LeCron Foster. *Peace and War: Cross-Cultural Perspectives.* New Brunswick, NJ: Transaction, 1989.

———, eds. *The Social Dynamics of Conflict: Culture in International Society.* Boulder, CO: Westview, 1988.

Ruddick, Sara. *Maternal Thinking: Toward a Politics of Peace.* New York: Ballantine, 1989.

Ruina, Jack. "More Is Not Better." *International Security* 12(1987): 187–92.

Rushdie, Salman. *Shame.* New York: Aventura, 1984.

Safire, William. "Friendly Dissuasion." *New York Times,* May 3, 2001.

———. "Giving Iraq Time." *New York Times,* November 12, 1990.

———. "The Saddam Bomb." *New York Times,* November 29, 1990.

———. "Support Your President." *New York Times,* February 19, 1998.

Sagan, Scott. *The Limits of Safety: Organizations, Accidents, and Nuclear Weapons.* Princeton, NJ: Princeton University Press, 1993.

———. "More Will Be Worse." In Scott Sagan and Kenneth Waltz, *The Spread of Nuclear Weapons,* 47–91. New York: Norton, 1995.

Sagdeev, Roald. "Russian Scientists Save American Secrets." *Bulletin of the Atomic Scientists* 49(1993): 32–36.

Said, Edward. *Orientalism.* New York: Vintage Books, 1978.

San Francisco Chronicle, "U.S. Ignored A-plant's Toxic Emissions," October 15, 1988.

Sanders, Ben. "Avoiding the Worst of All Possible Worlds." In Joseph Pilat and Robert Pendley, eds., *The Future of the NPT Regime Beyond 1995,* 47–91. New York: Plenum Press, 1990.

Sapolsky, Harvey. "The Politics of Risk." *Daedalus* 119(1990): 83–96.

Scarry, Elaine. *The Body in Pain: The Making and Unmaking of the World.* New York: Oxford University Press, 1985.

Scheer, Robert. "The Man Who Blew the Whistle on Star Wars." *Los Angeles Times Magazine,* June 17, 1982.

———. *With Enough Shovels: Reagan, Bush, and Nuclear War.* New York: Random House, 1982.

Schell, Jonathan. *The Abolition.* New York: Avon Books, 1986.

———. *The Gift of Time: The Case for Abolishing Nuclear Weapons Now.* New York: Owl Books, 1998.

Schelling, Thomas. "Abolition of Ballistic Missiles." *International Security* 12 (1987): 179–83.

———. *Arms and Influence.* New Haven, CT: Yale University Press, 1966.

———. *The Strategy of Conflict.* Cambridge: Harvard University Press, 1960.

Schirmer, Jennifer. *The Guatemalan Military Project: A Violence Called Democracy.* Philadelphia: University of Pennsylvania Press, 1998.

Schmitt, Eric. "Racing through the Darkness in Pursuit of Scuds." *New York Times,* February 24, 1991.

Schneider, Keith. "Decades of Plutonium Peril at an Arms Plant." *New York Times,* November 20, 1989.

———. "Report Warns of Impact of Hanford's Radiation." *New York Times,* July 13, 1990.

———. "U.S. Tells of Peril in '40's Radiation to the Northwest." *New York Times,* July 12, 1990.

———. "U.S. Temporarily Shutting Down Nuclear Plant for Safety Problems." *New York Times,* November 30, 1989.

Schoch-Spana, Monica. "Reactor Control and Environmental Management: A Cultural Account of Agency in the U.S. Nuclear Weapons Complex." Ph.D. dissertation, The Johns Hopkins University, 1999.

Schwarz, Michiel, and Michael Thompson. *Divided We Stand: Redefining Politics, Technology, and Social Choice.* Philadelphia: University of Pennsylvania Press, 1990.

Scott, James. *Domination and the Arts of Resistance.* New Haven, CT: Yale University Press, 1990.

Senate Policy Committee, Berkeley Division of the Academic Senate, University of California. "The University of California, the Lawrence Livermore National Laboratory, and the Los Alamos National Laboratory." Unpublished background paper, 1984.

Senghaas, Dieter. "A Clash of Civilizations: An Idée Fixe?" *Journal of Peace Research* 35 (1998): 127–32.

Shankland, Steve. "Lab's Rebound Test Detonated as Planned." *Los Alamos Monitor,* July 2, 1997.

Shapin, Steven, and Simon Schaffer. *Leviathan and the Air-Pump: Hobbes, Boyle, and the Experimental Life.* Princeton, NJ.: Princeton University Press, 1985.

Shapiro, Michael. *Violent Cartographies: Mapping Cultures of War.* Minneapolis: University of Minnesota Press, 1997.

Shelley, Mary. *Frankenstein.* Oxford: Oxford University Press, 1969.

Shroyer, Jo Ann. *Secret Mesa: Inside the Los Alamos National Laboratory.* New York: Wiley and Sons, 1998.

Sigal, Leon V. *Disarming Strangers: Nuclear Diplomacy with North Korea.* Princeton, NJ: Princeton University Press, 1998.

Simich, Laura. "Comiso: The Politics of Peace in a Sicilian Town." *IUAES Commission on the Study of Peace Newsletter* 5 (1987): 5–9.

Sjoberg, Lennart, ed. *Risk and Society: Studies of Risk Generation and Reactions to Risk.* Boston: Allen and Unwin, 1987.

Sloss, Leon. "A World without Ballistic Missiles." *International Security* 12 (1987): 184–89.

Sloyan, Patrick. "U.S. Has Policy Allowing Nuclear Attack on Iraq." *Irish Times,* February 3, 1998.

Smith, Andrew. "Genius, Resources Grace Facility." *Tri-Valley Herald,* September 9, 1990.

———. "Lab Spreads Radiation in Air." *Tri-Valley Herald,* August 4, 1990.

Smith, Hedrick. "A-Bomb Ticks in Pakistan." *New York Times Magazine,* March 6, 1988.

Smith, R. Jeffrey. "America's Arsenal of Nuclear Time Bombs." *Washington Post National* (weekly edition), May 28–June 3, 1990.

———. "Indian Tests Shatter West's Containment Policy." *San Francisco Chronicle,* May 12, 1998.

Snyder, Jack. "The Gorbachev Revolution: A Waning of Soviet Expansionism?" *International Security* 12(1987–88): 93–131.

Sokal, Alan. "A Physicist Experiments with Cultural Studies." *Lingua Franca,* May–June 1996, 62–64.

Solo, Pam. *From Protest to Policy: Beyond the Freeze to Common Security.* Cambridge, MA: Ballinger, 1988.

Spector, Leonard. *Nuclear Ambitions: The Spread of Nuclear Weapons, 1989–1990.* Boulder, CO: Westview Press, 1990.

Spence, Floyd. *The Clinton Administration and Nuclear Stockpile Stewardship: Erosion by Design.* U.S. House of Representatives, National Security Committee, 1996 (armedservices.house.gov/openingstatementsandpressreleases/104thCongress/spdocpap.pdf).

Spiro, David. "The Insignificance of the Liberal Peace." *International Security* 19(1994): 50–86.

Stack, Carol. *All Our Kin: Strategies for Survival in a Black Community.* New York: Harper and Row, 1974.

Starhawk. *Dreaming the Dark: Magic, Sex, and Politics.* Boston: Beacon Press, 1982.

Starn, Orin. "Missing the Revolution: Anthropologists and the War in Peru." In George Marcus, ed., *Rereading Cultural Anthropology,* 152–80. Durham, N.C.: Duke University Press, 1992.

Starr, Paul. "Seductions of Sim." *American Prospect* 17 (1994): 19–29.

Stevens, Austin. "General Removed over War Speech." *New York Times,* September 2, 1958.

Stewart, Kathleen. *A Space on the Side of the Road: Cultural Poetics in an "Other" America.* Princeton, NJ: Princeton University Press, 1996.

Stimson, Henry. "The Decision to Use the Atomic Bomb." *Harper's Magazine,* February 1947, 97–107.

Stober, Dan. "Lawrence Livermore Braces for Change." *San Jose Mercury News,* September 9, 1990.

——. "Weapons Lab Incinerator Permit Iffy." *San Jose Mercury News,* September 29, 1989.

Sturgeon, Noelle. "The Direct Action Movement." Paper presented at the annual meeting of the American Anthropology Association, Phoenix, AZ, 1988.

Sutton, John. "Organizational Autonomy and Professional Norms in Science: A Case Study of LLNL." *Social Studies of Science* 14 (1984): 197–224.

Tambiah, Stanley J. *Leveling Crowds: Ethnonationalist Conflicts and Collective Violence in South Asia.* Berkeley: University of California Press, 1997.

Taylor, Bryan C. "The Politics of the Nuclear Test: Reading Robert Oppenheimer's Letters and Recollections." *Quarterly Journal of Speech* 78(1992): 429–449.

——. "Remembering Los Alamos: Culture and the Nuclear Weapons Organization." Ph.D. dissertation, University of Utah, 1991.

———. "Reminiscences of Los Alamos: Narrative, Critical Theory, and the Organizational Subject." *Western Journal of Speech Communication* 54 (1990): 395–419.

Teller, Edward. "The Work of Many People." *Science* 121 (1955): 267–75.

Terdiman, Richard. *Discourse/Counter-discourse: The Theory and Practice of Symbolic Resistance in Nineteenth-Century France.* Ithaca, NY: Cornell University Press, 1985.

Thomas, Evan, and Barry, John. "War's New Science." *Newsweek,* February 18, 1991.

Thompson, E. P. *Beyond the Cold War: A New Approach to the Arms Race and Nuclear Annihilation.* New York: Pantheon Books, 1982.

——. *The Heavy Dancers: Writings on War, Past and Future.* New York: Pantheon Books, 1985.

Thompson, E. P., and Dan Smith, eds. *Prospectus for a Habitable Planet.* London: Penguin, 1986.

——. *Protest and Survive.* New York: Monthly Review Press, 1981.

Tirman, John, ed. *The Militarization of High Technology.* Cambridge, MA: Ballinger, 1984.

Tompkins, J. H. "Whose Livermore Is It Anyway?" *Diablo,* May 1990.

Toomay, John. "Strategic Forces Rationale—A Lost Discipline?" *International Security* 12(1987): 193–202.

Touraine, Alain. *The Voice and the Eye: An Analysis of Social Movements.* Cambridge: Cambridge University Press, 1981.

Traweek, Sharon. *Beamtimes and Lifetimes: The World of High Energy Physics.* Cambridge, MA: Harvard University Press, 1988.

Tri-Valley Herald. "Livermore Lab Hearings Needed" (editorial), November 7, 1988.

——. "Top Salaries at Lawrence Livermore Lab," February 22, 1991.

Turkle, Sherry. *Life on Screen: Identity in the Age of the Internet.* New York: Simon and Schuster, 1995.

———. *The Second Self: Computers and the Human Spirit*. New York: Simon and Schuster, 1984.

Turner, Paul, and David Pitt, eds. *The Anthropology of War and Peace: Perspectives on the Nuclear Age*. South Hadley, MA: Begin and Harvey, 1989.

Turner, Stansfield. *Caging the Nuclear Genie*. Boulder, CO: Westview, 1997.

Turner, Victor. *The Forest of Symbols: Aspects of Ndembu Ritual*. Ithaca, NY: Cornell University Press, 1967.

———. *The Ritual Process: Structure and Anti-Structure*. Chicago: Aldine, 1969.

Urban, Greg, and Benjamin Lee, eds. "Gender Reason and Nuclear Policy: Report of a Colloquium Held at the University of Chicago." *Working Paper of the Center for Psychosocial Studies*, Chicago, 1990.

U.S. Air Force. *Oral History of General Horace M. Wade*, October 10–12, 1978. K239.0512-1105, ASHRC.

Van Gennep, Arnold. *The Rites of Passage*. London: Routledge and Kegan Paul, 1909.

Veiluva, Michael, John Burroughs, Jacqueline Cabasso, and Andrew Lichterman. "Laboratory Testing in a Test Ban/Non-Proliferation Regime." Oakland, CA: Western States Legal Foundation, 1995; www.chemistry.ucsc.edu/anderso/UC_CORP/testban.html (accessed March 6, 1998).

Virilio, Paul, and Sylvère Lotringer. *Pure War*. New York: Semiotext(e), 1983.

Wald, Matthew. "Lab's Task: Assuring Bomb's Quality without Pulling Nuclear Trigger." *New York Times*, June 3, 1997.

———. "Plutonium Hazard Found at Nuclear Arms Plant." *New York Times*, October 7, 1989.

———. "Secrecy Tied to Hanford Tanks' Trouble." *New York Times*, August 1, 1990.

Walker, R. B. J. *Inside/Outside: International Relations and Political Theory*. Cambridge: Cambridge University Press, 1992.

Wallace, A. F. C. *Culture and Personality*. New York: Random House, 1970.

———. *The Death and Rebirth of the Seneca*. New York: Knopf, 1970.

Waller, Douglas C. *Congress and the Nuclear Freeze: An Inside Look at the Politics of a Mass Movement*. Amherst: University of Massachusetts Press, 1987.

Wallis, Jim, ed. *Peacemakers: Christian Voices from the New Abolitionist Movement*. San Francisco: Harper and Row, 1983.

Walt, Stephen. "Building Up New Bogeymen: The Clash of Civilizations and the Remaking of World Order." *Foreign Policy* 106 (1997): 177–89.

Waltz, Kenneth. "The Emerging Structure of International Politics." *International Security* 18(1993): 44–79.

———. "More May Be Better." In Scott Sagan and Kenneth Waltz, *The Spread of Nuclear Weapons*, 1–45. New York: Norton, 1995.

———. "Toward Nuclear Peace." In Dagobert Brito and Michael Intriligator, eds., *Strategies for Managing Nuclear Proliferation*. Lanham, MD: Lexington Books, 1982.

———. "Waltz Responds to Sagan." In Scott Sagan and Kenneth Waltz, *The Spread of Nuclear Weapons*, 93–113. New York: Norton, 1995.

Wartzman, Rick. "Rockwell Bomb Plant Is Repeatedly Accused of Poor Safety Record." *Wall Street Journal,* August 30, 1989.

Washington Post, "Second Best" (editorial), October 21, 1987.

Weart, Spencer. *Nuclear Fear: A History of Images.* Cambridge, MA: Harvard University Press, 1988.

Wedel, Janine. *Collision and Collusion: The Strange Case of Western Aid to Eastern Europe.* New York: St. Martin's, 1998.

Weiner, Tim. "U.S. and China Helped Pakistan Build Its Bomb." *New York Times,* June 1, 1998.

Weisman, Steven. "Nuclear Fear and Narcissism Shake South Asia." *New York Times,* May 31, 1998.

Welch, Jasper. "Assessing the Value of Stealthy Aircraft and Cruise Missiles." *International Security* 14(1989): 47–63.

Weldes, Jutta. *Constructing National Interests: The United States and the Cuban Missile Crisis.* Minneapolis: University of Minnesota Press, 1999.

Weldes, Jutta, Mark Laffey, Hugh Gusterson, and Raymond Duvall, eds. *Cultures of Insecurity: States, Communities, and the Production of Danger.* Minneapolis: University of Minnesota Press, 1999.

Welsome, Eileen. *The Plutonium Files: America's Secret Medical Experiments in the Cold War.* New York: Dell, 2000.

Weston, Kath. *Families We Choose: Lesbians, Gays, Kinship.* New York: Columbia University Press, 1991.

White, Diane. "Everyday Uses for Gulfspeak." *Boston Globe,* February 27, 1991.

White, Pepper. *The Idea Factory: Learning to Think at MIT.* New York: Plume Books, 1992.

Whitehead, Harriet. "Reasonably Fantastic: Some Perspectives on Scientology, Science Fiction, and Occultism." In I. Zaretsky and M. Leone, eds., *Religious Movements in Contemporary America,* 147–90. Princeton, NJ: Princeton University Press, 1974.

Whitemore, Hugh. *Breaking the Code.* BBC Productions. 1997.

Williams, Raymond. *Marxism and Literature.* New York: Oxford University Press, 1977.

Williams, Robert, and Philip Cantelon. *The American Atom: A Documentary History of Nuclear Policies from the Discovery of Fission to the Present.* Philadelphia: University of Pennsylvania Press, 1988.

Wilson, Andrew. *The Disarmer's Handbook of Military Technology and Organisation.* London: Penguin Books, 1983.

Wilson, Lynn. "Power and Epistemology: Rethinking Ethnography at Greenham." In Johnetta Cole, ed. *Anthropology for the '90s,* 42–58. New York: Free Press, 1988.

———. "Resistance to Nuclear Militarism: Greenham Common." *IUAES Commission on the Study of Peace Newsletter* 4 (1986): 2–10.

———. "Rethinking Resistance in Belau." Paper presented at the annual meeting of the American Anthropology Association, Chicago, November 21, 1991.

Winner, Langdon. *Autonomous Technology*. Cambridge, MA: MIT Press, 1977.

Wohlforth, William. "Realism and the End of the Cold War." *International Security* 19(1994–1995): 9–129.

Wohlstetter, Albert. "The Delicate Balance of Terror." *Foreign Affairs* 37 (1959): 211–34.

Wolf, Eric, and Joseph Jorgenson. "Anthropology on the Warpath in Thailand." *New York Review of Books,* November 19, 1970.

Wolfowitz, Paul. Testimony on Ballistic Missile Defense to Senate Armed Services Committee, July 12, 2001 (www.defenselink.mil/speeches/2001/s20010712-depsecdef.html).

Woodmansee, Martha. *The Author and the Market: Rereading the History of Aesthetics*. New York: Columbia University Press, 1994.

———. "On the Author Effect: Recovering Collectivity." In Martha Woodmansee and Peter Jaszi, eds., *The Construction of Authorship*, 15–28. Durham, NC: Duke University Press, 1994.

Woodmansee, Martha, and Peter Jaszi, eds. *The Construction of Authorship*. Durham, NC: Duke University Press, 1994.

Woolley, Benjamin. *Virtual Worlds: A Journey in Hype and Hyperreality*. New York: Penguin, 1993.

Wouters, Jorgen. "Nuclear Powder Keg." *ABC News*. American Broadcasting Corporation, May 28, 1998.

Yoneyama, Lisa. *Hiroshima Traces: Time, Space, and the Dialectics of Memory*. Berkeley: University of California Press, 1999.

York, Herbert. *Making Weapons, Talking Peace: A Physicist's Odyssey from Hiroshima to Geneva*. New York: Basic Books, 1987.

———. "The Origins of the Lawrence Livermore Laboratory." *Bulletin of the Atomic Scientists* 31 (1975): 8–14.

Younger, Stephen. *Nuclear Weapons in the Twenty-First Century*. Internal Document LAUR-00-2850. Los Alamos National Laboratory, 2000.

Zamora Collina, Tom. "South Africa Bridges the Gap." *Bulletin of the Atomic Scientists* 51(1995): 30–31.

Zerriffi, Hisham, and Arjun Makhijani. *The Nuclear Safety Smokescreen: Warhead Safety and Reliability and the Science Based Stockpile Stewardship Program*. Takoma Park, MD: Institute for Energy and Environmental Research, 1996.

———. "The Stewardship Smokescreen." *Bulletin of the Atomic Scientists* 52 (1996): 22–28.

Publication History

Chapter 1 previously appeared as "Becoming a Weapons Scientist," in George Marcus, ed., *Technoscientific Imaginaries: Conversations, Profiles, and Memoirs*, 255–74 (Chicago: University of Chicago Press, 1995). Copyright 1995 by the University of Chicago. All rights reserved.

Chapter 2 was previously published as "Nuclear Weapons and the Other in the Western Imagination," *Cultural Anthropology* 14 (1999): 111–43. Reprinted with permission from *Cultural Anthropology*.

Chapter 3 previously appeared as "Short Circuit: Watching Television with a Nuclear Weapons Scientist," in Chris Gray, ed., *The Cyborg Handbook*, 107–18. (New York and London: Routledge, 1995). Reprinted with permission.

Parts of chapter 4 were previously published as "Nuclear War, the Gulf War, and the Disappearing Body," *Journal of Urban and Cultural Studies* 2 (1991): 28–39.

Parts of chapter 4 were previously published as "Remembering Hiroshima at a Nuclear Weapons Laboratory," in Laura Hein and Mark Selden, eds., *Living with the Bomb: American and Japanese Cultural Conflicts in the Nuclear Age*, 260–76 (Armonk, NY: M. E. Sharpe, 1997). Reprinted with permission from M. E. Sharpe, Inc., Publisher, Armonk, NY 10504.

Chapter 5 previously appeared as "Presenting the Creation: Dean Acheson and NATO," in *Alternatives: Social Transformation and Humane Governance* 24 (1999): 39–57. Copyright 1999 by Lynne Rienner Publishers, Inc. Reprinted with permission of the publisher.

Chapter 6 previously appeared as "Missing the End of the Cold War in International Security," in Jutta Weldes, Mark Laffey, Hugh Gusterson, and Raymond Duvall, eds., *Cultures of Insecurity: States, Communities, and the Production of Danger*, 319–45 (Minneapolis: University of Minnesota Press, 1999).

Chapter 8 previously appeared as "Nuclear Weapons Testing: Scientific Experiment as Political Ritual," in Laura Nader, ed., *Naked Science: Anthropological Inquiry into Boundaries, Power, and Knowledge*, 131–47 (New York and London: Routledge, 1996). Reprinted with permission.

Chapter 9 was previously published as "The Virtual Nuclear Weapons Laboratory in the New World Order," *American Ethnologist* 28 (2001): 417–37. Reprinted with permission from the American Anthropological Association.

Chapter 10 previously appeared as "The Death of the Authors of Death," in Mario Biagioli and Peter Galison, eds., *Scientific Authorship: Credit and Intellectual Property in Science*, 281–307 (New York and London: Routledge, 2003). Reprinted with permission.

Chapter 11 was previously published as "How Not to Construct a Radioactive Waste Incinerator," *Science, Technology, and Human Values* 25 (2000): 332–51. Copyright 2000 by Sage Publications, Inc. Reprinted by permission of Sage Publications, Inc.

The Postscript was previously published as "Tall Tales and Deceptive Discourses," *Bulletin of the Atomic Scientists* 57 (2001): 65–68. Reprinted by permission of *Bulletin of the Atomic Scientists*. Copyright 2001 by the Educational Foundation for Nuclear Science, 6042 South Kimbark, Chicago, IL 60637. A one-year subscription is $28.

Index

Hugh Gusterson is associate professor of anthropology and science studies at the Massachusetts Institute of Technology and professor of public policy at the Georgia Institute of Technology. He studies the political culture of nuclear weapons scientists and antinuclear activists and has written on war, international relations, and the cultural study of science. He is author of *Nuclear Rites: A Weapons Laboratory at the End of the Cold War* and coeditor of *Cultures of Insecurity: States, Communities, and the Production of Danger* (Minnesota, 1999). The American Council of Trustees and Alumni, directed by Lynne Cheney, named him one of the most controversial intellectuals in the United States today. Visit his Web site at http://mit.edu/anthropology/faculty_staff/gusterson/index.html.